History of Computing

The History of Computing series publishes high-quality books which address the history of computing, with an emphasis on the 'externalist' view of this history, more accessible to a wider audience. The series examines content and history from four main quadrants: the history of relevant technologies, the history of the core science, the history of relevant business and economic developments, and the history of computing as it pertains to social history and societal developments

Titles can span a variety of product types, including but not exclusively, themed volumes, biographies, 'profile' books (with brief biographies of a number of key people), expansions of workshop proceedings, general readers, scholarly expositions, titles used as ancillary textbooks, revivals and new editions of previous worthy titles

These books will appeal, varyingly, to academics and students in computer science, history, mathematics, business and technology studies. Some titles will also directly appeal to professionals and practitioners of different backgrounds.

More information about this series at http://www.springer.com/series/8442

Aristotle Tympas

Calculation and Computation in the Pre-electronic Era

The Mechanical and Electrical Ages

 Springer

Aristotle Tympas
National and Kapodestrian University of Athens
Athens, Greece

The author(s) has/have asserted their right(s) to be identified as the author(s) of this work in accordance with the Copyright, Designs and Patents Act 1988.

ISSN 2190-6831   ISSN 2190-684X   (electronic)
History of Computing
ISBN 978-1-4471-7410-3   ISBN 978-1-84882-742-4   (eBook)
https://doi.org/10.1007/978-1-84882-742-4

Library of Congress Control Number: 2017952052

Printed on acid-free paper

This Springer imprint is published by Springer Nature
The registered company is Springer-Verlag London Ltd.
The registered company address is: The Campus, 4 Crinan Street, London, N1 9XW, United Kingdom

Preface

The research presented in this book started while I was a doctoral student in the United States, at the History, Technology and Society Department of the Georgia Institute of Technology. It was completed during the first sabbatical year available to me after joining the faculty of the History and Philosophy of Science Department at Greece's National and Kapodistrian University of Athens. It would take one more sabbatical year to turn these two rounds of research into a book. In the meantime, I had the opportunity to appreciate better the historiographical challenge involved in deciding to write a history of computing that would not project the analog-digital demarcation of the 1940s into the preceding history of computing—a history that would turn the analog-digital demarcation into a social question instead of treating it as technically answered. Aiming from the beginning at a history that would fully respect the fact that this demarcation was not there before the electronic era, I eventually had to accept that I would have to explain why and how this demarcation was prepared before the electronic era, through the long run formed by the mechanical era (from the emergence of the steam engine to that of the electric power network) and the electrical era (from the emergence of the electric power network to that of electronic computing). This required attention to the demarcations between (and associated classifications of) computing artifacts during the mechanical and electrical eras. In turn, this invited an emphasis on the history of comparisons of computing artifacts. In the end, it was this emphasis that was proven crucial in liberating from the effects of the projection of the analog-digital demarcation of the electronic era to the mechanical and electrical eras.

The arguments of the book are then developed around retrieving and interpreting a series of representative comparisons. Central here are comparisons involving the slide rule, an artifact with a uniquely rich history throughout the mechanical and the electrical eras. The book introduces it in two chapters, which offer an overview of the history of the use of the slide rule (Chap. 2) and details of its use in the context of electrification (Chap. 3). With the addition of a chapter that includes artifacts that represented the highest and the lowest ratio of machine to human computing capital, like the analyzers (Chap. 4) and the graphs (Chap. 5), respectively, the comparisons of the book open up to the whole range of computing artifacts—tools, instruments, mechanisms, machines—that have been historiographically devaluated through their a posteriori placement under the allegedly inferior class of analog computers. The book includes a chapter that focuses on comparisons undertaken from the other side, that of promoters of the class of the calculating artifacts—calculating and tabulating machines—that were a posteriori designated as preelectronic ancestors of the digital electronic computer (Chap. 6). By this chapter, all the elements are in place in order to retrieve the key role of the concealment of the laboring with the analog part of computing machines through its encasement (blackboxing), which left on display only a view of the machine as digital (numbers).

It follows that this is not a book about preelectronic analog or digital computers but about the how and why the two emerged as technically different in the electronic era—the one with the concealed analogy, representing, supposedly, an evolution from an inferior to a superior class of computers. Emerging through the long-run history of this book, the analog and the digital are neither alternatives nor complementary. They are inseparable, with their alleged difference having actually to do with a full or restricted view to the computing process. Removing from public view the labor to produce the computing analogy, each special use went hand in hand with presenting the computing artifact as general purpose, universal, independent from labor to adjust it to special uses, and therefore capable of intelligence. Underneath then the demarcations that prepared for the one between the digital and the analog, we find the pursuit of a political economy of computing that devaluated the human capital versus the machine one. A resistance to an extreme version of this pursuit was persistently manifested in the defense of socially situated comparisons of computing artifacts, when the accuracy was not treated in isolation from flexibility and other computing variables and when it was further related to the issue of cost (and, therefore, indirectly, to ownership of the computing artifact). In the book, we see representative instances of the history of the passionate defense of the political economy of a mode of computing production that was based on a combination of an inexpensive slide rule and skillful use.

Opening up historiographically to socially situated comparisons of computing technology opens the history of this technology to the long and widespread use of an understudied universe of computing artifacts. It brings into the fore a myriad of graphs, a multitude of slide rules, and a range of analyzers. The book can be read as a history that exposes to representative samples of all of the above. The main argument from this history is that what we find in the analog-digital demarcation is the outcome of demarcations accumulated through a long series of comparisons, which go back to the beginning of the capitalist mode of production (industrial and, before it, merchant—the book focuses on the industrial one). This suggests that the computing revolution did not start in the 1940s; it did not follow in the industrial revolution. The computing revolution was inseparable from the industrial revolution. It made possible the industrial revolution just as it was made possible by it.

Athens, Greece   Aristotle Tympas

Acknowledgments

The first round of support to the work that led to this book came from my former professors at Georgia Tech, especially Steve Usselman, Bruce Sinclair, Jim Britain, Nancy Nersessian, Steve Vallas, Mark Shields, Ken Knoespel, Phil Scranton, Dan Kleinman, Gus Giebelhaus, John Krige, Allice Bullard, and Greg Nobles. Barney Finn (my host at the Smithsonian), Rik Nebeker (from the IEEE History Center), and, more recently, Tom Misa (from the Charles Babbage Institute) came to add their support. A faculty sabbatical as a visiting scholar at MIT, thanks to David Mindell, made it possible to conclude the research that I had started while a doctoral student at Georgia Tech.

In Greece, the key support by Kostas Gavroglu started while I was searching my way to graduate studies in the field and has continued ever since, through our collaboration as department colleagues at the National and Kapodistrian University of Athens. My department colleagues Theodore Arabatzis, Jean Christianidis, Manolis Patiniotis, and Stathis Araposthathis have supported me in many ways, intellectual and practical. Dionysios Anapolitanos and Costas Dimitracopoulos have also been very supportive. Collaboration with former students who moved on to start their work as postdoctoral researchers and instructors has added one more layer of support. Katerina Vlantoni, Nancy Megremi, Spyros Tzokas, Costas Morfakis, Christos Karampatsos, and Eirini Mergoupi are the ones whom I have had the closest and longer collaboration with. A new generation of doctoral students is following course in supporting me through our collaboration. Costas Raptis, a model of braveness to our community, deserves special mentioning.

Upon my return to Europe, I have also been receiving support through my participation in the ToE (Tensions of Europe) and the ESST (European Studies of Society, Science and Technology) scholarly communities. Johan Schot (earlier at the Technical University of Eindhoven, now with the Science Policy Research Unit at SPRU) and Jessica Mesman (Maastricht University) have been the two most influential persons behind the development of my ties to these communities.

A series of international fellowships and grants allowed me to advance to my research. In reverse chronological order, these came from the Chemical Heritage Foundation (*Doan Fellowship*), the Dibner Library, the National Museum of

American History, the Smithsonian Institution *(Resident Scholar Fellowship)*, the History Center of the Institute of Electrical and Electronics Engineers (*Fellowship in Electrical History)*, the Smithsonian Institution (*Visiting Student Fellowship*), the Hagley Museum and Library (*Residential Fellowship*), the National Science Foundation (*Dissertation Improvement Grant*), and the Georgia Institute of Technology (*Presidential Fellowship*). I want to thank the persons who decided to award these fellowships to me and the administrators, archivists, and librarians who assisted me in my research while I was taking advantage of them.

An early round of help with proofreading and editing by Jeff Sherrill was crucial at the start of the process that led to this book. A more recent round of help with checking various parts of the manuscript that led to this book by Polyxeni Malisova has been very helpful.

I am more than indebted to Springer's Wayne Wheeler and Simon Rees who stood by me repeatedly through the efforts to finish this book amidst unpredictable difficulties. I am also very thankful to the editor and the members of the editorial board of the Springer series that this book is falling under.

Contents

List of Figures

Chapter 1
Introduction

Contents

1.1 Topic, Period, and Argument

This is a book on the history of computing technology before late capitalist modernity (historical capitalism)—in the vocabulary of the book, a history before the "electronic era." As I gradually enter into the narrative of the history of general slide rules (Chap. 2), electrification-related slide rules (Chap. 3), analyzers (Chap. 4), graphs and tables (Chap. 5), and calculating and tabulating machines (Chap. 6), I move on to refine my argument.

The book covers the concluding decades of what Eric Hobsbawm has called the "long nineteenth century" (1780s–1910s)—a century that started with the political revolution in France and the economic revolution in England and ended with World War I. This century was defined by the emergence and prevalence of industrial capital. In his trilogy on "the long nineteenth century," Hobsbawm refers to the concluding decades of this century as "the age of empire" (1875–1914). The book covers in more detail the interwar years that followed (1910s–1940s). According to Hobsbawm, this was the formative sub-period of "the short twentieth century." Because of the two global wars and the intervening economic crisis, he calls the decades between the 1910s and the 1940s "the age of catastrophe."[1] "The age of empire" was the concluding part of the heydays of what in this book I refer to as the "mechanical era," "the age of catastrophe" the climax of the "electrical era."

Historians of computing have so far separated between two periods of computing history: the period before World War II, described as the period of the "prehistory of

---

[1] See Eric Hobsbawm. 1987. *The age of empire, 1875–1914*. London: Weidenfeld & Nicolson, and Eric Hobsbawm. 1994. *Age of extremes: The short twentieth century, 1914–1991*. London: Michael Joseph.

© Springer-Verlag London Ltd. 2017
A. Tympas, *Calculation and Computation in the Pre-electronic Era*, History of Computing, https://doi.org/10.1007/978-1-84882-742-4_1

computing" or the period of "computing before computers," and the period of the actual history of computing, i.e., the period after World War II. According to this periodization, there was only one break in computing history, amounting to a computing revolution that took place in and around World War II. I argue that there is an historical continuity in computing technology throughout historical capitalism. The real break took place much earlier, and it coexisted with the revolution from pre-capitalist to capitalist social formations: from the time of the introduction of the slide rule and the calculating machine (which was also the time of the invention of the calculus). The difference between our computing technology (that of late capitalism) and that of earlier capitalism looks more like a similarity if considered from a non-capitalist perspective. In regard to the decades considered in this book and what precedes and follows, my main argument is that there was no real break in the pattern of computing technology, just an impressively expansive reproduction of the pattern of capitalist computing technology.[2]

1.2   Theoretical Framework

To classify the artifacts discussed in this book, slide rules (Chaps. 2 and 3), analyzers (Chap. 4), graphs (and tables) (Chap. 5), and calculating (and tabulating) machines (Chap. 5), I use as a criterion the ratio of machine to human—"constant" to "variable" in the Marxian vocabulary—capital involved in their use. Starting with the lowest ratio, we move from graphs, to slide rules, to calculating machines, to (some of the top-of-the-line of the) analyzers. In regard to the connection between labor and the use of these artifacts, I rely on an interpretation that contrast human "computers"—also known as "computors"—who stood on the basis of the computing pyramid and "analysts," who topped the pyramid.[3] Given that this is a book on the history of technology, I am not after the history of the whole of the social life of computors and analysts. The history of the book stays at retrieving and interpreting the process of a relative social differentiation between a computor

---

[2] See the pioneering collection that William Aspray (ed.). 1990. *Computing before computers.* Ames: Iowa University Press. For an early challenge to the technical superiority of digital computers, I refer to the study by Larry Owens on the history of the interwar development and use of the most known analog computer, Vannevar Bush's differential analyzer: Larry Owens. 1986. Vannevar Bush and the differential analyzer: The text and the context of an early computer. *Technology and Culture* 27(1): 63–95. For the most recent addition to approaches that perceptively challenge the decontextualized treatment of the digital as superior, which covers the postwar decades, see Care, Charles. 2010. *Technology for modelling: Electrical analogies, engineering practice, and the development of analogue computing.* London: Springer. Unlike, however, these two otherwise insightful approaches to analog computing, I don't accept the technical demarcation between analog and digital computing to start with.

[3] For a pioneering article on human computers, which set the stage for the subsequent literature on the topic that I refer to in the following chapters of the book, see Ceruzzi, Paul E. 1991. When computers were human. *Annals of the History of Computing* 13(1): 237–244.

and an analyst, as this interacted with the computing classifications produced via the comparisons that are the focus of the history of the book.[4]

I also experiment with a Wittgensteinian approach in order to argue that computing was part of the process of active nature making, not a passive representation of nature as it was. Instead of interpreting the computer by employing standard STS (Science and Technology Studies) concepts such as "cyborg," "actant," "heterogeneous engineering," etc., I further chose to use of more generic Lacanian concept "imago" (image): computing provided with an "imaginary" order—the images, the mirrors—so as to engineer the transformation of nature as it was (the Lacanian order of the "real") according to what nature was supposed to be (the Lacanian order of the "symbolic"). For the purpose of this book, the symbolic is in this book discussed as equivalent to the ideal.[5] I use this mostly when I seek to interpret the pursuit of ideally automatic computers.

I introduce my theoretical framework gradually so that it is in contact with the progressive introduction of the various artifacts from the history of computing. For example, I am not able to fully explain why I treat analyzers and graphs as the two poles of the "constant" (higher ratio of machine to human capital) and "variable" capital mode of computing—slide rules placed somewhere between—before reaching the chapter on graphs (Chap. 5).

1.3 Line of Argumentation

The book argues in favor of moving beyond the uncritical projection of the analog-digital computing demarcation to the whole of historical capitalism. Analyzers, slide rules, and graphs are understudied because they are now placed under analog computing. Most histories of computing have neglected analog computing altogether, on essentialist grounds, by assuming that it is technically different from (and inferior to) digital computing. A minority of historians study the history of analog computing advantages without, however, moving on to question the absolute and primary demarcation between analog and digital computing. I differ from both in that I suggest that we start by substituting a relative-social for an absolute-technical demarcation between the two.

In my opinion, what we now call digital computing corresponds to the perspective of the analyst, whereas what we now call analog computing corresponds to the perspective of the computor. Analog computing is what was ideologically devaluated as technically inferior so as to lower the variable computing capital (computing

---

[4] On theoretical analysis that suggests to treat differentiations like this as relative, see Nicos Poulantzas. 1975. *Classes in contemporary capitalism.* London: New Left Books.

[5] See Ludwig Wittgenstein. 1956. *Remarks on the foundations of mathematics,* ed. G.H. Wright, R. Rhees, and G.E.M. Anscombe and Trans. G.E.M. Anscombe. Oxford: Blackwell, and Jacques Lacan. 1977. *The four fundamental concepts of psycho-analysis,* ed. Jacques-Alain Miller and translated by Alain Sheridan. London: Hogarth Press.

wages) as a whole. Over the course of this book, I point to antecedents to the analog-digital computing debate in comparisons between classes of computing artifacts (e.g., slide rules versus calculating machines) and in comparisons within classes of computing artifacts (e.g., nomographs versus circle diagrams).

In my opinion, the history of the configuration of the prevalence of the aforementioned ideological devaluation is no different from the history of the formation of the hegemony of the ideology of presenting computers as intelligent-thinking machines. More specifically, the ideology of intelligent machines aimed at presenting the computing machine as the source of value so as to relatively lower the part of the capital that went to computing wages and, as a result, so as to allow for the extraction and accumulation of surplus computing value. The surplus computing value accumulated was transformed into new computing machines so that the capitalist mode of computing production could keep on expanding successfully—an expansion that was key for the expansion of the capitalist mode of production as a whole.

In parallel to providing with a perspective to interpret the ideology of intelligent computing machines, I suggest that we explain the easiness by which the electronic computer was embraced as an intelligent machine by reference to the previous history of presenting artificial lines and network analyzers as intelligent machines. Noticeably, even slide rules were actually presented as intelligent machines. This is why I am also interested in versions of the ideology of intelligent machines that came along versions of the analyst-computor relationship. To serve this interest, I make the study of engineering comparisons of computing techniques the center of this dissertation.

1.4   Strategy Regarding Primary Sources

In searching through the collections of old engineering journals and books, along with other technical material, I initially had to follow a tree and branch approach, letting one reference lead me to others. I gradually moved on to add a vertical reading of engineering journals. Moving backward from the history of, for example, the network analyzer of Vannevar Bush (see Chap. 4), this reading heuristic led me to the transition from the artificial line to the network analyzer. Moving forward to the present, this strategy led me to the transition from the network analyzer to the electronic computer.

Although both transitions are documented in the journals of the professional community of electrical engineers (*AIEE Transactions* and *AIEE Proceedings*), I realized that many other publications frequently offered ideas that are more engaging. For General Electric's participation in the development of the electrification and computation relationship, I found it useful to start with a full scanning of the *General Electric Review*; for Westinghouse's participation, I commenced with scanning of the pages of the *Electric Journal* and the *Westinghouse Engineer*.

Eventually, I ran into the limitations to reading vertically through an engineering journal specifically focused upon one series of artifacts identified primarily through index references. A horizontal search for other series of artifacts had much to suggest. Continuing the case concerning Vannevar Bush, in 1920, he not only supervised research on artificial line computing, which led to the network analyzer, but he published an article on power analysis utilizing a different form of analyzer—harmonic analyzer (Chap. 4)—and, even more suggestively, an article on power analysis using an artifact from the other end of the spectrum, namely, a graph (a nomogram, see Chap. 5).

Concerning archival research, I saved my most systematic research for the General Electric Archives in Schenectady, New York. Combined research at the Trade Catalogs Collection of the National Museum of American History at the Smithsonian Institution and at Schenectady allowed me, for example, to locate some important General Electric *Engineering Department Technical Letters* on calculation. My record remains, however, incomplete. As we move to the end of the spectrum that includes the least-mechanized mode of computing production, we frequently run into the problem of devaluated artifacts, which means resources overlooked and, accordingly, damaged.

References

Aspray W (ed) (1990) Computing before computers. Iowa State University Press, Ames

Care C (2010) Technology for modelling: electrical analogies, engineering practice, and the development of analogue computing. Springer, London

Ceruzzi PE (1991) When computers were human. Ann Hist Comput 13(1):237–244

Hobsbawm E (1994) Age of extremes: the short twentieth century 1914–1991. Michael Joseph, London

Hobsbawm E (1987) The age of empire, 1875–1914. Weidenfeld & Nicolson, London

Lacan J (1977) The four fundamental concepts of psycho-analysis (Miller JA (ed) and trans: Sheridan A). Hogarth Press, London

Owens L (1986) Vannevar Bush and the differential analyzer: the text and context of an early computer. Technol Cult 27(1):63–95

Poulantzas N (1975) Classes in contemporary capitalism. New Left Books, London

Wittgenstein L (1956) Remarks on the Foundations of Mathematics, edited by Wright GH, Rhees R, and Anscombe GEM and translated by Anscombe GEM. Blackwell, Oxford

Chapter 2
"The Delights of the Slide Rule"

Contents

2.1 Introduction

The centuries-long and widespread use of the slide rule qualifies it as one of the most important computing artifacts of historical capitalism to date. Yet, the literature on the history of computing with the slide rule is extremely limited. This chapter offers an introduction to the history of the slide rule based on the presentation of the slide rule in engineering and other technical texts. The emphasis is placed on retrieving and interpreting representative comparisons between the various versions of slide rules and between slide rules and other computing artifacts, mostly calculating machines (mechanical calculators).

The narrative of the chapter is organized around a set of interrelated themes:

The use of slide rules by protagonists of the mechanical and the electrical era, which went parallel to an interest in writing histories of the slide rule that confirm the historical importance of its use (Sect. 2.2)

The availability of a myriad of versions of slide rules and associated artifacts that defies any easy attempt at classifying them (Sect. 2.3)

The persistent presentation of the slide rule as an intelligent artifact, which could therefore save labor by being capable of universal (general-purpose) use (Sect. 2.4)

© Springer-Verlag London Ltd. 2017

A. Tympas, *Calculation and Computation in the Pre-electronic Era*, History of Computing, https://doi.org/10.1007/978-1-84882-742-4_2

The many methods to improve the accuracy of the slide rule without a corresponding increase in its size (Sect. 2.5)

The opening up of the comparison of computing artifacts to variables like flexibility,
while defending the accuracy of skillful computing with the slide rule against
those who sought to frame the slide rule as inherently inaccurate so as to promote
machines that represented higher computing capital (e.g. calculating machines)
(Sect. 2.6)

The overall replacement of an abstract technical conception of computing accuracy
by a socially situated one that did not ignore the low cost of a slide rule, which
gave the average engineer the opportunity to maintain ownership of the means of
computing production (Sect. 2.7)

The attention paid to the formal training in the slide rule at engineering and other
technical environments (Sect. 2.8)

The chapter includes a section that captures the flowing of the history of the slide
rule into the emergence of the electronic computer (Sect. 2.9).

2.2 "No Device Has Been of Greater General Interest"

Eugene Ferguson, an engineer and distinguished historian of technology of an earlier generation (1914–2004), knew from his own experience that the slide rule was
"the prime symbol of the engineering profession until the 1960s."[1] The considerable
contrast between the historical value of computing with the slide rule and its historiographical devaluation after the emergence of the analog-digital computing
demarcation in the 1940s is striking.[2] The history of the slide rule—now assumed to
be an exemplar of analog computing—was once considered important enough to

---

[1] Eugene S. Ferguson. 1992. *Engineering and the mind's eye*, 146. Cambridge: MIT Press.

[2] For historical works that confirm the importance of the history of the slide rule, see Peggy Aldrich
Kidwell. 2015, Jan–Mar. Useful instruction for practical people: Early printed discussions of the
slide rule in the US. *IEEE Annals of the History of Computing* 37(01): 36–43; Peggy Aldrich
Kidwell, and Amy Ackerberg-Hastings. 2014. Slide rules on display in the United States, 1840–
2010. In *Scientific Instruments on Display,* eds. Silke Ackermann, Richard Kremer, and Mara
Miniati. Brill; P.A. Kidwell. 2008. Useful instruction for practical people. In *Tools of American
Mathematics Teaching, 1800–2000,* ed. P.A. Kidwell, A. Ackerberg-Hastings, D.L. Roberts, 105–
122. Baltimore: Johns Hopkins University Press. A very useful record on slide rules is offered
through communities interested in the identification, preservation, and collection of slide rules and
documents of relevance to them, through publications like the *Journal of the Oughtred Society* and
the *Slide Rule Gazette*. For synthetic works from similar perspectives, see Dieter von Jezierski.
2000. *Slide rule: A journey through three centuries*. Mendham, NJ: Astragal Press; Peter M. Hopp.
1999. *Slide rule: Their history, models, and makers*. Mendham, New Jersey: Astragal Press; Philip
Stanley. 2004. *Source book for rule collectors*. Mendham, New Jersey: Astragal Press; I. J.
Schuitema, and H. van Herwijnen, 2003. *Calculating on slide rule and disk*. Mendham, New
Jersey: Astragal Press. On the extremely rich material culture of calculating wheels, with circular
sliding scales of all kinds that slide on top of each other, see Jessica Helfand. 2006. *Reinventing the
wheel*. New York: Princeton Architectural Press.

deserve long historical treatises. In fact, the history of the slide rule was considered more significant than the history of any other modern computing artifact, including the calculating machine—now assumed to be an exemplar of digital computing. In 1909, Florian Cajori, professor of mathematics and dean of the School of Engineering at Colorado College, started his book-long history of the slide rule by arguing that "[o]f the machines for minimizing mental labor in computation, no device has been of greater general interest than the Slide Rule." "Few instruments," he added, "offer a more attractive field for historical study. Its development has reached into many directions and has attracted men of various gifts."[3] In 1925, Eugene Smith, professor of mathematics at Columbia and pioneer historian of mathematics, added that "[f]ew such instruments have gained so much popularity in such a short time."[4]

"Skill in calculation and manipulation of numbers," found A. J. Turner, "although perhaps not essential to the functioning of 17th-century European society, was nonetheless of considerable and increasing importance." "Abaci," he clarified, "had existed for this purpose since Antiquity, but during the 17th century the slide rule, the sector, the scale rule, the mechanical calculator, and a wide range of instruments were invented."[5] We usually associate the slide rule and related computing artifacts with the names of John Napier, Henry Briggs, William Oughtred, and Edmund Gunter, who introduced the slide rule during the emergence of merchant capitalism. It is much less known that the use of the slide rule was indispensable at the steam engine Soho factory of James Watt and the Menlo Park electric network of Thomas Edison, the greatest symbols of industrial capitalism of the mechanical and electrical era, respectively. For the design of his slide rules, Watt had relied on the considerable technical skills of John Southern, who was also a skillful mathematician. Watt had employed the most skillful artists in order to construct the Soho slide rules.[6] It is even less known that in order to move forward with his electric network, Edison brought at Menlo Park a European engineer, the Austrian Herman Claudius, who combined PhD training with exemplar proficiency in the use of the slide rule.[7]

It has been argued that a great part of the success of both Soho and the Menlo Park was due to their systematic promotion as products of a divine ingenuity, that of Watt and Edison, respectively.[8] Acknowledging that the symbolic launch of the eras of steam and electricity was actually calculated by slide rules offers confirmation to this argument. At the same time, it suggests that computing was an integral part of

[3] Florian Cajori. 1909. *A history of the logarithmic slide rule and allied instruments*, iii. New York: The Engineering News Publishing Company.

[4] David Eugene Smith. 1925. *History of mathematics*, 206. Boston: Ginn.

[5] A.J. Turner. 1993. *Of time and measurement: Studies in the history of horology and fine technology*, 252. Norfolk, Great Brittain: Varorium.

[6] Jane Wess. 1997, Fall. The Soho rule. *Journal of the Oughtred Society* 6(2): 23–26.

[7] For a history of the Menlo Park calculations, which includes a reconstruction of the story of Herman Claudius, see Aristotle Tympas. 2001. *The computor and the analyst: Computing and power, 1870s–1960s*. PhD dissertation, Atlanta, Georgia Institute of Technology, chap. 2.

[8] See Ben Marsden. 2004. *Watt's perfect engine: Steam and the age of invention*. New York: Columbia University Press, and Charles Bazerman. 1999. *The languages of Edison light*. Cambridge: The MIT Press.

the industrialization; the industrial revolution came along a computing revolution. Computing was crucial during the symbolic birth moments of both the "first" (steam) and "second" (electricity) phase of the industrial revolution. This suggestion can only be reinforced by further acknowledging that relying on the use of the slide rule did not only define the origins of the factory and the industrial mode of production in the eighteenth century but, also, marked the paradigmatic scaling-up of this mode of production that gave the "Fordist" factory of the twentieth century, in interaction with "Taylorism." Noticeably, a version of slide rules was central to the implementation of the "scientific management" approach of Frederick W. Taylor. The slide rules of Carl G. Barth, the skillful collaborator of Taylor, were in fact the embodiment of the principles of this approach.[9]

Karl G. Bath presented these slide rules briefly in short articles in the *American Machinist* in 1902–1903 and, in detail, in a series of articles in *Industrial Management* in 1919. Taylor referred to them at the Annual Meeting of the American Society of Mechanical Engineers in 1906 in New York while giving his infamous talk "On the Art of Cutting Metals."[10] Several manufacturers offered linear and circular machine-time slide rules until the late 1950s. In his infamous *On The Art of Cutting Metals*, Taylor had stated that the benefit from his slide rules was greater than that from other inventions, because they made possible the transfer of control from the workers to the management and the associated replacement of empirical methods by scientific ones.[11]

To design and construct a slide rule that would include all the variables considered by Taylor turned out to be difficult. In his editorial comment in the *Industrial Management* 1919 series of articles by Barth, L. P. Alford stated that Taylor had provided with a "comprehensive, scientific treatise," but it was Barth who was called upon to supplement it with a "practical, engineering paper."[12] Special purpose slide rules were quite popular among Taylorites. In 1917, Lewis Jenkins started the first of his two article series on the design of special rules in *Industrial Management* by stating that "[a]mong all the means and tools to save mental labor in making computations the slide rule stands first."[13]

---

[9] Dieter von Jezierski, and Rodger Shepherd. 2000, Fall. Taylor, taylorism, and machine-time slide rules. *Journal of the Oughtred Society* 9(2): 32–36.

[10] Frederick W. Taylor. 1907. On the art of cutting metals *Transactions of the American Society of Mechanical Engin*eers 28: 31–279. For Barth's articles see Carl G. Barth. 1902a, July 31. Barth's gear slide rule *American Machinist*: 1075, Carl G. Barth. 1902b, November 20. Barth's lathe speed slide rules *American Machinist*, 1684–1685, and Carl G. Barth. 1919a, September. Supplement to Frederick Taylor's on the art of cutting metals. *Industrial Management* LVIII, 169–175, Carl G. Barth. 1919b, October. Supplement to Frederick Taylor's on the art of cutting metals. *Industrial Management* LVIII, 282–287, Carl G. Barth. 1919c, November. Supplement to Frederick Taylor's on the art of cutting metals. *Industrial Management* LVIII, 369–374, and Carl G. Barth. 1919d, December. Supplement to Frederick Taylor's on the art of cutting metals. *Industrial Management* LVIII, 483–487.

[11] von Jezierski, and Shepherd, *Taylor, taylorism, and machine-time slide rules*, 36.

[12] See "Supplement to Frederick Taylor's on the art of cutting metals," 71.

[13] A. Lewis Jenkins. 1917, November. Design of special slide rules. *Industrial Management* part I, 241.

We may conveniently differentiate between a period of slide rule history that corresponds to merchant capitalism and one that corresponds to industrial capitalism. The 1787 publication of a book on the various types used up to then, authored by William Nicholson, captures the break between the two periods of slide rule history.[14] Nicholson's self-conscious attempt at a history of the slide rule coincided with the appearance of Watt's Soho slide rules. Just like Watt's Soho steam engines, Watt's Soho slide rules can be treated as a symbol of the break between merchant and industrial capitalism. The first treatises on the slide rule capture this break. In 1822, B. Bevan, a civil engineer and an architect, wrote a treatise on the "sliding rule" that included two parts; the first focused on the use of the slide rule in trade and the second on its use in engineering. They covered the use of the slide rule in the context of merchant and industrial capitalism, respectively. Bevan, who had reported that he had used the slide rule extensively for 18 years, argued that the slide rule was a general-purpose computing artifact:

> The sliding rule is an instrument of general utility, for all purposes of expeditious calculations; and it may be said, that few instruments require less time and application for attaining a sufficient knowledge of their principles, to enable any person of sufficient knowledge of common education to become able to resolve all questions of common arithmetic with great ease and dispatch: a few hour's attention is sufficient to instruct a common schoolboy in the use of the Rule, for the usual questions that occur in common business; after which the progress is perfectly easy, to that of the more refined calculations required by the professional gentleman and man of science.[15]

In John Farey's pioneering treatise on the steam engine (1827) there was a special chapter on "Applications of the sliding rule for calculating the dimensions for the parts of Steam-Engines." Farey explained that computing with the logarithmic slide rule was based on mechanization of computing with logarithmic tables:

> This instrument is a mechanical application of logarithms; and to have a correct idea of its principle of action, we must consider the operation of logarithms, whereby they perform the multiplication and division of numbers. Logarithms are a series of artificial numbers, adapted in a particular manner to a series of real numbers, and arranged in a table, wherein every real number has its corresponding logarithm; so that by inspection of such a table, any number can be converted into its logarithmic representative; and conversely any logarithm can be converted into the real number which it represents...
>
> Hence logarithms tend to facilitate computations, by substituting the operations of addition and subtraction, for those of multiplication and division, which are more tedious and difficult to be performed.[16]

Farey's 1827 history of the preceding use of the slide rule leaves no doubt that Watt's Soho factory slide rules represented a breakthrough:

---

[14] Smith, *History of mathematics*, 206.

[15] B. Bevan. 1822. *A practical treatise on the sliding rule*, A2. London: Published by the author.

[16] John Farey. 1927. *A treatise on the steam engine*, 533. London: Longman, Rees, Orme, Brown, and Green. On the importance of this treatise, see A. P. Woolrich. 2000. John Farey and his treatise on the steam engine of 1827. *History of Technology* 22: 63–106.

These sliding rules were put into the hands of all the foremen and superior workmen of the Soho manufactory, and through them, the advantage of calculating by means of the sliding rule has become known amongst other engineers, and some do employ it for all computations of ordinary mensuration; but the habit of using it upon all occasions, is almost confined to those who have been educated at Soho.[17]

Farey had included a section entitled "Directions to Engineers for the Choice of a Sliding Rule" and a description of a "sliding rule" arrangement of his own design.[18] The slide rule figured prominently in his 1827 ground setting treatise on mechanical power engineering (steam engine engineering). The slide rule would also figure prominently in the ground setting treatise on electrical engineering mathematics by the infamous General Electric engineer Charles Proteus Steinmetz.[19] Because of its longevity, the slide rule offered the standard for computing comparisons for all those who claimed that a computing revolution was underway. Manufacturers, minor or major, frequently sought to promote their new computing artifacts as replacements of the slide rule. For example, in 1916–1917, Yu Wang announced that the slide rule was to be "replaced" by his own computing board, which he introduced to as a "new computer."[20] Over the course of this book, we will discuss several representative examples of promotion of computing artifacts through their comparison to the slide rule. As late as in the 1950s, the tradition of computing with the slide rule was so alive, and the connection between the slide rule and skillful-independent work so well established (see following sections of this chapter) that the slide rule figured prominently in a 1951 advertisement of the IBM 604 electronic computer that claimed that this computer could replace 150 engineers working with slide rules (Fig. 2.1) and in a 1956 Marlboro commercial that displayed a slide rule as a symbol of skill and independence (Fig. 2.2).

2.3   "A Machine for Putting Logarithms to Work"

Given that the history of the slide rule is centuries long, classifying a slide rule as such and placing the various slide rules to sub-classes is extremely difficult, especially considering that the concept "slide rule" was eventually used in order to describe a number of artifacts that were originally called by different names. In Clyde Clason's 1964 slide rule handbook, we find a description of what came to be considered as a standard slide rule:

---

[17] Ibid., 531.

[18] Ibid., 566–567 and 567–568, respectively.

[19] Charles Proteus Steinmetz. 1917. *Engineering mathematics*, 3rd rev and enlarg ed. New York: McGraw-Hill.

[20] Yu Wang. 1916, June 15. The slide rule replaced by a new computer. *Engineering News* 75(24): 1120, and Yu Wang. 1917. New parallel-line computer to replace slide-rule for rapid calculations. *Electrical Review and Western Electrician* 70(10): 22.

Fig. 2.1 Advertisement that introduces an IBM electronic computer as equivalent to 150 slide rules (1951)

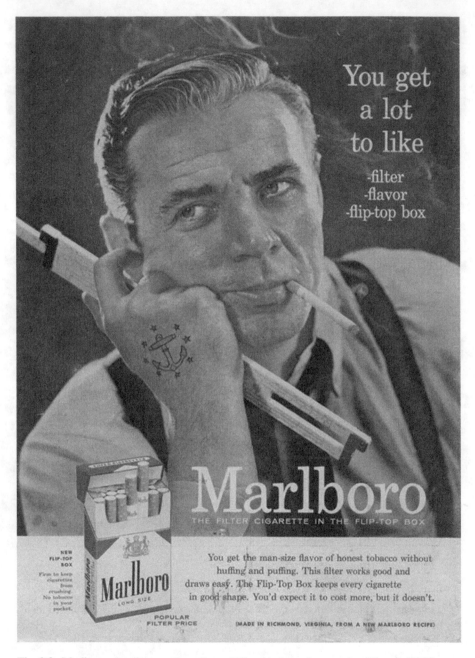

Fig. 2.2 Marlboro advertisement that relates skill and independence to the slide rule (1956)

> The slide rule is a machine for putting logarithms to work. It is one of the simplest machines ever constructed, having only three parts: (1) A framework with fixed scales, called the body or stock. (2) A sliding middle section with additional scales, called the slide; and (3) A transparent sliding indicator with a hairline or hairlines. The indicator is sometimes called the cursor, particularly in England.[21]

Depending on the use of a slide rule, the difference between scales placed on the "stock" or "stator" and scales placed on the "slide" or "tongue" of this slide rule can now be interpreted as a difference between general and special purpose hardware (by interpreting the stock as general-purpose hardware and the slide as special purpose hardware), as a difference between general and special purpose software (by interpreting the stock as an operating software system and the slide as the rest of the software), or as a difference between hardware and software (by interpreting the stock as hardware and the slide as software). The more general purpose a scale, the more likely that it would be eventually placed on the stock. Yet, as with the contents of the operating system of the electronic computer, the stock scales varied in time and place because old scales were modified, new scales were added, and/or old scales were dropped. The "Manheim," the "Rietz," and the "Darmstadt" seem to have been the most popular of the standard slide rule "scale systems."[22] There were many other significant special purpose scale systems, including one—the "Electro"—that was developed in the context of calculating the process of electrification.[23]

In his 1961 handbook on the slide rule, which was based on his experience with establishing a course on the slide rule at the University of Kansas, John P. Ellis, who was with the General Electric Power Transformer Department in Pittsburgh, introduced to the slide rule scale as a form of a "graphic table"—the logarithmic slide rule was a graphic logarithmic table.[24] Indeed, as with a calculating table or graph, the slide rule was made by the inscription of numbers and other signs that corresponded to pre-computed relationships. Unlike the soft material chosen for a table, the materials used for slide rules were harder, usually various pieces of cardboard, wood, metal, celluloid (or other synthetic material), and glass. As with the type of graphs known as "alignment charts," "nomographs," or "nomograms" (see Chap. 6), slide rules consisted of a network of scales. Unlike the fixed scales of the nomogram, the scales of the slide rule could be moved by sliding. As with pressing the key of a calculating machine so as to turn linked material parts upon which pre-computed relationships were inscribed (e.g., counter bearing shafts), computing with a slide rule was based on sliding linked material parts upon which pre-computed relationships were also inscribed. But, unlike with the calculating machine, no part of the motion of the linked material parts of the slide rule was encased so as to be removed from public view (see Chap. 7).

---

[21] Clyde B. Clason. 1964. *Delights of the slide rule*, 20. New York: Thomas Y. Crowell Company.

[22] von Jezierski, *Slide rule: A journey through three centuries*, 33–35, and Hopp, *Slide rule: Their history, models, and makers*, 95–98.

[23] Ibid.

[24] John P. Ellis. 1961. *The theory and operation of the slide rule*, 4. New York: Dover.

Such comparisons appear to be infinite, especially considering that we could compare the various slide rules to many more computing artifacts and, more importantly, that both the slide rules and the computing artifacts that we could compare them to were frequently hybrids deviating from the standard. For example, mechanical slide rules were combined with small mechanical or, later, electronic, calculating machines like the "Addiator" adding device, which was operated by using a stylus. The "Faber-Castell 67/98 Rb ELEKTRO" was a special combinatory model that was designed to compute electrical problems.[25] Equally difficult to identify and classify are the artifacts that could be conveniently considered as both a slide rule and as a different artifact. There were, for example, artifacts known as "slide charts."[26]

Slide rules were in fact frequently incorporated into other portable artifacts. This was the case with slide rules that were embodied in a pencil. One such slide rule was the "Voith Slide Rule and Mechanical Pencil Combination."[27] Some slide rules were to be used in conjunction with artifacts that were not computing devices. A five-piece combination gauging rod and slide rule described offers us an example.[28] One of the artifacts listed in the catalog of the 1914 Edinburgh Exhibition of computing technology was a slide rule that was especially designed to be used so as to correct the measurements of a saccharometer, which was used by brewers and officers of the Excise to determine the density of wort in the process of making beer. It was introduced by Professor Thomson of Glascow. In 1816, an Act of Parliament enacted that it should be used by the Excise. It was exhibited by John M. Mclean.[29]

Even after we exclude combinations of slide rules and other artifacts (computing or other), the remaining variance in the form of slide rules is great. For example, the same set of scales could be included in something as small as a portable slide rule, available in the form of a pocket or hand watch, or, alternatively, in something as big as a slide rule that could fill a room. Finally, even after we focus on a standard form, e.g., that of a 10-inch straight slide rule, we find an enormous variance in the placement and the content of the scales.

I will here use Section F of the handbook of the 1914 Exhibition in order to experiment with a classification of slide rules according to use. This section included an introductory article by G.D.C. Stokes, which contained aspects on the history of slide rules to 1850 that were extracted from Cajori's 1909 history of the logarithmic slide rule. It also contained sections on the classification of slide rules, on a standard

---

[25] Dieter von Jezierski. 1996, March. Faber-Castell combination rules. *Journal of the Oughtred Society* 5(1): 24, and Jezierski, *Slide rule: A journey through three centuries*, 57–58.

[26] Hopp, *Slide rule: Their history, models, and makers*, 219.

[27] Edwin Chamberlain. 1997, March. The Voith slide rule and mechanical pencil combination. *Journal of the Oughtred Society* 6(1): 27–28.

[28] Thomas Wyman. 1997, March. A five-piece combination gauging rod and slide rule. *Journal of the Oughtred Society* 6(1): 45–46.

[29] See Ellice Martin Horsburgh (ed.). 1914. *Modern instruments and methods of calculation: A handbook of the Napier tercentenary exhibition*, 173. London: Bell and Sons. On saccharometry, see James Sumner. 2001, September. John Richardson, saccharometry and the pounds-per-barrel extract: The construction of a quantity. *British Journal for the History of Science* 34(3): 255–273.

slide rule, on the mathematical principle of the slide rule, on functions read on the standard rule, and on poly-slide slide rules. This was followed by a description of the slide rules exhibited, which were arranged according to the exhibitor. Stokes, who admitted that he had no absolute technical classification criterion to offer, started by explaining that "[t]he term 'slide rule' has never been restricted to rules in which slide was an essential feature" and that "[t]here is thus a class of slide rules for which the name 'logarithmic computing scales' would be more appropriate." It is to this special class that he focused on. But first, he gave examples of slide rules classified according to the two classes "conveniently" identified by M. D'Ocagne, and a third, "intermediate" sub-class. More specifically, he differentiated between "rules by movable indices" (first class), "rules with adjacent sliding scales" (second class), and artifacts "in which sliding takes place without performing the function of displacing the scales relatively to one another" (intermediate class).[30]

Stokes placed "circular scales" and "spiral scales" under the first sub-class. He explained that in principle these rules were "Gunter scales," which means that in multiplying with them, the logarithm of a number was measured by some form of dividers and was added to the logarithm of another number by applying one arm of the dividers to this other number on the scale. Stokes estimated that the variety of rules coming under the second sub-class was "very great." It included "straight rules," "circular forms," and "cylindrical design." Providing examples of the intermediate class, Stokes mentioned a "straight rule" in which the slide carried no scale but took the place of the dividers, an "instrument" in which one dial moved relatively to the other, and "helical rules" in which one index was fixed and the scale made movable. The intermediate class slide rules were used by employing the Gunter method.[31]

Slide rules may also be classified according to the following parameters: name of manufacturer or retailer (there were hundreds of them worldwide), type (beaker, circular, grid-iron, linear, pencil, special function, tubular, watch type calculator, others), mode of construction (closed frame, closed frame duplex, duplex, folded metal, folded plastic, multi-disk circular, multi-cursor circular, open frame, others), material used (aluminum, bakelite, bamboo, celluloid, metal, paper/cardboard, plastic, wood, wood/celluloid, wood/painted), type of cursor (metal knife edge, metal/celluloid, metal/glass, metal/glass magnifying, metal/plastic, plastic, plastic folded, plastic magnifying), and placement of scales (stock/slide interface, reverse of slide, edge of slide rule, in well of rule, i.e., under the slide).[32]

The names used to describe slide rules varied extremely in response to variance of form or/and content. The names could vary even when the form and the content was the same due to an attempt to promote a slide rule by associating it to a concept that could bring more prestige. Depending on the time and the place, the same slide rule could be called, for example, "calculating rule," "calculating instrument," "calculating machine," or simply "calculator." The terms "computing" and "computer"

---

[30] Ibid., 156.

[31] Ibid.

[32] Hopp, *Slide rule: Their history, models, and makers*, 128–129.

(rule, instrument, machine) were also used in reference to a slide rule. "Computing" and "calculating" with a slide rule were usually used in reference to the routine work by low-ranking human "computers" ("computors") or the design work of high-ranking "analysts."[33]

2.4 "A Very Ingenious Instrument"

Like our electronic computer, the slide rule was ideologized as an intelligent and general-purpose machine for saving labor. In 1883, when Keuffel & Esser's long history of promoting the slide rule to American engineers had just started, the 17th edition of the company's trade catalog included a special page on "Engineers Slide Rules or Calculation Rules," which stated that the slide rule was "[a] very ingenious instrument, which performs many useful operations in arithmetic, with great facility and convenience," and that it was "[a] pocket companion useful for Mechanical and Civil Engineers, Machinists, Builders and Contractors, to make all kinds of calcula-tions." The two 10-inch engineering models with the instructions on how to use them were selling for $3.50 and $4.50. The difference between the two models had to do with the inclusion of a brass indicator. The price of these "ingenious" artifacts "for all kinds of calculations" was considerably higher than that of the common brass slide rule, which was then selling at $1.[34]

In 1903, when the slide rule was already more familiar to the American engineer, Charles N. Pickworth argued similarly in the context of promoting "A. W. Faber's Improved Calculating Rule."

> It is a somewhat surprising fact that in an age in which such an immense amount of attention is given to labour-saving tools and appliances generally, so little advantage has been taken of the Calculating Rule—an instrument which offers a ready means for mechanically per-forming all the varied calculations which are required by the engineer or architect, the chemist or the power user.[35]

In promoting its "Tag-Isom Blending Calculator" in the January 1928 issue of the journal *Instruments*, the Tagliabue Manufacturing Company referred to it as an "ingenious device" that "will not only do more than charts or formulae but it will do it quicker, more accurately and with much less effort on the part of the operator." It was a slide rule for "the practical oil man," designed "after years of experiments with different oils, the viscosities and gravities of which were accurately known."

---

[33] For an introduction to the historical difference between calculation and computation, see Tympas. *The computor and the analyst: Computing and power, 1870s–1960s,* and Aristotle Tympas. 2004. Calculation and computation. In *New dictionary of the history of ideas, vol. I,* ed. Maryanne Cline Horowitz, 255–259. New York: Charles Scribner's Sons.

[34] See Robert Otnes. 1995, October. A page from the 1833 Keuffel & Esser catalog. *Journal of the Oughtred Society* 4(2): 15.

[35] Charles N. Pickworth. 1903. *Instructions for the use of A. W. Faber's improved calculating rule,* 5. London: A. W. Faber.

"Handy to carry, easy to operate, no parts to wear out, no charts to replace," it could, supposedly, be used to work out "any" blending problem "in a few seconds." The editor of *Instruments* seized the opportunity to add a general comment about information, which he placed underneath the pictures of the slide rule:

> It is common experience that next to possessing information the ideal desideration is to know where to find it. This is especially true at present when the vast amount of information probably available on almost any subject is so great as to lie beyond the capacity of an individual. The problem is usually where to find what is wanted. The world-wide demand for information of all kinds has grown so rapidly that one is often at his wit's end to know where to look for it.[36]

The assumption was that the practical oil man could satisfy his demand for information based on the ingenuity of the slide rule. The slide rule was portrayed as a general-purpose computer, to be used everywhere and at all times. In the 1933 Keuffel & Esser catalog, which included tens of slide rule models, we find models that were called "Ever-There." There was an "Ever-There" standard Manheim and a "polyphase" slide rule.[37] Many individuals and manufacturers were calling their slide rules "universal." At the 1914 Edinburgh World Exhibition, Lewis Evans exhibited a "universal ring dial" of gilt brass on one side of which there was a circular slide rule from about 1700, J. M. Warden a "universal proportion table" that was made by J. D. Everett, and W. F. Stanley & Company of Glasgow a 10-inch "Universal" slide rule that was designed for "tacheometrical calculations." The designation "universal" was used to imply that a slide rule was suitable for all purposes or, as with the one designed for "tacheometrical calculations," that it was suitable for all sub-purposes within a given purpose.[38]

2.5 "High-Speed Scales"

Diachronically, promoters of computing artifacts that competed with the slide rule were investing on the assumption that its accuracy could not be increased without a corresponding increase in its size. In 1962, MIT students Ronald Pasqualini and Philip F. Hudock undertook an experiment that exemplified this assumption. They filled up a room-long table with a vertically placed slide rule that was "big enough to be seen from the rear of a lecture hall." Behind this slide rule, they had connected motors and chains to be used in order to provide with remote drives. The remote drives were based on feedback positioning mechanisms used in machine tools, radar antenna, and other industrial and military equipment in order to precisely position some large objects. The two MIT students used these drives to move the slide and

---

[36] The Tag-Isom blending calculator *Instruments* (January 1928): 64–65.

[37] *Keuffel & Esser Trade Catalog, 1933*, 18–19 (Smithsonian Institution, National Museum of American History, Trade Catalogs Collection, Mezzanine Library).

[38] See Horsburgh (ed.), *Modern instruments and methods of calculation: A handbook of the tercentenary exhibition*, 166, 171, and 175 respectively.

the cursor to positions corresponding to those on a small slide rule, which they hold in their hands. The reported positioning accuracy was 1/16th of an inch on the larger rule.[39]

In reality, there have been a multitude of methods to increase the accuracy of the slide rule without increasing its size. Some of them are as old as the slide rule.[40] Including a "runner," "cursor," or "indicator" was a popular method, followed systematically throughout the rich history of Keuffel & Esser slide rule improvements.[41] Reading through the pages of the catalog of the 1914 Exhibition indicates the wealth of the options tried. I here select a random sample of ten.

First, one could rely on subdivision of scales with addition of indices of transparent celluloid as in "Anderson's Patent Slide Rule," which was exhibited by Brigadier General F. J. Anderson. It was formerly manufactured by Messrs. Casella & Company of London. Second, one could rely on inclusion of a series of cursors that were movable relatively to one another but were constrained by the positive link mechanism known as "lazy tongs," by some other type of similar mechanism, by connecting springs, or by a mechanism to remain equidistant from one another. This was the case with a device exhibited as "A Patent Accessory to the Slide Rule" by R. F. Muirhead. Third, there was the option of introducing a fundamental scale in a reverse direction in order to provide a check and in order to reduce the work for certain uses. This was tried in "An Improved Slide Rule" that was exhibited by Professor E. Hanauer of Budapest. A fourth option was the incorporation of magnifying cursors. It was exercised in "Hellener," which was exhibited by John Davis & Son Limited of Derby. Another, fifth, option was based on the incorporation of a tongue on the cursor as in the slide rule "Yokota" that was also exhibited by John Davis & Son Limited of Derby. The incorporation of a registering cursor was a sixth option. Several of the "Castell" slide rules that were exhibited by A. W. Faber of London had incorporated it. A seventh option was the incorporation of a cursor with pointer attachment and divided line. It was tried in the "Perry Patent Slide Rule," which was exhibited by A. G. Thornton of Manchester. An eight option was available by jointing a slide that combined the accuracy of the larger slide with the portability of the smaller as in the "Stelfox" slide rule that was exhibited by John Davis & Son Limited of Derby. Inscription of special signs, e.g., signs for decimal, product, and quotient, was a ninth option. The second of the Castell slide rules that were exhibited by A. W. Faber of London had several such signs. A tenth option was the use of the sides of the slide rule for the inclusion of more scales. This was the option

---

[39] *The Technology Review* (March, 1962), 22.

[40] Bruce E. Babcock. 1995b, March. Two noble attempts to improve the slide rule. *Journal of the Oughtred Society* 4(1): 41–45.

[41] Mel Larson. 1993a, March. The runner. *Journal of the Oughtred Society* 2(1): 40–43. For an introduction to the subtleties of the difference between the terms "runner", "cursor", and "indicator," see Mel Larson. 1993b, March. Runner, cursor, or indicator? *Journal of the Oughtred Society* 2(1): 47–48.

chosen in the eleventh of the Castell slide rules that was also exhibited by A. W. Faber of London.[42]

The history of improving runners and associated slide rule accessories so as to improve the accuracy of computing with the slide rule without increasing its size is not the only one that was canonically neglected. Promoters of calculating machines and, later, electronic computers were actually neglecting the most obvious way to improve the accuracy of the slide rule, namely, to keep the size of the slide rule constant but double its accuracy by including only the half of the range that was required for a specific use (Stokes' first suggestion). In fact, by following this method, it was also possible to keep the size of the rule constant and increase the resolution by several times by decreasing the range an equal number of times. Moreover, one did not even have to miss any of range because an extra set of scales could be used so as to adjust the range to use. Indicative of the flexibility of the slide rule was the fact that any scale proven to be useful could be turned into a slide rule. An extreme example of this was the "boxwood rule" that was exhibited by Lewis Evans. The rule was from about 1720, but it was changed to a slide rule about a century later.[43] Noticeably, accuracy was not only an issue of slide rule length but, also, an issue of slide rule width. This was the case with lines of "wide-faced" slide rules for technicians. An example was the Blundell lines of slide rules.[44]

Given that the accuracy of the slide rule depended on the accuracy by which the inscriptions could be read, extended markings, background colors, colored numbers, slanted numbers, and gauge marks were extensively used in order to increase the accuracy of the slide rule without increasing its size.[45] A system of notation of scales, usually called "gauges" or "marks," could also help so as to avoid the introduction of new scales. It could also assist in special purpose computing through the inclusion of certain constants, which could be used to speed up a computation. The result was what Clason referred to as "high-speed scales".[46] It is estimated that there are literally dozens of such useful notation marks, which were added by the manufacturer or the owner for his own particular use or specialization. For example, one notation systems, W, was used for computing the weight of copper conductors. It was used regularly by electrical specialists.[47] We find an example of a process of an introduction of slide rule marks in the series of the 1905 *Electric Club Journal* articles that concluded with the recommendation to use a slide rule for the purpose of memorizing the wire table.[48]

---

[42] See Horsburgh (ed.), *Modern instruments and methods of calculation: A handbook of the tercentenary exhibition*, 167, 170–171, 173, 177, 178, 179, 180, 178, 179, and 179 respectively.

[43] Ibid., 166.

[44] Hopp, *Slide rule: Their history, models, and makers*, 145.

[45] von Jezierski, *Slide rule: A journey through three centuries*, 40.

[46] Clason, *Delights of the slide rule*.

[47] Hopp, *Slide rule: Their history, models, and makers*, 288–289.

[48] Charles F. Scott. 1905, April. How to remember the wire table. *Electric Club Journal* 11(4): 220–223; Harold Pender. 1905, May. Formulae for the wire table. *Electric Club Journal* 11(5): 327; Y. Sakai. 1905, October. How to use the slide rule on the wire table. *Electric Club Journal*

2.6   "The Habit of Attempting That 'Ficticious Accuracy'"

Turning from abstract to concrete comparisons, computing accuracy becomes a variable that depends on many factors (e.g., portability) and sub-factors (e.g., portability to hostile environments). Accessories like special leather cases or other, less standard items could here make a difference. For example, the "special" slide rule of John Davis & Son of Derby that was exhibited at the 1914 Exhibition was advertised as a "standard" rule that included "a steel back" and "three adjusting screws to make the slide travel smoothly." It was "[f]or use in hot or damp climates."[49] The fact that a slide rule could be conveniently carried around—even in the form of a stylus and a pocket or wristwatch—could make a difference in terms of portability in the field.[50]

The accuracy of computing with a slide rule depended, among other things, on how skillfully and carefully it was constructed. All evidence suggests that the experience and the talent of the user of the dividing engine could make a big difference. This explains why the workings of the Keuffel & Esser "dividing rooms" were always top-secret.[51] Critics of the slide rule tended to focus on the errors from wrong setting or/and reading of the scales. But there were errors that an engineer could not avoid, including errors in the data tables used to compute with a slide rule. Such errors have been found in the "carpenters' and engineers'" slide rules.[52] The computing accuracy of the slide rule depended not only on how much accuracy could be constructed by the use of a dividing engine but also by how much accuracy could be maintained by the proper care of the slide rule.[53] Most treatises on the slide rule gave instructions on how to make a slide rule and properly take car of it.[54]

The issue of computing accuracy in connection to an improved method to use the slide rule and/or in connection to improved slide rules was a theme that was consid-

---

11(10): 632–633, and Miles Walker. 1905, November. Calculating temperature rises with a slide rule. *Electric Club Journal* 11(11): 694–696.

[49] See Horsburgh (ed.), *Modern instruments and methods of calculation: A handbook of the tercentenary exhibition*, 177.

[50] Conrad Schure. 1997, March. Slide rule watches. *Journal of the Oughtred Society* 6(1): 47–48.

[51] Robert Otnes, *Keuffel and Esser and the American engineering slide rule*, Manuscript in the collection of the Division of Computers, National Museum of American History, 5.

[52] Philip E. Stanley. 1984. Carpenters' and engineers' slide rules (Part II Routledges' Rule). *Chronicle of the Early American Industries Association* 37(2): 25–27; Philip E. Stanley. 1987, March. Carpenters' and engineers' slide rules: Errors in data tables. *Chronicle of the Early America and Industries Association* 40(1): 7–8, and Philip E. Sranley. 1994, March. Letters. *Journal of the Oughtred Society* 3(1), 35–37. See, also, Bruce E. Babcock. 1993, October. An error on a slide rule for 50 years? *Journal of the Oughtred Society*. 2(2): 15–17, and Bruce E. Babcock. 1994, March. A guided tour of an eighteenth century Carpenter's rule. *Journal of the Oughtred Society* 3(1): 26–34.

[53] Hopp, *Slide rule: Their history, models, and makers*, and Jezierski, *Slide rule: A journey through three centuries*.

[54] On proper slide rule maintenance, see Clason, *Delights of the slide rule*, chapter 2.

ered important enough to deserve the attention of academicians. For example, finding the decimal point with the slide rule was an inexhaustible issue because it changed along modifications in the mode of constructing and using the slide rule. In 1929, William J. Alcott, Jr., Assistant Professor at Northeastern University in Boston, Massachusetts, wrote to *Engineering News-Record* to propose an improved method for locating the decimal point. Alcott stated the problem properly by explaining that:

> In slide rule computations involving complicated formulas or which involve either very large numbers or very small numbers, the position of decimal point is often determined with some difficulty. Such rules as are in use involving the manipulation of the rule, as, for instance, the direction in which the slide rule protrudes, fail when other scales than the *C* and *D* scales are used.[55]

Alcott wrote to argue that with a minimum of proper "memorization," this problem could be solved while, in addition, an independent check on the accuracy of the computation would be possible. Being considerably faster than computing by hand or with logarithmic tables, computing with the slide rule allowed the user to try out a few "what-ifs," in addition to providing the user with a good indication of the relevance of significant figures, i.e., of the importance of a proper approximation:

> If the third and the fourth figure cannot be ascertained because it means guessing at a difference less than the thickness of a hairline, then you realize how markedly insignificant it is compared to the digits to the left. But when folks began using calculators with ten-digit displays it was hard to persuade them to ignore the last six or seven, even when the input data was of doubtful accuracy and could not be guaranteed beyond the second of third digit.[56]

An important observation, which surfaced in the context of surveying slide rule decimal point location methods, is that most engineers who used a slide rule relied on inspection and approximation methods, because "they fit neatly with the engineer's training to visualize problems."[57]

As we saw, Clason referred to "speed scales" as an option for trading range of use (generality of purpose) for rapidity of use. Sensitive to all sorts of variable trade-offs, the economy of computing with a slide rule varied even with change in national context. Clason distinguished between an "American ideal of crowding the maximum possible number of scales into a single slide rule" and a "contrary philosophy," German and British, which was to provide "as large a number of different types of inexpensive slide rules as possible."[58] This seems to reproduce the general American

---

[55] William J. Alcott Jr. 1929, April 25. The decimal point with the slide rule. *Engineering News-Record* 102: 686.

[56] Cyrill Catt. 1999, Fall. Slide rule accuracy. *Journal of the Oughtred Society* 8(2): 5.

[57] Edwin J. Chamberlain. 1998, Spring. Slide rule decimal point location methods. *Journal of the Oughtred Society* 7(1): 38.

[58] Clason, *Delights of the slide rule*, 239.

tendency toward producing general-purpose machines, which came along the development of the "American System of Manufactures."[59]

It has been shown that technical variables—for example, speed in computing with prestigious electronic supercomputers—are socially constructed.[60] The history of the debates concerning the accuracy of the slide rule helps us to understand that computing comparisons actually involved a number of variables. To start with, with the exception of the "Curta," calculating machines were too heavy, too bulky, too fragile, or/and too dependent on power to be used outside the office—Curta was a handheld machine, 6.3 cm diameter and 11 cm high, not however available before World War II.[61] Portability—being able to fit the slide rule "in the pocket" and carry it "around" the plant—was also an important variable.[62] To the main trade-offs between accuracy and other variables—cost vs. accuracy, range vs. accuracy, speed vs. accuracy, portability versus accuracy, etc.—we could add many other secondary trade-offs. For example, as mentioned earlier, tolerance of the computing artifact to extreme temperatures was also a factor in field computations.

In 1901, Chas. A. Holden wrote that in engineering computations, one could actually often see "the habit of attempting that 'fictitious accuracy,'" a habit to be overcome by a minimum of proper training (more on Holden and his views on slide rule training below, in 2.8).[63] Assuming such training, engineers frequently took the pen to argue against those who sought to dismiss their beloved "slipstick" as an insufficient computing artifact of a bygone era. Clason instructions on maintenance called the slide rule "the mighty slipstick."[64] For Clason and for several generations of engineers before him, computing with the corresponding generations of slide rules was sufficient: "The slide rule has so many applications that it would be futile to attempt to list them. But, besides helping make the daily technical jobs easier, the slide rule can be a thorough satisfying hobby for those who, like the author, find pleasure in fooling around with mathematics."[65]

---

[59] For the history of the "American System of Manufactures" and its conclusion in Fordism, see David A. Hounshell. 1984. *From the American system to mass production, 1800–1932: The development of manufacturing technology in the United States.* Baltimore: John Hopkins University Press. For the analogy between this history and the history of software production, see Michael Mahoney. 1990. The roots of software engineering. *CWI Quarterly* 3(4): 325–334.

[60] Boelie Elzen, and Donald Mackenzie. 1994. The social limits of speed: The development and use of supercomputers. *IEEE Annals of the History of Computing* 16(1): 46–61; Donald MacKenzie. 1990. The influence of the Los Alamos and livermore national laboratories on the development of supercomputing. *Annals of the History of Computing* 13(4), 325–334.

[61] Catt, Slide rule accuracy. For Curta, see Peggy Aldrich Kidwell, and Paul E. Ceruzzi. 1994. *Landmarks in digital computing: A Smithsonian pictorial history*, 30. Washington, DC: Smithsonian Institution Press.

[62] W.L. Durand. 1922, May 2. Why not use a slide rule? *Power* 55(18): 705.

[63] Charlers A. Holden. 1901, May 30. The use of calculating machines. Engineering News 45(22): 405.

[64] Clason, *Delights of the slide rule*, Foreword.

[65] Ibid., x.

2.7 "The Poor Man's Calculator"

Clason entitled the chapter in which he gave slide rule construction and maintenance instructions "the poor man's calculator."[66] Reading the instructions on maintenance enforces the impression that computing with a slide rule allowed for individual ownership of the means of computing production. Individual ownership of a calculating machine by an engineer was much more unlikely than individual ownership of a slide rule. For most engineers, defending the accuracy of the slide rule against attacks from promoters of the calculating machine was akin to defending their ownership of the means of computing production.

In the 30th (1900) and in the 31st (1902) Keuffel & Esser trade catalogs, the most expensive slide rule listed was "Thacher's calculating instrument," which was a cylindrical slide rule that was selling for $35.[67] Purchasing a 3-inch reading glass that could be slid on brass bar and that was adjustable to any part of this instrument would cost an additional $10. The book with directions on how to use this instrument was available for an extra $1. "Fuller's spiral rule" was a little less expensive. Its cost was $30. These two slide rules were the most expensive. In comparison to the millions of slide rules sold, these two models sold a total of approximately 6,700 and 14,000 over 65 (1882 to the early 1950s) and 95 (1879–1973) years of continuous production, respectively.[68] Indicative of how expensive these two slide rules were is the fact that in the event that the Thacher slide rule scales became worn, they could be repaired by a special Keuffel & Esser service.[69]

For a maximum that was less than $50, there were slide rules that could be used so as to compute with extreme accurately. In an 1891 article on the accuracy of various calculating devices that was published in Keuffel & Esser's *The Compass*, William Cox reported that he had estimated the mean error of the cylindrical slide rule to have been 0.0031% or 1/32,000 and the mean error of the spiral rule to be 0.008% or 1/12,500. Such accuracy was far greater than the accuracy that most engineers thought that they needed in the majority of the cases that they worked with. In fact it would be difficult to find an engineering problem that required greater accuracy. The most demanding computations of those undertaken in connection to electric power transmission calculations did not require such accuracy.[70]

The Thacher slide rule was a relatively cumbersome device, large to be carried everywhere as easily as a simple slide rule, which was most likely designed to compete in business applications with the equally cumbersome Arithmometer, the first

---

[66] Ibid, Chapter 2.

[67] See David C. Garcelon. 1996, October. Solving the Keuffel & Esser catalog problem. *Journal of the Oughtred Society* 5(2): 52–53.

[68] Wayne E. Feely. 1997a, September. The fuller spiral slide rule. *Chronicle of the Early American Industries Association* 50(3): 93–98, and Wayne E. Feely. 1997b, December. Thacher cylindrical slide rules. *Chronicle of the Early American Industries Association* 50(4): 123–127.

[69] Feely, *Thacher cylindrical slide rules*, 127.

[70] See, for example, the computing accuracy recommended in William Nesbit 1919–1920. Electrical characteristics of transmission circuits. *Electric Journal*. 16–19, series of articles.

commercially available calculating machine.[71] The most expensive of the much more popular and portable slide rules was a 20-inch duplex slide rule with glass indicator and two "interchangeable slides," which was priced at $20—still a high price.[72] The majority of the engineers were pleased with a slide rule that would cost them very few dollars instead of a few tens of dollars. Like a 10-inch Manheim, one with a glass indicator, which was selling for less than $5.

The Keuffel & Esser "reckoning machine" (a calculating machine) was advertised as being suitable to laboratories and offices. It was selling at $193.25 for 6 grooves and 12 holes in upper row, $241.50 for 8 grooves and 16 holes in upper row, and $338.25 for 10 grooves and 20 holes in upper row.[73] In 1915, when P.H. Skinner sought to promote the introduction of calculating machines to engineering, he mentioned that they would cost about $400.[74] The average individual engineer could not be an owner of a calculating machine. For 1/100 of this cost, he could buy a common slide rule, or if extreme accuracy was necessary, for 1/10 of this amount, he could buy an exceptionally accurate slide rule. In either case, he would maintain ownership of the computing artifact, regardless of whether he worked for himself or for a company. Accordingly, most engineers had every reason to remain suspicious of those who, like Skinner, were attempting to attract them to calculating machines.

The last time that a Thatcher slide rule was listed to a catalog was in 1949. Its cost was $100.[75] In comparison to the cost of the electronic computers of the 1940s, this was very little money for plenty of accuracy. For most engineering purposes, the accuracy of this exceptional slide rule was still unnecessary. As late as in the 1940s, for most engineers, the accuracy of a common slide rule was actually all that they needed. Noticeably, the demand for Keuffel & Esser slide rules during World War II accelerated because colleges and schools were ordering double and triple the quantity they had ordered the previous year.[76] Nobert Wiener had called World War I the "Slide Rule War."[77] It may turn out that World War II should be called the same.

Engineering comparisons that involved computing with the slide rule were not rare. A comparison of slide rules, tables of logarithms, and calculating machines was offered by R. C. Carpenter, professor of experimental engineering at Cornell University, in his *Experimental Engineering*.[78] Two years earlier, Holden, who was

---

[71] Otnes, *Keuffel and Esser and the American engineering slide rule*, 2.

[72] Ibid., 4.

[73] Advertisement by Keuffell & Esser in J.Y. Wheatley. 1903. *The polar planimeter and its use in engineering calculations together with tables, diagrams, and factors*. New York: Keuffel & Esser.

[74] P.H. Skinner. 1915, January 7. Computing machines in engineering. *Engineering News*, 25–27.

[75] Robert Otnes. 1993, March. Thacher notes. *Journal of the Oughtred Society* 2(1): 21–25.

[76] William Franklin. 1967. *Partners in creating: The first century of Keuffel & Esser*, 24–25. New York: Keuffel & Esser.

[77] Thomas Wyman. 2001, Spring. Norbert Wiener and the slide rule or how American mathematicians came of age. *Journal of the Oughtred Society* 10(1): 46–47.

[78] R.C. Carpenter.1903. *Experimental engineering (and manual for testing)*, 5th rev and enlarg ed. New York: Wiley.

an instructor at the Thayer School of Civil Engineering at Hannover, New Hampshire, published the results of his research on the use of the "Manheim pocket slide rule," the "Thacher calculating machine," and other calculating machines in an article that was published in *Engineering News* under the title "The Use of Calculating Machines." Holden had sent out 100 copies of a questionnaire to individual engineers, professors of engineering schools, and business firms. He interpreted his results as showing "quite a haziness as to the extent to which the slide rule can be properly used." Taking the average accuracy of the slide rule as two tenths of 1%, he suggested that it could be used "for all preliminary and very many final estimates, perhaps three-fourths of the computations ordinarily required of an engineer." "If then," he moved on to wonder, "there is so large a field for the use of slide-rule, why it is not used to a greater extent?" After observing that some doubted the accuracy of the slide rule "without a definite idea as to the relationship between the accuracy of the slide rule and the data of most engineering problems," he identified the source of the problem in the lack of proper training, because about 50% of engineering schools were "remiss in this [teaching the use of the slide-rule] duty."[79] In the rest of his paper, Holden outlined a plan for instructing engineering students to the use of the slide rule so that they would be prepared for the business world.

2.8   "As Well as the Pianist Knows His Keyboard"

Writing in 1901, Holden was concerned with the issue of the mechanization of computing as a whole. Instruction to and use of a pocket Manheim slide rule was for him an index to such mechanization. Computing with calculating machines was competing against engineering computations by hand, with or without tables. The comparison of the use of the various calculating machines in Holden is very informative. For Holden, the concept "calculating machine" was actually referring mostly to a slide rule. As far as the use of the standard slide rule goes, the numbers for individual engineers and engineering schools were 39.5% and 37.5% for "constantly," 0% and 12.5% for "much," 34.2% and 33.3% for "little," 0% and 4.2% for "discouraged," and 26.3% and 12.5% for "none." The expensive slide rules were used more by engineering schools than by individual engineers. The only other calculating machine mentioned by name in Holden's article was the Arithmometer, which was used "constantly" in 4 out of the 13 business firms that responded. If any of the 38 individual engineers and the 24 engineering schools that replied used an Arithmometer or any other calculating machine, these were two few to show in Holden's analysis of the data.[80]

---

[79] Charlers A. Holden. 1901, May 30. The use of calculating machines. *Engineering News* 45(22): 405.
[80] Ibid.

These percentages indicate that the slide rule was already used extensively among American engineers, especially considering that several authors agree that slide rules in general and engineering slide rules in particular were not in wide use in the United States before the 1880s (in comparison to Great Britain and Europe in general).[81] Keuffel & Esser has developed the engineering slide rule business in the United States in the 1880s and in the 1890s by producing a large variety of rules of generally high quality and by educating the engineering community through a series of books, pamphlets, and articles in various magazines.[82] By 1900, the Keuffel & Esser models were about 30, and by 1906, 54.[83] Several retailers were already offering engineering slide rules to American engineers. In the fourth edition trade catalog of the Frederick Post Company of 1903–1904, six models were advertised as "Engineers' Slide Rule." At the time, the Frederick Post Company was a retailer of the German slide rules of Faber.[84]

The spread of the slide rule in engineering by 1901 seems more impressive if we take into account the fact that computing with the slide rule required education and reeducation. Holden's attention to engineering education was well justified. It explains the emphasis on demonstration slide rules for educational purposes,[85] the persistence of high school competitions that sought to promote the introduction to the slide rule until the late 1970s,[86] the development of a great number of student or beginner slide rules,[87] the slide rule manufacturers sales campaigns to engineering

---

[81] On engineering slide rules, see the following sample: Otnes, *Keuffel and Esser and the American engineering slide rule*, Robert Otnes. 1989, August and November. Keuffel & Esser slide rules *Historische Burowelt*: 15–20 and 21–26 respectively and Robert Otnes. 2001, Spring. Keuffel & Esser—1880 to 1899. *Journal of the Oughtred Society* 10(1): 18–28; Franklin, *Partners in creating: The first century of Keuffel & Esser*, 11; Kenneth D. Roberts. 1983, March. Carpenter's and engineer's slide rules, Part I: History. *Chronicle of the Early American Industries Association* 36(1): 1–5; Philip E. Stanley, Carpenters' and engineers' slide rules (Routledges' Rule and "Carpenters' and Engineers' Slide Rules: Errors in Data Tables" and "Letters"; Bruce E. Babcock, An Error on a Slide Rule for 50 Years? and A Guided Tour of an Eighteenth Century Carpenter's Rule; Conrad Schure. 1994a, March. The Scofield-Thacher slide rule. *Journal of the Oughtred Society* 3(1): 20–25; Wayne Feely. 1994, September. The Engineer's rule. *Journal of the Oughtred Society* 3(2): 48–49 and Wayne E. Feely 1996. Keuffel & Esser slide rules. *Chronicle of the Early American Industries Association* 49(2): 50–52; Thomas Wyman. 1996. October. The Thomas Dixon engineer's slide rule. *Journal of the Oughtred Society* 5(2): 68.

[82] Otnes, *Keuffel and Esser and the American engineering slide rule*, 10; Keuffel & Esser slide rules; and Keuffel & Esser—1880 to 1899.

[83] Wayne Feely, "Keuffel & Esser Slide Rules": 51.

[84] Robert Otnes. 1998a, Spring. Notes on Frederick post slide rules. *Journal of the Oughtred Society* 7(1): 7.

[85] von Jezierski, *Slide rule: A journey through three centuries*, 85–86.

[86] Mike Gabbert. 1999, Fall. Slide rule competition in Texas high schools. *Journal of the Oughtred Society* 8(2): 56–58.

[87] Bruce E. Babcock. 1995a, October. K&E student's and beginner's slide rules, 1897 to 1954. *Journal of the Oughtred Society* 4(2): 41–49.

students,[88] and the appearance of many engineering treatises that were based on courses introducing engineering students to the slide rule until very late.[89]

In his 1964 treatise on the slide rule, Clason used a set of engaging analogies in order to explain that the slide rule required an initial education in manual and mental skills and reeducation to new skills:

> True, practice is required to become proficient on the slide rule—just as practice is needed to learn how to pitch a curve ball, sail a boat, or play piano. However, the slide rule also requires you to use your mind. ...every good engineer is on the alert to add to his store of knowledge. He should know the scales of the slide rule as well as the pianist knows his keyboard. Generally he does. But slide rules change, though slowly, and the engineer may have gotten into a rust with his trusted old faithful from the 1930's.[90]

The history of slide rule instruction manuals suggests that computing with the slide rule was more complex that now assumed because it involved more than a piece or pieces of hardware.[91] With his 1891 Keuffel & Esser slide rule instruction manual, Cox set a pattern for these manuals. "There is a very general impression," stated Cox, "that the acquirement of a facile use of the Slide Rule is both tedious and difficult. This, however," he argued, "is not the case. It may be easily learnt in spare moments, advantage being taken of these to attain to proficiency by frequent practice."[92] In effect, Cox was admitting the need for instruction and practice. Accordingly, he moved on to provide with tables of settings, equivalents, and gauge points. He did the same in several articles. In the January 3, 1891, issue of *Engineering News,* he published a paper entitled "Equivalents or Useful Numbers for Simplifying Calculations and for Slide Rule Practice," which was described by the editor as "the most complete and useful table of the kind in print, in English at least."[93]

Ability to use the slide rule was assumed in almost every engineering class, even if the amount of course credit given to courses on the study of the use of the slide rule was not great. Demonstration of the ability to use a slide rule weighted heavily in the examination part of courses on the slide rule.[94] As late as in the 1970s, the slide rule was a symbol of one's identity as an engineering student: "the brown or black leather scabbard holding the rule could be suspended from his [the engineering student's] belt as he walked across the campus, identifying him from a

---

[88] Tomash Wyman. 1998, Fall. The slide rule in college. *Journal of the Oughtred Society* 7(2): 57.

[89] For a sample of late slide rule treatises, see Randolph P. Hoelscher, Joseph N. Arnold, and Stanley H. Pierce. 1952. *Graphic aids in engineering computation.* New York: McGraw-Hill; John P. Ellis, *The theory and operation of the slide rule* and Clason, *Delights of the slide rule.*

[90] Clason, *Delights of the slide rule,* viii–x.

[91] Robert Otnes. 1997, March. K&E instruction manuals. *Journal of the Oughtred Society* 6(1): 18–21, and Robert Otnes. 1998b, Fall. American slide rule instruction books before 1890. *Journal of the Oughtred Society* 7(2): 31–34.

[92] William M. Cox. 1891b. *The Manheim's slide rule,* 1. New York: Keuffel & Esser.

[93] William M. Cox. 1891a, January 3. Equivalents of useful numbers for simplifying calculations and for slide rule practice. *Engineering News-Record* 25: 6.

[94] Otnes, *Keuffel and Esser and the American engineering slide rule,* 10.

distance."[95] The use of the slide rule by engineering students was so pervasive that it was depicted in comics and cartoons.[96] The foundation of an engineering political economy that was based on keeping the capital spent on computing artifacts within individual control rested on an education that encouraged him to start with an inexpensive and simple student slide rule of less than $1 before making the next step into one or more expensive ones that would cost ten times this amount.

2.9 "Unfair to Compare"

After the mid-1950s, there was an unprecedented increase in slide rule manufacturing.[97] At the same time, there was also an absorbing of the tradition of computing with the slide rule by the emerging tradition of electronic computing. At Faber-Castell, machines for production of pocket electronic calculators were added in the slide rule production factory. The result was an electronic calculator and slide rule combination that appeared in 1972. The initial series of Faber-Castell pocket calculators consisted of models TR1, TR2, and TR3, all of which had slide rules attached to the back. The cases and keys were made in-house, and the chips and circuit boards were purchased from outside. Since models TR1 and TR2 could only be used for the four basic arithmetic operations, several scales of a built-in slide rule were included. Only the TR2 persisted. Subsequent models had no built-in slide rules.[98] The Faber-Castell slide rule and pocket electronic calculator combination can be interpreted as updates of the Addiator Faber-Castell slide rule and pocket calculating machine combination mentioned earlier in this Chapter (Sect. 2.3).

There is another suggestive connection between slide rules and pocket electronic calculators. To show it, we may consider some articles and advertisements published in the "Special HP-35 Anniversary Edition" of *The International Calculator Collector*.[99] The first article is a reprint from the June 1972 issue of *The HP Journal*. It was authored by Thomas M. Whitney, France Rode, and Chung C. Tung and was entitled "The HP-35—The 'Powerful Pocketful' an Electronic Calculator Challenges the Slide Rule." Once again, a new computing artifact was promoted through its comparison with the slide rule, which persisted against innumerable such comparisons:

> When an engineer or scientist needs a quick answer to a problem that requires multiplication, division, or transcendental functions, he usually reaches for his ever present slide rule. Before long, however, that faithful 'slip-stick' may find itself retired. There's now an elec-

---

[95] Ibid.

[96] Wyman, *The slide rule in college*.

[97] von Jezierski, *Slide rule: A journey through three centuries*, 60.

[98] Ibid., 60–61.

[99] "Special HP-35 Anniversary Edition. 1997, Summer. *International association of calculator collector*, 17.

tronic pocket calculator that produces those answers more easily, more quickly, and much more accurately.[100]

This comparison was quite abstract. For example, the cost of the two artifacts compared was not comparable. In the early 1970s, the HP-35 was much more expensive than the average slide rule. In a 1973 Hewlett-Packard advertisement that is reprinted in the HP-35 anniversary issue of *The International Calculator Collector*, the HP-35 complete with accessories was priced at 208 pound sterling.[101]

Wlodek Mier-Jedrzejowicz, author of *A Guide to HP Handheld Calculators and Computers*, remembered that in 1971 he had bought a top-of-the-range slide rule with help of a grant given to him by IBM that had 34 scales, the cursor "to make the equivalent to 35 keys," a case including a pocket for an instruction card, and a manual over 30 pages long. He had even bought a bottle of slide cleaner fluid as an accessory, but he did not buy the most expensive accessory, which was a cursor with a magnifier to give greater accuracy. "The slide rule," he thought, "was more than a tool—it was as much fun as a personal computer would be these days, and it was accurate to three whole significant figures." "In comparison," continued Mier-Jedrzejowicz, "my father's handheld and hand-cranked Curta gave eleven digit results, but could only carry out the four basic arithmetic operations." In other words, the two were not comparable in respect to use. By 1972, Mier-Jedrzejowicz had the opportunity to use somebody else's HP-35, but he could not afford one. The HP-35 was actually so expensive that only the student laboratories installed a row of them next year. Even if he could afford it, he could not use it for everything that he could use his slide rule for: "[i]t [HP-35] was even more fun than my slide rule—though unlike the slide rule it did not have hyperbolic functions."[102]

As we read in an editorial note to the aforementioned special HP-35 edition of *The International Calculator Journal*, Hewlett-Packard had a model in the market since 1968 that could be used, among other things, to compute the conversion from polar to rectangular conversion. But it weighted 40 pounds and cost just under $5000. The most expensive of the special slide rules that could be used for the same purpose, e.g., the Fuller style one mentioned earlier in this Sect. (2.7), cost 1/100 of this, i.e., it was two orders less expensive. Four-function electronic calculators of the mid- to late 1960s were less expensive than the first Hewlett-Packard (HP-9100). Their cost was between $1,000 and $2,500. This was also about 100 higher that the cost of a slide rule—for a maximum of $2.5, one could actually buy a four-function slide rule.

An advertisement republished in the special issue of *The International Calculator Collector* on HP-35 captures the continuity between the slide rule and the electronic calculator, especially in respect to engineering computations. The electronic calculator advertised was the "New Lloyd's Accumatic." It was presented as the "first real

---

[100] Ibid., 1.

[101] Ibid., 7.

[102] Ibid., 6 and 8.

alternative" to the HP-35. But, noticeably, it was not introduced to as an "electronic calculator" but as an "electronic slide rule":

> Hats off to Hewlett Packard! This remarkable company managed to hold its very own market position for almost two years selling its $300 to $400 slide rule calculators directly to the consumer.

> But good old American competition has produced what we feel to be a better alternative than Hewlett Packard's famous HP-35. And it costs considerably less! It's called the Lloyd's Accumatic electronic slide rule.[103]

The price of this electronic slide rule was $169.95. In the advertisement of the Lloyd Accumatic electronic slide rule quoted above, the emphasis was placed on the special features that made this artifact better for engineering computations. For example, in using it one could compute in radians or degrees, which was "a great help to civil and electrical engineers." More importantly, those who designed this electronic slide rule substituted addressable memory for scientific notation because they considered it to be "of greater value to engineering than scientific notation which they felt was a luxury similar to power seats on an automobile." Even though it was also advertised to engineers, HP-35 was promoted as "a powerful scientific calculator."[104]

In comparison to the HP-35, Lloyd's Accumatic was explicitly more for engineers than for scientists. Given that engineers historically preferred slide rules over calculating machines, calling Lloyd's Accumatic a slide rule was appealing to the engineering ideology and to the engineering economy that this ideology was articulated with. We saw that most engineers had traditionally tried to avoid "fictitious" technical superiority. It is to the same computing political economy of engineering that Lloyd counted on by dismissing the scientific notation that was provided by the competing firm as a "luxury."

The Hewlett-Packard calculators were also described as "slide rule calculators." Calling the first electronic calculators "electronic slide rules" was a generalized practice. The fact that Texas Instruments called its early models, e.g., SR-11 and SR-50, "electronic slide rule calculator" has been called the "ultimate irony" of the slide rule history:

> Because it is human nature to resist anything new or different, there was undoubtedly some reluctance on the part of many engineers and scientists to give up their tried-and-true Slide Rules. In order to overcome this resistance, one of the early electronic pocket calculators manufacturers (probably at the suggestion of their Madison Avenue advertising consultants) introduced a model which they heroically named The Electronic Slide Rule Calculator.[105]

There was actually an electronic calculator that came close to being a "real" electronic slide rule because multiplication with it was based on logarithmation. This made perfect sense at a time when "electronic multiplication was slow, and

---

[103] Ibid., 12.

[104] Ibid., 1.

[105] Conrad Schure. 1994b, September. The irony of it all. *Journal of the Oughtred Society* 3(2): 45.

expensive to implement." The electronic calculator was the Wang 300. It was intended for engineering computations.[106] The concept "electronic slide rule" pointed to a dynamic transformation of the slide rule into an electronic computing artifact, not to the static substitution of an electronic computing artifact by the slide rule. At the least, it suggests a continuity between slide rules and electronic calculators that invites to reconsider historical periodizations that assume that calculating machines were the only ancestors of electronic calculators.

Can we defend an essentialist demarcation between the computing of the recent decades and computing during the recent centuries based on "programmability" (a variant actually of "generality" of computing purpose)? Can we assume that our electronic digital general-purpose computing is different because it is the only one that is based on the "stored-program" principle? In my opinion, as demonstrated by the diachronic development of specialized slide rule scales, the operating principle of the slide rule was based on the same principle. For a synchronic comparison, I invite us to juxtapose a state-of-the-art general-purpose computer and a state-of-the-art slide rule by taking the end of the 1950s as a basis. This was the time of the appearance of a conscious division between hardware and software—as it is well known, without special purpose software, the (supposedly) general-purpose electronic computer could not be used for any purpose.[107] 1959 was the year that the "Direct Frequency Response Slide Rule" was introduced by Boonshaft and Fuchs of Hatboro, Pennsylvania. It included 25 plastic slides, each about 17″ long by 0.32″ wide and 0.18″ thick, with tabular data on each of their broader slides. It also included a slide holder that was a metal and plastic device about 12.6″ wide, by 5″ from top to bottom, and about 0.45″ thick. It had slots for holding up to 11 slides with the broader sides visible. There were leaf springs at both ends of all the slots that prevented the slides from moving while making calculations. The slide holder was transparent so that sides of the slides in it could be read. A runner for reading the scales was included, marked so that one column of information could be conveniently totaled. An owner of such slide rule wrote that, "[a]s slide rules go," this was "quite attractive."[108] The same slide rule was recently described on page 72 of the March 22, 1999, issue of *Electronic Design*, in the column "Forty Years Ago in Electronic Design." As I understand it, the 25 slides incorporated as an option in the "Direct Frequency Response Slide Rule" qualify it as a stored-program computer. From the perspective of the advance in storing programs for computing intensity and phase as function of network frequency, this slide rule was comparable to the electronic computer hardware and software combinations then available—not to mention that the hardware and the software of the electronic computer

---

[106] Ibid., 45.

[107] On the earliest emergence of the term software in the 1950s, see Fred R. Shapiro. 2000, April–June. Origin of the term software: Evidence from the JSTOR electronic journal archive. *IEEE Annals of the History of Computing* 22(2): 69–70.

[108] Robert Otnes. 1999, Spring. Direct reading frequency response slide rule. *Journal of the Oughtred Society* 8(1): 49.

cost much more and were not portable.[109] By the end of the twentieth century, the accumulated ideological force of abstract technical comparisons that sought to belittle computing with a slide rule became so strong that even the editor of the *Journal of the Oughtred Society* could state that "[w]hile this [his] slide rule may have been useful at the time (circa 1959), any low-grade PC running a BASIC interpreter could be set up to do a better job of solving the problem."[110] As I see it, the 1959 slide rule should only be compared to a 1959 electronic computer: the well-known fact is that in 1959 and for about two more decades, no PC to run a BASIC interpreter was available.

To indicate how problematic it may be to compare computing artifacts that differ by 2 electronic era decades, I refer to an advertisement that suggested that it may be unfair to compare electronic era computing artifacts that differ only by 2 years. I quote from the "New Lloyd's Accumatic electronic slide rule" 1974 comparison to the HP-35:

> Unfair to Compare
>
> It might be unfair to compare the HP-35 with the Lloyd's Accumatic. After all, the HP-35 is over two years old, and calculator technology has developed a great deal since then. What took five separate integrated circuits two years ago now takes just one in the Accumatic. The new larger florescent green display available on the Accumatic wasn't available when the LED display was first used in the HP-35. An unfair comparison? Maybe. But one thing is clear—the Lloyd's Accumatic represents today's most advanced feature package at a most reasonable price.[111]

My hypothesis then is that the social trade-offs of technical features involved in computing with the slide rule were incorporated in computing with an electronic computer. This requires that we question what is now canonically assumed, namely, the essentialist (technical) superiority of the electronic computer. Historiographically, it requires that we cease studying only the promoters of the electronic computer and we move on to add the study of promoters of the slide rule. It then requires that we try to understand why as late as in 1952, three professors of engineering introduced to their slide rule McGraw-Hill treatise by claiming that "[g]raphical and mechanical aids in engineering computations are coming to occupy an ever-increased field of usefulness. In particular, the slide rule, of both the standard and special types, and the nomogram have come into prominence."[112]

---

[109] I base this estimation on the findings of various articles on the history of software production: Mahoney, The roots of software engineering; Martin Campbell-Kelly. 1995. Development and structure of the international software industry, 1950–1990. *Business and Economic History* 24(2): 74–110; Michael A. Cusumano. 1991. Factory concepts and practices in software development. *Annals of the History of Computing* 13(1): 3–30; Stuart Shapiro. 1997. Splitting the difference: The historical necessity of synthesis in software engineering. *IEEE Annals of the History of Computing* 19(1): 20–54; Eloina Pelaez. 1999, June. The stored-program computer: Two conceptions. *Social Studies of Science* 29(3): 359–389.

[110] Otnes, *Direct frequency response slide rule*, 50.

[111] Special HP-35 Anniversary edition, 12.

[112] Hoelscher, Arnold, and Pierce, *Graphic aids in engineering computation*, v.

It also requires that we try to understand what it was that Clason, author of the *Delights of the Slide Rule*, had in mind when he introduced to his 1964 treatise along the following lines:

> The 'slipstick,' as generations of engineers have affectionately called their slide rules, detours the dreary labor involved in multiplication, division, raising numbers to powers, extracting roots, solving triangles, and so on. The mighty slipstick does all that anything short of the electronic computer can do. It does these jobs simply, quickly, and accurately enough for many practical applications. Best of all, the slide rule lies within the range of almost every purse…The slipstick is a fascinating instrument. It continually challenges the imagination. Its possibilities seem almost endless.[113]

To recapitulate, I argue that we should attribute the attachment of most engineers to their slide rules to the fact that a mode of production of engineering computations that was based on the slide rule allowed them to be owners of the means of computing production. Arguments against "fictitious", "illusory", and "luxury" computing sought to challenge the ideology of a decontextualized conception of computing technology.

2.10 Conclusion

All indices presented in this chapter for the importance of computing with the slide rule suggest that such computing was tremendously important. The history of presenting the slide rule as intelligent, on the grounds of its alleged universality, allows us to hypothesize that the ideology of intelligent machines is much older than canonically assumed. For the average engineer, the accuracy of the slide rule was sufficient, especially in conjunction to his proper training. The chapter has systematically followed the history of the average engineer's passionate defense of the accuracy of the slide rule. What clearly emerges from reading the sizable literature relevant to this history is the struggle of the average engineer to advance a socially situated conception of technical variables to strengthen his position. To make sense of this struggle, the chapter focused on the political economy of computing with the slide rule. This focus prepares for understanding the relatively limited adoption of the calculating machine by the very same engineers (Chap. 6). In comparison to computing with a calculating machine or an analyzer (Chap. 4), computing with a slide rule corresponded to a higher percentage of skilled labor than machine capital. The evidence presented within this chapter suggests a promising hypothesis: in computing with a slide rule, an engineer could maintain ownership of the computing artifact. Against the assumption that the slide rule was replaced by the electronic computer, the chapter provided hints that suggest that the slide rule was absorbed by the electronic computer. In sketching the history of the slide rule, I have here run

---

[113] Clason, *Delights of the slide rule*, viii.

into several similarities that prove worthy of exploring, between computing with the slide rule and electronic computing as we now know it. The relationship between general and special purpose slide rules (or general and special purpose slide rule scales) comes first to mind as a clear forerunner of the hardware-software (or the general and special purpose software) relationship of our times.

References

Alcott WJ Jr (1929) The decimal point with the slide rule. Eng News-Rec 102:686

Babcock BE (1993) An error on a slide rule for 50 years? J Oughtred Soc 2(2):15–17

Babcock BE (1994) A guided tour of an 18th century Carpenter's rule. J Oughtred Soc 3(1):26–34

Babcock BE (1995a) K&E student's and beginner's slide rules 1897 to 1954. J Oughtred Soc 4(2):41–49

Babcock BE (1995b) Two noble attempts to improve the slide rule. J Oughtred Soc 4(1):41–45

Barth CG (1902a) Barth's gear slide-rule. Am Mach 1075

Barth CG (1902b) Barth's lathe speed slide rules. Am Mach 1684–1685

Barth CG (1919a) Supplement to Frederick Taylor's 'on the art of cutting metals' I and II. Ind Manag 58(3):169–175

Barth CG (1919b) Supplement to Frederick Taylor's 'on the art of cutting metals' I and II. Ind Manag 58(4):282–287

Barth CG (1919c) Supplement to Frederick Taylor's 'on the art of cutting metals' I and II. Ind Manag 58(5):369–374

Barth CG (1919d) Supplement to Frederick Taylor's 'on the art of cutting metals' I and II. Ind Manag 58(6):483–487

Bazerman C (1999) The languages of Edison light. The MIT Press, Cambridge

Bevan B (1822) A practical treatise on the sliding rule. W. Turnbull, London

Cajori F (1909) A history of the logarithmic slide rule and allied instruments. The Engineering News Publishing Company, New York

Campbell-Kelly M (1995) Development and structure of the international software industry 1950–1990. Bus Econ Hist 24(2):74–110

Carpenter RC (1903) Experimental engineering (and manual for testing), 5th rev and enlarg edn. Wiley, New York

Catt C (1999) Slide rule accuracy. J Oughtred Soc 8(2):5

Chamberlain EJ (1997) The Voith slide rule and mechanical pencil combination. J Oughtred Soc 6(1):27–28

Chamberlain EJ (1998) Slide rule decimal point location methods. J Oughtred Soc 7(1):38–52

Clason CB (1964) Delights of the slide rule. Thomas Y. Crowell Co, New York

Cox WM (1891a) Equivalents of useful numbers for simplifying calculations and for slide rule practice. Eng News-Rec 25:5–6

Cox WM (1891b) The Manheim slide rule. Keuffel and Esser, New York

Cusumano MA (1991) Factory concepts and practices in software development. Annals Hist Comput 13(1):3–30

Durand WL (1922) Why not use a slide rule? Power 55(18):705

Ellis JP (1961) The theory and operation of the slide rule. Dover, New York

Elzen B, Mackenzie D (1994) The social limits of speed: the development and use of supercomputers. IEEE Ann Hist Comput 16(1):46–61

Farey J (1927) A treatise on the steam engine. Longman, Rees, Orme, Brown, and Green, London

Feely WE (1994) The engineer's rule. J Oughtred Soc 3(2):48–49

Feely WE (1996) Keuffel and Esser slide rules. Chron Early Am Ind Assoc Chron 49(2):50–52

Feely WE (1997a) The fuller spiral scale slide rule. Early Am Ind Assoc Chron 50(3):93–98

Feely WE (1997b) Thacher cylindrical slide rules. Early Am Ind Assoc Chron 50(4):123–127

Ferguson ES (1992) Engineering and the mind's eye. The MIT Press, Cambridge

Franklin W (1967) Partners in creating: the first century of Keuffel and Esser. Keuffel and Esser, New York

Gabbert M (1999) Slide rule competition in Texas high schools. J Oughtred Soc 8(2):56–58

Garcelon DC (1996) Solving the Keuffel & Esser Catalog problem. J Oughtred Soc 5(2):52–53

Helfand J (2006) Reinventing the wheel. Princeton Architectural Press, New York

Hoelscher RP, Arnold JN, Pierce SH (1952) Graphic aids in engineering computation. McGraw-Hill, New York

Holden CA (1901) The use of calculating machines. Eng News 45(22):405

Hopp PM (1999) Slide rule: their history models and makers. Astragal Press, Mendham

Horsburgh EM (ed) (1914) Modern instruments and methods of calculation: a handbook of the Napier tercentenary exhibition. Bell and Sons, London. Reprinted with an 'Introduction' by Michael R. Williams (Los Angeles: Tomash Publishers, 1982): ix–xxi

Hounshell DA (1984) From the American system to mass production 1800–1932: the development of manufacturing Technology in the United States. The John Hopkins University Press, Baltimore

Jenkins AL (1917) Design of special slide rules, Parts I and II. Ind Manag:241–389

Kidwell PA (2008) Useful instruction for practical people. In: Kidwell PA, Ackerberg-Hastings A, Roberts DL (eds) Tools of American mathematics teaching, 1800–2000. Johns Hopkins University Press, Baltimore, pp 105–122

Kidwell PA (2015) Useful instruction for practical people: early printed discussions of the slide rule in the US. IEEE Ann Hist Comput 37(01):36–43

Kidwell PA, Ackerberg-Hastings A (2014) In: Ackermann S, Kremer R, Miniati M (eds) Slide rules on display in the united states, 1840–2010 in scientific instruments on Display. Brill, Leiden

Kidwell PA, Ceruzzi PE (1994) Landmarks in digital computing: a Smithsonian pictorial history. Smithsonian Institution Press, Washington, DC

Kidwell PA, Ackerberg-Hastings A, Roberts DL (2008) Tools of American mathematics teaching, 1800–2000. Johns Hopkins University Press, Baltimore, especially pp 105–122

Larson M (1993a) The runner. J Oughtred Soc 2(1):40–43

Larson M (1993b) Runner indicator or cursor? J Oughtred Soc 2(1):47–48

MacKenzie D (1990) The influence of the los Alamos and Livermore National Laboratories on the development of supercomputing. Ann Hist Comput 13(4):325–334

Mahoney MS (1990) The roots of software engineering. CWI Q 3(4):325–334

Marsden B (2004) Watt's perfect engine: steam and the age of invention. Columbia University Press, New York

Otnes R (1989) Keuffel and Esser slide rules. Historische Burowelt:15–20

Otnes R (1993) Thacher notes. J Oughtred Soc 2(1):21–25

Otnes R (1995) A page from the 1883 Keuffel & Esser catalog. J Oughtred Soc 4(2):14–15

Otnes R (1997) K&E instruction manuals. J Oughtred Soc 6(1):18–21

Otnes R (1998a) Notes on Frederick post slide rules. J Oughtred Soc 7(1):7–10

Otnes R (1998b) American slide rule instruction books before 1890. J Oughtred Soc 7(2):31–34

Otnes R (1999) Direct reading frequency response slide rule. J Oughtred Soc 8(1):49–50

Otnes R (2001) Keuffel & Esser—1880 to 1899. J Oughtred Soc 10(1):18–28

Pelaez E (1999) The stored-program computer: two conceptions. Soc Stud Sci 29(3):359–389

Pender H (1905) Formulae for the wire table. Electr Club J 11(5):327

Pickworth CN (1903) Instructions for the use of A. W. Faber's improved calculating rule. A. W. Faber, London

Roberts KD (1983) Carpenters and engineers slide rules (Part I, History). Chron Early Am Ind Assoc 36(1):1–5

Sakai Y (1905) How to use the slide rule on the wire table. Electr Club J 11(10):632–633

Schuitema IJ, van Herwijnen H (2003) Calculating on slide rule and disk. Astragal Press, Mendham

Schure C (1994a) The Scofield-Thacher slide rule. J Oughtred Soc 3(1):20–25

Schure C (1994b) The irony of it all. J Oughtred Soc 3(2):45

Schure C (1997) Slide rule watches. J Oughtred Soc 6(1):47–48

Scott CF (1905) How to remember the wire table. Electr Club J 11(4):220–223

Shapiro S (1997) Splitting the difference: the historical necessity of synthesis in software engineering. IEEE Ann Hist Comput 19(1):20–54

Shapiro FR (2000) Origin of the term software: evidence from the JSTOR electronic journal
archive. IEEE Ann Hist Comput 22(2):69–70

Skinner PH (1915) Computing machines in engineering. Eng News, January 7, pp 25–27

Smith DE (1925) History of mathematics, vol II. Ginn, Boston

Stanley PE (1984) Carpenters' and engineers' slide rules (Part II, Routledges' rule). Chron Early
Am Ind Assoc 37(2):25–27

Stanley PE (1987) Carpenters' and engineers' slide rules (Part III, Errors in the data tables). Chron
Early Am Ind Assoc 40(1):7–8

Stanley PE (1994) Letters. J Oughtred Soc 3(1):35–37

Stanley PE (2004) Source book for rule collectors. Astragal Press, Mendham

Steinmetz CP (1917) Engineering mathematics, 3rd rev and enlarg edn. McGraw-Hill, New York

Sumner J (2001) John Richardson, saccharometry and the pounds-per-barrel extract: the construction of a quantity. Br J Hist Sci 34(3):255–273

Taylor FW (1907) On the art of cutting metals. ASME Trans 28:31–279

Turner AJ (1993) Of time and measurement: studies in the history of horology and fine technology.
Varorium, Norfolk

Tympas A (2001) The computor and the analyst: computing and power, 1870s–1960s. PhD dissertation, Georgia Institute of Technology, Atlanta. Chap. 2

Tympas A (2004) Calculation and computation. In: Horowitz MC (ed) New dictionary of the history of ideas, vol I. Charles Scribner's Sons, New York, pp 255–259

von Jezierski D (1996) Faber-Castell combination rule. J Oughtred Soc 5(1):24

von Jezierski D (2000) Slide rule: a journey through three centuries. Astragal Press, Mendham

von Jezierski D, Shepherd R (2000) Taylor, taylorism, and machine time slide rules. J Oughtred
Soc 9(2):32–36

Walker M (1905) Calculating temperature rises with a slide rule. Electr Club J 11(11):694–696

Wang Y (1916) The slide rule replaced by a new computer. Eng News 75(24):1120

Wang Y (1917) New parallel-line computer to replace slide-rule for rapid calculations. Electr Rev
West Electr 70(10):22

Wess J (1997) The Soho rule. J Oughtred Soc 6(2):23–26

Wheatley JY (1903) The polar panimeter and its use in engineering calculations together with
tables, diagrams and factors. Keuffel and Esser, New York

Woolrich AP (2000) John Farey and his treatise on the steam engine of 1827. Hist Technol 22:63–
106. 531, 566–567, 567–568

Wyman T (1996) The Thomas Dixon engineer's slide rule. J Oughtred Soc 5(2):68

Wyman T (1997) A five-piece combination gauging rod and slide rule. J Oughtred Soc 6(1):45–46

Wyman T (1998) The slide rule in college. J Oughtred Soc 7(2):57

Wyman T (2001) Norbert Wiener and the slide rule or how American mathematicians came of age.
J Oughtred Soc 10(1):46–47

Chapter 3
"Lightning Calculations Lightened"

Contents

3.1 Introduction

This chapter supplements the overview of the history of the slide rule of the preceding chapter by detailed histories of discussions concerning the slide rule in a key context of use, that of energy-related calculations. It starts with an introduction to the multitude of classes of slide rules that were used in this context (Sect. 3.2) before moving on to focus on discussions of relevance to the mechanical era, through research based on the journal *Power* (Sect. 3.3), and the electrical era, through research on a set of journals that included the *General Electric Review* (Sect. 3.4). Considering that the use of the slide rule for electricity-related calculations was especially wide, the chapter refers to it in order to elaborate on some of the issues raised in the preceding chapter: the presentation of the slide rule as intelligent and therefore universal computing artifact, the advance of an argument that attributed accuracy to skillful social use (and training to such use) rather than to some inherent technical advantage, and the refusal to consider accuracy independently from a broader set of variables, of which the most central was the cost (these are recurring issues in Sects. 3.4.1, 3.4.2, 3.4.3, and 3.4.4).

The more detailed approach of this chapter allows for attention to an additional set of issues, like the endless modification of a line of slide rules and associated hybrid artifacts so as to address the most demanding calculation issues, including the ones

© Springer-Verlag London Ltd. 2017

A. Tympas, *Calculation and Computation in the Pre-electronic Era*, History of Computing, https://doi.org/10.1007/978-1-84882-742-4_3

involved in the rapid lengthening and complex interconnection of the lines of transmission of electric power (Sect. 3.4.2), the functioning of interactive journal columns as media for training in the skillful use of the slide rule (see, especially, Sect. 3.4.3), and the pride by which engineers identified themselves with their slide rules (Sect. 3.4.4). The chapter includes a section that shows how the use of the slide rule reached into the era of electronics (Sect. 3.5) and an episode from electric power calculations that captures the exploitation of the deep historical experience with the slide rule by the emerging tradition of the electronic computer (Sect. 3.6).

3.2 "With Lightning Speed"

Accustomed as we are to assume that the ideology of intelligent and therefore autonomous machines, capable of self-acting, came along the electronic digital and general-purpose computer of the second half of the twentieth century, we may find it surprising that the "Palmer-Fuller" American circular slide rule from the 1840s could be formally introduced as an "Endless, Self-Computing Scale."[1] The following extracts from the two-page long poem that promoted the "Palmer-Fuller's Telegraph Computer" (ca. 1860s) are indicative of how a computing artifact could be presented no less than a century before the electronic computer:

> Progressive men of every nation,
> To business men in any station,
> We bring a true good working scale,
> A right good test-it cannot fail.
>
> You men of science, this invention
> May well invite your close attention;
> A magic rule you here will find;
> Well suited 'tis to train the mind....
>
> This well known Telegraph Computer
> Is learned with ease, without a tutor,
> Will trace mistakes with lightning speed—
> In this fast age what all men need.[2]

---

[1] For aspects of the history of this slide rule, see Peggy Aldrich Kidwell and Amy Ackerberg-Hastings "Slide rules on display in the United States, 1840–2010" in *Scientific Instruments on Display,* Silke Ackermann, Richard Kremer and Mara Miniati eds (Brill, 2014), chapter 9, 159–172; Bobby Feazel. 1994a, March. Palmer's computing scale. *Journal of the Oughtred Society* 3(1): 9–17, and Bobby Feazel. 1995, March. Palmer's computing scale revisited. *Journal of the Oughtred Society* 4(1): 5–8, and Colin Barnes. 1997b, Fall. Fuller's telegraph computer *Journal of the Oughtred Society* 6(2): 37–38.

[2] Reproduced in Barnes, Fuller's telegraph computer. Barnes informs that the poem was taken from one of the three Palmer-Fuller rules in the Whipple Museum of the History of Science, Cambridge University, England, and, that it appears twice in a folio edition. It seems to come from the 1860s.

Slide rule manufacturers were producing both general and special purpose slide rules as standard apparatus. "Special purpose" or just "specials" can be placed in subclasses, some of which included hundreds of different slide rules.[3] The special general-purpose distinction is relative. I would argue so by selecting some of the slide rules listed at the catalog of the 1914 Exhibition and by placing them in six classes.[4] According to this classification, an engineer could choose from: a general mathematical slide rule (class six), a special mathematical slide rule (class five), a general slide rule for engineering (class four), a special slide rule for engineering (class three), a slide rule for a special engineering work (class one), and a general slide rule for a cluster of similar special engineering works (class two).

In class one, I place slide rules like the wire table slide rules that I will consider below. In class two, I place "Callender's slide rule for determining the sizes of cables." In the same class, I also place the "Steam Engine Calculator" that was exhibited by A. C. Adams. It included scales for horsepower, piston speed, length of stroke, steam pressure per square inch, and cylinder diameter. Adams also exhibited a "Ram Pump Calculator," which included eight special scales.[5] It belongs to the same class. Moreover, under the second class, I include "Hudson's Horse Power Computing Scale," which was a two-slide rule to compute the engine power, the size of engine for a given power, the piston speed due to any stroke and number of revolutions per minute, the ratio the high- and low-pressure cylinders of compound engines bear to each other, and the proportion the "mean" bears to the "initial" pressure. It was exhibited by W. F. Stanley & Company of Glascow.[6]

In the third class, I place "Jakins" 11-inch slide rule by John Davis and Son of Derby, which was presented as "a quick and convenient instrument" for performing calculations in surveying and as "a most ingenious device." It was advertised as offering an accuracy of within 1 in 10,000 and at times greatly higher. Although intended primarily for surveyors, it was recommended as having "very wide" applicability.[7] I also place here a special "boxwood rule" with two adjacent slides that was designed by the engineer S. Milne and was patented in 1891. It was exhibited by Lewis Evans. This slide rule was suitable for the computing needs of paper makers.[8] In addition, I place in this class the "Essex Calculator for the Discharge of Fluids from Pipes, Channels, and Culverts" that was "designed to enable the engineer to ascertain rapidly and with fair accuracy the rates of velocity and discharge from sewers and water mains" as well as in order to find "the velocity of discharge in different forms of channel." It was available by W. F. Stanley & Company of

[3] Bobby Feazel. 1994b, September. Special purpose slide rules. *Journal of the Oughtred Society* 3(2): 43–44. For a survey of the Faber-Castell special slide rules, see Dieter von Jezierski. 1995, October. Special slide rules of Faber-Castell. *Journal of the Oughtred Society* 4(2).

[4] E.M. Horsburgh (ed.). 1914. *Modern instruments and methods of calculation: A handbook of the Napier tercentenary exhibition*. London: Bell and Sons.

[5] Ibid., 167.

[6] Ibid., 176.

[7] Ibid., 178.

[8] Ibid., 166.

Glasgow. Turning from a slide rule to compute the velocity of fluids to a slide rule that "gives at sight" various strengths of solids, we find "Hudson's Shaft, Beam, and Girder Scale." It was exhibited by the editor of the handbook of the 1914 Exhibition.[9] Still in solids, moving from metals to other materials, we find Auguste Esnouf's two forms of slide rules to compute reinforced concrete construction. Their names— "The Concretograph" (for complete design of slabs and beams) and "The Struttograph" (to determining the load which a strut or column could sustain safely)—indicate that the intended use could determine how a slide rule was named.[10]

In the third class, I also place the "electrical" 10-inch slide rule that was exhibited by John Davis and Son of Derby. "With this new type of rule," we read in the 1914 Exhibition handbook description, "practical electrical calculations can be most simply and quickly carried out." One or two movements of the slide were supposed to be "usually sufficient," whereas, with the old type of rule, several settings were needed to obtain the required result. The scales on the edge of the slide, and those on the stock adjacent to them, were the same as in ordinary slide rules so that the use of the instrument for the usual calculations "is not interfered with in any way."[11] I add to this class the 11-inch long "Castell electrical and mechanical engineers' slide rule" that was exhibited by A. W. Faber of London. G.D.C. Stokes had mentioned A. W. Faber's "Electro" slide rule as an example of a slide rule carrying a "log-log" scale.[12]

On the stock and beneath the slide, it included two special scales, one for calculating efficiency of dynamos, effective horsepower, etc., and the other for loss of potential, current strength, etc. Beyond the inclusion of special scales, the range of the general scales of a slide rule could vary according to the special purpose. For example, this Castell slide rule included a "log-log scale" in two sections, E and F, which were extended to ranges 1.1. to 2.9 and 2.9 to 10,000, respectively. Its description concluded with the statement that this "[i]n other respects [was] a standard rule."[13] This shows that a special slide rule for computing electrification could be made by the inclusion of a special mathematical scale—in this case a double logarithmic scale known as "log-log" (a scale based on a double logarithm so as to compute by addition, i.e., algebraically, the raising of variable into the power of a second variable). It then suggests that any slide rule classification like the one that I experiment with here is destined to be relative because there was a mix of features of different slide rule classes.

Into the third class, I also place special scientific slide rules such as the 10-inch slide rule for chemists that included a series of gauge points on scales A and B for the computation of logarithms of atomic and molecular weights to the same unit as on standard scales C and D. It was available by W. F. Stanley & Company of

[9] Ibid., 172.
[10] Ibid., 172.
[11] Ibid., 178.
[12] Ibid., 159.
[13] Ibid., 179.

London.[14] In the fourth class, I include general engineering slide rules such as the large "Tavernier-Gravet" slide rule, which was 6 feet 10 inches x 8 feet 5 inches long. It was an exhibit from the Engineering Department of the University of Edinburgh.[15] In the fourth class, I also place general technical slide rules such as the 11-inch "'technical' slide rule" by A. G. Thornton of Manchester.[16] In the fifth and sixth classes, I include special, e.g., logarithmic, and general mathematical slide rules, respectively. Along with logarithmic slide rules, in the fifth class, I place slide rules like the 10-inch "fix" slide rule for mensuration of round bodies. Scale A, which was a standard scale in design, was in this slide rule displaced $\pi/4$ to the left relative to the stock. It was exhibited by W. F. Stanley & Company of Glasgow.[17]

Accordingly, in respect to choosing a slide rule in order to compute electric power transmission, there were theoretically six options. I place an electric transmission wire table slide rule in the first class, a general electric transmission line slide rule like the one exhibited by the Electrical Engineering Department of the University of Glascow ("Callender's") in the second class, a general electrical engineering slide rule (like Faber's "Electro" or Davis' "electrical") in the third class, a general engineering slide rule like the one exhibited by the Engineering Department of the University of Edinburgh ("Tavernier-Gravet") in the fourth class, a general logarithmic slide rule (like Stanley's "fix") in the fifth class, and a general mathematical slide rule in the sixth class. Over the course of this chapter, I will consider examples from all classes.

At the other end of "universal" slide rules, there were explicitly special purpose slide rules like the electric power transmission slide rule that was called "Callender's slide rule for determining the sizes of cables." It consisted of a combination of slide rule and chart that gave "the size of cable required for transmitting electric power under given conditions of system of supply (k), voltage (u), power (w), length of route (y), power factor (f), and percentage loss of voltage (p)." This slide rule was an exhibit from the Electrical Engineering Department of the University of Glasgow.[18]

This notation was referring to a formula introduced by Stokes as corresponding to a four-slide design, the two slides of which were horizontal and adjacent and the other two vertical and adjacent. A "more compact and easy to read" three-slide version was possible, at the cost of ending up with a slide rule that was "less easy to read." Stokes explained that "[a]nalysis of the arrangement leads to the formula $R = 0.513kfy\text{W}/V^2p$." The equation was "reduced to the general form" of the algebraic equation of the slide rule and became: $\log R + 2\log V + \log p + \log 1/0.513 = \log k + \log f + \log y + \log \text{W}$. This furnishes us with an example of how the size of wire in electric power transmission, R, could be computed algebraically with the proper setting of a slide rule.[19]

---

[14] Ibid., 176.
[15] Ibid., 173.
[16] Ibid., 180.
[17] Ibid., 176.
[18] Ibid., 171–172.
[19] Ibid., 162.

"The chief mathematical interest in this instrument," argued Stokes, "lies in the combination of four slides with a logarithmic chart." This means that this slide rule was a hybrid artifact. Moreover, this slide rule offers us an example of a four-slide poly-slide rule, which, unlike the single-slide rule, had more than one sliding scale. Under poly-slide rules, Stokes discussed an "Ordinary Two-slide Rule" and "slides with dependent motion" as representative of the two ends, respectively. The contrast between standard slide rules models called "ordinary" and slide rules of uncommon design was quite common. Slides with dependent motion could be connected by a mechanism that required only one setting. Stokes mentioned the "Baines slide rule" as the only one of this type that "calls of notice." It had no scale-carrying stock, but four slides were connected by a parallelogram linkage. The only advantage over the single-slide rule was that "two special formulae (not even wholly independent) can be dealt instead of one." A 1904 article in the *Engineer* had described one such slide rule. According to Stokes, its advantage was "more apparent than real." "But," added Stokes, "the Baines rule is noteworthy for introducing a dependent motion of the slides, an idea which may lead to future developments."[20]

In a listing of slide rule scales that includes no less than 130, several scales of apparent interest to electrification are included. For a sample, I refer to the following 14: *dB* (decibels), attenuation for electrical calculations; *Dyn* (efficiency), efficiency scale for generators; *Eff* (efficiency), efficiency scale for generators and motors; *f* (frequency), used in electrical and radio calculators; *Ind* (inductance), used in electrical and radio calculations; *mv* (milli-volts), for electrical calculations; *Mot* (motor), motor efficiency; *neper* (attenuation), for electrical calculations; U_1, for cube scales in electrical calculations; U_2, for square scales in electrical calculation; *Vd* (volt dropage), for electrical calculations; *V* (in volts), for electrical calculations; *Volts* (also in volts), volt drop scales for motor and dynamo calculation; and *II* wavelength, for electrical and radio calculations.[21]

3.3 "Extreme Accuracy with a Slide Rule"

The general importance of computing with slide rules in engineering can be shown by the interest that it attracted in the technical press. The samples from articles in *Power* that I am about to present had its roots in a deep tradition of slide rules that were developed in connection to the mechanical engineering side of the power industry. Using slide rules to compute the generation of power from a mechanical engineering perspective was important since the days of James Watt and his Soho slide rules (see Chap. 2). The pocket watch circular slide rule that was called "The Mechanical Engineer" is testimony to the sophistication that the production of mechanical engineering slide rules has reached by the end of the nineteenth

---

[20] Ibid., 162.

[21] Peter M. Hopp. 1999. *Slide rule: Their history models and makers*, 285–287. Mendham NJ: Astragal Press.

century.[22] Upon the establishment of electrical engineering, slide rules to compute power from the mechanical and the electrical side supplemented each other. For example, in the 1933 Keuffel & Esser trade catalog, a "Power Computing Slide Rule" for steam, gas, and oil engineers was advertised right below the "Roylance Electrical Slide Rule." Computing the transmission of power with the "Roylance Electrical Slide Rule" started with the conversion of horsepower to kilowatts, while the horsepower generated in the first place was computed with the "Power Computing Slide Rule."[23]

In the *Power* column "Engineers' Study Course," an editorial series of three introductory articles that was entitled "The Slide Rule" was published in 1914.[24] Additional 1914 and 1915 editorial series of articles were devoted to issues such as how to read, or more generally, how to use a slide rule.[25] Several authors or the editors themselves contributed articles on general issues such as on the use of the slide rule for finding the number of integer places in a product or quotient, on the method for the location of the decimal point in slide rule calculations, on the mode of using the slide rule to compute quadratic equations, and on the suitability of the slide rule for interpolating logarithms.[26] At the same time, there were articles on special issues such the ones on a "power plant logarithmic calculator" that could be used as a slide rule, on calculating scales for computing engine horsepower and pipe areas, on a "handy flywheel calculator," and on a slide rule for steam flow that was introduced to as a "steam flow computer."[27] There was also an article on an "engineers improved slide rule."[28] The important issue of obtaining the wire resistance from an ordinary slide rule was also represented.[29] Discussions on these issues in *Power* persisted through the 1920s. For example, in 1923, through the column "Easy Lessons in Engineering," the editor of *Power* introduced to a series of general articles with the

[22] Bob De Cecaris. 1998, Spring. The mechanical engineer. *Journal of the Oughtred Society* 7(1): 23–24.

[23] *Keuffel & Esser Trade Catalog*. 1933, 21.

[24] The slide rule, part I. 1914, February 10. *Power* 39(6), 210–211, The slide rule, part II. 1914, 17 February. *Power* (7), 245–246 and The slide rule, part III. 1914, 24 February. *Power* (8), 283–284.

[25] How to read a slide rule. *Power* 42(6) (1915, August 10): 192–194, and Wyman T. 1915, December 14. Using a slide rule. *Power* 42(24): 825–826.

[26] F.R. Low. 1914, March 24. To find the number of integer places in a product or quotient. *Power* 39(12): 400–401; Charles G. Richardson. 1914, April 21. Fixing the decimal point in slide-rule calculations. *Power* 39(16): 551–552; Robert N. Miller. 1915, September 21. Slide rule quadratics. *Power* 42(12): 422–423; and H.B. Schell. 1916, March 28. Interpolating logarithms with the slide rule. *Power* 43(13): 451–452.

[27] Walter N. Polakov. 1913, April 29. Power plant log calculator. *Power* 37(17): 596–597; G.H. Bascome. 1913, March 4. Calculating scales. *Power* 37(9): 308–309; J.P. Morrison. 1915, November 16. Handy flywheel calculator. *Power* 42(20): 683; and J.M. Spitzglass. 1916. Slide rule and flow computer. *Power* 43(8): 257.

[28] D.E. Foster. 1914, April. Engineers' improved slide rule. *Power* 39(15): 537.

[29] A.F. Moore. 1913, February 4. Obtaining wire resistance on slide rule. *Power* 37(5): 151.

same title as before: "The Slide Rule." In addition, he edited special promotional pieces such as the one entitled "Extreme Accuracy With a Slide Rule."[30]

The edition or reedition of a slide rule handbook was immediately reported in the *Power* column "Books Received." Between the first and the second sample of articles mentioned above, four more reeditions were added to the total of the editions of C. N. Pickworth's *The Slide Rule,* raising this total to 17. Van Nostrand of New York was selling the 1915 edition for $1 and the 1921 for $1.50.[31] The readers, usually mechanical engineers and frequently professors of mechanical engineering, used general columns or the special columns "Correspondence" and "Comments from Readers" in order to introduce to their standings on the issue of computing with a slide rule or in order to present with improvements. These improvements included a general slide rule for addition and a special boiler room slide rule.[32] The readers also introduced to issues such as the one concerning the increase of the number of calculations in the boiler test code and, more generally, the issue of the relationship between the slide rule and the "power man."[33] The interest of the readers in the slide rule resulted in debates on issues as specific as how to interpolate logarithms or how to point off decimals and as general as that subsumed under the series of articles on "Why Not Use a Slide Rule?"[34] The editor himself was frequently involved in these debates by adding a brief editorial comment or by contributing longer pieces such as the one entitled "Extreme Accuracy With The Slide Rule."[35]

In a piece published in the column "Comments for Readers," W. E. Wines, assistant professor of Mechanical Engineering at the University of Wisconsin, "discontinued his struggle with the calculations of boiler tests" in order to publish an article entitled "Why So Many Calculations in the Boiler Test Code?" His purpose was to eliminate some repetitive steps in the use of the slide rule.[36] For the mechanical side of power engineering, computing was indeed a considerable job. What Raymond L. Drew wrote under the title "The Slide Rule and the Power Man," in an article published in the June 22, 1926 issue of *Power* is indicative of how indispensable computing with the slide rule has become:

---

[30] "The Slide Rule, I, Reading the scales: Multiplication and division". *Power* 57, no. 20 (1922, May 15): 774–755 and "The slide rule, II, Proportion, square and square roots, and cubes and cube routes". *Power* 57, no. 21 (1923, May 22): 812–813; Muller. 1923. Extreme accuracy with a slide rule. *Power* 58(23): 920.

[31] See *Power* 42, no. 16 (1915, October 19): 567 and *Power* 53, no. 8 (1921, February 22): 329.

[32] A.B. Solomon. 1919, September 9. An adding slide rule. *Power* 50(11): 437, and H. Payne, and Huylett O'Neill. 1922, April 4. A boiler-room slide rule. *Power* 55(14): 543–544.

[33] W.E. Wines. 1923, July 3. Why so many calculations in the boiler test code? *Power* 58(1): 27–28, and Raymond L. Drew. 1926, June. The slide rule and the power man. *Power* 63(25): 967.

[34] H.D. Fisher. 1916, May 16. Interpolating logarithms. *Power* 43(20): 703–704; R.O. Muller. 1916, June 20. Pointing off decimals with the slide rule. *Power* 43(25): 888; W.L. Durand. 1922, May 2. Why not use a slide rule? *Power* 55(18): 705, and V.K. Stanley. 1922, May 30. Why not use a slide rule? *Power* 55(22): 866.

[35] See his editorial comment in Muller, *Pointing off decimals with the slide rule*, and his editorial piece Muller, *Extreme accuracy with a slide rule*.

[36] W.E Wines, *Why so many calculations in the boiler test code?* 27.

This is written especially for those power-plant men and mechanical men in general who believe that the slide rule is a useless play-toy, to those who feel that it is a mysterious calculating machine that requires an operator endowed with the magical powers of a wizard, and to those who "just can't get the hang of using it.",...

Anyone should be able to follow given settings on the slide rule just as easily as he can follow a formula in a handbook, but in order to solve actual problems, an idea of the basic logarithmic principles upon which the rule is constructed, along with considerable practice, is necessary.

I say considerable practice, for that is the most important thing. In fact it may be truly said that the manipulation of the slide rule is an art than a science, and, like all arts, must be practice to be acquired. One or two trials—even a dozen trials—will not make one proficient with the slide rule.[37]

Beyond informing us that as late as in 1926 the slide rule could still be considered as a "mysterious calculating machine," Drew's article offers us a picture of computing with the slide rule that is incompatible with the views of those who sought to promote the slide rule as easy to use. Drew's article was actually concerned with the issue of the relationship between accuracy and skill, which was a key issue for engineers. To elaborate on this relationship, I retrieve and interpret some of the opinions of those who participated in debates through the pages of *Power*.

"Not long ago," stated Charles G. Richardson in his 1914 piece on how to fix the decimal point in computing with the slide rule:

The slide rule was frequently held up to ridicule, especially by those who could not or would not use it. It was termed a "guess-stick," and an error by the manipulator was hailed with satisfaction. This feeling now has given place to one of respect for its value as a great time and energy saver in mechanical calculations, but the idea seems to prevail that to acquire skill with the rule one needs unusual mental equipment.

In his opinion, "the inexcusably opaque 'instruction' books which have been distributed with slide rules are in a great measure responsible for these conditions." "Eight years of daily use of the method in a department requiring calculations of considerable complexity," informed Richardson in his conclusion, "has thoroughly demonstrated its value in promoting accuracy and rapidity."[38]

In his 1916 *Power* article on how to interpolate logarithms, H. B. Schell recommended the use of the logarithmic slide rule because he thought that it was "the quickest and most satisfactory method" he had found yet. "With some practice," he argued, "one should be able to read from the tables and the rule without writing down any figures but the result. The time savings is considerable." For Schell, the accuracy of interpolating logarithms by the use of a slide rule was adequate, especially considering that "[l]ogarithms themselves are but a means of close approximation," and the issue was with what "kinks" to make this approximation "very much closer."[39] In the following issue, H. D. Fisher came to doubt that great accuracy in interpolation was possible with Schell's method. For him this was "largely

---

[37] Raymond L. Drew, *The slide rule and the power man*, 967.

[38] Charles G. Richardson, *Fixing the decimal point in slide-rule calculations*: 551–552.

[39] Schell, *Interpolating logarithms with the slide rule*: 451–452.

illusory." Fischer thought that Schell was "stretching the method of directly proportional interpolation beyond the permissible limit." But, interestingly, what Fisher
was protesting against was not the inaccuracy introduced by Schell but the fact that
Schell was pursuing useless accuracy in the first place. What Fischer meant by
"largely illusory" accuracy was unnecessary accuracy. He also referred to this accuracy as "foolish and misleading":

> The true method of interpolation based on the principle of successive differences is rather
> complicated and may be found in textbooks on practical astronomy.
>   Engineers, however, have very little use for figures of this class as few measurements or
> basic data have an accuracy of better than 1/10 of 1 per cent, and it is foolish and misleading
> to carry out a figure to several places of decimals because the dividend does not happen to
> contain the divisor as a prime factor when both divisor and dividend may be uncertain to the
> extent of several hundreds.
>   The writer has no wish to decry accuracy in power-plant measurements, but if more
> trouble were taken to see that coal scales were checked occasionally and weights read prop-
> erly and less to figuring daily evaporations to three or four places of decimals, the results
> obtained would more nearly show under just what conditions the power plant is
> operating.[40]

Similarly, in 1916, when R. O. Muller complained that in a 1914 *Power* article
on fixing the decimal point the methods offered were not complete, the editor
responded by agreeing that Muller was right, but he added that "one would hardly
use a slide rule or a calculating machine" in the cases not treated in the 1914 article.[41] In other words, the issue was not simply one of producing enough computing
accuracy: it was also an issue of avoiding an excess of computing accuracy. In
response to some comments by the editor, in his "Why Not Use a Slide Rule" 1922
piece, W. L. Durand informed that he had found "from many years use that a slide
rule is decidedly more accurate than is required in the majority of engineering computations." "Also," he added, "most engineering problems require the use at some
point in the cycle of one or more variable constants based on experience," and,
accordingly, "[e]ven if the work is done with the exactness of 'long-hand' arithmetic, the results may in fact be in error by an amount many times in excess of that
which would be caused by the use of a slide rule."[42]

In the 1932 handbook on calculating electrification that was published in the
Audel series of popular technical publications, the accuracy of computing with a
standard slide rule was assumed to be no worse than 1/4 of 1 percent, which was
considered satisfactory for most purposes.[43] As with many other engineers who
cared about having sufficient computing accuracy without being caught in pursuing
unnecessary computing accuracy, Durand had done some tests that compared the
accuracy of multiplying with a 10-inch slide rule and with a multiplying (calculating) machine. From the results that he obtained, he found it certain that "the prob-

---

[40] H.D. Fisher, *Interpolating logarithms*, 703–704.

[41] R.O. Muller, *Pointing off decimals with the slide rule*, 888.

[42] W.L. Durand, *Why not use a slide rule?* 705.

[43] Frank D. Graham. 1932. *Audels new electric library: Mathematics calculations,* vol. XI, 235.
New York: Audel.

able error for any one operation should not exceed one-tenth of one percent and that for a series of operations the total error would not exceed one-fifth of one per cent due to the balancing of the plus and minus errors." "An error of this magnitude," he concluded, "is much less than the required accuracy for most engineering work." Accordingly, Durand shifted the issue from the technical accuracy of the artifact to the social skill of the user. "Of course," he clarified, "the personality of the observer enters to a large extent into any determination of this character, and other observers would probably obtain results either greater or less than those given herein." He nevertheless estimated that engineers as a whole would confirm his results as "the difference should not exceed 25 per cent."[44]

In the issue of *Power* that came out 3 weeks later, V. K. Stanley added his experience. I find it especially illuminating because it shows that engineers could also resort to a combination of slide rules to avoid the pursuit of an excess of accuracy:

> I have been interested in the comments on the issue of slide rule in answer to the editorial in the April 18 issue of *Power*. As a practical user of slide rules for various branches of engineering, I beg to verify W. L. Durand's statement in the May 2 issue.
> I have three slide rules of lengths 8, 10 and 18 in. The 8-in. rule I use for electric work alone, while the 10-in. polyphase rule will apply to almost any problem around the plant. I use the 18-in. rule in problems involving heavy multiplication and division.
> Every engineer should learn slide-rule operation. A little daily practice will enable him to go over his plant and know what the operating conditions are in a very short time. The slide rule takes up less space in the pocket than a handbook of tables and is a wonderful time saver.[45]

Even when it "occasionally happens, however," added the editor, "that greater precision is required," on the condition that the operator had "reasonable skill," the solution was not to be found in abandoning the slide rule but in "the intelligent use of a slide rule in connection with long-hand computations."[46]

3.4 "An Indispensable Companion"

3.4.1 "For the Exercise of His Ingenuity"

Taken together, the various versions of slide rules for calculating the flow of electric currents, weak (communications) and strong (energy), represented the most common form of slide rule for specialists. The number of slide rule models called "Electro" or "electrical" and the number of slide rules models that were described as especially designed for electrical engineers and electrotechnicians were in the order of 100.[47] Many standard slide rules were supplied with some capability for conversion

---

[44] W.L. Durand, *Why not use a slide rule?* 705.

[45] V.K. Stanley, *Why not use a slide rule?* 866.

[46] Muller, *Extreme accuracy with a slide rule*, 920.

[47] Peter M. Hopp. *Slide rule: Their history, models, and makers*, chapter VI.

to electricity-related calculations, even if it was only the conversion of electrical power from kilowatts to horsepower by means of additional markings on the cursor. Davis, Nestler, Unique, Faber, Faber-Castell, Keuffel & Esser, and Thornton had versions of electrical slide rules that differed in the placement of the scales and in the method of reading them. Slide rules for what we now call electronic engineering were effectively a subset of the electrical slide rule. For example, the John Davis Company supplied the "Davis-Martin Wireless Slide Rule," which included special scales of inductance and capacitance for computing wavelength.[48]

The "well" or "groove" of the stock was an obvious place to put special electrical scales, which required some form of additional cursor on one end of the slide. In the series of "Faber-Castell Electro" slide rules, the slide was fitted with a metallic chisel-edged fork at the left-hand end so that the electrical scales that were placed in the groove of the rule could be read and used along with the scales on the front of the rule. The "A.G. Thornton Electrical" had a rounded end and a hairline marked on the stem of the extension of the slide so that the scales could be read as if there was a cursor. The rounded end was fitted on slide rules just before World War II. The design of the rounded end has been attributed to a literature on user complaints concerning the sharpness of the chisel-edged fork.[49]

In order to construct his "Electro" slide rules, Faber started by combining two "log-log" ("LL") scales. In the first model of the series (Model 378), these scales were placed on the slanted lower edge of the stock and were used by means of an index "tongue" or "tab" on the lower end of the runner. Later, they were placed in the well of the stock and, eventually, in the top and bottom rows of the stock. This version of Model 378 was very successful and with few changes remained available through 1975. By then, both a wooden version (1/98) and a plastic version (111/98) were available.[50]

For one more index to the emergence of electrification slide rules, we can look at those mentioned by Florian Cajori. His 1909 list included the following:

"Faber's Improved Calculating Rule for Electrical and Mechanical Engineers," which became popular in the United States through Pickworth's writings,[51]
a "Slide Rule for Electrical Calculations," which was made by A. E. Colgate in New York[52]

---

[48] Ibid., 119.

[49] Ibid., 23.

[50] Dieter von Jezierski. 2000. *Slide rule: A journey through three centuries*, 37. Mendham NJ: Astragal Press.

[51] It was first described in *Der Praktische Maschinen-Constructeur (Unland)* 27 (1894), 8. Florian Cajori. 1909. *A history of the logarithmic slide rule and allied instruments*, 91. New York: The Engineering News Publishing Company.

[52] It was first described in the *American Machinist* 24 (1901): 339. See Florian Cajori, *A history of the logarithmic slide rule and allied instruments*, 97.

"Robert's Slide Rule for Wiring Calculations," which, according to E. P. Roberts
   who had designed it, was patented in 1894 and was sold for a time (though it was
   not on the market at the time of the writing of Cajori's book)[53]
a "Slide Rule for Calculating Sag in Wires," designed by R. J. C. Wood[54]
"Woodworth's Slide Rule for Electrical Wiremen" and "Woodworth's Slide Rule
   for Calculations with Volts, Amperes, Ohms and Watts," both designed by
   Professor P. B. Woodworth of the Lewis Institute, Chicago[55]

Some of the same slide rules were displayed at the 1914 Exhibition. In fact for a
third index to electrification slide rules, I refer to the sample of slide rules that I
selected from those displayed at the 1914 Exhibition (see earlier in this chapter,
Sect. 3.2).

"The slide-rule," we read in the 1909 *Electrical Review and Western Electrician*
article that introduced to Woodworth's slide rules, "has become an indispensable
companion of the technical man, since it makes possible a saving in time and mental
energy required in mathematical calculations that is attainable in no other way." The
article actually described more than Woodworth's slide rules. After explaining that
the slide rule is "but an assemblage of logarithmic scales" and that various forms of
which have been contrived for the solution of special problems, it sought to introduce to "special forms of slide rule" devised for the use of electrical engineers in
wiring calculations. It started with a description of a slide rule "for facilitating electrical calculations" that was described in an article in the *Elektrotechnischer
Anzeiger* and was put in the market by the firm of Albert Nestler of Lahr in Baden,
Germany. The "distinct feature" of this slide rule was "the solution of problems
relating to electrical conductors in a rapid and simple manner." More specifically, it
was constructed so as to compute any of the parameters involved in the formula
$K = li/ea$, in which l was the length of the conductor in meters, i the current strength
in amperes, e the voltage drop, a the cross-sectional area in square millimeters, and
K a constant depending upon the material. "With the ordinary slide rule," we read in
the article, "this operation is possible only by performing one variable of movements and placings, while the new rule requires only one setting."[56]

Woodworth's slide rule for wiring calculations was presented as a "independently designed, for similar purposes." Woodworth, a professor of electrical engineering, had developed it for the use of his students during the previous year. In
differed from the Nestler slide rule in that it could be used to compute the cross-
section of the wire but, also, its diameter and size. All values corresponded to
American copper-wire practice. The article referred to it as "The Woodworth

[53] It was first described in the *Electric Journal* 3 (1906), 116–118. See Cajori, *A history of the logarithmic slide rule and allied instruments*, 103.

[54] It was first described in the *Electrical World* 50 (1907), 402. See Florian Cajori, *A history of the
logarithmic slide rule and allied instruments*, 103.

[55] It was first described in the *Electrical Review and Western Electrician* 54(9) (February 27, 1909):
399. See Florian Cajori, *A history of the logarithmic slide rule and allied instruments*, 106.

[56] "Special Slide Rule for Electrical Engineers". *Electrical Review and Western Electrician* 54(9)
(February 27, 1909): 115.

Demonstration Slide-Rule for Electrical Wiremen." It was made up in pocket size of six-inch length but was also available in standard length. It was printed on bristol board and could be readily mounted and shellacked. The bristol board itself could be folded so as to make a "handy rule." Being "highly accurate," informed the author of the article, "these rules have been found a very convenient practical working tool." Anyone sending his name and address to the Lewis Institute would be furnished a copy of it, with the compliments of Professor Woodworth. The article concluded with informing that Woodworth had also "contrived a slide-rule arranged for facilitating calculations involving volts, amperes, ohms, megohms and watts."[57]

Decades after the article in *Electrical Review and Western Electrician*, at a time when a special slide rule for electrical engineers were anything but a novelty, the issue of choosing between a special and a general slide rule required an "ingenuity" that could still define an electrical engineer as such. I quote from an article that was published in the January 22, 1937 issue of *The Engineer*, which was the introduction to and entitled, "An Electrical Engineer's Slide Rule":

> The production of a slide rule to facilitate some special form of calculation which is of frequent occurrence offers to the mathematically minded inventor a considerable and tempting opportunity for the exercise of his ingenuity. In general however a specialized slide rule is of no value outside the particular field which it is designed to serve. Hence before a slide rule is evolved to deal with some specific form of calculation it is always desirable to consider carefully whether the balance of advantage will lie with it or with an ordinary slide rule reinforced by the addition of a few special graduations or perhaps by an additional scale. Electrical and hydraulic engineering, for instance, doubtlessly provide scope for the employment of specialized rules. It seems, however, certain that many electrical and hydraulic engineers would, if they were given a choice, prefer an ordinary rule, with its unrestricted applicability if it were adapted to their particular needs by the addition of certain graduations of an electrical or hydraulic character.[58]

The purpose of the author of the article was to introduce to an ordinary A. W. Faber slide rule that was "adapted to facilitate electrical engineering calculations. The "special electrical features" of this slide rule consisted of a three-line cursor, efficiency and voltage scales E and V, a short temperature scale, and special graduations. This slide rule furnishes us with a good example of slide rule improvements without an increase in the size of the artifact. Several graduations in the standard scales A, B, C, D, F, R, and LL could be used for special electrification purposes. The middle-line of the cursor was the same as in ordinary slide rules. But, with this slide rule, in conjunction with the left line, horsepower could be converted into kilowatts or vice versa with only a single setting. With a single movement of the left line of the cursor that was to be followed by a single movement of the slide, an electrical engineer could use the slide rule in computations involving π, e.g., he could compute the volume of a cylinder of given length and diameter.[59]

The scales E and V, revealed when the slide was partially withdrawn, could be read by means of short metal tongues projecting from the left-hand end of the slide.

---

[57] Ibid., 115.

[58] Ibid., 115.

[59] Ibid., 115.

Scale E was to be employed in computations involving the efficiency of dynamos and motors in horsepower. Input, output, and efficiency of a dynamo or a motor could be computed with one setting. Computing the drop of potential in a copper conductor of a given length and given cross-sectional area, i.e., computing the additional loss of power by connecting a generator and a motor, was possible by using scale V. With this slide rule, this computation could supposedly be done "automatically," based on the same formula as the one used in Woodworth's 1909 slide rule. Appropriate indications that were engraved at the origins of standard scales A and B were used to remind the user of conventions that could help him to locate the decimal point. With the use of scale G, the resistance of a conductor was related to its temperature.[60]

The Keuffel & Esser Number 4133 "Roylance Electrical Slide Rule," which was copyrighted in 1924, was another electrical slide rule. It was a modified 8-inch slide rule that was placed between a Manheim and a polyphase slide rule. It included several special graduations on the standard scales, special additional electrical scales, and a three-line cursor. With one setting of the slide and cursor, it was possible to read directly for any size of copper wire, the diameter in mils, area in circular mils, area in square inches, weight in pounds per 1000 ft. of bare wire, and the resistance in ohms per 1000 feet. at any temperature, in degrees centigrade.[61] In addition to its potential use in various kinds of power conversions, the same data could be used in any computation that was possible on the Manheim slide rule and in any computation involving any standard electrical formula. In his 1930 book on the history, principle, and operation of the slide rule, J. E. Thompson, who was with the Department of Mathematics at the Pratt Institute, Brooklyn, gave a detailed description of the "Roylance," which he considered to be an exemplar of a "special form of the slide rule."[62] Its prize, as listed in the 1933 Keuffel & Esser catalog, was $8.50, which was about two times the cost of a standard Manheim slide rule.[63]

A nonstandard slide rule for wiring computations was the one patented by Herbert Lutz of Ontario, Canada, in 1898. It has been described as an "Electrical Wireman's Combined Gage and Calculator" because two tools were combined into one. Anyone wishing to wire buildings for electric lights would have to compute the gauge of wire necessary to produce the required amperage at a known voltage for a given distance from the source. He would also have to measure the wire to ensure that it was of the proper size. Lutz's artifact could be used for both. This unique slide rule was made of plate steel. A later version of the same artifact that was patented by the Novelty Electric Company of Philadelphia.[64]

---

[60] Ibid., 115.

[61] Bobby Feazel. 1997b, Fall, The roylance electrical slide rule. *Journal of the Oughtred Society* 6(2): 39.

[62] J.E. Thompson. 1930. *A manual of the slide rule*, 206. New York: Van Nostrand.

[63] *Keuffel & Esser Trade Catalog*.1933.

[64] Bobby Feazel. 1997a, Fall. Electrical Wireman's combined gage and calculator. *Journal of the Oughtred Society* 6(2): 9–10.

Wire drawing consists in pulling a ductile metal wire through a hole in a hard die to reduce its cross-sectional area, elongate its length, and possibly change some of the properties of the metal. The wire drawing process is of great importance because it is used to produce gold or copper wire for various electrical purposes that can be smaller than one-thousand of an inch in diameter or steel cylinders that can be six or seven-tenths of an inch in diameter for suspension bridge cables or automobile shock absorber struts. As many as nine variables (and in some case more) must be considered in combination, which requires a complicated set of interacting computations. An elaborate nonstandard slide rule for these computations was made by A.G. Thornton of Manchester, in response to an order placed by a wire manufacturer, the Spencer Wire Company of Wakefield, England. It was called the "Spencer-Taylor Wire Die Draft Calculator." This slide rule actually consisted of a set of three slide rules: a fixed one at the top, a movable one in the center, and a rotating drum toward the bottom.[65]

The contrast between a standard and a nonstandard electrification slide rule was not simply one between slide rules manufactured in mass by a firm and slide rules constructed by an individual. It could also be a contrast between a standard slide rule and a nonstandard slide rule that were both manufactured by a firm. For an example of a mass manufactured slide rule of an unconventional form, I refer to Model L of the "Otis King Calculator." The Otis King Calculator was a cylindrical and spiral slide rule that consisted of two metal tubes, the smaller (cylinder) being free to rotate and slide within the larger (holder). Spiral scales were mounted on each of these tubes, while a third tube that was mounted on the holder formed a tubular cursor. A year after its introduction to the United States from England, it was advertised in the June 1928 issue of *Instruments* as "an instrument which in pocket size (6 in. when closed) provides, it is said, the calculating facilities of an ordinary slide rule 66 in. long." It was available in two models, "Model 'K' for general work and ordinary calculations, and Model L, with a log-arithmetic scale, especially adapted for electrical and chemical formulae, etc." In the United States it was sold by A. S. Aloe Company. "The calculator," we read in the *Instruments* promotional piece, "has met with approval of the leading engineers, universities and chemists throughout the United States."[66]

Model L had a single cycle and a log scale instead of a double cycle on the upper scale. The log scale corresponded to a 4-place logarithmic table and had 2,001 marks. Available from about 1920 to 1972, it was generally advertised as "as easy to read as a clock, and as plain to read as a yard stick." It has been described as a "curious device" that was a cylindrical slide rule, more closely related to the Fuller than the Thacher but in actuality having a distinct design. According to one estimate, the Otis King slide rules sold were as many as 250,000.[67] More conservative

[65] Howard Andrews, and Conrad Schure. 2001, Spring. A slide rule for wire drawing calculations. *Journal of the Oughtred Society* 10(1): 15–17.

[66] New calculator now sold in the United States *Instruments* (June, 1928): 294.

[67] Robert Otnes. 1991, October. The Otis king slide rule. *Journal of the Oughtred Society* 0(0): 7–8.

estimates place the number somewhere between 100,000 and 230,000.[68] Dating the Otis King slide rules has produced an interesting debate.[69] Even if the total number sold is closer to one than 200,000, it is still impressive for a slide rule that was much more expensive than an ordinary slide rule. Given the fact that one of the two basic models was explicitly advertised as suitable to electrification (Model L), it seems reasonable to expect that thousands of Otis King slide rules were bought by electrical engineers.

In the category of mass-produced slide rules that could be used for electrification, somewhere between a slide rule of a common form like the "Roylance" Keuffel & Esser slide rule and a slide rule of a unique form like the Model L Otis King slide rule, we can place "Type 400.D" and "Type 600.E" models of the "ALRO" circular (disk) slide rule. "Type 400.D" included several constants for "electrotechnics." "Type 600.D," which was especially designed for electrotechnics, included scales N, N2, L, and LL, plus scales for output and tension loss calculations.[70] ALRO was a Dutch firm that was not included in the list of major manufacturers, that did not start production before the 1930s, and that produced only slide rules of a special form. The "ALRO" circular slide rules were high-quality products that were used by many Dutch technicians in many technical fields. The total number of them produced is impressive: φ 6 cm: 25,000 standard and 25,000 especially ordered; φ 13 cm: 100,000 standard and 20,000 special order; and φ 16 cm: 5000.[71]

Beyond offering us a rare example of a non-American slide rule that was available in the United States during World War II in fair numbers, these Dutch slide rules can help us to elaborate on the importance of the relationship between slide rule form and purpose. The ALRO slide rule was promoted as offering a slide rule with many advantages: It could be operated with one hand; it did not include a runner that could be lost or broken; it would not warp in high temperatures as slide rules sometimes did; it was easy to carry in the pocket; specialized scales could be fitted; it was easy to read because the runner was a full circular transparent disk upon which one could put more several hairlines in distances of different constants; and it was more accurate because the length of the many scale line was about 7 cm longer than the scale on a normal slide rule (32 cm). Another advantage was that it was possible to use it by placing nomograms on the disk.[72]

---

[68] Peter Hopp. 1995, October. Otis-king update. *Journal of the Oughtred Society* 4(2): 33–40, and Peter Hopp. 1996, October. Otis-king: Conclusions? *Journal of the Oughtred Society* 5(2): 62–67.

[69] See Colin Barnes. 1997a, Fall. Dating Otis-king slide rules. *Journal of the Oughtred Society* 6(2): 35–36, and Richard Lyon. 1998, Spring. Dating of the Otis king: An alternative theory developed through use of the internet. *Journal of the Oughtred Society* 7(1): 33–37.

[70] Ysebrand Schuitema. 1993, October. The ALRO circular slide rule. *Journal of the Oughtred Society* 2(2): 28.

[71] Ibid., 30.

[72] Ibid., 25.

3.4.2 "A Transmission Line Calculator" for "the Most Tedious Problem"

In his 1921 comparison of computing with various artifacts, MIT's F.S. Dellenbaugh Jr. mentioned that one could compute quicker with a slide rule than with a Marchant calculating machine, but the errors were liable to be very great—he actually dismissed both the calculating machine and the slide rule in comparison to the electric analyzer that he sought to promote. Noticeably, Dellenbaugh did not compare the cost of computing with the slide rule and the cost of computing with the Marchant calculating machine—the calculating machine was much more expensive.[73] Electrical engineers kept computing by developing and using slide rules because concrete comparisons of available computing options suggested to them that a slide rule was better in most cases.

For example, in presenting a new "power-factor" slide rule in the July 1922 issue of the *General Electric Review*, P. L. Alger, who was with General Electric's Induction Motor Engineering Department, and H. W. Samson, who was with the General Electric's Data Section, offered a concrete comparison between this new slide rule and computing with the tables upon which the slide rule scales were based. According to the two General Electric engineers, "substitution of a printed table of figures for slide rule scales has the disadvantage of requiring two devices instead of one and of requiring laborious interpolations between the tabulated values. While very good accuracy is this obtainable, the time required is at least twice as long as by the new slide rule method."[74]

Alger and Samson also compared computing with this new slide rule to computing with two different slide rules. "Time trials" of a method based on an ordinary slide rule have shown that it took about one and ½ times as long, and the result was a little less accurate on account of the increase in the number of operations. Similar trials on a polyphase slide rule took one and ⅓ times as long. The result was still somewhat less accurate due to the use of two settings instead of one. Alger and Samson concluded that the new power-factor slide rule offered "distinctive advantage" and that it was probable that "it will in time be recognized as a very useful addition to the mathematician's tool chest." This new power-factor slide rule was "metamorphosed from" a standard 10-inch slide rule by the substitution of a power-factor scale, N, for the ordinary scale of squares, A, and by the addition of a new scale of square roots, M, on the lower edge of the face.[75]

"The familiar ten-inch polyphase slide rule," informed the two authors in their introduction, "has become an almost indispensable element in engineering calculations, and many newer, more complicated varieties of slide rule have become very

---

[73] Frederick S. Dellenbaugh, Jr. 1921, February. An electromechanical device for rapid schedule harmonic analysis of complex waves. *AIEE Journal*, 142.

[74] P.L. Alger, and H.W. Samson. 1922, July. A new power-factor slide rule. *General Electric Review* 25(7): 456.

[75] Ibid., 455–456.

popular." "However," they added, "none of the extant commercial forms of rule are adapted for the convenient solution of numerical problems involving the third side of a right triangle of which two sides are already known." Ordinarily, this was computed by squaring the other two sides, adding or subtracting, and extracting the root, a process which required "either pen and pencil, or at least some mental gymnastic and frequently requires a search for the decimal point." The new power-factor slide rule was designed so as to provide a more convenient solution of these problems. Its name was derived from its use in determining the power factor in alternating current power transmission.[76]

The two authors expected that, "[s]ince this power-factor slide rule affords a mechanical means of solving any right triangle with the same facility and the same accuracy as ordinary multiplications are performed, it will be useful in a great many kinds of engineering calculations." It could be used, for example, "in surveying and bridge design in civil engineering, stress determination, and steam flow calculation in mechanical engineering and all kinds of alternating current calculations in electrical engineering." "In general," explained Alger and Samson, "wherever the algebra of complex quantities involving the use of the symbol j for the square root of -1 has proved useful in the representation of physical phenomena, the new slide rule will also prove useful in the performance of the corresponding numerical calculations."[77] This was then a slide rule designed to be used in connection with the algebra of complex numbers in mind.

If computing with a slide rule in general could point to a human computer, usually a female, computing with the algebra of complex numbers pointed to an analyst, usually a male. Exemplars of analysts of the first generation of electrical engineers were General Electric's Charles Proteus Steinmetz and the Harvard-MIT professor Arthur Edwin Kennelly and, of the second, Vannevar Bush (see Chap. 4). It is not then accidental that the person who had actually designed the new power-factor slide rule was both a computer and an analyst. In the middle of their article, Alger and Samson mentioned that this person was no other than Kennelly's student Edith Clarke. Unable to find employment as an electrical engineer, Clarke had worked between 1919 and 1921 as a trainer and director of a small team of women computers, which was set up at General Electric's Turbine Engineering Department (Alger's department). James Brittain found that this team was created as a response to "an anomalous situation that created a temporary need for skilled calculators," needed in order to produce computations in relation to the unanticipated problems caused by rotor vibrations and metal fatigue. The work of the human computers was part of an intensive research program that included both experimental and theoretical analysis.[78]

Not having signed the article that introduced to the 1922 power-factor slide rule, Clarke is now associated only with another slide rule of the second period. She was

---

[76] Ibid., 455–456.

[77] Ibid., 457.

[78] James E. Brittain. 1985. From computor to electrical engineer: The remarkable career of Edith Clarke. *IEEE Transactions on Education* E-28(4): 185.

issued a patent for it in September of 1925. In comparison to the conventional form of Clarke's 1922 power-factor slide rule, her 1925 slide rule was of a unique form. It consisted of sliding charts. This slide rule was the subject of her first technical paper, which was published in the *General Electric Review* in 1923. The paper contained drawings of the parts of Clarke's computing artifact along with instructions on how to mount the parts on cardboard and assemble. We may place this artifact under the tradition of calculating artifacts that combined more than one class. Clarke called it "a transmission line calculator." It included a base chart and two calibrated radial arms that were attached to it. Clarke explained that she had designed it because transmission line calculations, "as ordinarily performed by means of the well-known series of hyperbolic formulas require a great deal of time and labor."[79]

It was used to compute the equation of electric power transmission through a relatively graphical orientation. Clarke introduced to it as being sufficiently accurate for computing overhead power transmission lines of up to 250 miles. She estimated that computing with it could cut down the time required for such computation to less than one-tenth. Clarke had reconfigured the transmission line equations so as to be suitable to the use of this artifact. The fact that distributed resistance, inductance, and capacitance were taken into account suggests that this was an artifact to be used for computing a phenomenon that was much more complex than the electrical wiring slide rules described earlier. Leakance was not taken into account, but Clarke clarified that it would be possible to design a slide rule that would include it. The theory upon which the design and use of this slide rule was based started from the transmission line equations of Steinmetz. In the patent application, Clarke explained that her transmission line slide rule was also based on the work of Oliver Heaviside and Kennelly.[80]

Important as Clarke's contribution was, it can be placed in a context of similar contributions. Only 9 years earlier, also in the *General Electric Review*, Robert W. Adams had published an article with the same title as Clarke's: "A Transmission Line Calculator." His introduction offered a clearly expressed justification of the interest in mechanizing power transmission computations through the use of special sliding rules and charts:

> Perhaps the most tedious problem which confronts the average electrical engineer is the accurate calculation of voltage drop and power loss in alternating-current transmission lines. This calculation is one that frequently has to be repeated several times before the most economical and efficient design is secured, and on this account the orthodox trigonometric method, while not in itself unduly difficult, becomes very laborious in its practical application.
>
> Accordingly, there have been proposed a number of 'short-cut' methods, designed to reduce the labor of computing voltage drop in lines of moderate length in which capacity can be neglected; and one of these, the Mershon chart, has been very successful in abbreviating a portion of the process without departing from the strict mathematical solution of the

---

[79] Edith Clarke. 1923, June. A transmission line calculator. *General Electric Review* 26(6): 380.

[80] James E. Brittain. *From computor to electrical engineer: The remarkable career of Edith Clarke*, 185.

vector diagram. This chart, however, in common with most of the other graphic methods, cannot be applied to a specific problem until a certain amount of arithmetical calculation has been performed, and it is this extra labor which is the most fruitful source of error and delay.[81]

"With the idea of shortening this labor and lessening the chance of error," Adams had condensed into two steps the preliminary work necessary to the graphic solution of the vector diagram. In order then to express graphically the whole of his simplified method, he had constructed a device that consisted of a circular slide rule scale for computing the value of the "transmission factor," which was to be used together with a wire diagram for locating the apex of the line-drop triangle and a transparent chart to indicate the actual drop in the percentage of the receiver voltage.[82]

Adams (1915) and Clarke's (1923) transmission line calculators were as special as a power transmission analyst's slide rule could be. More general-purpose slide rules of a more conventional form were also used by power transmission analysts. In 1923, H. Goodwin presented a paper on "Qualitative Analysis of Transmission Lines" that was based on computing with a standard slide rule. Computations as complex as those that had to do with the issue of transmission line regulation were discussed and debated with reference to standard slide rules scales A, B, C, and D.[83] The discussion of Goodwin's paper was exceptionally long because the issue of computing regulation was discussed at a time when even the most expensive of the available computing artifact (an "artificial line," see Chap. 4) was quickly becoming inadequate, and the computing artifact to be used so as to successfully address the issue was still a few years away (the "network analyzer," see Chap. 4). Several other alternatives or supplements were mentioned in the same discussion, including something as common as the computing graphs known as "circle diagrams" (see Chap. 6) and something as unique as Vladimir Karapetoff's special kinematic computing linkage that was named the "Heavisidion" (see Chap. 4).[84]

3.4.3 "If Querist Will Lay Out His Slide Rules"

In several cases, electrical engineers proudly published their personal contributions for computing with a slide rule. In 1929, M. K. Kruger, who was with the Bell Telephone Laboratories, published an article in *Instruments* with details on an improved slide rule for complex number transformation computations. Kruger informed the readers that six of them had been made for the use of the engineers at

---

[81] Robert W. Adams.1915, January. A transmission line calculator *General Electric Review* 18(1): 28.

[82] Ibid., 29.

[83] H. Goodwin. 1923, February. Qualitative analysis of transmission lines. *AIEE Transactions* 42, 25 and 27.

[84] Ibid., 40.

his department by Keuffel & Esser.[85] Engineering and other technical journals, just like home technology journals, have been key media for the dissemination of knowledge about new computing artifacts. We know that in the age of the electronic computer, interactive and other special columns in these journals, like the ones in *Power* that are discussed earlier in this chapter (Sect. 3.3), have offered a much needed forum for all kinds of knowledge exchanges as well as for sharing indispensable software.[86] Similar practices seem to have a deep past. Cutting the pages of technical journals in order to assemble computing artifacts from the parts printed on them was standard practice in the case of the machine tool nomograms offered through the pages of the *American Machinist*.[87] We find similar instances in the history of the slide rule. Noticeably, Clarke, who did not have to assign her patents to the General Electric because she was not yet a permanent employee, had written the article on her transmission line calculator so as to make it easy for any electrical engineer to construct his own slide rule by cutting the parts needed from the pages of her *General Electric Review* article and then assemble these parts by using glue to attach them to cardboard.[88]

For an example of a less demanding computing artifact, I choose an advertisement by the Ohmite Manufacturing Company of Chicago, which was placed in the *Index* of the September 1940 issue of *Instruments*. For a firm that was selling rheostats, resistors, and tap switches, it made perfect sense to offer an artifact that "solves any Ohm's Law problem with one setting of the slide." Beyond promoting the firm in general, the use of the special scales of this slide rule could habituate an engineer to the products of this firm. Just like a hematologist may now choose to prescribe a certain drug because the sliding scales offered to her by the firm that produces it offers her a handy way to compute a treatment scheme that is based on this drug, an electrical engineer could habitually order resistors or rheostats from a certain electrical manufacturer because of a promotional slide rule offered to him by this manufacturer. The Ohmite "Ohm's Law Calculator" was supposed to be "the handiest":

> Here's the handiest Ohm's Law Calculator ever devised. Figures Amperes, Volts, Watts, Ohms—quickly, easily, accurately! Requires no slide rule knowledge. All values are direct readings. Scales on both sides cover the current and wattage range for motors, generators, lamps, electrical apparatus and other applications up to 100 amperes or 1000 watts; also the low current high resistance radio, sound and electronic applications. Has convenient Stock Unit Selector—a setting of the slide tell the stock number of the resistor or rheostat you

[85] M.K. Kruger. 1929, July. A slide rule for filter computations. *Instruments*, 233–238.

[86] Aristotle Tympas, Fotini Tsaglioti, Theodore Lekkas. 2008. Universal machines vs. national languages: Computerization as production of new localities. In *Proceedings of Technologies of Globalization,* ed. Reiner Anderl, Bruno Arich-Gerz, Rudi Schmiede, Darmstadt: TU Darmstadt.

[87] See Aristotle Tympas and Fotini Tsaglioti. 2016. L'usage du calcul àla production: le cas des nomogrammes pour machines-outils au XXe siècle. In *Le monde du génie industriel au XXe siècle: Autour de Pierre Bézier et de machines-outils,* ed. Serge Benoit, and Alain Michel, 63–73. Paris: Collection Sciences Humaines et Technologie, Pôle editorial de l'UTBM.

[88] Edith Clarke, *A transmission line calculator.*

may need. Size 4 and 1/8"x9'.' Specially designed by Ohmite Engineers. Available for only 10c to cover handling cost.[89]

The industries involved in electrification were quite interested in promoting the use of the slide rule. In the column "Answers" to "Question Box" of the publication of the National Electric Lighting Association, which was edited by Stephen A. Sewall, computing with a slide rule was frequently a focus. Entry 0–85, published in the October issue of 1916 of *NELA Bulletin,* is quite typical:

> I am desirous of obtaining a pamphlet, book or chart working out the number of kilowatts one horsepower will consume per year on a 6-hour, 12-hour, 18-hour and 24-hour basis per day, under different load factors.
>
> Can you get me also the cost per horsepower per year under different charges per mil from 2 mils up? If I can get figures they will help me greatly in working out problems pressing at this time.
>
> E. E. Stark, City Electrical Engineer's Office Christchurch N Z—If Querist will lay out slide rules, he will find it a very simple job to make a scale and plot the logarithms he needs.
>
> Enclosed are three slide-rules that I have found very useful in my ordinary work.
>
> [Other replies in July and September Bulletins][90]

The following page was filled with drawings of these three special slide rules. They were straight slide rules with special scales to compute the parameters that Stark had mentioned. Sewall referred to them as "calculating rules." These slide rules had very specialized scales that were arranged in the most common slide rule form. For an example of the opposite from the same period, i.e., a slide rule of a very uncommon design with scales that were as little specialized as possible, I choose the slide rule presented in the September 11, 1915, issue of the *Electrical World.* It was called a "Five-Place Calculating Device." This device was manufactured by the Computer Manufacturing Company of San Francisco. Louis Ross was its designer. This "calculating device for engineers" was supposed to be "capable of performing operations for which a slide rule is generally employed having an accuracy of 1 in 100,000." Called "the Ross Precision Computer," it was a metallic instrument throughout. The graduations were engraved on silvered metal surfaces. The Ross Precision Computer consisted of a graduating dial rotating under a slotted curve, a floating guide, and a slide mounted at the right of the slot. Its diameter was only 8 inches.[91]

The operation of the dial was designed so as to be suitable for an accuracy of five significant figures. If an accuracy of three significant figures was sufficient, a miniature scale dial could be used. This dial was ordinarily used to check and point out the precise answer and to locate the decimal point. To multiply and divide any series of numbers, it was necessary to set each number in succession under the reading line of the slot and read the result under the slot line. The same slide rule could be used for logarithmic calculations involving as many as five significant figures and, also,

---

[89] Get this handy new Ohmite Ohm's law calculator. *Instruments* (Index 1941), 45.

[90] See *NELA Bulletin* 10, part III, New Series, no. 9 (1916), 782–783.

[91] A five-place calculating device. *Electrical World* 66 (1915, September 11): 604.

for complex calculations (power, roots, etc.). It was claimed that trigonometric computations could be made with an accuracy of from 3 to 5 s of arc.[92]

For a representative couple of slide rules from the following decades, I choose the "Slide-Disk Calculator" that G. S. Merrill described in the June 1946 issue of the *General Electric Review*, and the "Calcu-light-or" of the Westinghouse Lighting Division (Cleveland) that was advertised in the November 1948 issue of the *Westinghouse Engineer*. The General Electric artifact belonged to the second class. It was convenient for making root-mean-square computations and was especially adapted to statistical deviations from a mean. Merrill was with the Lamp Department of the Engineering Division of the General Electric Company. The artifact of the Lighting Division of Westinghouse was for computations of illumination problems, involving either the lumen or the point-by-point methods, in which case a distribution curve of the particular luminaire was also required. It was introduced to a "slide-rule-type device," which consisted of three scales that were drawn in the form of wheels. The Calcu-light-or was a simple and easy to use artifact that cost $1 to buy. With this slide rule, "Lighting Calculations Lightened."[93]

The General Electric slide rule was more complex. It consisted essentially of a disk with a center pin projecting a short distance from the back and sliding in a slot that was located under the disk. The upper side of the disk was covered with a material such as heavy drawing paper, into which the point of a pin could be pressed. Mounted at right angles to the slot was a movable arithmetic scale E, under which the disk could turn and slide. Judging from the graphical representation of the mathematical principle by which the instrument was to be operated, this artifact can be also interpreted as an attempt at mechanizing the process of computing with a nomogram.[94]

3.4.4 *"Equivalent to Millions of Dollars Annually"*

A record of pictures of engineers posing with their slide rules promises to be very suggestive in confirming that engineers were proud to be identified by working with their slide rules. For a sample, I have surveyed the pictures of the General Electric engineers that were presented in the column of the General Electric *Monogram* that was called "The Monogram Salutes..." It was a column with pictures of distinguished General Electric engineers. Electrical engineers frequently posed by placing their slide rule on the top of their desk. In several cases, the engineer held the slide rule set in the one hand and was pictured absorbed by the process of reading the result on the slide rule or recording the results. The 1940 picture of M. A. Whiting, application engineer in the Industrial Engineering Department at Schenectady is typical of this kind. Whiting was introduced to as having made

---

[92] Ibid.

[93] Lighting calculations lightened. *Westinghouse Engineer* 8 (1948, November): 174.

[94] G.S. Merrill. 1946, June. Slide-disk calculator. *General Electric Review* 49, 31.

"outstanding contributions particularly for adjustable- and variable-voltage control a-c systems."[95]

The 1941 picture of A. T. Sinks, who was with the engineering department at West Lynn Works, is typical of cases in which the open slide rule was placed on the desk while the engineer recorded the results (Fig. 3.1). Sinks was chosen for his "resourcefulness and untiring efforts" in improving the design of dry-type instrument transformers, on which he is recognized as "an authority."[96] A picture of Edith Clarke was also included in the same page. By the 1940s, Edith Clarke was recognized as an analyst.[97] She was with the Central Station Engineering Department at Schenectady. The *Monogram* saluted her "for her greatly simplified methods of calculating electrical performance of high-voltage transmission lines and her pioneering work in power systems stability." She was photographed holding in her hands her transmission line calculator (Figs. 3.1 and 3.2).[98]

The note that the editor of the *General Electric Review* wrote in order to introduce to Clarke's slide rules reveals why electrical engineers posed proudly with their general or special slide rules until so late: "While the ordinary slide rule is practically universal in its application, and can be credited with saving its users an amount of time equivalent to millions of dollars annually, there are special types of calculation that may be facilitated to a still greater extent by the use of a variation of the common style of rule."[99]

3.5 "Speed Up Computations of Many Sorts"

We can refer to the slide rules of Clarke for an example of a line of development of slide rules that brings us from electrical to electronics engineering. As Brittain has observed, her second slide rule, which she devised in order to compute electric transmission of power, was similar in function to the well-known "Smith chart" that would be developed by P. H. Smith of the Bell Telephone Laboratories in the late 1930s, for the purpose of computing the electric transmission of communication. It was also introduced to as a "transmission line calculator." Smith had actually devised an earlier form of it in 1931.[100] Both Clarke's and Smith's artifacts were slide rules of class two (see the classification in 3.2). They were also, both,

---

[95] The monogram salutes... *The GE Monogram* 17(10) (1940, October), 17.

[96] The monogram salutes... *The GE Monogram* 18(4) (1941, April), 17.

[97] Edith Clarke. 1944. Trends in power system analysis. *Midwest Power Conference Proceedings* 7, 172–180.

[98] The monogram salutes... *The GE Monogram* 18(4) (1941, April), 17.

[99] P.L. Alger, and H.W. Samson, *A new power-factor slide rule*, 455.

[100] Brittain, *From computor to electrical engineer: The remarkable career of Edith Clarke*, 186; P.H. Smith. 1939, January. Transmission line calculator *Electronics* 12, 29-31; and E.F. O'Neill ed. 1985. *A history of engineering and science in the Bell System: Transmission technology, 1925–1975*, 56. AT&T Bell Laboratories.

The Monogram Salutes . . .

EDITH CLARKE, Central Station Engineering Dept., Schenectady, for her greatly simplified methods of calculating electrical performance of high-voltage transmission lines and her pioneering work in power system stability.

JOHN EATON, Industrial Control Engineering Dept., Schenectady Works, whose ingenuity, particularly along mechanical lines, combined with sound common sense, has helped to establish G-E control in a position of leadership.

E. F. LUMBER, Lighting Division, Central Station Dept., Schenectady, for his important contributions in appearance design in the field of modern architectural lighting.

A. T. SINKS, Engineering Department, West Lynn Works, for his resourcefulness and untiring efforts in improving the design of dry-type instrument transformers, on which he is recognized as an authority.

Nominations of G-E engineers and others whose achievements merit recognition on this page should be sent the editor.

Fig. 3.1 General Electric engineers A. T. Sinks (bottom right) and Edith Clarke (top left) posing with a slide rule of standard design and a hybrid calculating artifact with sliding of personal design (1941) (a clean copy of this figure was provided through the courtesy of the miSci Museum of Innovation and Science, Schenectady, New York)

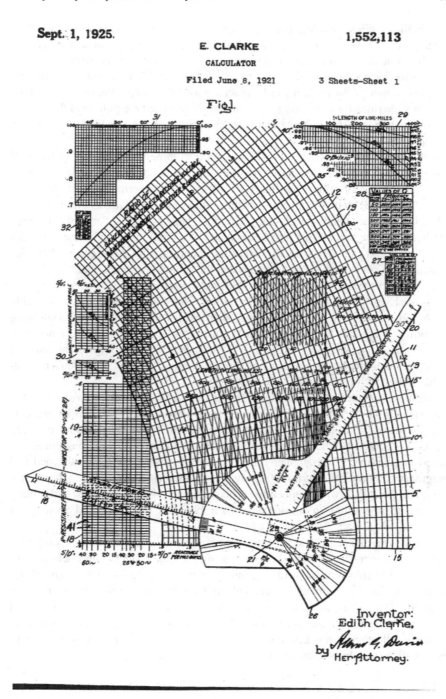

Fig. 3.2 Patent drawing of the hybrid calculating artifact with sliding by Edith Clarke (1925)

combinations of a slide rule and a graph. Clarke's first slide rule (power-factor slide rule), which was of the common straight-form slide rule design, can also be related to a slide rule development that was connected to electronic engineering, for it was a slide rule that could be used for engineering purposes that involved computing by complex numbers. As such, it can be placed under the line of the development of straight slide rules for computing the relationship between the polar and the rectangular form of a complex quantity that was described by Kruger in his 1929 article in *Instruments* (see 3.4.3).

For Kruger, who was with the apparatus development department of the Bell Telephone Laboratories, computing the transformation between the polar and rectangular form was of prime importance to electrical engineering network computations. "Electrical networks such as filters, attenuation equalizers, transformers, balancing networks and speech delay circuits," stated Kruger, "are used in large numbers in many parts of the telephone plant." We would now call these networks "electronic" and engineering them "electronics" engineering. After giving examples of their use, Kruger moved on to explain that these networks were made up of resistances, inductances, and capacitances and that in some cases the number of elements included could be a hundred or more. This had resulted in considerable computing complexity and an associated demand for improvements in computing techniques: "In order to ascertain their performance accurately, a large amount of mathematical computation is involved. Any consideration simplifying the work of computation are therefore deserving of serious thought, particularly when a considerable saving in time is thereby effected."[101]

All these networks involved alternating current transmission. In most cases, the analysis of such networks could be simplified by expressing the voltages and currents as vectors so as to show the magnitudes and the phase relationships between them. This could be done by representing them in polar form, with magnitude and direction given, or in rectangular form, by complex numbers giving the real and imaginary components. "Partly offsetting the advantages of this notation, however," noted Kruger, "is the work frequently involved in solving the equations, particularly the routine operations in transferring them between the polar and rectangular form."[102]

"Various mechanical devices, some of them especially designed for the purpose," explained Kruger, "have been used for reducing the time taken by this operation. An ordinary slide rule is used most commonly, but it was designed for general use rather than for this particular operation, and numerous settings of the rule are required." The numerous settings of the slide rule required for the transformation of the polar to the rectangular form (and vice versa) usually resulted in reduction of accuracy (all other things kept constant).[103] This was why Kruger was in favor of special slide rules for vector transformations.

---

[101] M.K. Kruger, *A slide rule for filter computations*, 233.

[102] Ibid., 233.

[103] Ibid., 233–234.

To place his own contribution within an historical context, Kruger started with the slide rule that F. A. Hubbard had designed in 1916—by 1929, Hubbard had become vice president and general manager of the Mexican Tel. & Tel. Company. With his slide rule, Hubbard had reduced to three the number of settings of slide and hairline required for a complete transformation. For Kruger, Hubbard's slide rule had two disadvantages. First, the scales were drawn so that this 20-inch long slide rule was no more accurate than a 10-inch one. Second, given that it was necessary to set up the numerical factors on an inverted scale and read from right to left, the chance of error from "carelessness on the part of the users" was increased because the reverse side was also used for multiplication and division. The other special slide rule that Kruger mentioned was that of M. P. Weinbach, who was a professor at the University of Missouri.[104] Weinbach, who was actually Professor of Electrical Engineering, was an author of a treatise on the electric transmission of power.[105] As Kruger explained, problems involving complex numbers could be solved with this slide rule as well, but four settings were required for a change from rectangular to polar form and six settings for the reverse transformation.[106]

Kruger reported that a 20-inch slide rule was designed to expedite the filter computations at the Bell Telephone Laboratories, with the scales arranged especially for vector transformations. Preliminary arrangements for its manufacture were made with the Keuffel & Esser Company early in 1928, and in the summer of the same year six slide rules were made for the Research Department and the apparatus development department. With this rule, only one setting of the slide and two settings of the hairline were needed in order to change a complex number from either form to the other.[107] Kruger described in detail the special scales placed on it and gave examples of how they ought to be used. He also argued that, although the slide rule was originally intended primarily for filter computations, its usefulness was not restricted to those engaged in designing filters. Kruger outlined certain modifications that could make a 10-inch size slide rule of the same kind "in many ways advantageous for general engineering and student use." "Since complex numbers enter into computations in many other fields than those of telephone filters," concluded Kruger, "a rule so made would speed up computations of many sorts, and at the same time fit the general types of computation for which a slide rule is commonly used."[108]

Kruger's was neither the only nor the last slide rule for computing complex vector transformations. The "vector slide rule" by Blundell Rules, which was patented in 1951, was a "massive and quite interesting to look at" slide rule that was used for the same purpose.[109] Evidently, more than one company developed slide rules for

---

[104] Ibid., 234.

[105] M.P. Weinbach. 1948. *Electric power transmission*. New York: Macmillan.

[106] M.K. Kruger, *A slide rule for filter computations*, 234.

[107] Ibid., 234–235.

[108] Ibid., 238.

[109] Robert Otnes, and Conrad Schure. 1996, March. The Blundell vector slide rule. *Journal of the Oughtred Society* 5(1), 19.

the same purpose. The "Hemmi 255 slide rule," which was designed "for expert electrical engineer, deserves mentioning." The Blundell slide rule could be used more generally and over a wider range, but it was more expensive than the Hemmi.[110] The Hemmi 255 slide rule was manufactured around 1950. Hemmi was a Japanese manufacturer. The total number of slide rules of all kinds that Hemmi manufactured between 1895 and 1973 is estimated to be approximately 15 million. Hemmi slide rule production peaked in 1963 at 1,000,000 per year.[111]

In the September 1961 issue of *Electronic Technology*, D. J. Whythe described a special Fuller (cylindrical-helical) slide rule as a "slide rule for complex numbers." It appears to be the last of the Fuller style slide rules made and sold by W. F. Stanley of London. It was a slide rule made by using the complex plane representation of complex numbers with logarithmically divided components. It could be used to multiply or divide complex numbers with the same facility and accuracy with which a conventional slide rule could be used to multiply or divide real numbers. The result was indicated in both a rectangular and polar form. Clason called it "remarkable" and argued that it differed in principle from all others by explaining that "[w]hereas real numbers and their logarithms can be presented as points on a line, complex numbers and their logarithms must be represented as lines on a surface."[112] As with all Fuller slide rules, it was more expensive than conventional slide rules.[113]

Considerable emphasis was also placed on a modified use of an ordinary slide rule. Given that special slide rules were more expensive, the option of using a conventional slide rule for the conversion of the complex form of vectors to its equivalent exponentials—that is from a form suitable for addition and subtraction to a form suitable for multiplication and division—was never abandoned. For example, a few months after University of Missouri's Weinbach presented his special slide rule in his 1928 *AIEE Journal* paper, Elbert G. Allen, who was a consulting engineer with Stone & Webster of Boston, described how to use an ordinary polyphase slide rule for the same purpose in the *Electrical World*.[114]

3.6 "Uses Slide Rule"

There are several ways to indicate that the relationship between the centuries-long history of computing with the slide rule and the decades-long history of electronic computing is much more dialectical that canonically assumed. I started with the history of the line of development of slide rules that became useful for electronics

---

[110] Ibid., 19.

[111] Peter M. Hopp, *Slide rule: Their history, models, and makers*, 183–187.

[112] Clyde Clason. 1964. *Delights of the slide rule*, 225. New York: Thomas Y. Crowell Co. Clason also described it in detail in pages 240–241.

[113] The Whythe complex slide rule in fuller style. *Journal of the Oughtred Society* 8(1) (1999, Spring): 15–17.

[114] Elbert C. Allen. 1928, 25 April. Slide rule calculation of vectors. *Electrical World* LIV(8), 362.

engineering (3.5). Another way would be to start by acknowledging that established and new manufacturers moved on to produce special slide rules for electronics engineering. As mentioned earlier, Nestler of Germany, which has been in business from 1878 to 1978, had introduced a slide rule for wiring computations in 1909. For years, Nestler was a prime manufacturer of several models with special electrical scales designated "Electro." Starting with the 1967 catalog, an "electronic" slide rule was added in the Nestler line product. It had special scales for electronics.[115] There were also newcomers in the slide rule for electronic engineering business. The Australian firm Reed of Sydney is known from one slide rule for "Service Electronic Engineers."[116]

The flowing of the slide rule tradition into the emergence of the electronic computer is captured by the following examples, which come from the history of transmission line calculations ('power system analysis'). At the 1955 American Power Conference, C. A. Imburgia, G. W. Stagg, L. K. Kirchmayer, and K. R. Geiser presented a paper on a "straightforward electrical analog computer," which they called "Penalty Factor Computer." It was designed and constructed to be used in conjunction with the existing incremental fuel cost slide rule. Their study:

> indicated that the overall requirements of the American Gas and Electric system, namely, economic allocation of generation and evaluation of losses associated with intercompany transactions, could best be satisfied by the Penalty Factor Computer which could be used with the existing incremental cost slide rule.[117]

The importance of computing with this slide rule was not questioned by the four authors, who had stated that their "criterion of economic performance has been applied widely by the electric utility industry through use of an incremental fuel cost slide rule."[118] This criterion was based on the incremental fuel rate, which was a small change in the output divided by the corresponding change in the input. The overall issue concerned the best allocation of plant generation to effect optimum system operating economy. It was an issue of primary importance. The proper consideration of transmission losses in the dispatching of plant generation had resulted in savings of over $200,000 a year for the American Gas and Electric Company. The computer was used to quickly compute quickly transmission loss penalty factors, which were then used to adjust the relative position of the incremental fuel strips of the incremental fuel cost slide rule in order to include the effect of transmission losses.[119]

The four authors gave an example of a simple slide rule for a two-generator network, which consisted of a logarithmic calibration scale, a movable strip for each generator unit, and a fuel adjustment scale. The calibration scale was graduated in

[115] Peter M. Hopp, *Slide rule: Their history, models, and makers*, 202–206.

[116] Ibid., 212.

[117] C.A. Imburgia, G.W. Stagg, L. Kirchmayer, and K.R. Geiser. 1955. Design and application of a penalty factor computer. *American Power Conference Proceedings* 17, 697.

[118] Ibid., 689.

[119] Ibid., 687.

mills per kwhr to a logarithmic scale. Each movable strip was calibrated in Mw and indicated the relation between the incremental fuel cost as shown on the calibration scale and the output of each generator unit as shown on its movable strip. Differences in fuel cost could be accounted for by displacing a given generator strip to line up the bottom of the strip with the appropriate position on the fuel cost adjustment scale. This position corresponded to the ratio of the plant fuel cost to a base cost. The individual generator outputs could then be read directly from the strips, and the value of the total generation could be computed by summing these individual readings. The incremental cost of power could be read from the calibration scale.[120]

The four authors informed that subsequent to the decision to install this computer, significant advances were made in the development of computing and control equipment to allocate generation automatically on a continuous and economic basis. They expected that development of the penalty factor computer and incremental slide rule combination would result in significant changes in forecasting generation and capacity schedules and in determining losses associated with interconnection sales.[121]

A 1959 editorial in the *Electrical World* was written so as to update on the activities of a manufacturing-utility task force with several working groups that was set to experiment with the "gaming" concept of planning, which was based on statistical analysis of utility records. It was headed by Westinghouse's J. K. Dillard and Public Service E&G's H. K. Sels. Arizona PS's Americo Lazzari reported fuel savings of $100,000 or more per year by equal incremental scheduling of all thermal machines on two interconnected utility systems. As with the aforementioned example, incremental transmission losses were included by assigning penalty factors. For assigning such factors, the Arizona PS "personnel" has developed a "unique" slide rule. According to the editor, this slide rule "offers a convenient way to demonstrate to system dispatchers the savings available from various schedules." It could also be used for actual scheduling, for merging the load schedules of both systems to serve each with less installed generation, for making fuller utilization of existing facilities, and for enabling new generating equipment to be added in more economical unit sizes and timing. Eight main slides were provided for station incremental cost curves, each containing a sub-slider to allow for variations in heat content of the natural gas.[122]

The *Electrical World* editor had started by claiming that "[m]odern mathematics, coupled by high speed computers, offers electric utilities a powerful new approach to the perpetual problem of expanding system capacity economically to meet load requirements." One would expect to read only about the supposedly revolutionary electronic computer. But the explanatory title of a section incorporated in this editorial was betraying the continuity of computing techniques that the plan for expansion was capitalizing on: "Uses Slide Rule."[123]

---

[120] Ibid., 689.

[121] Ibid., 697.

[122] Task Force Plans System Expansion. *Electrical World* (1959, July 20): 88–89.

[123] Ibid.

3.7 Conclusion

The research presented in this chapter confirms that the slide rule has been used extensively and for very long. In the context of energy-related calculations, the slide rule may have been the most important computing artifact of the mechanical and the electrical eras, ever present, all the way from the boiler room of the steam engine to the office where the fast increase of the length and the complexity of electric power transmission lines was calculated. Just like the electronic era, the mechanical and the electrical era were perceived as being marked by the speed around. And just like the present day computer, the slide rule was thought as an exemplar of an age that was fast. Its speediness was crucial to the calculation of the fastening of change, while it was itself constantly changing to catch up with this fastening. The result was a myriad of special slide rules, standards adjusted in use or altogether new ones, which could, in due time, become themselves standard. The research in this chapter further confirms that the slide rule was found to be perfectly adequate, in this case by the power man of both steam and electricity. There was nothing from the technical side that could restrict its accuracy. On the contrary, the issue for many of its users was the pursuit of an excess of accuracy, under the influence of the fastness of the age, so as to be carried away by the technical potential of the slide rule instead of staying at the accuracy needed socially. The slide rule could be used to speed up calculations of all kinds. The most demanding calculating issues could be addressed by the use of slide rule, even the ones surfacing in the context of long transmission of electrons for communication. This could lead to considerable profits. The substantial space devoted to discussions about the proper use and appropriate modification of the slide rule in the technical press (in this case in energy-related journals) only confirms the importance of its history. Last but not least, by leaving aside the assumption that the slide rule was just displaced by the electronic computer, the chapter has added one more representative moment of the emergence of the electronic computing through the incorporation (rather than the displacement) of preceding computing traditions.

References

Adams RW (1915) A transmission line calculator. Gen Electr Rev 18(1):28–30
Alger PL, Samson HW (1922) A new power-factor slide rule. Gen Electr Rev 25(7):455–457
Allen EC (1928) Slide rule calculation of vectors. Electr World 92(8):362
Andrews H, Schure C (2001) A slide rule for wire drawing calculations. J Oughtred Soc 10(1):15–17
Barnes C (1997a) Dating Otis-king slide rules. J Oughtred Soc 6(2):35–36
Barnes C (1997b) Fuller's telegraph computer. J Oughtred Soc 6(2):37–38
Bascome GH (1913) Calculating scales. Power 37(9):308–309
Brittain JE (1985) From computor to electrical engineer: the remarkable career of Edith Clarke. IEEE Trans Educ E-28(4):184–189
Cajori F (1909) A history of the logarithmic slide rule and allied instruments. The Engineering News Publishing Company, New York

Clarke E (1923) A transmission line calculator. Gen Electr Rev 26(6):380–390
Clarke E (1944) Trends in power system analysis. Midwest Power Conf Proc 7:172–180
Clason CB (1964) Delights of the slide rule. Thomas Y. Crowell Co, New York
De Cesaris B (1998) The mechanical engineer. J Oughtred Soc 7(1):23–24
Dellenbaugh FS Jr (1921) An electromechanical device for rapid schedule harmonic analysis of complex waves. AIEE J:135–144
Drew RL (1926) The slide rule and the power man. Power 63(25):967
Durand WL (1922) Why not use a slide rule? Power 55(18):705
Feazel B (1994a) Palmer's computing scale. J Oughtred Soc 3(1):9–17
Feazel B (1994b) Special purpose slide rules. J Oughtred Soc 3(2):43–44
Feazel B (1995) Plamer's computing scale revisited. J Oughtred Soc 4(1):5–8
Feazel B (1997a) Electrical Wireman's combined gage and calculator. J Oughtred Soc 6(2):9–10
Feazel B (1997b) The Roylance electrical slide rule. J Oughtred Soc 6(2):39
Fisher HD (1916) Interpolating logarithms. Power 43(20):703–704
Foster DE (1914) Engineers' improved slide rule. Power 39(15):537
Goodwin H (1923) Qualitative analysis of transmission lines. AIEE Trans 42:24–41
Graham FD (1932) Audel's new electric library: mathematics-calculations, vol XI. Audel, New York
Hopp PM (1995) Otis-king update. J Oughtred Soc 4(2):33–40
Hopp PM (1996) Otis-king: conclusions? J Oughtred Soc 5(2):62–67
Hopp PM (1999) Slide rule: their history models and makers. Astragal Press, Mendham
Horsburgh EM (ed) (1914) Modern instruments and methods of calculation: a handbook of the Napier tercentenary exhibition. Bell and Sons, London. Reprinted with an 'Introduction' by Michael R. Williams (Los Angeles: Tomash Publishers, 1982): ix–xxi
Imburgia CA, Stagg GW, Kirchmayer L, Geiser KR (1955) Design and application of a penalty factor computer. Am Power Conf Proc 17:687–697
Kidwell PA, Ackerberg-Hastings A (2014) Chapter 9: Slide rules on display in the United States, 1840–2010. In: Ackermann S, Kremer R, Miniati M (eds) Scientific instruments on display. Brill, Leiden, pp 159–172
Kruger MK (1929) A slide rule for filter computations. Instruments:233–238
Low FR (1914) To find the number of integer places in a product or quotient. Power 39(12):400–401
Lyon R (1998) Dating of the Otis-king: an alternative theory developed through use of the internet. J Oughtred Soc 7(1):33–37
Merrill GS (1946) Slide-disk calculator. Gen Electr Rev 49:30–33
Miller RN (1915) Slide rule quadratics. Power 42(12):422–423
Moore AF (1913) Obtaining wire resistance on slide rules. Power 37(5):151
Morrison JP (1915) Handy flywheel calculator. Power 42(20):683
Muller RO (1916) Pointing off decimals with the slide rule. Power 43(25):888
O'Neill EF (ed) (1985) A history of engineering and science in the bell system: transmission technology 1925–1975. AT&T Bell Laboratories, Indianapolis
Otnes R (1991) The Otis-king slide rule. J Oughtred Soc 0(0):7–8
Otnes R, Schure C (1996) The Blundell vector slide rule. J Oughtred Soc 5(1):18–19
Payne H, O'Neill H (1922) A boiler-room slide rule. Power 55(14):543–544
Polakov WN (1913) Power plant log calculator. Power 37(17):596–597
Richardson CG (1914) Fixing the decimal point in slide-rule calculations. Power 39(16):551–552
Schell HB (1916) Interpolating logarithms with the slide rule. Power 43(13):451–452
Schuitema Y (1993) The ALRO circular slide rule. J Oughtred Soc 2(2):24–37
Smith PH (1939) Transmission line calculator. Electronics 12:29–31
Solomon AB (1919) An adding slide rule. Power 50(11):437
Spitzglass JM (1916) Slide rule and flow computer. Power 43(8):257
Stanley VK (1922) Why not use a slide rule? Power 55(22):866
Thompson JE (1930) A manual of the slide rule. Van Nostrand, New York

Tympas A, Tsaglioti F (2016) L'usage du calcul à la production: le cas des nomogrammes pour machines-outils au XXe siècle. In: Benoit S, Michel A (eds) Le monde du génie industriel au XXe siècle: Autour de Pierre Bézier et de machines-outils. Collection Sciences Humaines et Technologie, Pôle editorial de l'UTBM, Paris, pp 63–73

Tympas A, Tsaglioti F, Lekkas T (2008) Universal machines vs. national languages: computerization as production of new localities. In: Anderl R, Arich-Gerz B, Schmiede R (eds) Proceedings of technologies of globalization. TU Darmstadt, Darmstadt

von Jezierski D (1995) Special slide rules of Faber-Castell. J Oughtred Soc 4(2):50–52

von Jezierski D (2000) Slide rule: a journey through three centuries. Astragal Press, Mendham

Weinbach MP (1948) Electric power transmission. Macmillan, New York

Wines WE (1923) Why so many calculations in the boiler test code? Power 58(1):27–28

Wyman T (1915) Using a slide rule. Power 42(24):825–826

Chapter 4
"Like the Poor, the Harmonics Will Always Be with Us"

Contents

4.1   Introduction

From the perspective of the degree of mechanization (machine to human capital, constant to variable capital), some of the machines presented in this chapter should be placed at the one end of the spectrum of technologies of calculation-computation of the mechanical and electrical eras, whereas some of the graphs presented in Chap. 5 should be placed at the other. The calculating machines (mechanical calculators) presented in Chap. 6 and the slide rules presented in Chaps. 2 and 3 would fill the space in between. If we had to choose one name to refer to the great variety of the machines and associated mechanisms of this chapter, this would have to be "analyzer."

There were several lines of analyzer development. The most known is the one that culminated in the interwar "differential analyzers." Also known are the "network analyzers" of the same period, which built on a century-long experience with "artificial lines" for communication and power and on an early interwar experience with "calculating boards." Differential and network analyzers are considered to be representatives of general mathematical and special modeling calculating artifacts of the period before the electronic computer. This distinction is relative, as the use of network analyzers was successfully extended to a whole range of engineering and scientific uses, well beyond the analysis of electric power networks. A third line of analyzer development gave the "harmonic analyzers." What we know about them comes mostly from their use as "tide predictors." These three lines of analyzers incorporated an endless array of mechanisms

© Springer-Verlag London Ltd. 2017   75
A. Tympas, *Calculation and Computation in the Pre-electronic Era*, History of
Computing, https://doi.org/10.1007/978-1-84882-742-4_4

and related components, mechanical and electrical, from various "integrators" (and "differentiators") and "linkages" to diagrams like the "indicator diagram" of the steam engine and the "oscillograph" of the electric power network. The chapter starts with an introduction to the historiography and history of all these analyzers (Sect. 4.2).

Some of the analyzer components were also stand-alone calculating artifacts. This was the case with the various "planimeters." They are the focus of a special section (Sect. 4.3), which sets the stage for the history of aspects of the unknown history of the use of harmonic analyzers in the context of electrification in general and electric power transmission calculation in particular (Sect. 4.4). By way of indicating the richness of analyzer-related artifacts, the chapter continues with a section on the understudied idiosyncratic artifacts of electric power transmission by Vladimir Karapetoff, a Cornell professor of electrical engineering (Sect. 4.5). The extremely unique "isograph" and the family of calculating artifacts known as "linkages" are also discussed in this chapter, because they were closer to analyzers (or components of analyzers) than to slide rules and calculating machines (Sect. 4.6).

In recent years we started to know more about the human "computers" or "computors" of the period before the electronic computer, whose work status was at the other end of that of the designers of analyzers, the "analysts." The chapter suggests passages to the history of a related class of computing workers, who were called "operators." Operators were to analyzers what computors were to slide rules and calculating machines. In the context of pointing to the relatively invisible yet indispensable laboring with analyzers (that of operators), the section also introduces to the equally indispensable yet equally understudied work required to construct analyzers (Sect. 4.7). As argued throughout this book, the dynamic expansion of historical capitalism was bringing along a constant revolution in computing technology. In this chapter, this is shown through a representative instance of pursuing an "ideal analyzer" (in this case an ideal harmonic analyzer), one to be defined as such by its ability to eliminate human labor (Sect. 4.8).

4.2 "Mathematician *Par Excellence*"

The uncritical projection of the analog-digital demarcation to the whole of the history of computing and the associated historiographical devaluation of what is now placed on the side of the supposedly inferior analog has resulted in a paradox: while nobody doubts that the state-of-the-art working computing artifacts before electronic computing come from the line of development of analog computers like the nineteenth century "harmonic analyzers" analyzer of Lord Kelvin and the twentieth century "differential analyzer" and "network analyzer" of Vannevar Bush, the emphasis is placed on the development of the digital calculating and tabulating machines.[1] Analyzers, just like all standard and idiosyncratic integrating-differenti-

---

[1] For an introductory placement of Bush's contribution within the history of computing in the long-run, see Brian Randell. 1982. From analytical engine to electronic digital computer: The contributions of Ludgate, Torres, and Bush. *Annals of the History of Computing* 4(4): 327–341. The articles

ating (and related) mechanisms (most notably the "planimeter") and machines that were independent computing artifacts or key components of larger analyzers, are now canonically placed under analog computing, which is identified by its dependence on a minimum of mathematization.[2] But, in historical time, especially when

---

by Larry Owens on Bush's differential analyzer and MIT's subsequent struggle to distance itself from Bush's analyzer have set the scholarly standard for studies on the history of analog computing. See Larry Owens. 1986. Vannevar Bush and the differential analyzer: The text and the context of an early computer. *Technology and Culture* 27(1): 63–95, and Larry Owens. 1996, October–December. Where are we going Phil Morse? Challenging agendas and the rhetoric of obviousness in the transformation of computing at MIT, 1939–1957. *IEEE Annals of the History of Computing* 18(4): 34–41. For an exemplar book-length study on interwar computing and Bush's role in it, see David Mindell. 2004. *Between human and machine.* Baltimore: Johns Hopkins University Press. On Bush's top administrative role in World War II and his influential role in shaping post-World War II science and technology policy, see Larry Owens. 1994, Winter. The counterproductive management of science in the Second World War: Vannevar Bush and the Office of Scientific Research and Development. *Business History Review* 68: 515–576; Daniel J. Kevles. 1977. The National Science Foundation and the debate over postwar research policy, 1942–1945: A political interpretation of 'Science: The endless frontier'. *ISIS* 68(241): 4–26; Stanley Goldberg. 1992. Inventing a Climate of Opinion: Vannevar Bush and the Decision to Build the Bomb. *ISIS* 83: 429–452; Daniel Lee Kleinman. 1994. Layers of interests, layers of influence: Business and the genesis of the National Science Foundation. *Science, Technology, and Human Values* 19(3): 259–282. For Bush in general, see G. Pascal Zachary. 1997. *Endless frontier: Vannevar Bush, engineer of the American century.* New York: Free Press. For more on the context of the development of Bush's analyzers and MIT, see, also, Karl L. Wildes, and Nilo A. Lindgren. 1985. *A century of electrical engineering and computer science at MIT, 1882–1982.* Cambridge: MIT Press. For a more general angle on MIT, see Bruce Sinclair (ed.). 1986. Inventing a genteel tradition: MIT crosses the river. In *New perspectives on technology and American culture*, 1–18. Philadelphia: American Philosophical Society Library no. 12, and Larry Owens. 1990. MIT and the Federal 'Angel': Academic R&D and Federal-Private Cooperation Before World War II. *ISIS* 81: 188–213. Also from a more general angle, see Christophe Lecuyer. 1995. MIT, progressive reform, and 'Industrial Service', 1890–1920. *Historical Studies in the Physical Sciences* 26(1): 35–38, and Christophe Lecuyer. 1992. The making of a science based technological university: Karl Kompton, James Killian, and the reform of MIT, 1930–1957. *Historical Studies in the Physical Sciences* 23: 153–180. For the suggestive variance in the perception and persistence of the differential analyzer tradition according to variance of national context, see Mark D. Bowles. 1996, October–December. U.S. Technological enthusiasm and British Technological Skepticism in the Age of the Analog Brain. *IEEE Annals of the History of Computing* 18(4): 5–15.

[2] For an introduction to the history of analog computing, see Aristotle Tympas. 2005a. Computers: Analog. In *Encyclopedia of 20th–Century Technology*, ed. Colin Hempstead, 195–199. London: Routledge, and Aristotle Tympas. 2005b. Computers: Hybrid. In *Encyclopedia of 20th–Century Technology*, ed. Colin Hempstead, 202–204. London: Routledge. See also the relevant chapter by Alan Bromley. 1990. In *Computing before computers*, ed. William Aspray. Ames: Iowa State University Press. For book-length historical studies, see Mindell, *Between human and machine*; James S. Small. 2001. *The analogue alternative: The electronic analogue computer in Britain and the USA, 1930–1975.* London: Routledge; Charles Care. 2010. *Technology for modelling: Electrical analogies, engineering practice, and the development of analogue computing.* London: Springer; Trevor Pinch, and Frank Trocco. 2004. *Analog days: The invention and impact of the moog synthesizer.* Cambridge, MA: Harvard University Press. For surveys of post-World War II analog computing, see, also, James S. Small. 1993. General-purpose electronic analog computing, 1945–1965. *IEEE Annals of the History of Computing* 15(2): 8–18, and James S. Small. 1994. Engineering, technology, and design: The Post-Second World War development of electronic ana-

they were first introduced, analyzers were actually considered to be mathematical tools and machines.

In the classificatory scheme of the handbook of the 1914 Edinburgh first World Exhibition on computing—a scheme that sought to take into account the impressive development of computing technology since early capitalist modernity, they were placed under the class of "Other Mathematical Laboratory Instruments."[3] Only a few years before the appearance of the late modern analog-digital computing demarcation, top analysts referred to the same class of artifacts as exemplars of a mode of computing that was based on computing mathematization. Classifications of analyzers, just like detailed comparisons of between analyzers and other computing artifacts and between the various versions of analyzers attracted considerable resources at MIT and elsewhere (Fig. 4.1). In his 1936 classificatory survey, leading electrical engineering analyst and pioneer of the mathematization of electrical engineering Vannevar Bush, then an MIT professor, thought of them as mathematical machines with great potential.[4] In his influential classification of computers, Thornton C. Fry, a mathematical analyst at the Bell Labs who led in the movement known as "industrial mathematics," referred to them as machines for use of

logue computers. *History and Technology* 11: 33–48. For a sample of case studies, see James E. Tomayko. 1985. Helmut Hoelzer's fully electronic analog computer. *Annals of the History of Computing* 7(3): 227–241; Frank Preston. 2003, January–March. Vannevar Bush's network analyzer at the Massachusetts Institute of Technology. *IEEE Annals of the History of Computing*: 75–78; Kent H. Lundberg. 2005, June. The history of analog computing. *IEEE Control Systems Magazine*: 22–28; Chris Bissell. 2007, February. The Moniac: A hydromechanical analog computer of the 1950s. *IEEE Control Systems Magazine*: 69–74; Jonathan Aylen. 2010. Open versus closed innovation: Development of the wide strip mill for steel in the United States during the 1920s. *R&D Management* 40(1): 67–80, and Jonathan Aylen. 2012, January. Bloodhound on my trail: Building the Ferranti Argus process control computer. *International Journal for the History of Engineering and Technology* 82(1): 1–36. The importance of analog computing in European contexts is suggested by several authors. See, for example, Jan Van Ende. 1992. Tidal calculations in the Netherlands, 1920–1960. *IEEE Annals of the History of Computing* 14(3): 23–33; Per A. Holst. 1996, October–December. Svein Rosseland and the Oslo Analyzer. *IEEE Annals of the History of Computing* 18(4): 16–26; Magnus Johansson. 1996, October–December. Early analog computers in Sweden—with examples from Chalmers University of Technology and the Swedish Aerospace Industry. *IEEE Annals of the History of Computing* 18(4): 27–33, and Wilfried De Beauclair. 1986. Alvin Weather, IPM, and the development of calculator/computer technology in Germany, 1930–1945. *Annals of the History of Computing* 8(4): 334–350.

[3] See Ellice M. Horsburgh (ed.). 1914. *Modern instruments and methods of calculation: A handbook of the Napier Tercentenary Exhibition.* London: Bell and Sons.

[4] Vannevar Bush. 1936. Instrumental analysis. *Transactions of the American Mathematical Society* 42(10): 649–669. For the placement of Bush's differential analyzer within the history of the mathematization of electrical engineering, see Susan Puchta. 1996. On the role of mathematics and mathematical knowledge in the development of Vannevar Bush's early analog computers. *IEEE Annals of the History of Computing* 18(4): 49–59, and Susan Puchta. 1997. Why and how American electrical engineers developed heaviside's operational calculus. *Archives Internationales d'Histoire des Sciences* 47: 57–107.

142   DELLENBAUGH: HARMONIC ANALYZER   Journal A. I. E. E.

The time required by graphical methods renders them practically useless except for determining one or two harmonics. They have the advantage of picking out anyone harmonic within the accuracy of the construction, but do not seem to lend themselves readily to large groups of analyses.

The two best known instrumental methods are the Henrici-Coradi machine (Bibl. 55, 65) and the Westinghouse-Chubb polar analyser, (Bibl. 51 and 52). The former consists of five glass spheres, rolling within a carriage so that their displacement is proportional to the ordinates of the curve. The curve in cartesian form is plotted to fairly large scale and followed with a tracer point. Motion of the tracer point in the time-axis direction rotates cages around the glass spheres, the cages carrying planimeter wheels in contact with the spheres. Thus the radius of the circle upon which the planimeter wheel rolls is proportional to sin $k\theta$ and the motion of the spheres is proportional to y. The resulting displacement of the wheel is the solution of the Fourier integral given in the first part of the paper. Each cage carries two wheels at right angles. Thus for one tracing of the curve, the sine and cosine components of five harmonics may be determined. Resetting of the pulleys upon the top of the cages allows another five to be determined with another tracing of the curve.

The Westinghouse-Chubb analyser requires a curve in polar form, obtained from the polar oscillograph, from which a template must be made of cardboard. This is placed upon a platen, which is given a combined rotational and harmonic translational motion. An arm carrying a roller traverses the edge of the template and guides a polar planimeter in its extremity. After one complete trace of the template the reading of the planimeter gives one component of the harmonic for which the machine was set. Gears are then shifted for another harmonic and the process repeated. Unfortunately, the author has no records of time required for analysis by this machine. If high order harmonics are required, the time is rather long, but this is not fair to the machine, since it may easily be motor-driven and other work done while it is grinding out the analysis. Transferring curves from cartesian form to polar form requires a good deal of time and introduces a good deal of chance for error, so it is not satisfactory unless used with polar curves.

Some of the times required for analyses are as follows:

Method	Time	No. harmonics determined	Minutes per coeff.	Authority
Steinmetz	10 hr.	10	60	D. C. Miller
Schedule	3 hr.	8	22.5	D. C. Miller
Schedule	1 hr.	8	7.5	F. W. Grover
Schedule	2.5 hr.	17	10.6	Author
Schedule	15 min.	3	5	D. C. Miller
Coradi Mch	13 min.	10	1.3	D. C. Miller
Coradi Mch	7 min.	5	1.4	D. C. Miller
Schedule	30 min.	6	5.0	Author
Electric Mch	3.5 min.	6	.6	Author

The figures are not all comparable. They should be corrected for the number of harmonics determined, as the labor is not proportional with the different methods. The figures for the Coradi machine assume the curve already drawn. If the curve has to be enlarged from an oscillograph film, the added time for this should be included. The last two sets of data are based upon the time for doing the actual calculation, the readings from the curve having already been made, and being the same in each case, both times being for analysis of the same curve. The schedule analysis was performed upon a Marchant calculating machine. It can be done quicker with a slide rule, but the errors in the cosine components are then liable to be very great.

CONCLUDING COMPARISON

In conclusion, it may be of interest to compare the advantages and disadvantages of the different methods.

SCHEDULE METHOD

ADVANTAGES	DISADVANTAGES
Simple	Very laborious and slow for more than a few coefficients.
Requires only a small chart for direction.	Not accurate where harmonics exist outside range of schedule.
Fairly accurate within theoretical limitations.	Subject to error unless calculating machine used, particularly in cosine components.
Reasonably fast for a small number of coefficients.	

WESTINGHOUSE-CHUBB

ADVANTAGES	DISADVANTAGES
Accurate	Requires cardboard template of polar form.
Easy to operate	Difficult to use with curves in Cartesian form.
May be motor-driven and so require little labor.	Requires separate trace for each component.
Semi-portable	Moderately expensive.
Not difficult to obtain	Construction requires much machine work.
Easy to maintain	

HENRICI-CORADI

ADVANTAGES	DISADVANTAGES
Accurate	Requires large curve.
Easy to operate	Special table, tracks, etc., must be provided.
Quick	Can only be manufactured by expert instrument makers.
Five harmonics completely determined with one trace.	Expensive.
	Difficult to obtain
	Requires care for maintenance.
	Not portable.

ELECTRIC

ADVANTAGES	DISADVANTAGES
Easy and simple to operate.	Subject to limitations inherent with schedule method.
Moderately accurate and eliminates many chances for error.	Subject to usual difficulties of electric networks.
Very quick, as only one group of readings required from curve.	Not extremely accurate.
Reads coefficients either in actual values or per cent of fundamental sine component.	Number of resistances increases rapidly with order of harmonics.

Fig. 4.1 Page with tables of quantitative (left) and qualitative (right) comparisons of methods-artifacts of harmonic analysis by MIT's Frederick Dellenbaugh (1921)

Fig. 4.2 Sketches of the replacement of adults with calculating machines by children with a network analyzer in a *Westinghouse Engineer* editorial (1944)

mathematics.[5] As late as in 1948, Francis J. Murray, an author of an influential treatise on computing, identified them as exemplars of mathematical machines.[6]

In 1944, an editorial on the history of the network analyzer in the *Westinghouse Engineer* could refer to the network analyzer as a "Mathematician *Par Excellence*", who was introduced as the state of the art in machine intelligence after the calculating machines were proven inadequate to compute the dramatic interwar lengthening and interconnection of electric power networks that were about to produce "Frankensteins out of Control" (Fig. 4.2).[7]

---

[5] Thornton C. Fry. 1941, July. Industrial mathematics. *Bell System Technical Journal* 20(3): 255–292. For an earlier promotion of 'industrial mathematics' at Bell Labs, see George A. Campbell. 1924, October. Mathematics in industrial research. *Bell System Technical Journal* 3: 550–557. See, also, George A. Campbell. 1925, September. Mathematical Research. *Bell Laboratories Record* 1(1): 15–18.

[6] Francis J. Murray. 1961. *Mathematical machines, Volume II: Analog devices.* New York: Columbia University Press.

[7] "Network Calculator...Mathematician *Par Excellence*," *Westinghouse Engineer* 4 (July 1944), editorial. For an introduction to the analyzer tradition as developed and used in the context of computing electric power networks, see Aristotle Tympas. 1996. From digital to analog and back: The ideology of intelligent machines in the history of the electrical analyzer, 1870s–1960s. *IEEE Annals of the History of Computing* 18(4): 42–48, and Aristotle Tympas. 2003. Perpetually laborious: Computing electric power transmission before the electronic computer. *International Review of Social History* 11(Supplement): 73–95, and Aristotle Tympas. 2012. A deep tradition of computing technology: Calculating electrification in the American West. In *Where minds and matters meet: Technology in California and the West*, ed. Volker Janssen, 71–101. Oakland: University of California Press; Aristotle Tympas, and Dina Dalouka. 2007. Metaphorical uses of an electric power network: Early computations of atomic particles and nuclear reactors. *Metaphorik* 12: 65–84, and Aristotle Tympas. 2007. From the historical continuity of the engineering imaginary to an anti-essentialist conception of the mechanical-electrical-electronic relationship. In *Tensions and*

Representing the highest ratio of machine ("constant") to human ("variable") computing capital before the electronic era, the largest of the analyzers were ideologized as exemplars of machine intelligence from early on. The 1914 presentation of a sizable tide predictor in *Scientific American*, which followed in the tradition of the harmonic analyzers of the nineteenth century, is indicative of the extremes reached in presenting computing artifacts as intelligent machines during the mechanical and the electrical eras. C. H. Claudy, the author of the article, introduced this harmonic analyzer as "A Great Brass Brain: A Unique Engine, on the Accuracy of Which Depend Millions of Dollars and Thousands of Lives." This "great brass brain" was defined by its capacity to do "mathematical calculations":

> Roger Bacon, man of letters and of science, who lived in the thirteenth century, is supposed to have manufactured a brazen head or android, which spoke and revealed "dreaded secrets of the past and future." But no brass brain has come down to the present day from antiquity which can even think, let alone articulate through a brass mouth.
>
> But a mechanism, built for this United States of ours, can truly be called a "brass brain", in that it does the mathematical calculations which would otherwise require a hundred flesh and blood brains to do; and if it does not actually articulate its results, at least it indicates them plainly enough, not only by dials, but by writing them down. Still more does it claim kinship with that ancient and fabled brass brain of Bacon's, in that it, too, foretells the future, though no "dread secret" does it make it known.[8]

Moreover, as late as in 1949, the differential analyzers were included in listings of "Giant Brains, or, Machines that Think."[9] All of the above challenge the assumption that only the electronic computer has been promoted as capable of machine

---

convergences: Technical and aesthetic transformation of society, ed. Reinhard Heil, Andreas Kamiski, Marcus Stippak, Alexander Unger, and Marc Ziegler, 173–184. Germany: Verlag. For articles that are focused on individual contributions, see Gordon S. Brown. 1981. Eloge: Harold Locke Hazen, 1901–1980. *Annals of the History of Computing* 3(1): 4–12. See, also, William Aspray. 1994. Calculating power: Edwin L. Harder and analog computing in the electric power industry. In *Sparks of genius: Portraits of electrical engineering excellence*, ed. Frederik Nebeker, 159–199. New York: IEEE Press, and William Aspray. 1993. Edwin L. Harder and the Anacom: Analog computing at Westinghouse. *IEEE Annals of the History of Computing* 15(2): 35–52. See, also, Bernard O. Williams. 1984. *Computing with electricity, 1935–1945*. Diss. University of Kansas. For a primary source that provided with a survey of the general uses of the various analyzers and a survey of particular uses within electrification right at the emergence of the analog-digital demarcation, see H.A. Peterson, and C. Concordia. 1945, September. Analyzers...For use in engineering and scientific problems. *General Electric Review*: 29–37. For an update that was focused on the spread of network analyzers, see Eric T.B. Gross. 1959. Network analyzer installations in Canada and the United States. *American Power Conference Proceedings* 21: 665–669. For the intervening emergence of the suggestive concept "digital differential analyzer" and the *a posteriori* designation of Bush's differential analyzer as the "analog differential analyzer," see Sprague, Fundamental methods of the digital differential analyzer method of computation," and John F. Dovan. 1950. The serial-memory digital differential analyzer. In *Mathematical tables and other aids to computation*: 41–49 and 102–112 respectively. For the eventual subsuming of the history of the analyzer computing tradition under the history of analog computing, see the "Historical Survey" in Stanley Fifer. 1961. *Analogue computation: Theory, techniques, and applications*, vol. I. New York: McGraw-Hill, section 1.8.

[8] See C.H. Claudy. 1914, March 7. A Great Brass Brain. *Scientific American*: 197.

[9] Edmund Callis Berkeley. 1949. *Giant Brains, or, machines that think*. New York: Wiley.

intelligence. The history of the ideology of intelligent computing machines before the electronic era has yet to be studied systematically. As I have suggested elsewhere, this study may be profitably start with the ideology displayed during the long history of analyzers and related artifacts.[10]

Focused as it is on the history of civilian computing, this chapter will not cover an extremely important class of military computers from the mechanical and electrical eras, which were also a posteriori devaluated as analog computers. Many of which included mass produced and relatively inexpensive integrators and differentiators like those used in the "computing bombsight" (and its *alter ego*, the "anti-aircraft director"). Their history is obscured by the attention drawn to the Electronic Numerical Integrator and Computer (ENIAC). But it was not the digital ENIAC but an analog computing bombsight that could fit in Enola Gay so as to be used to compute the drop of the first atomic bomb. We have yet then to study the greatest perhaps technological irony of historical capitalism, namely, the use of a maximally accurate computer (the Enola Gay bombsight) in order to compute the drop of a bomb that required the minimum of accuracy.[11]

I am here staying at the history of civilian electrical engineering computations and, more specifically, on the computation of electric power transmission. But, as I understand it, the mechanization of the calculation of the control of electric power transmission is actually the civilian counterpart to the mechanization of the calculation of the fire control of external ballistics—power generation and distribution correspond to internal and terminal ballistics, respectively. This explains why the two—calculation in the context of transmission of electric power through an array of analyzers and calculation in the context of external ballistics through computing bombsights and a myriad of related navy, army, and air-force artifacts—were actually developed in close relationship during the interwar period, frequently through the same institutions (most notably MIT).[12]

The world of civilian computing with analyzers was extremely rich. In this section I briefly survey and classify the various analyzers to prepare for my introduction to analyzers for power analysis, which I present in the following sections. What we know about analyzers and related computing artifacts come from studies that

---

[10] For an overview of the history of the ideology of intelligent machines before the electronic era, which focuses on network analyzers and related artifacts, see Tympas, From digital to analog and back: The ideology of intelligent machines in the history of the electrical analyzer, 1870s–1960s.

[11] There are several articles and books that include histories of the development and use of army, navy, and air-force fire control computing but most of them are written from a general military history perspective rather than the perspective of the history of computing technology. For a vivid description of the use of a bombsight in computing the drop of the atomic bomb, see Stephen L. McFarland. 1995. *America's pursuit of precision bombing, 1910–1945*. Washington: Smithsonian Institution Press. Published reminiscences also point to the importance of the class of computing artifacts under consideration in fire control. See, for example, A. Ben Clymer. 1993. The mechanical analog computers of Hannibal Ford and William Newell. *IEEE Annals of the History of Computing* 15(2): 19–34, and W.H.C. Higgins, B.D. Holbrook, and J.W. Emling. 1992, July. Defense research at Bell Laboratories. *Annals of the History of Computing* 4(3): 218–244.

[12] See Mindell, *Between human and machine*.

Fig. 4.3 Photograph of engineers absorbed by an artificial line at the calculating laboratory of MIT's electrical engineering department as shown in an article by Frederick Dellenbaugh (1923)

focus only on the most impressive of them, the differential and the network analyzer of Bush. As I had shown elsewhere, the late interwar and postwar history of the network analyzer can be inserted not only in the early interwar history of "calculating boards" but in the long history of an artifact known as the "artificial line" (Fig. 4.3). Computing with artificial power lines followed in (and after some point, interacted with) computing with artificial communication lines, which goes back to the mid-nineteenth introduction of telegraphic networks.[13] Building on the contrast between the philosophy of artificial lines that was advanced at laboratory settings at MIT (and General Electric, the leading electrical manufacturer) and the history of their local use in the most challenging natural environments by electric utilities (most notably that of California), I had argued that Bush, the undisputed star of interwar computing technology, should be treated as a key contributor to the emergence of digital computing, not as a pioneer of analog computing.[14]

In this chapter, I will add an important yet understudied dimension of the history of computing with analyzers and related artifacts by offering instances from the use of harmonic analyzers in electricity-related calculations. The history of Bush's contribution to computing development makes much more sense if, in addition to his

---

[13] Tympas, *Perpetually laborious: Computing electric power transmission before the electronic computer*.

[14] Tympas, *A deep tradition of computing technology: Calculating electrification in the American West*.

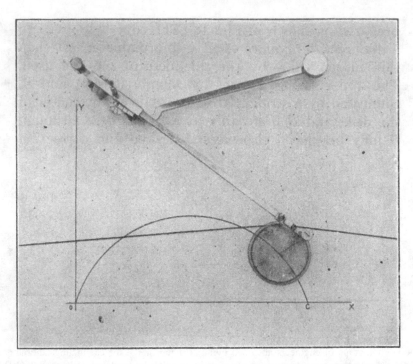

Fig. 4.4 Photograph of a planimeter-based simple harmonic analyzer by MIT's Vannevar Bush (1920)

celebrated differential analyzer and the network analyzer of the 1930s, we also associate him with the little known "new mechanical integrator" that he introduced to in 1920 as a "simple harmonic analyzer," so as "to fill a need, particularly among electrical engineers, for a simple inexpensive device of this nature",[15] and, further, to the nonmechanical calculating graph, a nomograph, which he wrote about in the same year (1920) (on the "nomographs" or "nomograms" or "alignment charts," see Chap. 5) (Figs. 4.4 and 4.5).

In his introduction to the 1982 reedition of the catalog of the 1914 Edinburgh Exhibition, Michael Williams writes that Section G on "Other Mathematical Laboratory Instruments," which followed in the section on the slide rule, "contains descriptions of so many analog instruments, ranging in nature from mechanical to hydraulic, that to comment on each would require this [his] introduction to be as long as the *Handbook* itself." He invites us to take special notice of tide predictors like the one by Lord Kelvin. For Williams, the computing artifacts placed in Section G "reached a still higher level development as calculating devices during the period between the two World Wars," in the form of "the large mechanical analog calculating machines, called "differential analyzers,"" of Douglas Hartree, of Manchester University, and Vannevar Bush, of MIT. I take this as another indi-

---

[15]Vannevar Bush. 1920, October. A simple harmonic analyzer. *AIEE Journal*: 903.

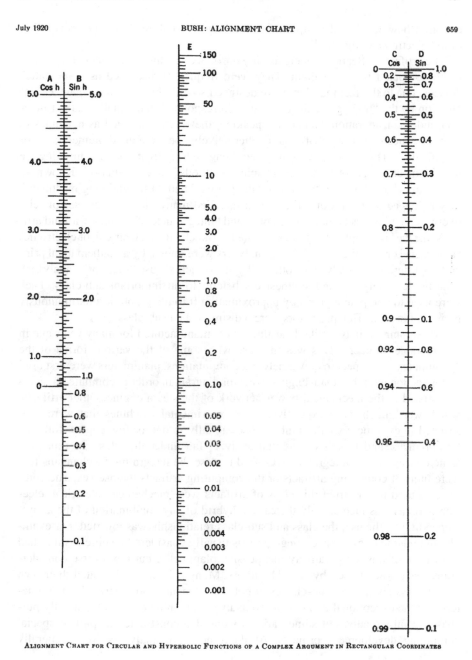

ALIGNMENT CHART FOR CIRCULAR AND HYPERBOLIC FUNCTIONS OF A COMPLEX ARGUMENT IN RECTANGULAR COORDINATES

Fig. 4.5 Nomograph (alignment chart) for some of the circular and hyperbolic functions involved in electrical engineering calculations by MIT's Vannevar Bush (1920)

cation of how developed computing technology was before the alleged revolution of the electronic computer.[16]

The artifacts in Section G were usually introduced by the mathematical functions to be computed by using them. They were frequently discussed as "kinematic" devices, due to the fact that they were designed so as to be used to produce a computation by the "tracing" of the curve that corresponded to the mathematical function under consideration. Generally speaking, they were classified as machines to compute mechanically what could, alternatively, be computed numerically or graphically.[17] This explains why in general engineering treatises on computing we find them under chapters on "mechanical methods" of computation. Known as "integrators" and "differentiators" or "integrating" and "differentiating machines," they belonged to a class of artifacts that included many more sub-classes of relatively standard artifacts like "integraphs" and "integrometers" or one-of-a-kind artifacts like the "isograph." They are all related to (mechanical, electrical, or electronic) "analyzers" or "synthesizers." Some analyzers were known by a mathematical principle (differential analyzer), others by a principal use (network analyzer). "Harmonic" analyzers and synthesizers belong to an important sub-class. They were used to compute a graph by approximating it to the graph of a harmoniously periodic function. Tide predictors were a distinguished sub-class.

Some commercially available artifacts were manufactured for many years and in considerable numbers. This was the case with some of the various forms of the "planimeter." In respect to power network computations, planimeters were first used in connection with the steam engine indicator diagram in order to compute phenomena related to the mechanical power network of the steam engine. Other artifacts, which were much more expensive, were experimental machines that were constructed in extremely small numbers, occasionally in one or few copies. Kelvin's tide predictor and Bush's differential analyzer fall under this class. At times the same concept, e.g., "integrator," was used to describe integrating mechanisms that were units of computing artifacts or the computing artifacts themselves. The components used to construct this class of artifacts were mechanical, electrical, electronic, or, as was increasingly the case, a hybrid of any combination of the above. Depending on the use, the class and sub-class relationship was inverted. For example, the relatively expensive integraph was usually considered a sub-class that had grown out of the comparatively inexpensive planimeter, but the inverse consideration was also endorsed by several authors. Many sub-classes included their own sub-classes. There were sub-classes of both the standard and inexpensive planimeters and the exceptional and expensive analyzers. Planimeters were generally purchased commercially, but some variants were also constructed as part of special computing development projects. At the other end, analyzers were generally

---

[16] See Michael Williams. 1982. Introduction. In *Modern instruments and methods of calculation: A handbook of the Napier Tercentenary Exhibition,* ed. Ellice M. Horsburgh, re-edition. Los Angeles: Tomash Publishers, xviii and xiv.

[17] For an influential placement of the artifacts under consideration in the class of 'mechanical methods', see Joseph Lipka. 1918. *Graphical and mechanical computation.* New York: Wiley.

constructed as part of special computing development projects, but some variants were also available commercially.

4.3 "A Marvel of Mechanical Skill and Mathematical Accuracy"

Planimeters were used to compute the area enclosed by a curve. For convenience, they were usually divided into two types; one consisted of those that were used to compute directly the areas and another of those that were used in connection to the boundary of the areas to be computed. The "integrometer," also called "moment planimeter," was used to compute integrals of a variable raised in a given power. The "curvometer" was used to compute the arc length of a curve. The integraph was used to compute the graph of a function for which the derivative was given. In certain developments, this became a device for computing differential equations. The harmonic analyzers were used to compute the Fourier coefficients of a function. A good description of these artifacts was given by A. M. Robb, who wrote a piece on the use of "mechanical integrating machines" in naval architecture for the handbook of the 1914 Exhibition. Robb divided them into three main classes: planimeters to compute areas, integrators for computing areas and first and second moments of these areas about chosen axes, and integraphs for tracing directly the integral curve of any curve round which the machine was guided. Robb informed that the first two classes were "absolutely essential" to the naval architect, but the last class was not in common use. He estimated that there were no more than three or four of integraph of this class in the country. As far as the first class goes, Robb had found that of the several types of planimeters, only the polar planimeter was in common use.[18]

G. A. Carse and J. Urquhart, who wrote the piece on planimeters for the handbook of the 1914 Exhibition, differentiated between "rotation" planimeters and planimeters "with an arm of constant length." One artifact of the class under consideration could be reconfigured so as to give another. For example, a planimeter of the rotation type could be used as a basis for an integraph or a harmonic analyzer. Planimeters with an arm of constant length included, among other sub-classes, "polar" and "linear" planimeters. In terms of use, Carse and Urquhart found that there also existed planimeters for "special purposes." At the other end, as with slide rule models, there were planimeter models that were called "universal." Special purpose planimeters included, for example, a "spherical" planimeter for computing areas of a spherical surface, a "stereographic" planimeter for computing spherical areas by computing the corresponding area on the stereographic projection, a "mean ordinate planimeter" to compute the mean ordinate of a polar diagram, and a planimeter to be used when the diagram was recorded on a drum that was of a varying

---

[18] For the integrometer and the curvometer, see Horsburgh ed., *Modern instruments and methods of calculation: A handbook of the Napier Tercentenary Exhibition*, 187–189 and 181–187 respectively. For Robb, see 206–207.

scale. In comparing the Durand and Schmidt "mean ordinate" planimeters, Carse and Urquhart touched on the trade-off involved in choosing a planimeter: Schmidt's gave "a high degree of accuracy" but was "complicated in construction." Exhibitors had their own way of classifying their planimeter models. From Zurich, G. Coradi's version exhibits included a "rolling," a "rolling-sphere," and "rolling-disc" planimeter. And from Kempton, A. Ott's version exhibits included various "compensating" planimeters and the aforementioned "universal" planimeter.[19]

Carse and Urquhart also wrote a piece on harmonic analysis, which they divided into "mechanical," "arithmetical," and "graphical" methods of analysis. The part on mechanical methods contained an inclusive history of harmonic analyzers up to 1914. The two authors gave detailed descriptions of some "computing forms" that could be used in connection to harmonic analysis, which were developed at the University of Edinburgh mathematical laboratory. The range of artifacts exhibited under "Other Mathematical Laboratory Instruments" was great. D. Gibb described a "hydrostatic solution of equations or system of equations," i.e., a hydrostatic balance that was used as a computer. There were other versions of a balance that could be used as a computer. For an indication of how broad the use of the planimeter was, but, also, of how inventive a society that depended on mechanizing computation had to be, I refer to a 1903 article by Ulrich Peters, of Wilkinsburg, Pennsylvania. Peters had proposed computing the laying out of passes for mills rolls by substituting the use of a "balance lever as a calculating machine" for the use of a planimeter.[20]

The use of the computing artifacts of this class in engineering was important enough to deserve several special treatises. We understand why by reading what J. Y. Wheatley's wrote in his 1903 book, which was entitled *The Polar Planimeter and Its Use in Engineering Calculations Together With Tables, Diagrams, and Factors*: "Of the many instruments which have been devised at various times to facilitate the long and tedious calculations which claim so large a share of the time and labor of the Engineer, the Polar Planimeter is easily the most valuable." For Wheatley, the polar planimeter was a general purpose machine: "Forming one of a class of similar instruments usually designated 'planimeters,' and standing midway between the simple planimeter with its limited range and restricted field of operation and the complicated and costly integraph and like instruments, the polar planimeter can advisedly be said to be adapted to the solution of almost every problem arising in the engineer's practice." He called the planimeter a "co-laborer of the engineer in almost every detail of his professional life" and "one of the most valuable, if not *the* most valuable, of the engineer's mechanical assistants." For Wheatley, the accuracy and rapidity by which this instrument could "perform" was "unequalled by any other known means." Considering that "it has in addition," he continued, "a range of application so wide as to include almost *every* form of operation incident to engineering work, we are able to gain some adequate appreciation of the value

---

[19] Ibid., 193, 194–199, 190, 204–206, 199, and 200–206.
[20] Ulrich Peters. 1903, July 23. The balance lever as a calculating machine. *Iron Age* 72: 12–13. For Carse and Urquhart and for Gibb, see Horsburgh ed., *Modern instruments and methods of calculation: A handbook of the Napier Tercentenary exhibition*, 220–248 and 264–265 respectively.

and importance of the instrument." After briefly reviewing the history of the planimeter, from its introduction by professor Shaw in 1814 and the exhibition of the first completed planimeter by Oppikofer in Paris in 1836 to the planimeters by Coradi of Zurich and by professor Amsler Laffon of Schaffhausen, Wheatley concluded by stating that the "Polar Planimeter of to-day is a marvel of mechanical skill and mathematical accuracy, performing the operations for which it was designed in a manner which leaves little to be desired."[21]

As I read him, Wheatley assumed that he was writing for a computer society: "When we consider how few of the details of professional, commercial or domestic life there are to which do not to a greater or less extent require the employment of some one or more of the operations of mathematical computation for their solution, the importance of any instrument which will lessen in any degree the mental and physical labor involved in such computation is at once apparent." In the case of "the Engineer, the Scientist, Statistician and others of whose work mathematical calculations form by far the greatest part," he added, "the subject of mechanical aids in those labors assumes an importance which cannot be over-estimated." Consumed by mechanizing computation as engineers may appear to be, they were actually interested in spending only as little capital as necessary. To serve this interest, Wheatley argued in favor of combining the use of the polar planimeter with computing tables, diagrams, and constants. Wheatley devoted a special chapter on how much computing accuracy could be produced by using this combination in several concrete computing purposes (Chapter XI). In a section entitled "Explanation of Tables," Wheatley stated that the tables were "intended to give at once by inspection and without further calculation the data necessary to adjust the Planimeter for use in the solution of most of the more frequently occurring problems arising in the Engineer's practice." As with the special scales of a slide rule, the tables to be used along with a planimeter could function as (what we would now call) special purpose software. For Wheatley, with the development and use of such tables, a planimeter, like our programmable electronic computer, could be turned into a general purpose computing artifact—to be used so as "to facilitate the work of the calculator": "The Tables have been calculated and checked by both Logarithmic and Slide Rule methods, and contain all the factors necessary for adjustment of the Planimeter for any operation."[22]

"Planimetry" deserved a special section in Frederik A. P. Barnard's 1869 report on the 1867 Paris Exposition. For Barnard, "for many purposes of great utility," it was "[A]n expeditious mode of ascertaining the area of irregular plane figures." "Apart from the obvious advantages of such a method as applied to the measurement of plots of ground in surveying," he explained, "its uses to mechanical engineer in determining the amount of work performed by a machine by means of dynamometrical curves and the tracing of indicators attached to steam cylinders, in which the contours of the figures to be measured are irregularly variable, is very

---

[21] J.Y. Wheatley. 1903. *The polar planimeter and its use in engineering calculations together with tables, diagrams, and factors*, 17–18. New York: Keuffel & Esser.

[22] Ibid., 11 and 14.

great."[23] In extensive discussions of the planimeter in special chapters that we can find in treatises on the steam engine indicator, the planimeter, in its various forms, was used extensively for the computation of steam engine operation related phenomena. We find similar discussions in editorials or articles on new ways to use the planimeter or/and various new forms of planimeters.[24]

For Professor Henry S.H. Shaw, the various forms of planimeters were mechanical integrators. His article on mechanical integrators became so popular that it was reprinted in the form of a small book by Van Nostrand in 1886. "Mechanical aids to mathematical computations," we read in a prefatory note to this book, "have always been regarded with interest. Aside from the labor-saving quality which most of them possess, they have a value arising from the fact that they represent thoughts of more or less complexity expressed in mechanism." "They are of many kinds," continued the author of this note, "and serve widely different purposes. The reader will find in the essay descriptions of many that are useful directly or indirectly to engineers."[25]

For one of the participants in the discussion that followed the presentation of the paper by Shaw, the usefulness of these devices was not the most interesting part. I quote the exchange of opinions between Charles Babbage's heir and Shaw because it is one of the earliest and clearest anticipations of more recent computing debates, e.g., the digital-analog one:

---

[23] See Frederik A.P. Barnard. 1869. *Paris Universal Exposition, 1867: Report on machinery and processes of the industrial arts and apparatus of the exact sciences*, 620. New York: Van Nostrand.

[24] For a sample of early references on the use of the planimeter in treatises on indicator diagram computations, see Thomas Pray. 1899. Twenty years with the indicator. *Boston Journal of Commerce and Publishing* 1; L. Elliott Brookes. 1905. *The calculation of Horsepower made easy.* Chicago: Frederik Drake and Company; William Houghtaling. 1899. *The steam engine indicator and its appliances.* Bridgeport: The American Industrial Publishing, and F.R. Low. 1910. *The steam engine indicator*, third revised and enlarged edition. New York: McGraw-Hill. For a sample of articles from the same period, see Indicator diagrams. *Electrician* (1894, April 20): 690–691; The Hatchet Planimeter. *Electrician* (1894, June 1): 137–138, and W.L. Butcher. 1905. A device for averaging certain kinds of continuous records by the planimeter. *Engineering News* 53(26): 685. For the persistence of the interest on the development of planimeter forms and computation methods, see 1922, May 2. Measuring area of indicator diagram. *Power* 55(18): 693–696; Walter Block. 1930, September. Measurements: Industrial and scientific. *Instruments*: 577–580, and Waldo Kliever. 1941, May. Integrator for circular ordinates. *Instruments*: 121. For a systematic promotion of the planimeter during the interwar period, see the cluster of articles by John L. Hodgson. 1928, November. Integration of diagrams. *Instruments*: 479–482, John L. Hodgson. 1929a, March. Integration of 'Orifice Head' charts by means of special planimeters. *Instruments*: 95–96, and John L. Hodgson. 1929b, July. The radial planimeter. *Instruments*: 227–231. For the historiographical importance of computations of relevance to the indicator diagram, see, Eugene Ferguson. 1992. *Engineering and mind's eye.* Cambridge: MIT Press; Thomas L. Hankins, and Robert Silverman. 1995. *Instruments and the imagination.* Princeton: Princeton University Press, and Robert M. Brain, and M. Norton Wise. 1999. Muscles and engines: Indicator diagrams and Helmholtz's graphical methods. In *The science studies reader*, ed. Mario Biagioli, 50–66. New York: Routledge.

[25] See Henry S. Shaw. 1886. *Mechanical integrators, including the various forms of planimeters.* New York: D. Van Nostrand, Preface.

Major-General H. P. Babbage remarked that what most interested him was the contrast between arithmetical calculating machines and these integrators. In the first there was absolute accuracy of result, and the same with all operators; and there were mechanical means for correcting, to a certain extent, slackness of the machinery. Friction too had to be avoided. In the other instruments nearly all this was reversed, and it would seem that with the multiplication of reliable calculating machines, all except the simplest planimeters would become obsolete....

The author [Shaw] was obliged to express his disagreement with the opinion of General Babbage, that all integrators except the simplest planimeters would become obsolete and give place to arithmetical calculating machines. Continuous and discontinuous calculating machines, as they had respectively been called, had entirely different kinds of operations to perform, and there was a wide field for the employment of both. All efforts to employ mere combinations of trains of wheelwork for such operations as were required in continuous integrators had hitherto entirely failed, and the author did not see how it was possible to deal in this way with the continuously varying quantities which came into the problem. No doubt the mechanical difficulties were great, but that they were not insuperable was proved by the daily use of the disk, globe, and cylinder of Professor James Thomson in connection with tidal calculations and meteorological work, and, indeed, this of itself was sufficient refutation of General Babbage's view.[26]

A notable use of the term "continuous" computer was made by Macon Fry in his influential 1945–1946 series of articles in *Machine Design*. Fry was with the W. L. Maxson Corporation, which had cooperated with Sperry and the army in the construction of fire control computers in World War II. The purpose of these post-World War II series of articles on continuous computers of the mechanical type was "to gather together the basic information regarding the design of elements composing present-day fire-control equipment, in the hope that designers in other fields will find new applications of these mechanisms." Instead of a demarcation between continuous and discontinuous computers, he divided, for "convenience," between "continuous" and "cyclic" mechanisms or computers: "The cyclic computer, exemplified by the familiar adding-calculator used in every engineering office, performs only one operation for a given setup, and deals with integral numbers. The continuous computer, with which this series of articles is concerned, deals with continually varying inputs which may assume any value, integral or fractional, and yields a continuing solution based upon the instantaneous values of those variables and the relationship connecting them."[27]

Fry wrote his series of articles a few years before the emergence of the analog-digital demarcation. In my opinion, the analog-digital technical demarcation of the recent decades is not the same as Fry's continuous-cyclic convenient demarcation (as present day historiographical substitutions of the analog-digital demarcation for the continuous-cyclic frequently assume). For Fry, both classes of computers dealt with numbers. They differ in that the one, the cyclic, was limited to integral values. As such, it was a limited case of the other, the continuous, which was not limited to integral values. Accordingly, the accuracy of either was socially situated, i.e., it depended on concrete use, which means that there was no technical criterion to

---

[26] Ibid., 207 and 211.

[27] Macon Fry. 1945, August. Designing computing mechanisms. *Machine Design*: 103–104.

abstractly determine accuracy. This is why he employed a relative division that was based on "convenience" that is on use.[28] By contrast, the analog-digital demarcation assumes a technical demarcation that is not supposed to depend on use.

An inspection of a recent trade catalog of an engineering-drafting office supplies firm can be quite suggestive in regard to how the planimeter relates to the analog-digital computer demarcation. In addition to the familiar "mechanical" planimeters, there are now several "digital" planimeters models available.[29] The analog side of computing, which consists in the tracing of the curve to be computed, is indispensable in both types. The difference between the digital and the non-digital has only to do with the recording and counting part of the mechanism. But, mechanical, electrical, or electronic, this digital part is (and always was) inseparable from the analog side. It seems to me that we have here an excellent opportunity to acknowledge the inseparability of analog and digital computing but, also, the relative difference between the two: unlike the tracing of the curve (analog side of computing), the counting that accompanied this tracing was the part of computing with the planimeter that could be automated (digital side of computing). We encounter here another instance of the relationship between constant (stored, accumulated, dead computing labor: digital computing, mechanical counting) and variable computing capital (living computing labor: analog computing, manual tracing).

4.4 "Eminently Satisfactory"

"There are many forms of mechanical integrators for this purpose, some of which are excellent," wrote Bush in introducing to the first of his series of analyzers for electric power analysis, "but they are usually too expensive for the small engineering office or laboratory." He gave the example of "Chubb's polar form" analyzer, which was "particularly useful" in connection with a polar oscillograph, but "inconvenient in other connections, and quite complicated," and the Coradi analyzer, which was "probably the most convenient machine" since it could be used to work in rectangular coordinates and to determine several components simultaneously, but, which was also not widely used because of its "cost."[30]

Below Bush in the hierarchy of computing research at MIT was Frederick S. Dellenbaugh, Jr., Secretary of the Research Division of MIT's Electrical Engineering Department. He had done extensive research on the history of numerical, graphical, and mechanical methods of analysis, which resulted in the compiling of an impressive bibliography on computing alternatives. Based on his studies and the studies of others, he had also produced series of tables of comparative results that related accuracy and time of computation. Dellenbaugh published his bibliography on the computing alternatives and the tables with the comparative results in a 1921 article

---

[28] Ibid.

[29] Sam Flax. 1995. *The tools to create.* Trade Catalog, ca. 1995, 77.

[30] Bush, *A simple harmonic analyzer"*, 903.

that introduced to an MIT analyzer, which he called an "electric analyzer" (Fig. 4.1). In 1923, Dellenbaugh introduced to another MIT harmonic analyzer, which was devised by David O. Woodbury, while he worked at the MIT Research Division Laboratory. In writing about this second analyzer, Dellenbaugh seized the opportunity to update his computing comparisons. During the early 1920s, Dellenbaugh had also studied the history of the artificial line in order to choose the approach that was best for the MIT interests. In the early 1920s, MIT historical researches provided Bush and the rest of the MIT analysts with a holistic perspective on computation that offered the basis for the traditions that (interactively) led to the differential analyzer (product of the culmination of the tradition of the MIT development of integrators and associated tools and machines) and, also, to the network analyzer (product of the culmination of the tradition of the MIT development of artificial lines).[31]

The MIT electrical engineers, usually in partnership with their colleagues at General Electric, were not the only engineers who had to start from history in order to mechanize power analysis. In 1914, Westinghouse's L. W. Chubb introduced to a mechanical harmonic analyzer for the computation of electric power phenomena after surveying the history of mechanical harmonic analyzers (Figs. 4.6 and 4.7). According to Chubb, even though there was already a rich tradition of mechanical analyzers—going back to Lord Kelvin's analyzers—analyzers have not been used extensively in electrical engineering. This is not to say that harmonic analysis as a whole was an alien to electrical engineering. On the contrary, the development of numerical and graphical methods of power analysis received constant attention. Arguments in favor of numerical or graphical approaches to harmonic analysis—we would now call them digital and analog, respectively—were actually running into circles. In a 1904 *Electrician* article entitled "Harmonic Analysis Reduced to Simplicity," Sylvanus P. Thompson dismissed the graphic methods for being "both laborious and inaccurate for higher harmonics" and the potential use of harmonic analyzers (mechanical methods) for representing an expense that "puts them out of reach of many" and for being "less rapid in operation than the arithmetical method which has been in use at the Technical College, Finsbury, for the last year or so [by him]."[32]

The debate between proponents of graphical and numerical methods was generally fought out as a debate between "geometrical" and "algebraical" approaches. The two-series article that John Hopkinson had published in the *Electrician* in 1894 on "The Relation of Mathematics to Engineering," an editorial comment that noted that Hopkinson's article was actually only on "The Relation of Cambridge

---

[31] See Frederick S. Dellenbaugh, Jr. 1921. February. An electromechanical device for rapid schedule harmonic analysis of complex waves. *AIEE Journal*: 135–144, and Frederick S. Dellenbaugh, Jr. 1923a, January. Another harmonic analyzer. *AIEE Journal*: 58–61, and Frederick S. Dellenbaugh, Jr. 1923b. Artificial lines with distributed constants. *AIEE Transactions* 42: 803–819 (discussion, 820–823).

[32] Sylvanus P. Thompson. 1905, May 5. Harmonic analysis reduced to simplicity. *Electrician*: 78. For Thomson, see A.C. Lynch. 1989. Sylvanus Thompson: Teacher, researcher, historian. *IEE Proceedings* 136(Part A, 6): 306–312. For the MIT-GE partnership see, W. Bernard Carlson. 1988, July. Academic enterpreneureship and engineering education: Dugald C. Jackson and the MIT-GE cooperative engineering course, 1907–1932. *Technology and Culture* 29(3): 536–567.

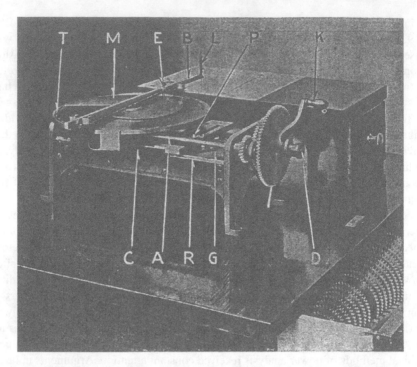

Fig. 4.6 Photograph of the harmonic analyzer by L. W. Chubb in a Westinghouse trade catalog (1916)

Mathematics to Engineering," and the response by Hopkinson can be read as an earlier episode of the same debate. Hopkinson explained that in his own work on characteristic curves or alternating currents, he relied "more frequently" on geometrical than algebraic methods, but he stated his belief in the fact that "algebraic methods have been useful for discovery more frequently than geometrical." The debate was not simply between promoters of numerical and graphical approaches to harmonic analysis. In 1904, based on his own historical account, Thomson attributed the preference to graphical approaches to the inadequacy of the numerical approaches offered up to then, including a recent one by S. M. Kinter. Accordingly, after clarifying that he "need say nothing about the instruments called harmonic analyzers," he focused on explaining the proper numerical approach. Thompson thought that he had provided "a method of harmonic analysis which reduces to extreme simplicity the hitherto very laborious calculations," but the dynamic expansion of electrification turned out to require the development of new methods.[33]

---

[33] John Hopkinson. 1894. May 11 and 18. The relation of mathematics to Cambridge Engineering. *Electrician*: 41–43, and 78–80, 85 respectively. For the editorial response, see 1894, May 11. The relation of Cambridge mathematics to engineering. *Electrician*: 44–46. For Thompson, see Thompson, Harmonic analysis reduced to simplicity: 78. For Kinter, see S.M. Kinter. 1904, May 22. Alternating current wave-form analysis. *Electrical World and Engineer* 63(22): 1203. For the context that prepared for these debates, see Bruce J. Hunt. 1983. Practice vs. theory: The British

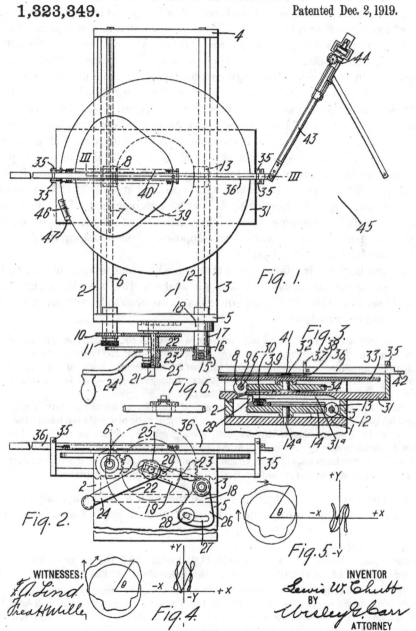

Fig. 4.7 Patent drawing of the harmonic analyzer by Westinghouse's L. W. Chubb with the planimeter and the oscillograph shown to the left and to the right, respectively (1919)

In a cluster of articles published in the *Electrical World* in 1909, there were contributions on an "experimental" method by P. G. Agnew, a "graphical" method by Charles S. Slichter, and a description of an artifact called an "electrical device for solving equations" by Alexander Russel and Arthur Wright, which consisted of a set of resistance-coils slide rules with conductances that could be summed automatically by a specially designed Wheatstone bridge. All contributors defended a socially situated conception of computing accuracy. For example, Slichter dismissed the numerical methods of harmonic analysis of alternating current curves "usually given in books" as "tedious" and insufficient. In addition, he found that mechanical methods such as the ones provided by harmonic analyzers were "very valuable for difficult work" but unnecessary for the usual alternating-current curves that were of so simple a type that it was quite possible to dispense with the more elaborate methods. The results obtained with his own graphical method were presented as comparable with a Michelson harmonic analyzer of 80 elements. It was comparisons of this sort that Dellenbaugh had collected in his 1921 tables of comparative results (Fig. 4.1). Moving to the 1910s, the complexity of methods was rapidly increasing. In response, several other methods and sub-methods were proposed, including R. Beattie's method on, supposedly, "the best form of the resonance method of harmonic analysis."[34]

The rapid, however, lengthening of transmission lines was bringing about a rapid advance of mechanical methods of harmonic analysis. This was clearly stated by Chubb in his 1914 *Electric Journal* article that introduced to his special harmonic analyzer for power analysis:

> The ever increasing complications and variations in electrical circuits and apparatus make desirable a method of harmonic analysis which is quick, accurate, can be easily be used by rule of thumb and without a working knowledge of the mathematics involved. It is important also to have a method which does not require replotting of the curve, the subdivision of the time axis or the measurement of any ordinates.
>
> Several mathematical, graphical and mechanical schemes for harmonic analysis have been devised. The mathematical methods are too laborious to be practical even when tables and carefully arranged blank forms are used. Some graphical methods are very useful to extract the harmonics by groups, such as the third group consisting of the third, ninth, fifteenth and higher harmonics of three. Graphical methods are, however, slow and inaccurate for a complete analysis and are not practical for wave containing high harmonics.[35]

Chubb moved on to introduce to a special mechanical harmonic analyzer, into which a planimeter was incorporated. The editor of the *Electric Journal* was opti-

---

electrical debate, 1888–1891. *ISIS* 74: 341–355; D.W. Jordan. 1985. The cry for useless knowledge: Education for a New Victorian Technology. *IEE Proceedings* 132(Part A, 8): 587–601.

[34] For Slichter, see Charles S. Slichter. 1909, July 15. Graphical computation of Fourier's constants for alternating current waves. *Electrical World* 54: 146. For Beattie, see R. Beattie. 1912, April 19. The best form of the resonance method of harmonic analysis. *Electrician* 69: 63. For the rest of the references, see P.G. Agnew. 1909a, July 15. Experimental method for the analysis of E.M.F. waves. *Electrical World* 54(3): 142–147, and P.G. Agnew . 1909b, July 15. An electrical device for solving equations. *Electrical World* 54(3): 144–146.

[35] L.W. Chubb. 1914, February. The analysis of periodic waves. *Electric Journal* 11(2): 93.

mistic that such "ingenious" methods could save considerably in computing labor and "should greatly stimulate the analysis of wave forms in general and should give us the true cause for many phenomena heretofore considered obscure." He found that although the mathematical theory of the analyzer may seem "somewhat complex, the apparatus itself is beautifully simple and easy to operate." The original analyzer has been in constant use for over a year, and, according to the editor of the *Electric Journal*, it has been found "eminently satisfactory."[36]

For Chubb, the development of "short cuts and new methods of calculation" ought to interact with the development of the method used to produce the curves. Later in the same year, consistent with his emphasis on the need for the compound development of a mechanical analyzer for harmonic analysis of curves and of methods to produce these curves mechanically, Chubb moved on to write an article of polar and circular oscillographs and their practical application. "In our complicated life," wrote J. B. Johnson of the Bell Labs in introducing to his early 1930s oscillograph innovation, "we find that we need a great many aids to our primary sense organs. The processes of the modern world demand that we make correct estimates of things that are too large or too small, too intense or too feeble, for our poor senses." "For recording long times," he added, "we have clocks and calendars; for making a record of happenings that take place in a time too short for us to think of, we use oscillographs." What we generally know about the history of the development of oscillographs seems to confirm that there was indeed a co-development of the mechanization of analysis and the mechanization of the generation of the curves to be analyzed (for analysis of the wave form see also the chapter on the history of computing with models).[37]

The mid-1910s, which is when Chubb's analyzer for power analysis was introduced, was also the time of the rapid development of artificial lines and calculating boards. They were all—special harmonic analyzers for power analysis, artificial lines, and calculating boards—responses to the rapid increase in the complexity of electric power transmission. They were also, all of them, expensive machines. Evidently, Westinghouse expected to make profit by manufacturing and selling analyzers. In a 1916 Westinghouse trade catalog, an analyzer like Chubb's was advertised as a harmonic analyzer that belonged in the class of "curve analyzing and recording devices" (Figs. 4.6 and 4.7). It was priced at $365, a circular oscillograph attachment at $35, the Keuffel & Esser number 4212 planimeter to be used along with it at $14, one dozen pieces of sensitized bristol board, 10 inches by 10 inches, for $2.50, and one dozen sensitized films 10 inches diameter, 3/8-inch hole for

---

[36] The analysis of wave forms. *Electric Journal* 11(2) (1914): editorial.

[37] L.W. Chubb. 1915, May. Polar and circular oscillograms and their practical applications. *Electric Journal* 11(5): 262. For Steinmetz's experience and, also, for the development of oscillographs, see Edward L. Owen. 1998. A history of harmonics in power systems. *IEEE Industry Applications Magazine* 4(1): 6–12. For Johnson, see J.B. Johnson. 1932, January. The cathode ray oscillogram. *Bell System Technical Journal* 11: 1–27. For the development of oscillographs, see, also, Frederick Bedell. 1942. History of A-C wave form, its determination and standardization. *AIEE Transactions* 61: 864–868; V.J. Philips. 1985, December. Optical, chemical and capillary oscillographs. *IEE Proceedings* 132(Part A, 8): 503–511.

$6.50. The total cost was over $400. Great as it may be in comparison to a slide rule, this cost was roughly the same as that of a calculating machine such as those then promoted as being suitable to engineering.[38]

Bush found that this cost was high enough to have blocked the wide use of this instrument. This is why in 1920, through the pages of the *AIEE Journal*, he responded with his "simple harmonic analyzer." Like Chubb's harmonic analyzer, Bush's 1920 simple harmonic analyzer had incorporated the more inexpensive form of the most standard and inexpensive form of an integrator, the planimeter. In comparison to Chubb's, Bush's harmonic analyzer was a more simple but less accurate version of a planimeter reconfiguration (Fig. 4.4). The computation of change of phenomena by the use of machines like harmonic analyzers was based on the computation of the change in the shape of an analog curve (graph, diagram). The paradigmatic case was the indicator diagram of the periodic mechanical phenomena produced by the use of the mechanical network of a steam engine. This, as mentioned above, was computed by a planimeter. Computing the periodic electric phenomena that were produced by the use of a steam engine through the mediation of an alternator (generator), i.e., computing electric power generation, transmission, and distribution, required increased computing accuracy. Since the electric power network was a reconfiguration that was based on the expansive reproduction of the mechanical power network of the steam engine, computing it required a reconfiguration that would be based on the expansive reproduction of the planimeter.[39] This explains why Bush started in 1920 with a reconfiguration of a simple integrator, the planimeter. The anticipated interconnection of transmission lines presented him and the rest of the MIT electrical engineers with new computational complexity. Starting in 1927, they moved on to present with reconfigurations of a complex integrator, the integraph.[40]

The MIT development of the integraph had both engineering and scientific audiences in mind. The celebrated outcome of this collaboration was the differential analyzer and the network analyzer. Less known is the influence that this line of electrical engineering development of computers exercised the development of in integrators and differentiators that were developed by the community of electrical scientists. In presenting an "all electric integrator for solving differential equations" in the January 1942 issue of the *Review of Scientific Instruments*, Robert N. Varney of the Physics Department of Washington University, St. Louis, Missouri, followed

---

[38] *Westinghouse Instruments and Relays (Catalogue 3-B)*. East Pittsburgh: Westinghouse Electric and Manufacturing Company, July 1916; Smithsonian Institution, National Museum of American History, Trade Catalogs Collection, Mezzanine Library. For the cost of calculating machines for engineering in the mid-1910s, see P.H. Skinner. 1915, January 7. Computing machines in engineering. *Engineering News*: 25–27.

[39] For the interpretation of the electrical power network as an expansive reproduction of a mechanical power network, see Tympas, From the historical continuity of the engineering imaginary to an anti-essentialist conception of the mechanical-electrical-electronic relationship.

[40] For the integraph, see Vannevar Bush, F.D. Gage, and H.R. Stewart. 1927, January. A continuous integraph. *Franklin Institute Journal*: 63–84; Vannevar Bush, and Harold L. Hazen. 1927, November. Integraph solutions of differential equations. *Franklin Institute Journal*: 575–615, and T.S. Gray. 1931, July. A photo-electric integraph. *Franklin Institute Journal*: 77–102.

Bush and his associates in using a watthour meter as an integrator, as suggested in their 1927 article on the integraph.[41]

A cluster of articles in the same journal from the same period indicates the considerable variety of similar efforts. In March 1943, J. Morris Blair of the Department of Physics at the University of Wisconsin reported the use of an "improved current integrator" and briefly reviewed the history of similar efforts. One of the authors mentioned by Blair was Otto H. Schmitt, who was with the Physics Department at the University of Minnesota. Schmitt and his colleague Walter E. Tolles had reviewed the development of electronic differentiators in the March 1942 issue of *Instruments*. As suggested by these references, by the early 1940s, electrical and even electronic integrating and differentiating components were becoming quite common. Beyond the names "integrator" and "differentiator," special names were used. In the November 1942 of the *Review of Scientific Instruments,* S. Leroy Brown and Lisle L. Wheeler of the University of Texas at Austin published an article on how to use a mechanical synthesizer that they had previously devised for graphic types of functions and for solution of pairs of nonlinear simultaneous equations. They called it the "mechanical multiharmonograph."[42]

"By various applications of these units," claimed Varney in his article on his all electric integrator, "with perhaps considerable ingenuity, virtually any differential equation may be solved." Perhaps "the most outstanding feature" of his integrator, he found, was the separation into units so that additional units could be added without any alteration of the existing equipment in the event that a rather large number of integrators and multipliers would be required for complicated equations. The normal cost of a single unit was not exceeding $200. Hence, he estimated that a machine with 10 integrators and 10 multipliers should be available at "a fairly reasonable cost, particularly when compared with costs of existing mechanical devices." The internal dependence of scientific to computational development was clear to Varney, who moved on to add: "Many problems in theoretical physics are dropped after considerable expenditure of effort because a numerical solution is out of ready reach. Many of these problems could be solved in a few hours time with an integrator similar to the one described above and at a cost not greatly exceeding that of two adding calculators."[43]

---

[41] See Robert N. Varney. 1942, January. An all electric integrator for solving differential equations. *Review of Scientific Instruments* 13: 10. For Norbert Wiener's involvement in the MIT development of analyzers for harmonic analysis, see Norbert Wiener. 1929, April. Harmonic analysis and the quantum theory. *Franklin Institute Journal* 207: 525–534, and Norbert Wiener. 1930. Generalized harmonic analysis. *Acta Mathematica* 55: 118–258.

[42] Morris Blair. 1943, March. An improved current integrator. *Review of Scientific Instruments* 14(3): 64–67; Otto H. Schmitt, and Walter E. Tolles. 1942, March. Electronic differentiation. *Review of Scientific Instruments* 13: 115–118. See, also, S. Leroy Brown, and Lisle L. Wheeler. 1941, March. A mechanical method for graphical solution of polynomials. *Franklin Institute Journal* 231(3), and S. Leroy Brown, and Lisle L. Wheeler. 1942, November. Use of a mechanical multiarmonograph for graphic types of functions and for solution of Pairs of non-linear simultaneous equations. *Review of Scientific Instruments* 13: 493–495.

[43] Varney, *An all electric integrator for solving differential equations*, 15.

Ideally positioned within the engineering community, the MIT analysts sought to immediately incorporate improvements from fields as traditional as mechanics and as novel as electronics. In supervising this line of development, Bush had a general purpose computing machine in mind from the beginning. Along with several other features, cross-connections and link motions were added to the MIT integraph so as to give an artifact that would be suitable for many uses. Bush and his associates claimed that, in general, the "[E]rrors of this machine [the 'continuous integraph'] have been reduced to an average of 1 per cent," which was adequate "for common uses." Its use in connection with electrical circuits was mentioned first.[44]

The developed MIT-General Electric partnership provided with the best environment for experimenting with this particular use. In an article published in the July 1928 issue of the *General Electric Review,* Leo Teplow, an MIT graduate, reported the use of an MIT "recording product integraph and multiplier" in order to compute a regulation problem, that of the stability of synchronous motors under variable-torque loads. Teplow mentioned that this integraph was first developed for the computation of the transient state in three-phase electric power transmission, but, after years of use, it was used for several other purposes. The *General Electric Review* editor introduced to Teplow's article by attributing the integraph to a society that was already defined by the development of intelligent machines: "The human difficulties encountered in the increasingly complex operations of modern life have resulted in the development of remarkably ingenious mechanisms, aptly called 'Robots.' These were made the subject of an article by Dr. S. W. Stratton and Frank Stockbridge in the *Saturday Evening Post* of January 21, 1928. The application of one of these devices to the solution of a particular problem appears below."[45]

Teplow included a special section on the computing approximations and the associated errors that were involved in using this integraph in the context of power analysis. He provided with a special table with comparisons of the results by computing with the recording product integraph and the computations made by A. R. Stevenson, Jr., of the General Electric Company, which were considered to have provided the most accurate previous solution available. He concluded that computing this special problem with the integraph gave a "high degree of accuracy" but moved on to attach a special section on the problems introduced by approximations made of the actual conditions existing in the motor.[46]

---

[44] Bush, Gage, and Stewart, *A continuous integraph*, 63.

[45] Leo Teplow. 1928, July. Stability of synchronous motors under variable-torque loads as determined by the recording product integraph. *General Electric Review* 31(7): 356. For the cooperative climate between MIT and GE, see Carlson, Academic entrepreneurship and engineering education: Dugald C. Jackson and the MIT-GE cooperative engineering course, 1907–1932: 536–567.

[46] Teplow, *Stability of synchronous motors under variable-torque loads as determined by the recording product integraph*, 363.

4.5 "With a Reasonable Accuracy"

Computing electric line transient phenomena "with a reasonable accuracy" was the motivation behind another university development of a special form of an integraph, that of Vladimir Karapetoff, Professor of Electrical Engineering at Cornell. Karapetoff's integraph was based on parallel double tongs. It could be used for a mechanical integration or differentiation of a given curve. Karapetoff mentioned that it was found to be useful in problems of hunting of machinery, flywheel design, ship stability, etc. It was described in 1922 in an article in the *Journal of the Optical Society of America* and in the *Review of Scientific Instruments*. In 1925, Karapetoff described a further development of this single integraph, which was to be generally used in computations involving linear partial differential equations with constant coefficients. The motivation behind its construction was its special use for mechanical integration of the differential equations of electric transients. Karapetoff referred to it as a "double integraph for electric lines transients."[47]

By 1923, the line of kinematic devices designed by Karapetoff in order to compute the performance characteristics of various kinds of electrical machinery and circuits included the following: a device for computing the performance of an electromagnetic clutch used in the Owen magnetic car;[48] the "Secomor," which was a device to compute the performance of a polyphase series-connected commutator;[49] the "Indumor" and its modification, the "Schucomor," which were devices to compute the performance of a polyphase induction motor and a shunt-connected commutator motor, respectively;[50] an artifact described as "generalized proportional dividers" that was developed by Karapetoff in the course of the construction of a piece of electrical apparatus;[51] the "Blondelion," which consisted of a properly constrained kinematically combination of adjustable bars, linkages, and straight and curved guides that could be set to be analogous of, to a certain scale, a vector diagram of the electric phenomena associated with the operation of a synchronous generator or motor of any desired constants (also featuring a saturation curve of an adjustable shape)—named after the noted French scientist and engineer Andre Blondel, upon whose theory of two armature reactions in a synchronous machine the devise was built;[52] the "Heavisidion," named after Oliver Heaviside;[53] and the

---

[47] Vladimir Karapetoff. 1925. Double integraph for electric line transients. *Sibley Journal of Engineering* 39: 243–260.

[48] See *Sibley Journal of Engineering* XXXII (1918, January): 550.

[49] See *AIEE Transactions* XXXVII, Part I (1918): 329.

[50] See *AIEE Journal* XLI (1922): 107.

[51] Vladimir Karapetoff. 1922, January. Generalized proportional dividers. *Sibley Journal of Engineering* XXXVI(1): 5–6.

[52] Vladimir Karapetoff. 1923a, February. The 'Blondelion': A kinematic device which indicates the performance of a polyphase synchronous generator or motor. *AIEE Transactions* 42: 144–156.

[53] Vladimir Karapetoff. 1923b, February. The 'Heavisidion': A computing kinematic device for long transmission lines. *AIEE Transactions* 42: 42–53.

"C.P.S'er," named for C. P. Steinmetz, prepared for the automatic addition of imped-
ances in series and admittances in parallel.[54]

The double integraph for electric transients and the Heavisidion were representatives of a reconfiguration of a standard computing artifact (the integraph) and of an
initial configuration of a new computing artifact, respectively, which were both used
for a special calculating purpose, that of calculating electric power transmission.
Given the period that they come from (first part of the 1920s), it is hardly surprising
that they were both used to compute long and extra-long transmission lines. They
were even used for the computation of the regulation of power transmission from
the perspective of the transient state. The double integraph for electric transients
was described by Karapetoff as a development of his single integraph and as a "ten-
tative device built in a relatively short time, with as simple means as possible,
mainly to test the soundness and the feasibility of the principle." The numerical
example considered in the case of the integraph referred to a transmission line
500 km. long.[55]

In the case of the Heavisidion, even an extra-long 1000 miles long line was
included. According to Karapetoff, the agreement between computed and measured
values was found to be quite satisfactory. The Heavisidion was a kinematic device
designed to compute vectorially the voltage and the current at any point of a long
transmission line with uniformly distributed properties and with a given load. It
consisted basically of steel and celluloid bars, proportional dividers, parallel double
tongs, and other elementary kinematic linkages. It also included two sharp-edged
wheels that were similar to those used in the planimeter (Figs. 4.8 and 4.9). It was
named after Heaviside because he was among the first to establish and compute the
basic differential equations of a long transmission line. Its components were made
to represent flexibly different positions that corresponded to different points of the
line. Current, voltage, and power factor could be read off directly on the Heavisidion
for any desired point of the line, including the generator and the load end. The
Heavisidion was to be used in conjunction with tables, various conventional graphs
(Fig. 4.10) or a nomograph (Fig. 4.11).[56]

The history of the understudied line of the development of computing artifacts at
Cornell by Karapetoff during the 1910s and the 1920s provides us with a supplement to the historiography of Bush's MIT much more known computing artifacts of
the same period. Karapetoff gave unique names to his computing artifacts. Analysts
from other institutions, who were more restricted by an institutional tradition, stayed
at variations of the name "analyzer," especially in connection to the development of
harmonic analyzers. The development of analyzers described in connection with the
Bell Labs included an "electrical frequency analyzer" that was described by R. L.
Wegel and C. R. Moore, several analyzers that were described by J. W. Horton, an

[54] It was "in preparation" in February 1923, see Karapetoff, The 'Heavisidion': A computing kinematic device for long transmission lines: 44, and The 'Blondelion': A kinematic device which
indicates the performance of a polyphase synchronous generator or motor: 145.

[55] Karapetoff, *Double integraph for electric transients*, 259–260.

[56] Karapetoff, *The 'Heavisidion': A computing kinematic device for long transmission lines*.

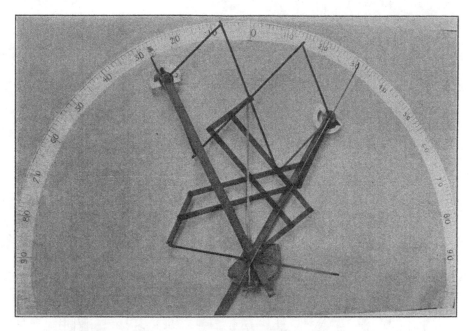

Fig. 4.8 Photograph of the first experimental Heavisidion by Cornell's Vladimir Karapetoff (1923)

analyzer for voice range that was described by C.R. Moore and A. S. Curtis, an "optical analyzer" that was described by H. C. Montgomery, and an "automatic vibration analyzer" that was described by F. G. Marble. There were several other analyzers that were developed in the 1920s. An "electrical harmonic analyzer" was described by J. D. Cockroft, R. T. Coe, J. A. Tyacke, and M. Walker in the *IEE Journal* in 1925 and another one by A. Blondel in the *Revue General de l'Electricite*, also in 1925. In the meantime, George A. Campbell was advancing the theory of electrical engineering harmonic analysis. [57]

[57] R.L. Wegel, and C.R. Moore. 1924, February. An electrical frequency analyzer. *AIEE Transactions*: 457–466; J.W. Horton. 1928, June. The empirical analysis of complex electrical waves. *Bell Telephone Laboratories Record Reprints* B-320; C.R. Moore, and A.S. Curtis. 1927, April. An analyzer for the voice frequency range. *Bell System Technical Journal* 6: 217–247; H.C. Montgomery. 1938, July. An optical harmonic analyzer. *Bell System Technical Journal* 27: 406–415; F.G. Marble. 1944, April. An automatic vibration analyzer. *Bell Laboratories Record* 22(7): 376–380; J.D. Cockroft, R.T. Coe, J.A. Tyacke, and Miles Walker. 1925, January. An electric harmonic analyzer. *IEE Journal* 63(337): 69–113, and A. Blondel. 1925, March 7. Une Methode Potentiometrique d'Analyze Harmonique des Orders des Comants Alternatifs des Alternateurs. *Revue Generale de l' Electricite*. For the parallel development of the theory of harmonic analysis, see George A. Campbell. 1928, October. The practical application of the Fourier integral. *Bell System Technical Journal* 7, 639–707, and George A. Campbell, and Ronald M. Foster. 1931, September. Fourier integrals for practical applications. *Bell Telephone System Monographs* B-584.

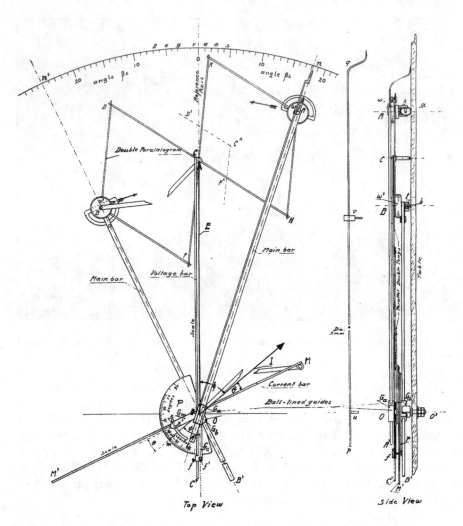

Fig. 4.9 Drawing of top and side view of a Heavisidion with the parallel double-tongs left out (1923)

The line of development of harmonic and other analyzers that were used in the computation of electric communication networks interacted with the line of development of analyzers that were used in the computation of electric power networks. This interaction was of particular importance in the case of the computation of the inductive coordination of power and telephone networks because the induced instability in telephone circuits occurred largely at frequencies corresponding to the harmonic components in the current and voltage waves of neighboring power systems. In a 1929 review article, AT&T's R. G. McCurdy and P. W. Blye referred to analyzers used in telephony and power analysis as "telephone circuit analyzers" and "power circuit analyzers," respectively. Taking Dellenbaugh's 1921 extensive bibli-

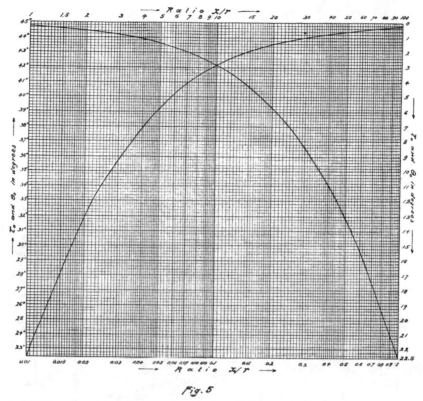

FIG. 5—A CHART OF VALUES OF IMPERFECTION ANGLE τ_0 AND OF DIFFERENTIAL ANGLE θ_0 FOR LINES OF ZERO LEAKAGE $(g = 0)$; IN THIS CASE $\theta_t = \tau_0$. Examples: $x/r = 3$, $\tau_0 = 10$ DEG. 13 MIN.; $x/r = 0.4$, $\tau_0 = 34$ DEG. 06 MIN.

Fig. 4.10 Graph for use together with the Heavisidion (1923)

ography as their bibliographical basis, McCurdy and Blye briefly surveyed the development of analyzers for electric network analysis up to 1929. They informed their readers that these analyzers "have been in active service in the field for some time and have permitted the obtaining of much valuable data as to coefficients of induction between power and telephone systems, the wave shape of power machinery and systems, and analyses of noise currents on telephone circuits." The analyzers have been available in "suitable form for use either in the laboratory or in the field and in some cases have been mounted in specially equipped testing trucks." In respect to accuracy, the two authors explained that their "over-all accuracy" depended "upon the conditions of their use." Under average conditions, the overall accuracy was within 5 percent of the quantities measured. Given that for an engineer the computing accuracy was inseparable from the time needed to produce it, the two AT&T engineers moved on to clarify that obtaining a complete harmonic analysis

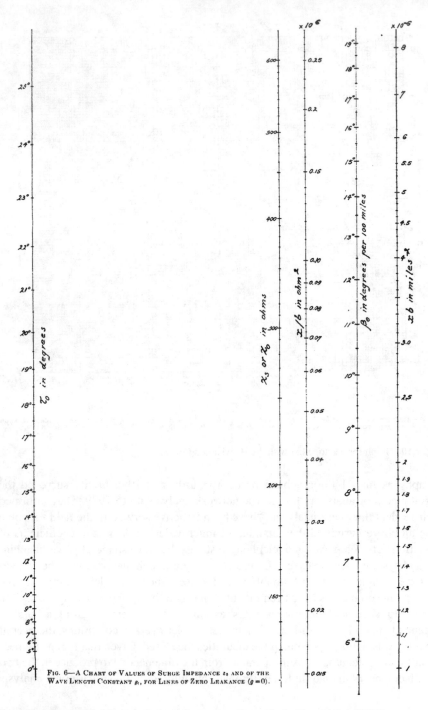

FIG. 6—A CHART OF VALUES OF SURGE IMPEDANCE z_0 AND OF THE WAVE LENGTH CONSTANT β_i, FOR LINES OF ZERO LEAKANCE ($g = 0$).

Fig. 4.11 Nomograph (alignment chart) for use together with the Heavisidion (1923)

of a complex wave of frequency up to 3000 cycles should not require more than "one man-hour."[58]

4.6 "Quickly and Easily"

The incorporation of multipliers and computing units that later became known as "computing mechanisms and linkages" was important to the construction of artifacts that were based on integrating or differentiating units. Some of the most uniquely designed artifacts of the class under consideration may also classify as complex versions of computing mechanisms and linkages that happened to include integrating units. A multiplier was a central component to Bush's 1927 integraph mentioned above. The Bell Labs isograph can be seen as a 1930s computing artifact that was based on linkages (see below). The 1940s University of Texas mechanical multiharmonograph of Brown and Wheeler and, also, some of the 1920s Cornell University uniquely designed artifacts of Vladimir Karapetoff were also based on linkages (see above). The development of computing mechanisms and linkages, including "bar-linkage computers," reached a peak in World War II, through the designs of Antonin Svoboda, which were later disseminated by the Office of Scientific Research and Development of the National Defense Research Committee.[59]

Several artifacts of those described in Section G of the handbook of the 1914 Exhibition also qualify for classification under computing mechanisms and linkages: the apparatus for solving polynomial equations that was described by R. F. Muirhead, the artifacts for the "mechanical description of conics" or "conography" that was described by D. Gibb, and some of the instrumental methods for the computation of equations that were also described by Gibb. This, I think, is also the case with some of the artifacts described in the Section I on "Mathematical Models" of the handbook of the 1914 Exhibition: the "closed linkages" that were described by R. L. Hippisley, the "double-four mechanism" that was described by G. T. Bennett, the "parallel motions" described by E. M. Horsburgh, and some of the artifacts placed under "miscellaneous."[60]

Computing devices that are based on linkages are some of the most difficult to identify because of their great variety, which came along a correspondingly great variety of names. The many uses that Joseph Eugene Row mentioned in connection to his "instruments for the solution of triangles and other polygons" furnish us with an example. Row was director of the Extension Department of the College of William and Mary. In his article, which was published in the August 1928 issue of *Instruments*, Row claimed that "[D]epending entirely upon the quality of the work-

[58] R.G. McCurdy, and P.W. Blye. 1929. Electrical wave analyzers for power and telephone systems. *Bell Telephone Laboratories Reprints* B-439: 2–3.

[59] Antonin Svoboda. 1948. *Computing mechanisms and linkages.* New York: McGraw-Hill.

[60] See Horsburgh ed., *Modern instruments and methods of calculation: A handbook of the Napier Tercentenary Exhibition*, 267–269, 253–258, and Section I.

manship employed in its construction," his instruments were supposed to compute "as accurately as required in ordinary problems," even more accurately than 1%.[61]

In 1910, Charles Vickery Drysdale described a linkage mechanism for the computation of inductance-resistance and capacitance-resistance circuits and showed examples of its use based on his work at the Northampton Institute. Among its basic components were, first, a Tee-square with a slot in the vertical arm, which carried a free sliding block on which a swiveling crutch was mounted, and, second, a parallelogram linkage upon which the whole of the mechanism was placed so that it could always be moved across a drawing board parallel to itself. Drysdale called it "planimeter," which, as C. F. Amor correctly points out, is a name that was usually associated with a different, unconnected, instrument (the one described earlier in this chapter).[62]

The Bell Labs' isograph included ten mechanical linkages of the "pin and slot" type with wires to sum up their motions—a pin and slot mechanism was employed to derive two linear motions from a rotation. The mechanism to accomplish the curve tracing was an elaboration of a harmonic analyzer built years ago by professor D. C. Miller of the Case School of Applied Science. The construction of the isograph furnishes us with another example of a hybrid artifact that incorporated more than one classes of computing artifacts. Cylindrical slide rules, consisting of cylindrical drums that carried a 10-inch logarithmic scale, were incorporated as an auxiliary device for the purpose of computing the crank settings mechanically. They were driven through friction clutches by the use of a gear mechanism that was identical to the one used in order to drive the crank. It was formally called the "mechanical root-finder." The isograph was introduced as a machine to compute the roots of the polynomial equations involved in the computation of an electrical network (we would now call it an electronic network)—the mechanical multiharmonograph was also used for the computation of a polynomial equation. It was a machine that was supposed to be mathematical, accurate, and labor-saving.[63]

R. L. Dietzold of the Bell Labs Mathematical Research Department introduced to it by explaining that an eight-degree polynomial that had arisen in design work some time ago had previously required 4 days for its solution but, with the isograph a problem like this, could be computed "quickly and easily." Only the most important problems could previously justify the allocation of 4 computing days, and as a result, in most cases it was necessary to employ less satisfactory methods, in which the behavior of small sections of the network was analyzed separately. With the isograph this was supposed to change. It was designed by Thornton C. Fry, the director of the Bell Labs Mathematical Research Department, a key figure in the development of computing technology in the interwar period

---

[61] Joseph Eugene Row. 1928, August. Instruments for the solution of triangles and other polygons. *Instruments*: 355.

[62] C.F. Amor. 1986. The graphical methods of Sumpner, Drysdale, and Marchant: Solving the Kelvin Equation. *IEE Proceedings* 133(Part A, 6): 389.

[63] R.L. Dietzold. 1937, December. The isograph: A mechanical root finder. *Bell Laboratories Record* 36(4): 131.

Fig. 4.12 Photograph of Rose Araneo, a Bell Labs computer at the department headed by Thorton Fry, working with a Millionaire calculating machine (1925)

(Figs. 4.12, 4.13 and 4.14). The machine's precision was found to be "at least as good as that of a ten-inch slide rule," which was thought to be "satisfactory."[64]

Taken together, the Bell Labs analyzers for power analysis, the analyzers for power analysis from the MIT-General Electric tradition of the same period, Westinghouse's contemporaneous analyzers, and Cornell's artifacts for power analysis provide us with an insight to the broader context that further explains the emergence of the differential and network analyzer. There were other institutions that became involved in supporting research on mechanization of power analysis. The American Committee on Inductive Coordination had published a bibliography on this issue in 1925. From a January 1928 National Electric Light Association (NELA) document that was entitled "Harmonic Analyzers for Use on Power Circuits," we learn that W. V. Lovell of the NELA Headquarters Engineering Staff had worked for 2 years to develop a portable and easy to operate analyzer. On the first page of the report, its authors stated that plans were made to have a small number of these instruments manufactured commercially to be used (and further developed) by larger operating companies. The purpose of the report was to describe the principles and construction of this harmonic analyzer for use on power circuits, "to the end that operating engineers of member companies may become familiar with it and apply it to their coordination problems as occasion may arise." It was hoped that "ultimately" it would "fill a very definite need in the

---

[64] Ibid.

Fig. 4.13 Photograph of Jessie Smith, a Bell Labs operator, working with a Coradi integraph, with Thorton Fry, standing next to her (1925)

Fig. 4.14 Photograph of women operators working with the Bell Labs isograph of Thorton Fry (1937)

field." The cost of one such electrical harmonic analyzer was estimated to be in the neighborhood of $400, which is about the same as the cost of the Westinghouse mechanical harmonic analyzer mentioned above. The cost of the NELA document was 10 cents for members and 15 for the rest.[65]

Westinghouse's Chubb, who was one of the first to suggest the replacement of graphical and numerical methods of power analysis by designing a mechanical method that was based on the development of a special harmonic analyzer, explained that he had pursued a method, quick and accurate, that could "easily be used by rule of thumb and without a working knowledge of the mathematics involved." Fry, the aforementioned director of the Bell Labs Mathematical Research Department and designer of the isograph, articulated the same pursuit in general terms in the context of arguing in favor of the systematic development of the class of computing machines of which the isograph was a member: "These are all mechanical methods for saving mathematical labor, but they are more than that, for they all rest upon a foundation of mathematical theory. They are, in fact, examples of the use of mathematics to avoid the use of mathematics."[66]

Fry argued so in the context of a World War II report on industrial mathematics, prepared for the National Research Council. He did it in presenting with the eighth and final reason that, for him, justified the development of industrial mathematics, namely, that "mathematics frequently plays an important part in reducing complicated theoretical results and complicated methods of calculation to readily available working form." For the head of the Bell Labs Mathematical Research Department, "the services falling in this category" were "[S]o many and so varied" that it was difficult to illustrate them by means of examples. Among the examples that he ended up choosing was "the postulation of an 'image current' as a substitute for the currents induced in a conducting ground by a transmission line above it, an "analyzing network" for computing "automatically" the dynamic stability of rotating machinery, a "tensor gauge which registers the principal components of a strain in a stressed membrane without advance knowledge of the principal axes," and "slide rules for a great variety of special purposes." Fry added that, perhaps, the list ought to include the use of "soap-bubble films for the study of elastic stresses in beams, the use of current flow in tanks of electrolyte for the study of potential fields, and the use of steel balls rolling on rubber membranes stretched over irregular supports as a means of studying the trajectories of electrons in complicated electric field."[67]

---

[65] *Harmonic analyzer for power circuits*, NELA, Publication Number 278–22. Washington, DC: Edison Electric Institute Library Archives. This publication was a Serial Report by the Inductive Coordination Committee of the 1927–1928 Engineering National Section.

[66] Chubb, The analysis of periodic waves: 93, and Fry, Industrial mathematics: 281.

[67] Fry, *Industrial mathematics*, 280–281.

4.7 "The Skill of the Expert Mechanical Technicians"

The analog-digital demarcation was not yet in place in 1941. All the computing artifacts that Fry mentioned as examples of use of mathematics to avoid the use of mathematics were soon placed under the class of analog computers. Based on Fry's classification, we can make sense of his seemingly schizophrenic reference to analyzers as "examples of the use of mathematics to avoid the use of mathematics" (see above). As I understand it, this reference points to two social agents, not one: Fry argued about a use of mathematics by leading electrical engineering, analysts, to avoid the use of mathematics by human computers, back then called "computers" or "computors."[68]

The analysts—mathematicians oriented toward engineering like himself or engineers oriented toward mathematics like Bush—were those responsible for "reducing complicated theoretical results and complicated methods of calculation to readily available working form" (see above quote of Fry). Their purpose was indeed to use mathematics to design analyzers in order to avoid the dependence on skilled computors who would have to be paid more because they would also use mathematics. But dependence on skilled work was not avoided by this supposedly static substitution. Skilled work was required to construct (and to maintain) the designed analyzer in the first place and, also, to trace the curve to be computed with the use of the constructed analyzer. There was then computing before and after an analyst's design of analyzer: construction and use. They both point to the work of those who, in comparison to analysts, i.e., in comparison to those who designed the analyzers, were computors.

In the technical literature of the use of analyzers, the position of the computor was usually indicated by the use of the term "operator." There were MIT operators: "When the machine [Bush's integraph] is used for integrating two functions, two operators are necessary, one for following each curve. The special case where only one function is to be integrated required only one operator, the other slider being then set at a fixed value." There were also Cornell operators: "Two persons roll the integraph along a guide rail, one operator following the *e* curve with a stylus, the other following the *i* curve with the other stylus. The two pencils then automatically trace the next *e* curve and the next *i* curve on two other sheets of paper. These sheets are then placed under the integraph and the operation repeated any desired number of times." There were also Bell Labs operators. I quote from the presentation of Fry's isograph in Dietzold's article: "It was found that the equation of the eight degree with no real roots, whose solution by previously existing methods required 4 days, can now be solved with the help of the isograph. A more significant advance,

---

[68] We introduced to human computers in Chapter 3, in the context of discussing the case of Edith Clarke. For a book-length study on the history of human computers, see David Alan Grier. 2007. *When computers were human*. Princeton: Princeton University Press.

however, is that the mechanical solution requires no special skill and produces no fatigue in the operator, so that costly errors are avoided."[69]

Having retrieved the fact that operators were actually needed, I can only leave it to a labor historian to decide if it would be worth studying if the operators were actually less tired after an analyzer was introduced. As an historian of technology, I shall simply suggest that the labor historian may want to question if there was a decrease in fatigue by producing computations according to the mode described in the concluding sentence of the presentation of Fry's isograph in an article by R. O. Mercner: "A bench in front of the isograph permits the operators to move readily from position to position as they set the slide rules or the arms of the elements" (Fig. 4.14).[70]

My other suggestion to a labor historian would be to study the labels in published pictures of analyzers because they habitually devaluated the human computing work. Instead of a focus on the human operators, in the picture placed in the first page of his 1937 *Bell Laboratories Record*, Dietzold focused on the artifact that they operated with (Fig. 4.14): "The instrument [the isograph] is shown in use in the illustration at the head of this article."[71]

The pattern of pictorial representations of computing work that were focused on the computing machine instead of the human operator is captured by the 1925 *Bell Laboratories Record* article that introduced to Fry's Mathematical Research Department. A picture in this article featured Jessie Smith, who was sitting and tracing a curve by holding an integraph, and Fry, standing up to her left and overwatching the tracing. The action was provided by Smith's tracing of the curve but the label suggested otherwise (Fig. 4.13): "A Scientific Instrument in Action: Miss Jessie Smith operates the Coradi Integraph, while Dr. Fry watches the resulting integral curve appear." Jessie Smith, who was introduced by the label as a mere operator of the integraph, was actually a college graduate (of St. Lawrence). Without the blending of gender bias and technological determinism that was necessary for devaluating the computing labor required to compute after an analyzer was designed—better, without gender bias making technological determinism possible, we cannot explain two events: first, why a woman with a college degree was only an "operator" who could be devaluated in texts and pictures and, second and related, why the work of a college graduate was only an "operation" that could be devaluated—as if, once designed by an analyst, an analyzer could compute by itself.

Once designed, an analyzer could not compute because it would first have to be constructed. Analysts comparisons of the savings by mechanizing analysis were customarily failing to incorporate the constructional labor power in the comparisons favoring the mechanization of analysis—not to mention that they failed to acknowledge that design was not only influenced by mathematical theory but also by con-

[69] Bush, F.D. Gage, and H.R. Stewart, A continuous integraph; Karapetoff, Double integraph for electric transients: 244, and R.L. Dietzold, The isograph: A mechanical root finder: 134.

[70] R.O. Mercner. 1937, December. The mechanism of the isograph. *Bell Laboratories Record* 26(4): 140.

[71] Dietzold, *The isograph: A mechanical root finder*, 130.

structional practice. For the considerable skill required for the construction of the isograph, I turn from Dietzold's article on the isograph to the one by R. O. Mercner:

> To attain the highest results, precision of the highest order had to be maintained in building all the essential parts of the isograph. The machine was built in the Laboratories' shop so as to utilize the skill of the expert mechanical technicians. The main foundation of the machine is a cast-iron bed plate eight feet long and two feet wide made in the form of a box with shallow sides and ends about three inches high. No machining was performed on the casting for several months so as to allow sufficient aging time, and thus hold the warping to a minimum....
>
> Although the mechanisms involved are not complicated, the construction of a satisfactory isograph is long and difficult because of the extreme precision with which all parts must be made and assembled. Loose motion or "back lash" must be reduced to almost undetectable amounts. After being cut, the gears were fitted to the bearings with an accuracy of 0.0001 of an inch for play and concentricity. The slide bars are lapped and fitted individually to their bronze guides to secure a minimum friction and no play. The guides are then screwed to the base plate, and then pinned in place after the final adjustment. All the pulleys have ball bearings, and are accurately adjusted for alignment. The scale by which the arm length is set is graduated to 0.025 of an inch and may be read with the vernier to 0.001 of an inch. With a little skill, however, it is possible to read to one-quarter amount.[72]

Construction of computing artifacts required skilled constructional work at special institutional settings. Like Fry, Karapetoff was an expert theorist—a specialist in the mathematization that defined electrical engineering theory as such. Karapetoff's expertise was indispensable for the design of his computing artifacts. As with artificial line construction, graduate students and various assistants produced the construction and the tests of these artifacts. The Heavisidion was constructed at Karapetoff's experimental shop at Cornell University during the year 1922. It was Karapetoff's assistant O. K. Marti who actually built the Heavisidion and produced all the computations described in Karapetoff's article on it. Beyond Marti, Karapetoff also thanked C. H. Dagnall, an instructor in electrical engineering at Cornell University, for making some preliminary investigations, computations, and measurements. In addition, he thanked Professor A. E. Wells of Mechanic Arts, D. B. Gree, Foreman of the machine shop, G. A. Culligan, Mechanician, all of the staff of the College of Engineering, for giving "generously their time and skill in the making of parts of the device" and for their "hearty cooperation" that made possible the completion of the devices "within a comparatively short time."[73]

Marti had also constructed the Blondelion and the double integraph. All three artifacts were developed with the support of a grant from the Heckscher Foundation for the Advancement of Research, established by August Heckscher at Cornell University. Like Bush, Karapetoff was uniquely positioned to take advantage of the latest in mechanics. For example, he knew the latest on the "parallel double tongs" that were used in several of his devices, e.g., in the double integraph.[74]

---

[72] Mercner, *The mechanism of the isograph*, 137 and 140.

[73] Karapetoff, *The 'Heavisidion': A computing kinematic device for long transmission lines*, 53.

[74] Karapetoff, *Double integraph for electric transients*, 245.

4.8   "Still Not the Ideal Analyzer"

As we saw, Fry actually argued about the availability of analyzers, designed by analysts, who would reduce mathematical work to mere operation. MIT's analysts argued similarly while insisting on pursuing an extremely complex and costly "ideal analyzer" that would not require "intelligent operation" even after the inexpensive and simple analyzer in hand was "very satisfactory" with "negligible" wear and tear. I quote from Dellenbaugh's 1923 paper:

> While this analyzer [his 1923 harmonic analyzer] requires intelligent operation and it is not fully automatic, it offers the advantages of simplicity, ease of construction, and rapidity of operation. It also frees the operator from the extremely wearisome amount of multiplication, addition and subtraction required by any extensive analysis with the usual schedule methods, and any one reading may be checked in a few moments without going through a series of calculations....
>
> Recently in the Research Division Laboratories analysis of all odd harmonics up to and including the 41st were made quite easily, the time required not being measured, but being far less than that necessary for any computational method, and the personal wear and tear being negligible instead of extreme. In general it might be stated that for certain classes of work this analyzer is extremely convenient and can be easily manufactured. It is still not the ideal analyzer but must be used with an understanding of its limitations, under which conditions it is very satisfactory.[75]

Never eventually pleased by the analyzer at hand, the MIT analysts were constantly after an ideal analyzer, fully automatic so as to not require intelligent operators.

Interestingly, the conception of the computer as an imago (an image) that connects the real and the ideal makes interesting appearances in texts by analysts. For example, Fry spoke about of the postulation of an "image current" as a substitute for the currents induced in a conducting network by a transmission line above it.[76] In a special section on the computing procedure to be followed with "Extra-Long Lines" of electric power transmission, Karapetoff spoke of the use of the Heavisidion (Figs. 4.8 and 4.9) as "*its own optical image*": "The circular scale of the Heavisidion as actually built extends only up to about 100 deg. On each side of the center zero. Therefore, for an extra-long line, or at a high frequency, the bars AA' and BB' may be at the limits of the scale before the other end of the line has been reached. In such a case the Heavisidion is used as *its own optical image*."[77] Karapetoff here reversed between computing with the Heavisidion as an optical image of real long lines (constructed and used) to computing with it as its own optical image in the case of ideally extra-long lines (to be designed). Giving priority to the ideal over the real through the mediation of their computing artifact, to computing being explicitly normative rather than descriptive, was based on the stretching of the use of the ana-

---

[75] Dellenbaugh, *Another harmonic analyzer*, 60.

[76] Fry, *Industrial mathematics*, 280. For the concept of the imago as used in the context of the three Lacanian orders—Real, Imaginary, Symbolic, see Ellie Rangland-Sullivan. 1996. *Jacques Lacan and the philosophy of psychoanalysis*. Chicago: University of Illinois Press.

[77] Karapetoff, *The 'Heavisidion': A computing kinematic device for long transmission lines*, 50.

lyzer to the limit. This defined a top analyst as such. In this case, it defined Cornell's Karapetoff, through the explicitly normative use of the Heavisidion.[78]

In the mechanical era, the circuit of the steam engine was computed by its image, which was the indicator diagram. In the electrical era, the image of the electric network, from which it was computed, was the "oscillogram." The indicator diagram was computed by being traced by planimeters. The oscillogram was being traced by the incorporation of planimeters into harmonic analyzers. The similarity between the indicator diagram and the polar form of the electric power network oscillogram is suggestive—we can generalize by adding similar electronic power network diagrams like the Nyquist diagram.[79] The purpose of calculation was to engineer so as to have an indicator diagram that would not differ from the ideal steam engine circuit. The same was the case with the oscillogram of an electric network. The calculation was in this case based on a comparison between the record from the oscillogram and an ideal electric power network record. This is what "harmonic analysis" by mechanical, numerical, or graphical methods was all about. The irregularity within the periodicity of the actual oscillogram was broken into components ("harmonics") that could be composed so to give an ideal regularity. The process stopped when the irregular components left out—as surplus—were considered to be negligible and the diagram was considered to be sufficiently approximate to the ideal one. Being ideal, these components were standard, and the process could be mechanized. This explains the emergence of the first special harmonic analyzers for computing electrical power networks.

On the other hand, in order to compute the further lengthening and interconnection of the lines of these networks, new analyzers had to be devised, because the components involved in approximating real irregularity to ideal regularity changed. Other things being equal, a calculation that required an increase in the number of harmonics included—called calculation of "higher harmonics"—required a corresponding increase in the mechanization of harmonic analysis. By definition, the electrical engineer had to work so as to produce a reality according to the harmony produced by the ideal of the electrical scientist. In electrical science, the alternating current was harmonic. In electrical engineering, it had to be engineered so as to become harmonic. The successful advance of capitalism depended on perpetual success in calculating such a harmony.

In 1920, Bush, the most known electrical engineer of his generation, expressed this in the esoteric vocabulary of his discipline by writing that the principal use of the first of his tremendously successful analyzers would be "the determination of the harmonics of an irregular function, such as the problem of splitting an oscillograph curve of current or voltage into its components." [80] The most known electrical engineer of the preceding generation, Charles Proteus Steinmetz, had prepared for

---

[78] A I have shown elsewhere, Bush did the same with the artificial line. See Tympas, A deep tradition of computing technology: calculating electrification in the American West."

[79] For the Nyquist diagram, see David Mindell. 2000, July. Opening black's box: Rethinking feedback's myth of origin. *Technology and Culture* 41(3): 405–434.

[80] Bush, *A simple harmonic analyzer*, 903.

this esoteric vocabulary by arguing that the familiarity of the electrical engineer with wave shapes so as to be able to compute the "resolution" of the "higher harmonics" that are "superimposed on the fundamental wave" was of "the greatest importance" and "indispensable."[81]

In trying to define the "wave form" while reviewing the history of the analysis of the wave form of the alternating current up to 1942, Frederick Bedell concluded with the expression "whatever that [the wave form] may be".[82] In his 1998 update of the history of harmonics in power systems, Edward Owen confirmed the difficulty to define the "wave form" in an ideal way:

> Wave forms of potential (voltage) and current in electric power systems are seldom the idealized functions on which engineering work is based. Harmonic analysis can be used to resolve time-based wave forms into spectral components. History teaches us that as new problems with harmonics arise, new instruments to measure the phenomenon will be offered and tighter limits on allowable deviations will probably be pushed. The old problems return to take on new forms.[83]

Analysts frequently called the alternating current a "freak." In 1942, Bedell argued in favor of aiming at the "assignment of penalties to different harmonics"—a "penalty to fit the crime" of this freak. Upsetting the idealized design of an analyst was a crime for which the higher harmonics—surplused during the mechanization of power analysis—had to be punished. In September 9, 1916, J. B. Fisken employed an external analogy that I find it to be quite illuminating in respect to what was the low social side of the technical surplusing of higher harmonics: "We operating men, I think, all agree that we have harmonics. I think we all agree that, like the poor, the harmonics will always be with us. If we could get rid of them, we would be very glad to do so."[84]

4.9 Conclusion

Like computing with the slide rule, computing with analyzers represented a deep technical tradition. This chapter offers an overview of this tradition, which makes relatively known computing artifacts like the differential and the network analyzer look a little less exotic, products of evolution rather than revolution. Retrieving the presence of this tradition shows that important as it was, MIT's Vannevar Bush celebrated contribution to computing electric power networks was only one of many. The use of harmonic analyzers for the same purpose, just like the sophistication of what Vladimir Karapetoff was doing at Cornell, are two important examples.

---

[81] Charles Proteus Steinmetz. 1917. *Engineering mathematics*, 3rd Rev. and Enlarg ed., 255. New York: McGraw-Hill.

[82] Bedell, *History of A-C wave form, its determination and standardization*, 866.

[83] Owen, *A history of harmonics in power systems*, 11.

[84] Bedell, *History of A-C wave form, its determination and standardization*, 866. For the quote from Fisken, see Owen, *A history of harmonics in power systems*, 6.

The variety of artifacts that we find within analyzers is as notable as the variety of artifacts considered in the chapters on the history of the slide rules. Considering everything, it is the development of analyzers that came to signify advance in the highest technical composition of computing capital (highest machine to human computing capital). Not surprisingly then, those working with these machines were devalueated by the rhetoric about analyzers. Like the high harmonics left out of consideration in the context of harmonic analysis, they too were left out of the dominant discourse. Within this chapter, I have pointed to rare passages that show that the operators were actually there, conducting their indispensable work.

References

Agnew PG (1909a) Experimental method for the analysis of E.M.F. waves. Electr World 54(3):142–147
Agnew PG (1909b) An electrical device for solving equations. Electr World 54(3):144–146
Amor CF (1986) The graphical methods of Sumpner, Drysdale, and Marchant: solving the Kelvin equation. IEE Proc 133(Part A, 6):389
Aspray W (1993) Edwin L. Harder and the Anacom: analog computing at Westinghouse. IEEE Ann Hist Comput 15(2):35–52
Aspray W (1994) Calculating power: Edwin L. Harder and analog computing in the electric power industry. In: Nebeker F (ed) Sparks of genius: portraits of electrical engineering excellence. IEEE Press, New York, pp 159–199
Aylen J (2010) Open versus closed innovation: development of the wide strip mill for steel in the United States during the 1920s. R&D Manag 40(1):67–80
Aylen J (2012) Bloodhood on my trail: building the Ferranti Argus process control computer. Int J Hist Eng Tech 82(1):1–36
Barnard FAP (1869) Paris universal exposition, 1867: report on machinery and processes of the industrial arts and apparatus of the exact sciences, 620
Beattie R (1912) The best form of the resonance method of harmonic analysis. Electrician 69:63
Bedell F (1942) History of A-C wave form, its determination and standardization. AIEE Trans 61:864–868
Ben Clymer A (1993) The mechanical analog computers of Hannibal Ford and William Newell. IEEE Ann Hist Comput 15(2):19–34
Berkeley EC (1949) Giant Brains, or, machines that think. Wiley, New York
Bernard Carlson W (1988) Academic enterpreneureship and engineering education: Dugald C. Jackson and the MIT-GE cooperative engineering course, 1907–1932. Technol Cult 29(3):536–567
Bissell C (2007) The Moniac: a hydromechanical analog computer of the 1950s. IEEE Control Syst Mag 27:69–74
Blair M (1943) An improved current integrator. Rev Sci Instrum 14(3):64–67
Block W (1930) Measurements: industrial and scientific Instruments: 577–580
Blondel A (1925) Une Methode Potentiometrique d'Analyze Harmonique des Orders des Comants Alternatifs des Alternateurs. Revue Generale de l' Electricite
Bowles MD (1996) U.S. technological enthusiasm and British technological skepticism in the age of the analog Brain. IEEE Ann Hist Comput 18(4):5–15
Brain RM, Norton Wise M (1999) Muscles and engines: indicator diagrams and Helmholtz's graphical methods. In: Biagioli M (ed) The science studies reader. Routledge, New York, pp 50–66

Bromley A (1990) In: Computing before computers. Aspray W (ed). Iowa State University Press, Ames

Brown GS (1981) Eloge: Harold Locke Hazen, 1901–1980. Ann Hist Comput 3(1):4–12

Bush V (1920) A simple harmonic analyzer. AIEE J 903

Bush V (1936) Instrumental analysis. Trans Am Math Soc 42(10):649–669

Butcher WL (1905) A device for averaging certain kinds of continuous records by the planimeter. Eng News 53(26):685

Campbell GA (1924) Mathematics in industrial research. Bell Syst Tech J 3:550–557

Campbell GA (1925) Mathematical research. Bell Lab Rec 1(1):15–18

Campbell GA (1928) The practical application of the Fourier integral. Bell Syst Tech J 7:639–707

Campbell GA, Foster RM (1931) Fourier integrals for practical applications. Bell Telephone System Monographs B-584

Care C (2010) Technology for modelling: electrical analogies, engineering practice, and the development of analogue computing. Springer, London

Chubb LW (1914) The analysis of periodic waves. Electr J 11(2):93

Chubb LW (1915) Polar and circular oscillograms and their practical applications. Electr J 11(5):262

Claudy CH (1914) A Great Brass Brain Scientific American 197

Cockroft JD, Coe RT, Tyacke JA, Walker M (1925) An electric harmonic analyzer. IEE J 63(337):69–113

De Beauclair W (1986) Alvin Weather, IPM, and the development of calculator/computer technology in Germany, 1930–1945. Ann Hist Comput 8(4):334–350

Dellenbaugh FS Jr (1921) An electromechanical device for rapid schedule harmonic analysis of complex waves. AIEE J:135–144

Dellenbaugh FS Jr (1923a) Another harmonic analyzer. AIEE J:58–61

Dellenbaugh FS Jr (1923b) Artificial lines with distributed constants. AIEE Trans 42:803–819

Dietzold RL (1937) The isograph: a mechanical root finder. Bell Lab Rec 36(4):131

Dovan JF (1950) The serial-memory digital differential analyzer. In: Mathematical tables and other aids to computation: 41–49 and 102–112

Elliott Brookes L (1905) The calculation of horsepower made easy. Frederik Drake and Company, Chicago

Ferguson E (1992) Engineering and mind's eye. MIT Press, Cambridge

Fifer S (1961) Analogue computation: theory, techniques, and applications, vol 1. McGraw-Hill, New York

Flax S (1995) The tools to create (Trade Catalog, ca.), 77

Fry TC (1941) Industrial mathematics. Bell Syst Tech J 20(3):255–292

Fry M (1945) Designing computing mechanisms. Mach Des: 103–104

Goldberg S (1992) Inventing a climate of opinion: Vannevar Bush and the decision to build the bomb. ISIS 83:429–452

Gray TS (1931) A photo-electric integraph. Franklin Inst J 211:77–102

Grier DA (2007) When computers were human. Princeton University Press, Princeton

Gross ETB (1959) Network analyzer installations in Canada and the United States. Am Power Conf Proc 21:665–669

Hankins TL, Silverman R (1995) Instruments and the imagination. Princeton University Press, Princeton

Higgins WHC, Holbrook BD, Emling JW (1992) Defense research at Bell Laboratories. Ann Hist Comput 4(3):218–244

Hodgson JL (1928) Integration of diagrams Instruments: 479–482

Hodgson JL (1929a) Integration of 'Orifice Head' charts by means of special planimeters. Instruments: 95–96

Hodgson JL (1929b) The radial planimeter. Instruments: 227–231

Holst PA (1996) Svein Rosseland and the Oslo analyzer. IEEE Ann Hist Comput 18(4):16–26

Hopkinson J (1894) The relation of mathematics to Cambridge Engineering. Electrician: 41–43, and 78–80, 85

Horsburgh EM (ed) (1914) Modern instruments and methods of calculation: a handbook of the Napier Tercentenary Exhibition. Bell and Sons, London

Horton JW (1928) The empirical analysis of complex electrical waves. Bell Telephone Lab Rec Reprints B-320

Houghtaling W (1899) The steam engine indicator and its appliances. The American Industrial Publishing, Bridgeport

Hunt BJ (1983) Practice vs. theory: the British electrical debate, 1888–1891. Isis 74:341–355

Indicator diagrams. Electrician (1894): 690–691

Johansson M (1996) Early analog computers in Sweden—with examples from Chalmers University of Technology and the Swedish Aerospace Industry. IEEE Ann Hist Comput 18(4):27–33

Johnson JB (1932) The cathode ray oscillogram. Bell Syst Tech J 11:1–27

Jordan DW (1985) The cry for useless knowledge: education for a New Victorian Technology. IEE Proc 132(Part A, 8):587–601

Karapetoff V (1922) Generalized proportional dividers. Sibley J Eng XXXVI(1):5–6

Karapetoff V (1923a) The 'Blondelion': a kinematic device which indicates the performance of a polyphase synchronous generator or motor. AIEE Trans 42:144–156

Karapetoff V (1923b) The 'Heavisidion': a computing kinematic device for long transmission lines. AIEE Trans 42:42–53

Karapetoff V (1925) Double integraph for electric line transients. Sibley J Eng 39:243–260

Kevles DJ (1977) The National Science Foundation and the debate over Postwar Research Policy, 1942–1945: a political interpretation of 'Science: the endless Frontier. Isis 68(241):4–26

Kinter SM (1904) Alternating current wave-form analysis. Electr World Eng 63(22):1203

Kleinman DL (1994) Layers of interests, layers of influence: business and the genesis of the National Science Foundation. Sci Technol Hum Values 19(3):259–282

Kliever W (1941) Integrator for circular ordinates. Instruments: 121

Lecuyer C (1992) The making of a science based technological university: Karl Kompton, James Killian, and the reform of MIT, 1930–1957. Hist Stud Phys Sci 23:153–180

Lecuyer C (1995) MIT, progressive reform, and 'Industrial Service', 1890–1920. Hist Stud Phys Sci 26(1):35–38

Leroy Brown S, Wheeler LL (1941) A mechanical method for graphical solution of polynomials. Franklin Inst J 231(3)

Leroy Brown S, Wheeler LL (1942) Use of a mechanical multiarmonograph for graphic types of functions and for solution of Pairs of non-linear simultaneous equations. Rev Sci Instrum 13:493–495

Lipka J (1918) Graphical and mechanical computation. Wiley, New York

Low FR (1910) The steam engine indicator, third revised and enlarged edition. McGraw-Hill, New York

Lundberg KH (2005) The history of analog computing. IEEE Control Syst Mag 22–28

Lynch AC (1989) Sylvanus Thompson: teacher, researcher, historian. IEE Proc 136(Part A, 6):306–312

Marble FG (1944) An automatic vibration analyzer. Bell Lab Rec 22(7):376–380

McCurdy RG, Blye PW (1929) Electrical wave analyzers for power and telephone systems. Bell Telephone Lab Reprints B-439:2–3

McFarland SL (1995) America's pursuit of precision bombing, 1910–1945. Smithsonian Institution Press, Washington, DC

Measuring area of indicator diagram (1922) Power 55(18): 693–696

Mercner RO (1937) The mechanism of the isograph. Bell Lab Rec 26(4):140

Mindell D (2000) Opening black's box: rethinking feedback's myth of origin. Technol Cult 41(3):405–434

Mindell D (2004) Between human and machine. Johns Hopkins University Press, Baltimore

Montgomery HC (1938) An optical harmonic analyzer. Bell Syst Tech J 27:406–415

Moore CR, Curtis AS (1927) An analyzer for the voice frequency range. Bell Syst Tech J 6:217–247

Murray FJ (1961) Mathematical machines, volume II: analog devices. Columbia University Press, New York

Owen EL (1998) A history of harmonics in power systems. IEEE Ind Appl Mag 4(1):6–12

Owens L (1986) Vannevar Bush and the differential analyzer: the text and the context of an early computer. Technol Cult 27(1):63–95

Owens L (1990) MIT and the federal 'Angel': academic R&D and federal-private cooperation before World War II. ISIS 81:188–213

Owens L (1994) The counterproductive management of science in the Second World War: Vannevar Bush and the Office of Scientific Research and Development. Bus Hist Rev 68:515–576

Owens L (1996) Where are we going Phil Morse? Challenging agendas and the rhetoric of obviousness in the transformation of computing at MIT, 1939–1957. IEEE Ann Hist Comput 18(4):34–41

Pascal Zachary G (1997) Endless Frontier: Vannevar Bush, engineer of the American century. Free Press, New York

Peters U (1903) The balance lever as a calculating machine. Iron Age 72:12–13

Peterson HA, Concordia C (1945) Analyzers…for use in engineering and scientific problems. Gen Electr Rev 48:29–37

Philips VJ (1985) Optical, chemical and capillary oscillographs. IEE Proc 132(Part A, 8):503–511

Pinch T, Trocco F (2004) Analog days: the invention and impact of the moog synthesizer. Harvard University Press, Cambridge, MA

Pray T (1899) Twenty years with the indicator, vol 1. Boston Journal of Commerce and Publishing, Boston

Preston F (2003) Vannevar Bush's network analyzer at the Massachusetts Institute of Technology. IEEE Ann Hist Comput 75-78

Puchta S (1996) On the role of mathematics and mathematical knowledge in the invention of Vannevar Bush's early analog computers. IEEE Ann Hist Comput 18(4):49–59

Puchta S (1997) Why and how American electrical engineers developed heaviside's operational calculus. Archives Internationales d'Histoire des Sciences 47:57–107

Randell B (1982) From analytical engine to electronic digital computer: the contributions of Ludgate, Torres, and Bush. Ann Hist Comput 4(4):327–341

Rangland-Sullivan E (1996) Jacques Lacan and the philosophy of psychoanalysis. University of Illinois Press, Chicago

Row JE (1928) Instruments for the solution of triangles and other polygons. Instruments 355

Schmitt OH, Tolles WE (1942) Electronic differentiation. Rev Sci Instrum 13:115–118

Shaw HS (1886) Mechanical integrators, including the various forms of planimeters. D. Van Nostrand, New York

Sinclair B (ed) (1986) Inventing a genteel tradition: MIT crosses the river. In: New perspectives on technology and American culture. American Philosophical Society Library no. 12, Philadelphia, pp 1–18

Skinner PH (1915) Computing machines in engineering. Engineering News: 25–27

Slichter CS (1909) Graphical computation of Fourier's constants for alternating current waves. Electr World 54:146

Small JS (1993) General-purpose electronic analog computing, 1945–1965. IEEE Ann Hist Comput 15(2):8–18

Small JS (1994) Engineering, technology, and design: the Post-Second World War development of electronic analogue computers. Hist Technol 11:33–48

Small JS (2001) The analogue alternative: the electronic analogue computer in Britain and the USA, 1930–1975. Routledge, London

Steinmetz CP (1917) Engineering mathematics, 3rd rev. and enlarg edn. McGraw-Hill, New York, p 255

Svoboda A (1948) Computing mechanisms and linkages. McGraw-Hill, New York

Teplow L (1928) Stability of synchronous motors under variable-torque loads as determined by the recording product integraph. Gen Electr Rev 31(7):356

The Hatchet Planimeter (1894) Electrician: 137–138

Thompson SP (1905) Harmonic analysis reduced to simplicity. Electrician: 78

Tomayko JE (1985) Helmut Hoelzer's fully electronic analog computer. Ann Hist Comput 7(3):227–241

Tympas A (1996) From digital to analog and back: the ideology of intelligent machines in the history of the electrical analyzer, 1870s–1960s. IEEE Ann Hist Comput 18(4):42–48

Tympas A (2003) Perpetually laborious: computing electric power transmission before the electronic computer. Int Rev Soc Hist 11(Supp): 73–95

Tympas A (2005a) Computers: analog. In: Hempstead C (ed) Encyclopedia of 20th–century technology. Routledge, London, pp 195–199

Tympas A (2005b) Computers: hybrid. In: Hempstead C (ed) Encyclopedia of 20th–century technology. Routledge, London, pp 202–204

Tympas A (2007) From the historical continuity of the engineering imaginary to an anti-essentialist conception of the mechanical-electrical-electronic relationship. In: Heil R, Kamiski A, Stippak M, Unger A, Ziegler M (eds) Tensions and convergences: technical and aesthetic transformation of society. Verlag, Germany, pp 173–184

Tympas A (2012) A deep tradition of computing technology: calculating electrification in the American West. In: Janssen V (ed) Where minds and matters meet: technology in California and the West. University of California Press, Oakland, pp 71–101

Tympas A, Dalouka D (2007) Metaphorical uses of an electric power network: early computations of atomic particles and nuclear reactors. Metaphorik 12:65–84

Van Ende J (1992) Tidal calculations in the Netherlands, 1920–1960. IEEE Ann Hist Comput 14(3):23–33

Vannevar B, Gage FD, Stewart HR (1927) A continuous integraph. Franklin Inst J 203:63–84

Varney RN (1942) An all electric integrator for solving differential equations. Rev Sci Instrum 13:10

Wegel RL, Moore CR (1924) An electrical frequency analyzer. AIEE Trans:457–466

Wheatley JY (1903) The polar planimeter and its use in engineering calculations together with tables, diagrams, and factors. Keuffel & Esser, New York, pp 17–18

Wiener N (1929) Harmonic analysis and the quantum theory. Franklin Inst J 207:525–534

Wiener N (1930) Generalized harmonic analysis. Acta Math 55:118–258

Wildes KL, Lindgren NA (1985) A century of electrical engineering and computer science at MIT, 1882–1982. MIT Press, Cambridge

Williams M (1982) Introduction. In: Horsburgh EM (ed) Modern instruments and methods of calculation: a handbook of the Napier Tercentenary Exhibition, re-edition. Tomash Publishers, Los Angeles, pp xviii and xiv

Williams BO (1984). Computing with electricity, 1935–1945. PhD dissertation, University of Kansas

Chapter 5
"The Inner Satisfaction That Comes with Each Use of the Alignment Chart"

Contents

5.1 Introduction

Calculating tables and graphs, the two classes of calculating artifacts covered in this chapter, exemplify a mode of computing that seems to have been as little (if at all) mechanical as possible. They are treated together for an additional reason: tables were usually generated from graphs and vice versa. In many cases, the two were also used complementary. The construction and use of calculating tables and graphs could actually involve several other calculating artifacts, from slide rules to ones that exemplified the highest degree of mechanization (some versions of analyzers). In some cases, tables and graphs were used as components of an expensive standard or unique calculating artifact; in others, expensive calculating artifacts had been used to generate a table or a graph. The process could start from empirical data, collected at the interface of engineering or other encounter with nature, or, from the other end, plans to change nature according to laboratory rehearsals.

The chapter starts with a section that introduces to a computing agenda that explicitly counted on graphs as visualizations of the alleged beauty of engineering—the beauty, in other words, of representing the world in the context of intervening in this world. It makes it all the more suggestive that the beautification of this intervening through computing graphs (and the tables that they were induced from) was

© Springer-Verlag London Ltd. 2017

A. Tympas, *Calculation and Computation in the Pre-electronic Era*, History of Computing, https://doi.org/10.1007/978-1-84882-742-4_5

inseparable from a division of computing labor. This helps to add on the analyst-computor demarcation introduced in the preceding chapters. It also helps to introduce better to the more general (and therefore more difficult to grasp) demarcation between "calculators" and "computors," and "calculation" and "computation" (Sect. 5.2).

The section that follows is the one devoted to tables. It is anchored in an introduction to the rich line of table development that had to do with electric power transmission. Retrieving this line of development confirms the importance of journals as prime media for both the modification and dissemination of computing technology (Sect. 5.3). Building on this, the chapter includes a section that introduces to a rich series of handbooks on calculation as indexes to the broader importance of computing technology, from much earlier that canonically assumed (Sect. 5.4).

The remaining of the chapter is devoted to graphs. It starts with a general introduction, which contains the first exposure to a class of computing graphs—the so-called nomographs or nomograms or (earlier) alignment charts—that help us understand the sociotechnical trade-offs involved in computing in general and graph-making (as well as graph-using) in particular (Sect. 5.5). It is followed by an introduction to a history of nomograms used in the context of advancing electrification (Sect. 5.6). This is coupled by a section that introduces to the same context but from a perspective of a class of calculating graphs—the "circle diagrams"—that were frequently discussed as the opposite of nomographs because they afforded visualization (Sect. 5.7). As with the rest of the chapters of this book, I here include a section that offers a flavor of the incorporation of the experiences with nomography into electronic computing (Sect. 5.8).

5.2   "A Perfect Poem: The Most Lovely Exposition of Mathematics in Simple Form"

The leadership of General Electric's Charles Proteus Steinmetz and Harvard-MIT's Arthur Edwin Kennelly during the first generation of electrical engineering was founded on their mastery of the calculation technology developed and used to rehearse the rapid lengthening and interconnection of electric power transmission lines. They were both pioneers in the introduction of calculating methods and artifacts for analysts, from the appropriation of imaginary numbers to electrical engineering calculations to analyzers that exemplify the mechanization of these calculations. The first calculating board came out of Steinmetz's General Electric Department; Kennelly was the protagonist in the development of the tradition of artificial lines for electric power calculations, which set the stage for the network analyzer of the following generation—led by Vannevar Bush, his dissertation advisee (Chap. 4). Both Steinmetz and Kennelly were actually experts in the full range of the calculating technology that was used to launch the electrical era. In this section, I will rely on their views regarding artifacts that come from the other end of the spectrum of calculating technology, the least mechanical: calculating tables and graphs.[1]

In his influential textbook on engineering mathematics, Steinmetz devoted a long discussion to the issue of "intelligibility" of numerical calculations. It was focused on how to advance from plotting the carefully arranged values of tables to a curve or a series of curves. He considered this "necessary, since for most engineers the plotted curve gives a much better conception of the shape and the variation of a quantity than numerical tables."[2] On the other hand, he argued that "for recording numerical values, and deriving numerical values from it, the plotted curve is inferior to the table due to the limited accuracy possible in a plotted curve, and the further inaccuracy resulting when drawing a curve through the plotted calculated points." Curves and numbers were feeding on each other. "To some extent," explained Steinmetz, "the numerical values as taken from the plotted curve, depend on the particular kind of curve rule used in plotting the curve."[3]

The point that I want to introduce to concerns the interdependence and the complementary use of the table and the graph, the two artifacts that are the focus of this chapter. The curve was a graph produced by plotting empirical data. Throughout his textbook, Steinmetz made it clear that it was the "empirical" curve that gave the "rational" or "empirical" equation from which the table was produced. In practice, the curve and the table—lines and numbers, we would now say the analog and the digital—were used complementary. They were also used along with the slide rule and other calculating artifacts, not against them. For example, in addition to curves, tables, and slide rules, in his chapter on numerical calculations, Steinmetz also mentioned semilogarithmic and logarithmic paper. "Such paper," he advised, "was to be used in instances when the values of a relationship extended over such a wide range as to make it impossible to represent all of them in one curve, and then a number of curves had to be used with different scales. A disadvantage of the logarithmic scale was that it could not extend down to zero, which made it inappropriate for an entire range of relationships."[4]

Under the issue of the "intelligibility" of calculation, Steinmetz advised on how to properly, first, record and, second, communicate a calculation. "Any engineering calculation in which it is worthwhile to devote any time," he stated, "is worth being recorded with sufficient completeness to be generally intelligible." He expected that, beyond "the name and the date," the calculator ought to add "a complete record of the object and purpose of calculation, the apparatus, the assumptions made, the data used, reference to other calculations or data employed, etc. . . , in

---

[1] On Steinmetz, see Ronald R. Kline. 1987. Science and engineering theory in the invention and development of the induction motor 1880–1900. *Technology and Culture* 28(2): 283–313. On Kennelly, see James E. Brittain. 2006, September. Arthur E. Kennelly. *Proceedings of the IEEE* 94(9): 1773–1775.

[2] Charles Proteus Steinmetz. 1917. *Engineering mathematics*, 3rd ed. Rev. and Enlarged, 283. New York: McGraw-Hill.

[3] Ibid., 284.

[4] Ibid., 288–289.

short, all the information required to make the calculation intelligible to another engineer without further information besides that contained in the calculations, or in the references given therein." Steinmetz was absolute about the need for a proper report of the calculation products. For him the report was an "essential and important part of the work," and, accordingly, he described as "very foolish" the attitude of an engineer or scientist "who is so much interested in the investigating work, that he hates to 'waste' the time of making proper and complete reports." Such attitude, added Steinmetz, "in general destroys the value of the work."[5]

For Steinmetz, the "most important and essential requirement of numerical engineering calculations" was "their absolute reliability." A single error in an important calculation could render "the most brilliant ability, theoretical knowledge, and practical experience of an engineer" useless. This is why he moved on to argue that "rapidity of calculation, while by itself useful, is of no value whatever compared with reliability—that is, correctness."[6] Like so many engineers before and after him, Steinmetz dismissed the assumption that the slide rule was inherently inaccurate. Reliability and intelligibility was determined by intelligent use. "Even for most exact engineering calculations," he argued, "the accuracy of the slide rule is usually sufficient, if intelligently used, that is, used so as to get the greatest accuracy." This was also his argument regarding tables. "For most engineering calculations," he wrote, "logarithmic tables are sufficient for three decimals, if intelligently used, and as such tables can be contained on a single page, their use makes the calculation very much more expeditious than tables of more decimals." "Expedition in engineering calculations," he concluded, "thus requires the use of tools of no higher accuracy than required in the result, and such are the slide rules, and the three decimal logarithmic and trigonometric tables." His next sentence points to the same conclusion from the reverse angle:

> The use of these [three decimal logarithmic and trigonometric tables], however, make it necessary to guard in the calculation against a *loss of accuracy*. Such loss of accuracy occurs in substituting or dividing two terms which are nearly equal, in some logarithmic operations, solution of equations, etc., and in such cases either a higher accuracy of calculation must be employed—seven decimal logarithmic tables, etc.—or the operation, which lowers the accuracy, avoided.

After considering the issue from both sides, Steinmetz concluded even more strongly in regard to the importance of skill in calculation: "[I]t is in the methods of calculation that experience and judgment and skill in efficiency of arrangement of numerical calculations is most marked."[7]

For Steinmetz, reliability depended on things as simple as "neatness and care in the execution of the calculation" by writing with ink on white ruled paper and erasing instead of striking out the changes. In his opinion, "the appearance of the work" was "one of the best indications of its reliability." Accordingly, he recommended the arrangement in tabular form when a series of values were calculated. Steinmetz

---

[5] Ibid., 290.
[6] Ibid., 293.
[7] Ibid., 281.

further argued that "[e]ssential in all extensive calculations" was "a complete system of checking the results, to insure correctness." One way to have reliability would be "to have the same calculation made independently by two different calculators, and then compare the results." Another would be "to have a few points of the calculation checked by somebody else." Neither, admitted Steinmetz was satisfactory, "as it is not always possible for an engineer to have the assistance of another engineer to check his work, and besides this, an engineer should and must be able to make numerical calculations so that he can absolutely rely on their correctness without somebody else assisting him." Steinmetz had a few methods to offer other than resorting to perform every operation twice, preferably in a different manner. For example, he suggested that when multiplying or dividing with the slide rule, the multiplication or division should be repeated mentally, approximately as a check.[8]

The following passage leaves no doubt about the importance of curves in engineering calculations, assuming a skilled human calculator:

> When a series of values is calculated, it is usually easier to secure reliability than when calculating a single value, since in the former case the different *values check each other*. Therefore it is always advisable to calculate a number of values, that is, a short curve branch, even if only a single point is required. After calculating a series of values, they are plotted as a curve to see whether they give a smooth curve. If the entire curve is irregular, the calculation should be thrown away, and the entire work done anew, and if this happens repeatedly with the same calculator, the calculator is advised to find another position more in agreement with his mental capacity. If a single point of the curve appears irregular, this points to an error in its calculation, and the calculation of the point is checked; if the error is not found, this point is calculated entirely separately, since it is much more difficult to find an error which has been made than it is to avoid making an error (italics added).[9]

For Steinmetz, an engineer was defined as such by his skill in calculation. His "calculators" were engineers who sought to become (or had already established themselves as) designers-analysts. "Calculation" was closer to design (in this case, of electric power networks). We may refer to some passages from Kennelly to introduce to "computation," work from the other end of the division of labor involved. Here we will find human "computers" or "computors."[10] To retrieve their presence,

---

[8] Ibid., 293a.

[9] Ibid., 293a–293b.

[10] For computational projects that were based on computors, usually women, see David Alan Grier. 2007. *When computers were human*. Princeton: Princeton University Press; Jennifer S. Light. 1999, July. When computers were women. *Technology and Culture* 40(3): 455–483; and James E. Brittain. 1985. From computor to electrical engineer: the remarkable career of Edith Clarke. *IEEE Transactions on Education* E-28(4): 184–189. See, also, Margaret W. Rossiter 1980. 'Women's work' in science. *ISIS* 71(258): 123–140; I. Gratan-Guinness. 1990. Work for the hairdressers: the production of de Prony's logarithmic and trigonometric tables. *Annals of the History of Computing* 12(3): 177–185; Paul Ceruzzi. 1991. When computers were human. *Annals of the History of Computing* 13(1): 237–244; Lorraine Daston. 1994, Autumn. Enlightenment calculations. *Critical Inquiry* 21(1): 182–202; Harry Polachek. 1995, Fall. History of the journal 'Mathematical tables and other aids to computation' 1959–1965. *IEEE Annals of the History of Computing* 17(3): 67–74; Andrew Warwick. 1994. The laboratory of theory or what's exact about the exact sciences? In *The values of precision*, ed. M. Norton Wise, 311–351. Princeton: Princeton University Press; Martin Campbell-Kelly, and William Aspray. 1996. *Computer: A history of the*

one has to pay attention, literally, to the footnotes of treatises authorized by an analyst. A footnote in one of Kennelly's series of treatises on electrical engineering computations of the 1910s offers us a representative example. These treatises included a book with equations (applications of hyperbolic functions to electrical engineering), a book with tables (tables of complex hyperbolic and circular functions), a book with graphs (chart *Atlas* of complex hyperbolic and circular functions), and a book on the theory, mode of construction, and uses of artificial lines.[11]

In the 1914 preface to the first edition of his treatise on electrical engineering tables, Kennelly proudly stated that to solve the same electrical engineering problem, "to a like degree of precision without aid from these functions, and by older methods, would probably occupy hours of labor and cover several sheets of computing-paper."[12] A lot of valuable labor could supposedly be saved by using the capital accumulated in the form of Kennelly's computing tables. But a lot of computing labor had been appropriated in order to produce these tables in the first place. In an explanatory appendix of this book, Kennelly informed that the steps between computations were larger than he originally intended them to be because his applications for financial assistance in the computation of the tables—150 pages of them—were unsuccessful. Even after compromising in respect to how large the steps between computations should be, Kennelly's computational project was large. For example, as Kennelly himself explained, to control against errors, all tables had to be computed twice by using two different formulas of the equation. All the tables had to be subsequently reduced to graphic form in the book with the charts—which Kennelly called the *Atlas*—by marking off each entry of the tables on its proper chart with a sharp needle. Then a ruling pen should be used to draw through the successive punctures. The graphs (charts) of Kennelly's *Atlas* of electrical engineering were not a passive picture of the tables because in the process of drawing, errors were discovered and rectified. This is why the tables were computed three times before they were set up in type. After this, they were proofread three times. Notably,

---

information machine. New York: Basic Books, Chapter 1; Jennifer S. Light, "When Computers Were Women"; and Mary Croarken, and Martin Campbell-Kelly. 2000, October–December. Beautiful numbers: The rise and decline of the British Association Mathematical Tables Committee, 1871–1965. *IEEE Annals of the History of Computing* 22(4): 44–46. For Blanch, see David Alan Grier. 1997. Gertrude Blanch of the mathematical tables project. *IEEE Annals of the History of Computing* 19(4): 18–27; David Alan Grier. 1998. The math tables project of the work project administration: The reluctant start of the computing era. *IEEE Annals of the History of Computing* 20(3): 33–49, and David Alan Grier. 2000, January–March. Ida Rhodes and the dreams of a human computer, *IEEE Annals of the History of Computing* 22(1): 82–85.

[11] Arthur E. Kennelly. 1925. *The application of hyperbolic functions to electrical engineering problems.* New York: McGraw-Hill. First edited in 1912 and reedited in 1919), Arthur E. Kennelly. 1914a. *Tables of complex hyperbolic and circular functions.* Cambridge, MA: Harvard University Press, Arthur E. Kennelly. 1914b. *Chart Atlas of complex hyperbolic and circular functions.* Cambridge, MA: Harvard University Press, and Arthur E. Kennelly. 1928. *Electric lines and nets: Their theory and electrical behavior.* New York: McGraw-Hill. First edited in 1917.

[12] Kennelly, *Tables of Complex Hyperbolic and Circular Functions*, Preface.

as Kennelly explained, if the two initial computations differed, "the steps of the computation were gone over afresh."[13]

Who provided with the labor required for this large computational project given that the budget for it was limited? We cannot find out by reading Kennelly's preface, in which he only mentions some of his fellow electrical engineering analysts who had exercised an indirect influence on his computing project. To learn who did the bulk of the work, we would have to stay lucky and manage not to overlook an appendix footnote, on the bottom of page 209. There, in small letters, Kennelly expressed "his acknowledgment" to four female "assistants." The footnote reads: "[t]he author desires to express his acknowledgment of the care and painstaking efforts of his assistants engaged in computation, namely Miss Ethel Smith, A.B. Radcliffe, 1911, Miss A. F. Daniell, A.B. Radcliffe, 1911, Miss Mary M. Devlin, A.B. Radcliffe, 1912, and Miss Hope M. Hearn, A.B. Radcliffe, 1912."[14]

Kennelly's computational project had actually started earlier. We get an idea of how much computing labor had to be accumulated in order to have Kennelly's computing treatises by considering how impressed were the 1895 discussants by the work required to produce a single computing graph. Plate I of a 1895 paper that Kennelly had co-authored, was a "diagram," which could become, "practically, to a moderate degree of approximation, a graphic table of hyperbolic sines and cosines" over a range which was "sufficient for most problems that present themselves." It was offered together with an appendix with formulas for computing beyond this range. Alexander Pupin, a pioneer of the use of the artificial line in communications, remarked that: "It is a very useful thing to have certain mathematical functions, with which we are not very well acquainted, worked out numerically, and, if possible, reduced to graphical representation." He therefore thought of obtaining one: "I think Professors Houston and Kennelly deserve great credit for the extremely careful way in which they have worked out the figure of Plate I, and I am glad to hear that anyone who wishes to have this plate can have it in an enlarged form, because it really simplified numerical calculations very much."[15]

Pupin's guest, the physicist Arthur G. Webster, started his comments by acknowledging that computing required much labor:

Not being an engineer myself, and not knowing engineers as well as I wish I did, I had supposed that an engineer was an extremely busy man and that he was mostly occupied in doing practical things which brought him in a certain amount of very pleasant returns which are not open to people in my position. But I came to the conclusion that there are engineers who delight in doing other things, who are willing to do arithmetic, which I may say for myself I find a terrible grind. If I have been fortunate enough to get certain experimental results and put them down in my notebook, when it comes to working the calculations over, I should prefer to send them several hundreds miles rather than do it myself. But I have come to the conclusion that business is probably a little slack in Philadelphia. I have always had the impression that there were more hours in the day in Philadelphia than in New York.

---

[13] Ibid., 102.

[14] Ibid., 102.

[15] See Edwin J. Houston, and A.E. Kennelly. Resonance in alternating current lines, *AIEE Transactions* 12: 139; for Pupin, see: 159–160.

But I see that there must be many more days in the week, and if I might take the liberty I should be glad to ask Mr. Kennelly privately how long it took him to draw that diagram. I was extremely interested in that part.[16]

In his reply, Kennelly proudly shared the story of the machine that he imported in order to plot Plate I: "In order to draw that diagram," explained Kennelly, "we had to send to Europe for a machine. We could not find anywhere in this country a machine which would draw the lines accurately enough."[17]

Taking his treatises on computation together, Kennelly argued that "it may be said that hyperbolic functions applied to alternating-current circuits have risen from the state of theory outlined in the first edition of this book, to a stage of practical utility; because problems which would take hours of labor to solve by other methods, may be solved in a few minutes by the use of the hyperbolic Tables and curve sheets." Kennelly appraised his computing artifacts by moving on to portray them as "a practical engineering tool of great swiftness and power." For a comparison, he contrasted his graphs to a slide rule. The savings in living labor seemed impressive: "In fact, with the [his] atlas open at the proper chart, any complex hyperbolic function can be read off within a few seconds of time, ordinarily, to at least such a degree of precision as is offered by a good 25-cm slide rule."[18]

Kennelly's political economy of computing, which included laboratory artificial lines that were used to produce tables and then tables to produce graphs, went side by side with an ideology that presented these graphs as manifestations of the naturalness of engineering, in this case electrical engineering. His graphs, based as they were on starting with his artificial lines, were not simply useful. They were also revelations of the beauty of this naturalness through the mediation of the laboratory. In his 1913 article on the artificial line, Kennelly coupled notions of convenience, realization, and practicality by notions of naturalness, expressiveness, and revelation:

> The distribution of voltage and current on long alternating-current lines in the steady state is most conveniently realized and practically demonstrated by the use of artificial lines in the laboratory. While the theory of these distributions finds simple and natural expression in hyperbolic functions, the experimental facts are revealed most simply by means of measurements on artificial lines composed of uniform sections of resistance, capacitance and leakance.[19]

The experimental results, argued Kennelly in his 1913 article, "may appear anomalous or even incredible to the student who is not familiar with the subject," but through his computing artifacts, the student could "familiarize himself with the underlying principles and formulas." For Kennelly, electrical engineering had a "natural entrance" and an "interior." When one entered electrical engineering through his computing technology, it appeared "very useful, comprehensive, and

---

[16] Ibid., 160–161.

[17] Ibid., 168.

[18] Kennelly, The application of hyperbolic functions to electrical engineering problems, vii.

[19] Arthur E. Kennelly. 1913, June 14. A convenient form of continuous-current artificial line. *Electrical World* 61(24): 1311.

beautiful." Top analysts of electric transmission of communication agreed. For AT&T's John Carlson, electrical engineering had an "inner meaning" that could be revealed by "a systematic and comprehensive program of computation."[20] Kennelly had provided such a program for electric transmission of power.

The climax of his presentation of computations as revelations of the beauty of electrical engineering was his *Atlas* of electrical engineering charts. Like all atlases, Kennelly's was drawn to attract to a journey. As mirrored in the pages of the Kennelly *Atlas*, Kennelly's image of electrical engineering looked like an attractive trip, riding an alternating current oscillation to territories where lines harmoniously converge or disappear (for an example, see Fig. 5.1). It was as if the electric lines to be calculated were manifestations of an ideal symmetry behind a material chaos. Deep inside, as revealed by the square-shaped charts of the *Atlas*, electrical engineering was a revelation of harmony. The *Atlas* was the virtual (computed) reality gallery of this harmony. It offered magnetizing portraits of a mysterious but controlled phenomenon, not of the risks from high voltage transmission instability and the labor required to avoid them.[21]

According to Vannevar Bush and Edith Clarke, Kennelly's two MIT students, employing mathematical simplicity so as to reveal the naturalness of electrical engineering was indeed what Kennelly was doing best. In her 1942 periodization of the history of power system analysis, Clarke quoted what a contemporary had said of Kennelly:

> Of all beautiful expositions of profound mathematical work in the simplest language … there is nothing in the literature of our time to come up to the writings of Mr. Kennelly. … The article [one of Kennelly's articles]…showing…how a person utterly ignorant of hyperbolic functions, quaternions, or anything else of that sort can treat the whole mathematics, is a perfect poem…the most lovely exposition of mathematics in simple form I have ever read.[22]

In his 1943 piece on Kennelly, written as an entry to the *National Academy of Sciences Biographical Memoirs*, Bush argued that "Kennelly's great work" was that he satisfied the need for an individual who could "regularize, interpret, simplify, and extend the mathematical approach in order to create a keen working tool."

---

[20] For Kennelly, see Kennelly, A convenient form of continuous-current artificial line: 1311, and Arthur E. Kennelly. 1912, August 10. An investigation of transmission line phenomena by means of hyperbolic functions: the distribution of voltage and current over pi artificial lines in the steady state. *Electrical World* 60(6): 306–311. For Carson, see John Carson. 1919. Theory of the transient oscillations of the electrical networks and transmission systems. *AIEE Transactions* 38(1): 386.

[21] Kennelly, *Chart Atlas of complex hyperbolic and circular functions*.

[22] See Vannevar Bush. 1943. Arthur Edwin Kennelly, 1861–1939. *National Academy of Sciences Biographical Memoirs* 22: 89, and Edith Clarke. 1944. Trends in power system analysis. *Midwest Power Conference Proceedings* 7: 177.

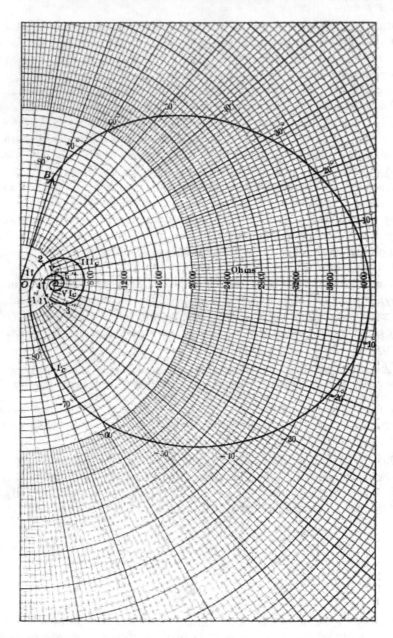

Fig. 5.1 Chart of electrical characteristics ("impedance") that was constructed through calculation with a "smooth" version of an artificial line, from a treatise by Harvard-MIT electrical engineering professor Arthur Edwin Kennelly (1917)

5.3 "A Convenient Table: A Welcomed Help"

The "perfect poem" that Kennelly's electrical engineering was supposed to be could not be revealed without taking, first, the form of tables. But how were tables to be produced and used? The introduction to a pioneering collection of contributions to the long-run history of mathematical tables offers an invaluable introduction to the historiographical challenges involved in studying the history of tables.[23] The first challenge has to do with acknowledging the diverse roles involved in the panorama of activities associated with tables, among them theoretician, constructor, scribe, printer, and consumer. Equally important is sensitivity to the range of types of tables, communities of table makers and consumers, and modes of production of tables. The aforementioned collection focuses on astronomical, mathematical, and actuarial communities. In this section we follow its lead by adding examples from engineering tables. Table making had been the subject of big table-making projects, which employed batteries of human computers but, also, of efforts by smaller groups or individuals. No big table-making projects—tables involving a considerable number of human computers—will actually be presented below. Even when the table-making engineering initiatives were big, they were carried out by relatively small teams or individuals. This may be the case when we move from more mathematical tables, for broader use, to tables for special communities, like the various communities and subcommunities of engineering.

Engineers, just like many others, also used general mathematical tables, which they had to adjust to the context of use. The focus here is on tables that started from the other end, i.e., special tables produced by the initiatives of engineers. The difference between table making from empirical data and mathematical formula, brought to our attention by the aforementioned collection, is, I would argue, relative. Engineers in general and electrical engineers in particular were interested in both. The very difference between the two was actually challenged when the empirical context determined, for example, the choice of mathematical formula, the adaptation of the formula to this context, the policy regarding approximations, and the density and the other features of the table (e.g., the number of decimals to be taken into account). The same seems to be the case with the difference between curves formed out of empirical data and graphs made out of mathematical formula. As we shall also see, tables could be based on graphs (and curves) and vice versa. We will actually have the opportunity to acknowledge that several more classes of computing artifacts could be involved. Slide rules and calculating machines were rather common, as was, also, long-hand calculation. I here pay special attention to instances of top-of-the-line artifacts, like the artificial lines used to produce tables

---

[23] M. Campbell-Kelly, M. Croarken, R. Flood, and E. Robson. 2003. *The history of mathematical tables: From sumer to spreadsheets*. Oxford/New York: Oxford University Press. For the diversity or the roles of those involved in table-making and using, the difference between tables based on empirical data and mathematical formula, the role of communities of table makers and users, and the styles of table making, see pages 2, 4, 5–9, and 9, respectively.

and graphs. The range of artifacts involved in the production of tables and the mode of this production (and the associated division of labor) were co-shaped.

The aforementioned pioneering collection further differentiates between five styles of table making: the solitary table maker, communal computing, computing bureaus, mechanized computing, and finally computerization. Since this section refers to examples from the preelectronic era, computerization (which means use of an electronic computer) was not an option. The teams of table-making human computers that I encountered in my research were placed within the company that used the tables or the academic laboratory. In many of the cases presented below, it is assumed that the work of table making was done by one or few engineers. In the case of an engineering team, the (always relative) analyst-computor demarcation was reproduced within the ranks of engineering. In the context of the decades considered here, the analyst-computor demarcation that I work with can be interpreted as a historically specific version of the long-run demarcation between the theoretician and the scribe.

As for the users-consumers of engineering tables (e.g., the electric power transmission ones), they were usually the producers themselves or other engineers. In the case of tables published in popular calculation handbooks on electricity (like some of the books discussed in the following section), the community of table users was broader. The present section and the one that follows also pay attention to the media used to share, disseminate, or access tables, from special and general engineering and other books to engineering and other technical journals. The picture from the journals that I studied points directly to a community of table (and graph) makers and users, which was similar to the communities that used journals to exchange information about modifying the slide rule and using it as skillfully as possible in concrete contexts (see Chap. 3). Discussions concerning accuracy and its cost are not absent from the literature. But they were much less passionate than the ones connected to the slide rule. Ownership of tables (or graphs) was not, for sure, defining an engineer as such. After all, unlike the slide rule, tables (and graphs) could be reproduced. Journals were used as the prime medium for such reproduction. On the other hand, we will register a case of series of corporate technical letters that specialized on tables that were not for public dissemination. This seems to explain why the few copies that survived are usually scattered in corporate archives. Evidently, tables have been of low priority when it came to preserve computing artifacts. Still, the general picture from the samples of tables that I present below leaves no doubt that table making and using was indispensable to engineering.

In exceptional cases, tables could be the product of a mental genius. Mental calculation actually played a role, only a very limited one. In his book on the history of great mental calculators, Steven Bradley Smith mentions the case of John Von Neumann (1903–1957), a well-known pioneer of electronic computing. Smith refers to Robert Jungk, who, in his *Brighter Than a Thousand Suns* (1958), had described a calculation typical of those that contributed to the development of the atomic bomb. "Whenever," writes Smith a calculation was needed, "Von Neumann, Fermi, and Feynman would begin to calculate, each after his own fashion. Fermi juggled his slide rule, Feynman pounded a desk calculator, and Von Neumann calculated in his head." According to an unnamed observer, Von Neumann would usually finish first, and the outcomes of the three independent computations were remarkably close.[24]

In the history of computing electrification, stories about mental calculation mark the passage from myth to history. Benjamin Garver Lamme (1864–1924), chief engineer at Westinghouse during the first subperiod, was thought to be a mental calculator. Lamme relied on his ability for mental calculation on several computational projects, including the one that prepared for the celebrated electric transmission of the power from the Niagara Fall. In his autobiography, Lamme mentioned that he could take a table of data and see relationships and sometimes even a law that were not apparent to the rest. The fact that Lamme also mentioned that, in his early years, he used a slide rule as an experimental exercise, for a short period, before he soon realized that he was losing his quantitative sense and his ability to do mental calculation, is worth noting for two reasons: first, because it suggests that the way the computing artifact is structured imposes its own computing pattern (structuring tables in order to form a slide rule prevented Lamme from having the picture that he preferred), and, second, because it confirms that the slide rule served as the standard of computing comparisons.[25]

At the myth of the origins of General Electric, the other giant of electrical manufacturing, we find another mental calculator, Steinmetz, who was actually a friend of Westinghouse's Lamme. Steinmetz's case suggests that the calculating ability of a corporate employee could in fact be exaggerated. In popular biographies, Steinmetz was presented as a mental calculator. It seems that Steinmetz was talented, but not exceptional. As with James Watt and Thomas Edison (see Chap. 2), we find in Steinmetz a contrast between his private picture and his public presentation by General Electric as an unparalleled genius.[26]

Tables were in fact formally connected to gift in mental calculation. Section C on "Mathematical Tables" in the catalog of the 1914 Edinburgh Exhibition included three sections—"Historical," "Sang's Tables," and "Working List of Mathematical Tables"—and a special subsection that was entitled "Notes on the Development of Calculating Ability," which was written by W. G. Smith, Lecturer in Psychology at the University of Edinburgh. In it, Smith discussed the phenomenon of individuals who have an exceptional calculating ability. The reason for including this subsection under mathematical tables is not now obvious.[27] With the advance of the

[24] Steven Bradley Smith. 1983. *The great mental calculators*, 343–344. New York: Columbia University Press.

[25] See F.A. (Tony) Furfari. 1999. Benjamin Garver Lamme: Electrical engineer. *IEEE Industry Applications Magazine* 5(6): 13.

[26] For an example of the historiographical promotion of Steinmetz as being gifted with exceptional mental faculties, see Jonathan Norton Leonard. 1932. *Loki: The life of Charles Proteus Steinmetz*, 148–149. Garden City: Doubleday, Doran, and Company. For Brittain's corrective account, see the chapter on Steinmetz in James E. Brittain. 1970. *B. A. Behrend and the beginnings of electrical engineering, 1870–1920*, diss., Case Western University.

[27] See page xiv in the "Introduction" by Williams R. Williams in the reprint edition (Los Angeles: Tomash Publishers, 1982) of E.M. Horsburgh. (ed.). 1914. *Modern instruments and methods of calculation: A handbook of the Napier tercentenary exhibition*. London: Bell and Sons.

mechanical era and the addition of the electrical and the electronic eras, production of tables became, increasingly, machine-mediated. Moreover, as it has been convincingly argued in a study of the introduction of calculating machines to the context of producing mathematical tables, mental calculation is a "fragile skill that is distributed very unevenly among human beings; it could not act as a substitute for machine-based calculation in a highly numerate society like our own."[28]

Even, for example, if we were to agree that both direct current distribution and alternating current transmission were initially calculated by the genius of a mental calculator, the electrical engineering tables required for calculating the lengthening of transmission distances could only be produced in connection to an appropriate institutional environment. Electrical engineers that were authors of series of articles that included extensive sets of tables on transmission line calculations were supported by such environments: M. W. Franklin by General Electric, William Nesbit by Westinghouse, Arthur Kennelly by Harvard University and MIT, Dressel Dewitt Ewing by Purdue University, Frederick Kurt Kirsten by the University of Washington, Frederick Eugene Pernot by the University of California, and T. R. Rosebrugh by the University of Toronto.[29]

From the perspective of what was needed in order to calculate the advance of electrification, Kennelly found the existing tables of these functions to be covering "a very restricted range." This is why he moved on to direct the production of special complex hyperbolic and circular functions for use in electrical engineering. Kennelly elaborated on this point in his annotated bibliography on the history of the production of such tables. He there explained that he had to make choices in respect to which functions to present in a tabular form and in respect to how to compute the values to be tabulated. These choices were determined by the fact that his tables were to be used by electrical engineers.[30]

Kennelly's choices in respect to the accuracy and reliability of computing with his tables were also tailored to an electrical engineering computational context. For example, the content of his tables was shaped by the expected mode of interpolation, which, in turn, was adjusted to what was suitable to electrical engineering. As

---

[28] For Warwick, see Warwick, The laboratory of theory or what's exact about the exact sciences?, 343.

[29] See M.W. Franklin. 1909, September. Transmission line calculations, Part I. *General Electric Review* 12(9): 447–451; William Nesbit. 1919–1920. Electrical characteristics of transmission circuits. *Electric Journal.* article series; Dressel Dewit Ewing. 1923. *Tables of transmission line constants.* Lafayette: Purdue University Press; Frederick Kurt Kirsten. 1923–1929. *Transmission line design*, series of publications. Seattle: University of Washington Press; David Eugene Pernot. 1916. *Formulae and tables for the design of air-core inductance coils.* Berkeley: University of California Press, and T.R. Rosebrugh. 1919. *The calculation of transmission line networks*, Bulletin of the School of Engineering Research 1. Toronto: University of Toronto Press. For Kennelly's and Pernot's more general tables, see Kennelly, *Tables of complex hyperbolic and circular functions*, and Frederick Eugene Pernot. 1918. *Logarithms of hyperbolic functions to twelve significant figures.* Berkeley: University of California Press.

[30] See Kennelly, *Tables of complex hyperbolic and circular functions*, Preface and 209–212.

Kennelly explained in an introductory passage, interpolation was supposed to be produced by the complementary use of his tables and his Atlas of charts so as to have, initially, a first expectation and, eventually, a last check of the outcome of interpolation. The scale of Kennelly's charts was chosen to accommodate a range that corresponded to the mode of variation of phenomena within limits set by the theory of electrical engineering. It follows that the tables corresponding with Kennelly's charts were also adjusted for electrical engineering. In the unlikely event that the same functions would be of interest to a mechanical engineer, it was very likely that he would prefer to interpolate from a different scale, which, in turn, would correspond to an emphasis on a different range. It follows that a mechanical engineer would prefer a different tabularization of the same function. Electrical engineers, as a whole, were interested in how the use of a chart could affect the computation-interpolation relationship. For an example from electric power transmission, I refer to MIT Professor L. F. Woodruff, author of a handbook on electric power transmission. Woodruff, who was also an author of electrical engineering charts, thought of the two (charts and tables) as inseparable.[31]

Tables with transmission line calculations belong to a subclass of special-purpose tables that is different from the general-purpose mathematical tables (logarithmic and other) that we know more about. There were in fact no mathematical tables per se but tables that were more mathematical than others from the perspective of a synchronic comparison of the range of their uses (for comparable accuracy and reliability). Most of the electrical engineering tables were, explicitly, special-purpose ones. This was the case with most of the tables for transmission line calculations. Within, however, the rich domain of such tables, some were actually to be used more generally than others. For example, a wire table that related transmission wire parameters (usually diameter) to one electric phenomenon (usually resistance) was much more specific than a general transmission line calculation table that contained many more parameters. Similarly, tables of two variables were usually more specific in respect to the relation of these two variables than tables of many variables that happened to include these two variables.

For a macro-historical indication of the pace of growth of tables of transmission line calculations, we can compare Franklin's *General Electric Review* and Nesbit's *Electric Journal* series of articles and tables of the 1910s to an article and a table from the 1880s. In the 1880s, one table and one very short article sufficed to exhaust the issue. Lemuel W. Serrell Jr.'s *Electrical World* 1889 article (and the table that it contained) presents us with a representative case. "In view of the great interest that is being taken in the conversion of water power into electric energy, and distributing the same for light and power purposes over long distances," thought Serrell, "a

---

[31] See Kennelly, *Chart Atlas of complex hyperbolic and circular functions*, appendix. For Woodruff, see L.F. Woodruff. 1938. *Principles of electric power transmission*, 115–116. New York: Wiley, and Complex hyperbolic function charts. *Electrical Engineering* (May 1935).

convenient table for calculating the amount of wire necessary to transmit different amounts of power over various distances and under different efficiencies would probably be a welcomed help to engineers who have this subject to deal with." All this he was able to treat in the one table of his brief article. Moreover, Serrell's table included calculations covering the transmission line and both generation and consumption. He considered 20 transmission distances, ranging from 0.5 to 10 miles. For Serrell, this was already long-distance transmission. In Franklin (early 1910s) and Nesbit (late 1910s), the maximum distance considered was at least an order of magnitude higher, 100 and 500 miles, respectively. In response, due to the additional complexity, Franklin and Nesbit had to provide with an extensive set of tables.[32]

For a micro-historical indication of the interest in tables, I refer to a 1905 set of four articles on how to remember the wire table. In the April issue of the *Electric Club Journal*, Charles F. Scott published an article with mnemonic rules for memorizing the wire table with acceptable accuracy. Scott's interest in tables of electric power transmission calculations was permanent: at his capacity as editor of the *Electric Journal*, he later wrote the piece that introduced to Nesbit's series of articles. Harold Pender followed in the next issue of the *Electric Club Journal* with a formula that could serve the same purpose. In an editorial footnote placed at the end of Pender's article, it was stated that "[m]any will doubtless find the rules [Scott's rules] more easily remembered and applied than the formulae [Pender's formula]." In the October issue of the same journal, Y. Sakai suggested that Scott's rules or Pender's formulas could be related to the sliding of some of the standard scales of a general-purpose slide rule. One issue later, Miles Walker suggested fitting a special scale to a general slide rule to be able to calculate temperature rises.[33]

Beyond offering us an indication of the importance of tables, this cluster of articles also indicates the interaction between tables and slide rules. The evolution of the titles of the four *Electric Club Journal* articles is suggestive. The title of the first article was "How to Remember the Wire Table." By the time of the third article this was changed to "How to Use the Slide Rule on the Wire Table." These series of articles also offer as an example of how scales were modified in use by the replacement of useless scales or by the reconfiguration of others. Walker, the author of the last of the four articles, explained:

> The scale for this purpose can be laid out on any part of the slide that is not required for ordinary work, as on the reverse side of the sliding stick; or a new slide may be made for the

---

[32] See Lemuel Serrell. 1889, May 25. Calculations for long-distance power transmission. *Electrical World*: 292. For Franklin and Nesbit, see Franklin, Transmission line calculations, Part I, and Nesbit, Electrical characteristics of transmission circuits.

[33] See Charles F. Scott. 1905, April. How to remember the wire table. *Electric Club Journal* 11(4): 220–223; Harold Pender. 1905, May. Formulae for the Wire Table. *Electric Club Journal* 11(5): 327; Y. Sakai. 1905, October. How to use the slide-rule on the wire table. *Electric Club Journal* 11(10): 632–633; and Miles Walker. 1905, November. Calculating temperature rises with a slide rule. *Electric Club Journal* 11(11): 694–696. For Scott's sustained interest on the issue, see Charles F. Scott. 1919, July. Finding the size of wire. *Electric Journal* 16(7): editorial.

purpose. To construct the scale, if the old slide is used, rub out the scale that is not wanted with fine sandpaper and repolish. Place the slide in the rule so that this clean surface will be opposite to the left-hand end of the lower scale.[34]

Walker then described how the new inscriptions were to be drawn.

For an additional macro-historical index to the growth of electric power transmission tables, we can compare two popular handbooks on calculation. In an 1895 handbook in the Audel series, electric power transmission was treated in one table column. The rest of the columns were about competing modes of power transmission. Noticeably, unlike the electric mode of transmission of power, these competing modes of power transmission were further treated in separate tables. There were, for example, tables of breaking loads for various wire ropes or iron chains. This changed dramatically in the following decades. In the 1932 edition of another special handbook on calculation in the Audel series, there were no tables on other modes of power transmission. Moreover, the electric mode of power transmission was now treated in an extensive series of tables.[35]

The impressive diachronic growth of electric power transmission tables is a given fact regardless of whether we focus on tables for analysts or on tables for computors. However, a synchronic comparison of tables for analysts and tables for computors points to an important difference. Popular handbooks on electrical engineering calculation were stuffed with tables like the wire tables but contained no tables like Kennelly's tables of complex hyperbolic and circular functions. On the other hand, wire tables were excluded from Kennelly's conception of electrical engineering tables for analysts. Evidently, the hierarchy that corresponded to the analyst-computor demarcation interacted with an associated hierarchy of tables.[36]

The study of the technical journals can help us to elaborate on the electrification-calculation relationship.[37] The journals of General Electric—Steinmetz's host institution—offer us a good index to the development of the electrification-computation relationship. The number of articles on calculation in the pages of the *General Electric Review* and the (General Electric) *Monograph* was no less than impressive. Equally impressive was the variety of the computing methods and artifacts men-

---

[34] Walker, Calculating temperature rises with a slide rule: 694.

[35] For 1895, see N. Hawkins. 1895. *Handbook of calculations for engineers and firemen*, 79–82 and 296. New York: Audel. For 1932, see Frank D. Graham. 1932. *Audel's new electric library, mathematics-calculations*, vol. XI. New York: Audel.

[36] Compare Graham, *Audel's new electric library, mathematics-calculations* to Kennelly, *Tables of complex hyperbolic and circular functions*.

[37] For the historiographical significance of studying technical journals, see Eugene Ferguson. 1989. Technical journals and the history of technology. In *In context: History and the history of technology (Essays in Honor of Melvin Kranzberg)*. eds. Stephen H. Cutliffe, and Robert C. Post, 53–70. Bethlehem: Lehigh University Press; James E. Brittain. 1989. The evolution of electrical and electronics engineering and the proceedings of the IRE: 1913–1937 and 1938–1962. *Proceedings of the IEEE* 77(6): 837–856 and 78, no. 1 (1990): 5–30; and P. Strange. 1979. Early periodical holdings in the IEE Library. *Proceedings IEE* 126(9): 941–94, and P. Strange. 1985. Two electrical periodicals: The electrician and the electrical review 1880–1890. *IEE Proceedings* 132, part A(8): 575–581.

tioned—from tools as humble as a slide rule to machines as prestigious as an analyzer. I will focus on calculation of electric power transmission.

I will actually start with a periodical publication that was not supposed to fall in the hands of anybody outside the General Electric, the confidential *Engineering Department Technical Letters*. Several of these letters were exclusively devoted to the issue of calculation. Electric power generation calculations were described in a 36-page-long publication entitled "Hydro Electric Calculations," which was published in September of 1911 and was republished at least once (in November of 1913).[38] There was also a set of two *Engineering Department Technical Letters* on transmission line calculations, 36 pages each. The basic one, entitled "Transmission Line Calculations," was published in September of 1909 and was republished in July of 1911.[39] I was able to locate a copy of its supplement that was published in July of 1911, but no copy from an earlier date. Its title was "Tables for Transmission Line Calculations."[40] These were not the only *Engineering Department Technical Letters* that were devoted to transmission line calculation. An eight-page-long one, entitled "Overhead Line Calculations," covered short transmission distances (up to 60 miles at 25 cycles and 40 miles at 60 cycles, not exceeding 55,000 volts delivered). It was published in November of 1911.[41] This was superseded by another one, an edition of which came out in February 1919.[42] On the bottom of the first page of this one, we read "Fifth Edition" and "Supersedes No. 318." It then seems likely that some of these confidential publications were published more than once.

The publication dates of the *Engineering Department Technical Letters* on transmission line calculations that I was able to locate (1909–1919) coincide with the period of the rapid increase of transmission distances. These publications were approved by chief engineer E. W. Rice and were issued by David B. Rushmore, engineer for the Power and Mining Department. The 1911 edition on overhead line calculations was written with the assistance of L. L. Perry and C. T. Wilkinson. The 1909 version on transmission line calculations and its supplement were written with the assistance of W. L. Franklin. Its supplement contained 38 tables relating electric line transmission phenomena to various choices of transmission materials. The

---

[38] General Electric Company. 1911a, September. Hydro-electric calculations. *Engineering Department Technical Letter*, no. 316 and 316A (November, 1913). Schenectady/New York: General Electric Archives.

[39] General Electric Company. 1909, September. Transmission line calculations. *Engineering Department Technical Letter* (no. 309, September 1909 and no. 309A, July 1911). Washington, DC: Smithsonian Institution, National Museum of American History, Trade Catalogs Collections, Mezzanine Library.

[40] General Electric Company. 1911b, July. Tables for transmission line calculations. *Engineering Department Technical Letter*, no. 309-A. Washington, DC: Smithsonian Institution, National Museum of American History, Trade Catalogs Collections, Mezzanine Library.

[41] General Electric Company. 1911c, November. Overhead line calculations. *Engineering Department Technical Letter*, no. 318. Schenectady: General Electric Archives.

[42] General Electric Company. 1919, February. Overhead line calculations. *Engineering Department Technical Letter*, no. 335D. Schenectady: General Electric Archives.

basic one described these phenomena and gave the relationships involved, in the form of equations or graphs, upon which the calculation of the tables was based. Starting with the September 1909 issue of the *General Electric Review*, Franklin published some of the information contained in these confidential publications in a series of articles on transmission line calculations.[43] For the persistent need for tables at General Electric until late, I refer to the tables included in Appendix B of Volume I of Edith Clarke's 1943 book in the General Electric Series, which was entitled *Circuit Analysis of A-C Power Systems*.[44]

The basic of the set of the two *Engineering Department Technical Letters* on transmission line calculations included an example of "a complete calculation of a transmission line." We can read it as an index to how complex electric power transmission calculations already were. Eleven variables, four of which contained several sub-variables each, had to be determined, based on data about eight given variables. The given variables were kilowatts load, length of line, power factor of load, frequency, number of phases, estimated cost of power per kw. year, cost of conductor per pound, and interest rate on line investment. The unknown variables and sub-variables were voltage, choice of conductor, most economic loss, cross-sectional area of conductor (based on four equations), pounds of conductor, total cost of conductor, interest on line investment, resistance of line, skin effect, recalculation of loss for cable selected, kilowatts loss on line, kilowatts delivered, kilovolts amperes delivered, line spacing of conductors, capacity, charging current, self-induction, inductive reactance, natural period of time, voltage and current at generating end under full load conditions, and regulation of line. In the example considered, applying the data to the formulas and going directly to the presentation of the results took the space of eight pages, one-fourth of the whole publication. The calculating work left even after the analysis of the calculating process into a set of variables, equations, graphs, and tables was still considerable. This, I think, explains the emphasis that an analyst like Steinmetz was placing on knowledge about how to make calculation efficient by experience, judgment, and skill.

From a static perspective, experience, judgment, and skill could bring efficiency. But the dynamic lengthening of the transmission distance and the beginning of the interconnection of lines into networks brought about new variables. The result was an absolute increase in calculating complexity. The transmission distance in the aforementioned example was 100 miles, which was the maximum possible according to the first of the tables. Within a decade, as contemplating transmission distances that were ten times higher became standard, the only solution was to count on a developed tradition of artificial lines. Similarly, as the interconnection of lines into networks also became standard, developing the tradition of calculating boards became necessary. The calculation of stability was the lengthiest of all. A mere reading of the variables considered reveals the inseparability of the technical and the social in transmission line calculations. In the example men-

---

[43] Franklin, Transmission line calculations, Part I: 447–451.

[44] Edith Clarke. 1943. *Circuit analysis of A-C power systems: Symmetrical and related components*, vol. I. New York: Wiley.

tioned above, an interest on line investment of 5%, i.e., an economic variable of profit, and a calculated regulation of 9.4%, i.e., a technical variable of stability, were treated as ontologically interchangeable. On the other hand, placing profit at the "given" variables and stability at the variables "to be determined" suggests that there was a causal relationship: increased calculating work was the outcome of the pursuit of increased profits.

The number of articles and editorials on electric power transmission calculation in the *Electric Journal* and, later, in the *Westinghouse Engineer* is as impressive as the number of articles on the same issue in the *General Electric Review*. Charles F. Scott's editorial in the July 1919 issue of the *Electric Journal* provides us with a brief outline of the history of the period. "Years ago," stated Scott, "a simple table giving the ampere-feet for a given drop was sufficient to determine the size of wire to be used in a lighting circuit." "In a modern power transmission system, however," he continued, "new and varied elements arise so that the problem of finding the size of wire becomes difficult and involved." With the prevalence of alternating current (higher) transmission voltages the complexity introduced was considerable: "[t]he entire transmission problem of determining the size of wire is really a question of not exceeding permissible limits in any one of a dozen particulars. Some features which may be insignificant in ninety-nine cases may become the dominating one in the hundredth."[45] The purpose of Scott's editorial was to introduce to the series of 13 articles that William Nesbit published in the *Electric Journal* between 1919 and 1920.[46] Nesbit, informed Scott, "has adopted transmission line data as a sort of hobby and for quite a number of years past has been collecting this material and arranging it in convenient form."[47]

A slight revision plus a large addition to Nesbit's original articles was soon published in a book form by Westinghouse. A 1926 third edition of this book, presented as a collected work by Westinghouse engineers that was compiled by Nesbit, was published by the Westinghouse Technical Night School Press.[48] The amount of data included in Nesbit's series of articles in the form of equations, tables, and graphs was nothing sort of breathtaking. In the first of his series of articles, Nesbit explained that he had incorporated everything published up to then, including Kennelly's and Steinmetz's data on the most complex transmission scenario possible. He claimed that his series of articles "undoubtedly contains the most complete data on this subject which has ever been published."[49] To illustrate the use of the various methods of calculation, Nesbit included 64 examples, covering lines from 10 to 500 miles in length. Like the General Electric *Engineering Department Technical Letter* on transmission line calculations, considerable space was here devoted to an introduc-

---

[45] Scott, Finding the size of wire: editorial.

[46] Nesbit, Electrical characteristics of transmission circuits: parts I–XIII.

[47] Scott, Finding the size of wire: editorial.

[48] William Nesbit. 1926. *Electrical characteristics of transmission circuits*, 3rd Edn. East Pittsburgh: Westinghouse Technical Night School Press.

[49] Nesbit, Electrical characteristics of transmission circuits: part I, 279.

tory discussion of the electrical phenomena involved, so that "this series of articles may prove of great value to many engineers who have not had the advantage of a technical education, or who have become rusty on such subjects." Nesbit admitted that the mathematical solutions could only be followed by those who have had some mathematical training, but, he predicted that for those who have not had such a training, the charts and the tables should prove "of immense help."[50]

In the last of the series of his articles, Nesbit tabulated his own comparison of some of the various approaches considered, ranking them according to the error introduced by employing each method in the calculation of the receiving-end voltage. He included receiving-end loads that varied between 10,000 and 200,000 volts, transmission distances that varied between 20 to 500 miles, two frequencies (25 and 60 cycles), various types of conductor, different spacing, and several other variables. Nesbit explained that the tabulated values were relative because the inherent error corresponding to various calculating methods would vary widely for conductors of various resistances and, to some extent, for different receiving-end loads. He compared the errors of eight methods by taking as his errorless standard the calculation of a method that he called the "rigorous solution." The values of the "rigorous solution" were obtained by calculating values for the auxiliary constants by means of convergent series and then calculating the performance mathematically." The "rigorous solution" was actually only a relatively rigorous solution: "[t]he calculations," explained Nesbit, "were carried out to include the sixth place, and terms in convergent series were used out to the point where they did not influence the result."[51] In our vocabulary, we would say that the computing analogy was extended to (and limited by) a sixth place of digitalization.

The eight methods compared to the standard were the "semi-graphical solution," the "complete graphical solution," "Dwight's 'K' formulas," four "localized capacitance methods," and the "impedance method." The "semi-graphical solution" combined a mathematical solution for the auxiliary constants and a graphical solution from there on, whereas in the "complete graphical solution," the auxiliary constants were taken from available charts. Taking Nesbit's interpretation of his comparisons as our reference, we can conclude that the "complete graphical solution" was adequate for transmission distances up to 300 miles. Since distances over 300 miles were the exception in this period, we can further conclude that an explicitly graphical calculation was generally adequate. Given, however, that analysts were already considering transmission distances that were much longer than 300 and even 500 miles, both the "completely graphical solution" and the "rigorous solution" would soon become inadequate (the purpose of those in charge of the artificial line project at MIT, which started in 1920, was to calculate distances as long as 1,500 miles[52]).

"The impedance method," which took no account of capacitance, was included by Nesbit simply to show how great the error could be (as high as around 70% for

---

[50] Ibid.

[51] Ibid., part XIII, 1920, 531.

[52] Frederick S. Dellenbaugh, Jr. 1923. Artificial lines with distributed constants. *AIEE Transactions* 42: 803–819. Discussion: 820–823.

60 cycles and transmission distance of 500 miles). Nesbit mentioned that some electrical engineers preferred to use this method for circuits of fair length and allow for error, thereby trading accuracy for flexibility (e.g., rapidity). "Dwight's 'K' formulas," based on Herbert Bristol Dwight's *Transmission Line Formulas: A Collection of Calculation for the Electrical Design of Transmission Lines*, were sufficiently accurate for all the distances considered for 25 cycle circuits and for distances up to 300 miles for 60 cycle circuits.[53] The "K" formulas were based upon the hyperbolic formula expressed in the form of convergent series. They were available in simple algebraic form that avoided the complex numbers by assuming that the capacitance multiplied by the reactance of nonmagnetic transmission conductors is a constant quantity to "a fairly close approximation." Nesbit recommended it for those "not familiar or not in position to make themselves familiar" with the operation of complex numbers. Of the four "localized capacitance methods," the most accurate appeared to be a method by Steinmetz that was known as "Steinmetz's three condenser method." Nesbit thought that it would be "interesting to note the high degree of accuracy inherent" in this method.[54]

In the footsteps of Nesbit, Donald M. Simons (a development engineer with the Standard Underground Cable Company of Pittsburgh) published in the *Electric Journal* a survey article with equations, tables, and graphs on calculation on the electrical problems of transmission by underground cables, which contained an appendix with 283 references on the issue.[55] Nesbit's 1920 comparison of methods was taking into account only the issue of computing accuracy. It was implied that more accuracy would require more capital—measured, for example, by the time that it took to compute by each method. A less precise comparison of methods of calculation that had the advantage of including the time that it took to compute according to each method was provided by MIT's Francis Dellenbaugh in 1921 (Fig. 4.1). Dellenbaugh had taken the data concerning the time that it took to compute by each method from various authors, which means that there was no common basis of comparison. Another problem with his data was that the basis of comparison was not the same because the various computations could not be reduced to the calculation of the same number of "harmonics". These problems aside, detailed investigation (which, for Dellenbaugh, was the prerequisite of progress) was often delayed even though the procedure was well understood because of the large amount of labor involved in handling cumbersome formulas or mathematical processes. Steinmetz's method, which was found to be fairly

---

[53] Herbert Bristol Dwight. 1925. *Transmission line formulas: A collection of methods of calculation for the electrical design of transmission lines*, 2nd Rev. and enlarged edition. New York: Van Nostrand, first edition, 1913).

[54] Nesbit, Electrical characteristics of transmission circuits: part XIII, 532.

[55] Donald M. Simons. 1925, August. Calculation of the electrical problems of transmission by underground cables. *Electric Journal* 22(8): 366–384.

accurate (Nesbit), required 10 h of work for the determination of the tenth harmonic.[56]

Dellenbaugh claimed that the electric analyzer that he introduced provided impressive savings of time. For the computation of the sixth harmonic, he estimated a time of 3.5 min. This radical gain in computing speed came along a substantial loss in computing accuracy. According to Dellenbaugh's own evaluation, his electric analyzer had the advantage of being "very quick" and the disadvantage of being "not extremely accurate." Adding (what we would now call) software disadvantages (problems due to the combination of the mathematical processes in a schedule) to hardware disadvantages ("usual" difficulties of electric networks and "rapid" increase of number of resistances with order of harmonics) gave an even less rosy picture in regard to the accuracy of computing with his electric analyzer.[57]

Dellenbaugh had compiled an impressive bibliography of 88 references on this issue (22 on "Mathematical and Selected Ordinate Methods," 10 on "Graphical Methods," 23 on "Instrumental and Mechanical Methods," and 23 on "Theory and Miscellaneous") and offered it "with no pretension of completeness."[58] I read it as another indication of how developed and how important calculation was by then. It is also indicative of how all this impressive accumulation of work on calculation was inadequate for computing the further lengthening of transmission lines and their interconnection. Based on Dellenbaugh's survey, those at MIT decided to compute the lengthening by turning to an advanced artificial line. Taking into account the pursuit of the interconnection of lines so as to form networks, they also turned to what soon concluded in the network analyzer.

Though a critical one, the calculation of electric power transmission was only one of the components of the calculation of electrification. From early on, there were also computing tables on all other aspects of electrification, including electric power generation. For an example, I refer to the set of tables included in series of 1894 articles on practical dynamo calculation that were published in *The Electrical Engineer* by Alfred E. Wiener.[59] Moreover, the calculation of electric power transmission included more than the calculation of electrical phenomena. The calculation of the mechanical phenomena of electric power transmission was also quite complex. There were then series of articles with equations, tables, and graphs for calculating the mechanical phenomena of electric power transmission, just like the series of articles with equations, tables, and graphs for calculating the electrical phenomena of electric power transmission already mentioned. For an example that is contemporary to those mentioned above, I refer to L. E. Imlay's series of articles of the mid-1920s, which were published in the *Electric Journal* under the general

---

[56] Frederick S. Dellenbaugh, Jr. 1921, February. An electromechanical device for rapid schedule harmonic analysis of complex waves. *AIEE Journal*: 142.

[57] Ibid., 142.

[58] Ibid., 143.

[59] Alfred E. Wiener. 1894, June 1/June 15. Practical notes on dynamo calculation. *The Electrical Engineer*: 640–641 and 701–703.

title "Mechanical Characteristics of Transmission Lines."[60] As the voltage was increased, the mechanical structure to support the transmission of power in the electric form also increased. For a taste of the persistent complexity of calculating the mechanical support of electric power transmission by the 1940s, I refer to the paper that the Italian L. Maggi presented at the 1946 International Conference on Large Electric Systems (*CIGRE*), which covered the demanding calculation of block foundations for transmission line towers. Maggi sought "to establish on a standard by eliminating the more considerable discordances existing among the formulae which are in greatest use."[61]

5.4   "New Catechism of Electricity"

Beyond the General Electric and the Westinghouse series of articles, there were series of calculating treatises and handbooks that that were published by various presses. We already mentioned Steinmetz's and Kennelly's treatises in a preceding section of this chapter (Sect. 5.2). In the University of California Press, Frederick Eugene Pernot published several transmission line calculation handbooks: *Formulae and Tables for the Design of Air-Core Inductance Coils*, *Logarithms of Hyperbolic Functions to Twelve Significant Figures*, and *An Extension of the Step-By-Step Method of Transmission Line Computation.*[62] In the Purdue University Press, Dressel Dewitt Ewing published his *Tables of Transmission Line Constants.*[63] In the University of Washington Press, Frederick Kurt Kirsten published a series of volumes under the title *Transmission Line Design*. It included plates, tables, and diagrams.[64] In the University of Toronto Press, T. R. Rosebrugh published *The Calculation of Transmission Line Networks.*[65] American electrical engineers also reached out to transmission line calculations included in publications in other languages. The 1920 and 1921 articles by M. L. Thielemans and P. Thielemans, respectively, were standard references.[66]

---

[60] L.E. Imlay. 1925, February. Mechanical characteristics of transmission lines II: Span formulae and general methods of calculation. *Electric Journal* 22(2): part II, 53–57.

[61] L. Maggi. 1946. The calculation of block foundations for transmission line towers. *International Conference on Large Electric Systems (CIGRE)* 2(220): 1.

[62] Frederick Eugene Pernot. 1919. *Formulae and tables for the design of air-core inductance coils* and *logarithms of hyperbolic functions to twelve significant figures* and *an extension of the step-by-step method of transmission line computation*. Berkeley: University of California Press.

[63] Ewing, *Tables of transmission line constants*.

[64] Kirsten, *Transmission line design*.

[65] Rosebrugh, *The calculation of transmission line networks*.

[66] M.L. Thielemans. 1920. Calculs et Diagrammes Des Lignes De Transport De Force A Longue Distance. *Comptes Rendus*, 1170, and P. Thielemans. 1920. Calculs, Diagrammes et Regulation Des Lignes De Transport D' Energie A Longue Distance. *Revue Generale De L'Electricite*: 403, 435, 475, 515, and (1921): 451.

Some of the most widely used handbooks on computing electrification were the one published in the Audel series of popular technical handbooks. "Audel's New Electric Library" comprised 12 volumes, the eleventh of which, written by Frank D. Graham and copyrighted by Theodore Audel and Company in 1932, was devoted to calculation for engineers and mechanics. "This book with its entirely different presentation," we read in the foreword, "it is hoped will inspire a wider interest in mathematics, because it puts at the student's finger ends a greater knowledge of applied mathematics, simplified for home study and ready reference."[67] The book was divided into four sections: "Mathematics," "Electrical Calculations," "Mechanical Calculations," and "Slide Rule." This classification suggests that putting applied mathematics at the finger ends was indeed the criterion that determined classification: the slide rule was by itself elevated into something like the whole of mathematics, the whole of mechanical calculations, and the whole of electrical calculations. At the very minimum, this classification indicates the importance of the tradition of computing with the slide rule.

The tradition of special Audel handbooks on calculation was old. Before there was a special handbook on calculation in the Audel Electric Library, data on calculating electrification, in various forms, was included in general technical handbooks on calculation that were part of the Audel Library, including the one written by N. Hawkins and published in 1895 as *Handbook of Calculations for Engineers and Firemen, Relating to the Steam Engine, the Steam Boiler, Pumps, Shafting, Etc.* In it, those interested in calculating power transmission could find something as general as a 13-page-long table containing the diameters, circumferences, and areas of circles along with something as specific as a third-of-a-page short table that compared the "commercial efficiency" of power transmission by electricity, hydraulic means, pneumatic means, and wire.[68] A mere look at this table suffices to show that transmission by electricity was more efficient than, for example, transmission by wire rope only after the transmission distance was over 15,000 feet. Since the transmission distances were then around or below this range, the eventual victory of electricity was not inevitable. Two years later (1897), in his widely read *New Catechism of Electricity*, another book in the Audel series, Hawkins argued that "while the current can be readily transmitted over enormously great distances—several hundred miles—practically speaking, such transmissions will probably be exceedingly rare for many years to come."[69] The problem, as Hawkins explained, had to do with the fact that "the first cost of installation" was "greater."[70] According then to this calculation handbook, the electric mode of power transmission required some previous accumulation of capital.

Tables and slide rules were only two of the many computing artifacts presented in handbooks on calculating electrification. There was, however, a notable contrast. In popular handbooks, we find no expensive electrical calculating artifacts like the

[67] Frank D. Graham, *Audel's New Electric Library*, *Mathematics-Calculations*, Preface.

[68] Hawkins, *Handbook of calculations for engineers and firemen*, 296.

[69] N. Hawkins. 1897. *New catechism of electricity: A practical treatise*. New York: Audel, 331.

[70] Ibid., 329.

artificial lines or, a generation later, like the network analyzer. By contrast, we find such artifacts in academic and industrial handbooks written by analysts. As I read them, the Audel popular handbooks on calculating electrification pointed more to the perspective of the low-ranking analyst (or chief computor), whereas handbooks on calculating electrification, like Kennelly's or, a generation later, Kennelly's student Bush, pointed more to the perspective of the higher-ranking analyst.

There were also handbooks that were written explicitly for the analyst (as distinct from the computor). Kennelly's treatise on the artificial line was an exemplar of this type of books. More representative of the average technical professional are books like Alfred E. Wiener's *Practical Calculation of Dynamo-Electric Machines: A Manual for Electrical Engineers and a Text-Book for Students of Electro-Technics* and Frederick Bedell's and A. C. Crehore's *Alternating Currents: An Analytical and Graphical Treatment for Students and Engineers*, both published by W. J. Johnston Company of New York.[71] As late as in 1917, both books were still promoted as addressing a more inclusive audience. I quote from the advertisement of these books in the back pages of the 1917 reedition of Steinmetz's *Engineering Mathematics* (1911). "Although intended as a text-book for students and a manual for practical dynamo-designers," we read in the advertisement of Wiener's book, "any one possessing but a fundamental knowledge of algebra will be able to apply the information contained in the book to the calculation and design of any kind of continuous-current dynamo."[72] Similarly, the chapters of the first part of the third edition of the Bedell and Crehore book contained "the analytical development" from simple to complex alternating current phenomena and circuits, a "feature" of which was "the numerical calculations given as illustrations," but the chapters of the second part were "devoted to the graphical consideration of the same subjects, enabling a reader with little mathematical knowledge to follow the authors, and with extensions to cases that are better treated by the graphical than by the analytical method."[73]

Wiener's treatise was addressed to both the designer and the calculator, and, as such, it was different from an analyst's handbook that excluded the computor:

> Differing from the usual text-book methods, in which the application of the various formulas requires more or less experience in dynamo-design, the present treatise gives such practical information in the form of original tables and formulas derived from the result of practical machines of American as well as European make, comprising all the usual types of filed magnets and armatures, and ranging through all commercial sizes.[74]

---

[71] Alfred E. Wiener. 1898. *Practical notes of dynamo-electric machines: A manual for electrical engineers and a text-book for students of electro-technics.* New York: W. J. Johnston, and Frederick Bedell, and A. C. Crehore. 1893. *Alternating currents: An analytical and graphical treatment for students and engineers.* New York: W. J. Johnston Company. For Bedell and Crehore, see James E. Brittain, *B. A. Behrend and the Beginnings of Electrical Engineering, 1870–1920.*

[72] Charles Proteus Steinmetz, *Engineering mathematics*, advertisement (First edition, 1911).

[73] Ibid.

[74] Ibid.

More specifically, I find here an implied contrast between design of ideal machines and, on the opposite end, calculation of practical machines. The fact that Wiener's book contained over 100 such tables indicates how much of an issue calculation already was, especially considering that it was a book focused on dynamo-design related calculations. The same can be shown by a simple exercise in bibliometrics. 10 out of the 49 publications of the W. J. Johnston Company listed in an advertisement that was placed at the end of the 1897 edition of Steinmetz's *Theory and Calculation of Alternating Current Phenomena* were directly related to calculation. Beyond Steinmetz's, Wiener's, and Bedell and Crehore's book, there were books with revealing titles such as *Standard Tables for Electric Wiremen* (Charles M. Davis), *Central-Station Bookkeeping* (H. A. Foster), *Universal Wiring Computer* (Carl Hering), *Tables of Equivalents of Units of Measurements* (Carl Hering), *Electric Lighting Specifications* (E. A. Merrill), *Reference Book of Tables and Formulae for Railway Engineers* (E. A. Merrill), and *Chart of Wire Gauges* (Schuyler S. Wheeler). If we subtract from the total the titles that referred to journals, to journal indexes, to directories, to the history (by Edwin J. Houston) or sociology (*Lightning Flashes and Electric Dashes: Humorous Sketches, Illustrated*) of electricity, and to the exhibition of electricity at World Fairs (by Carl Hering), the total number of the publications drops to 42. I think that we get a fair picture of how important calculation already was by the fact that 10 out of 42 of the technical publications advertised were written from the perspective of calculation.[75]

5.5 "It Would Lead Too Far to Explain Here in Detail the Laying Out of an Alignment Chart"

What we know from the history of "alignment charts" or "nomograms" or "nomographs" (the terms are here used interchangeably) suggests that they were very important to engineering and other technical works. This was certainly the case with machine-tool industry nomograms available continuously through the pages of the *American Machinist* for several decades during the twentieth century.[76] Historian Thomas L. Hankins wonders why we know so little of the origins of graphs in the eighteenth century, their development in the nineteenth-century engineering practice, and their importance in the twentieth century for describing physical and chemical systems: "[f]or us, in the age of supersonic missiles and electronic computation, it is hard to believe that gunners in World War I used nomograms to direct

---

[75] Charles Proteus Steinmetz (with the Assistance of Ernst J. Berg). 1897. *Theory and calculation of alternating current phenomena.* New York: W. J. Johnston Company, advertisement.

[76] Aristotle Tympas, and Fotini Tsaglioti. 2016. L'usage du calcul à la production: le cas des nomogrammes pour machines-outils au XXe siècle. In *Le monde du génie industriel au XXe siècle: Autour de Pierre Bézier et de machines-outils,* eds. Serge Benoit and Alain Michel, 63–73. Paris: Collection Sciences Humaines et Technologie, Pôle editorial de l'UTBM.

anti-aircraft fire. . . . I have never heard of them until last year, which is either a profession of personal inadequacy or a comment on the narrowness of our field."[77]

Beyond Hankins's introduction to the general context behind the development of a special-purpose nomogram for blood analysis, there is a pioneering contribution to the history of nomography for mathematics, which, like Hankin's, acknowledges the centrality of d'Ocagne's late nineteenth- and early twentieth-century contribution. Its author writes that "it appears" that d'Ocagne's nomography reached the United States through a series of 1908 articles by J. B. Pebble in the *American Machinist*.[78] Hankins finds that d'Ocagne's influence was mediated by the MIT community. Before a specialist in blood analysis went on to see d'Ocagne in 1921–1922, while traveling in Europe, he had learned, by asking E. B. Wilson at MIT, that what he himself had produced in the 1910s by superimposing several charts on the same graph like the ones that d'Ocagne had already baptized "nomograms." Once introduced, the branch of graphic calculation that became known as "nomography" became known rapidly, especially among engineers. Nomograms were centrally placed in the 1918 handbook on calculation by MIT's Joseph Lipka, which indicates that they had become quickly known to some US engineering analysts. Bush did not have to go very far to learn about alignment charts. We already saw that Bush has authored an alignment chart (Fig. 4.5). The alignment chart by Cornell's Vladimir Karapetoff that was also introduced earlier in this book (Chap. 4) is an example of a nomogram (Fig. 4.11) that was to be used together with an analyzer (Heavisidion, Figs. 4.8 and 4.9) and a more conventional graph (Fig. 4.10).[79]

Nomograms and the rest of graphs can be interpreted as technical "representations," the production and use of which is actually inseparable from the formation of social "power." I place nomograms—just like graphs and in fact all of the calculating artifacts considered in this book—in the order of the imaginary, which links through its mediation the real and the ideal (symbolic) (see also the relevant discussion in Chap. 4, in connection to the interpretation of Karapetoff's artifacts). I then think that it is correct to associate the history of production and use of scientific graphs (and scientific apparatus in general) with "imagination."[80] Starting from a review of recent work in the historiography of science, a scholar interested in diagrams of biological evolution that became important in the context of the Scopes

---

[77] Thomas L. Hankins. 1999. Blood, dirt, nomograms: A particular history of graphs. *ISIS* 90: 71.

[78] H.A. Evesham. 1986, October. Origins and development of nomography. *Annals of the History of Computing* 8(4): 331. On Pebble's article (actually a series of articles), see J.P. Pebble. 1908, May 30, September 19, and November 13. The construction of graphical charts. *American Machinist*.

[79] Hankins, Blood, dirt, nomograms: A particular history of graphs: 74–76.

[80] Thomas L. Hankins, and Robert J. Silverman. 1995. *Instruments and imagination.* Princeton: Princeton University Press.

Trial Debate argued that diagrams are active mediations.[81] I argue the same by starting from the other end, that is, from the history of technology.[82]

Another useful comparison is offered by a pioneering contribution to the history of the mediation of technical drawings between design and construction. As I see it, in drawings we have another example of representations, which can be placed right next to graphs.[83] W. L. Heard's Edison *Electric Institute Bulletin* 1946 article on one component of electric power drawings—drawings' standardization symbols—is suggestive of the importance of drawings in the history of the development of electric power transmission. The name of the committee that Heard chaired at the time is revealing of the importance of drawings: "ASA Sectional Committee on Graphical Symbols and Abbreviations for Use on Drawings." Interested in the development of a "unified system" of graphical symbols for electric power and electric control drawings, Heard took the pen to hail the 1946 approval of a step toward a universal symbolism of drawings of electric transmission of power and communication. For an example from electric power transmission, I refer to the six-page table with symbols of equivalent circuit of power and regulating transformers that the Westinghouse engineers included in an appendix to their handbook on electric power transmission.[84]

In the context of presenting with aspects of the history of electric power analysis by slide rules, models, calculating-tabulating machines, artificial lines, and analyzers, I am in this book interested in different historical variants of the constant-variable (machine-human) computing capital ratio during the process of the development of the mechanization of electric power analysis. In other words, I am mostly interested in what was known as "mechanical methods" of power analysis. In this chapter, however, I also cover what was actually considered an alternative to mechanical methods, namely, "graphical methods" of electric power analysis. Graphical computation as a whole was inescapable in engineering in general and electrical engineering in particular—for an introduction to the priority, in the last instance, of graphical methods, I refer to Steinmetz's relevant argument in his infamous handbook on engineering mathematics (see Sect. 5.2). While I will survey examples of various graphs for electric power analysis, I will maintain a focus on nomograms. Nomograms were usually made by the superposition of several particular graphs to produce a more general one. Nomograms were then exactly what

---

[81] Constance Areson Clark. 2001, March. Evolution for John Doe: pictures, the public, and the scopes trial debate. *Journal of American History* 87(4): 1278–1279, footnote no. 5.

[82] See Steven Lubar. 1995, April. Representation and power. *Technology and Culture* 36(2 Suppl): 54–82.

[83] See John K. Brown. 2000, April. Design plans, working drawings, national styles: Engineering practice in Great Britain and the United States, 1775–1945. *Technology and Culture* 41(2): 195–238.

[84] W.L. Heard. 1946. Coordinated graphic symbols for electric power and control drawings. *Edison Electric Institute Bulletin* 14(9): 311, and Central Station Engineers of the Westinghouse Manufacturing Company. 1944. *Electrical transmission and distribution reference book,* 612–618. East Pittsburgh: Westinghouse Electric and Manufacturing Company.

their name implies: graphs of a more general relationship that could be treated as a law, a *nomos*.[85]

A demarcation between graphical and mechanical methods was the most meaningful to MIT's Lipka. He was so explicit about it that he entitled his influential 1918 handbook "Graphical and Mechanical Computation." For Lipka, networks of computing scales could be used to compute either in the graphical form of a nomogram or in the mechanical form of a slide rule. The two analysts who had influenced Lipka were also of the opinion that any meaningful computing classification ought to start with the generic demarcation between graphical and mechanical computation. The first, a mathematician, the University of Edinburgh Professor of Mathematics E. T. Whittaker, the main actor behind the organization of the 1914 Edinburgh first World Exhibition on computing, was the one from whom Lipka had imported the emphasis on computing at a mathematical laboratory. He was a leading promoter of mechanical methods. The second, an engineer, the Ecole Polytechnique Professor of Geometry Maurice d'Ocagne, was the one from whom Lipka had imported the emphasis on situating mathematical computing in engineering practice. He was a leading promoter of graphical methods in general and the nomogram in particular.[86]

The canonical projection of the analog-digital demarcation into the whole of the history of computing has resulted in interpreting d'Ocagne as having made this (the analog-digital) demarcation central to his classification. As I read him, in reviewing "mechanical" (e.g., computing with a calculating machine), "graphical," "graphomechanical" (e.g., computing with a planimeter), "nomographic," and "nomomechanical" (e.g., computing with a slide rule) methods of calculation, d'Ocagne was actually assuming that the crucial demarcation was that between mechanical and graphical methods. The graphomechanical and nomomechanical methods corresponded to the mechanization of graphical and nomographic calculation, respectively. The title of d'Ocagne's basic treatise is quite revealing: D'Ocagne did not write a book on the analog and the digital; he wrote a book on "Calculus Simplification by Mechanical and Graphical Processes."[87]

---

[85] See Steinmetz, *Engineering mathematics*. For articles on the history of nomography, see Evesham, Origins and development of nomography: 323–333, and Hankins, Blood, dirt, nomograms: A particular history of graphs: 50–80.

[86] For Whittaker, see Warwick, The laboratory of theory or what's exact about the exact sciences?, 311–351. For d' Ocagne, see H.A. Evesham, "Origins and Development of Nomography". For Lipka's reference to Whittaker's pioneering mathematical laboratory, see the opening pages in Joseph Lipka. 1918. *Graphical and mechanical computation*. New York: Wiley. For Whittaker's role in the organization of the 1914 Edinburgh Exhibition, see the opening pages in Horsburgh, *Modern instruments and methods of calculation: A handbook of the Napier tercentenary exhibition*.

[87] See Maurice d' Ocagne. 1928. *Le Calcul Simplifie par les Procedes Mecaniques et Graphiques*, troisieme edition. Paris: Gauthier-Villars. For the interpretation of d' Ocagne as having made the analog-digital demarcation central, see the recent edition of d'Ocagne's treatise in English, which was translated by J. Howlett and M.R. Williams (Los Angeles: Tomash Publishers, 1986).

The examples of F. J. Vaes's design of engineering slide rules by the reconfiguration of the geometrical orientation of the nomogram into the algebraic orientation of the slide rule, G. S. Merrill's configuration of a slide disk calculator through the mechanization of a relationship conceived through a nomogram, Antonin Svoboda's "three-bar-linkage nomogram," and Douglas P. Adams' incorporation of nomography into "nomographic-electronic computation" indicate that the nomogram was the last stage in the transition from pre-mechanical to mechanical calculation. Vladimir Karapetoff's suggestion to combine the use of a nomogram and his "Heavisidion", a computing kinematic device for long transmission lines (Figs. 4.8, 4.9, 4.10 and 4.11), the promotion of the ALRO circular slide disk engineering rules as allowing for the option to place nomograms on them, and Steve M. Slaby's complementary use of nomograms and electronic computers indicates that the nomogram could occasionally remain recognizable after its subordination to a mechanical method of calculation.[88]

Nomograms were exemplary easy to use but, also, exemplary complex to design. Cornell University Electrical Engineering Professor Kaparettof introduced to the power nomogram that he presented in a 1923 issue of the *AIEE Transactions* by stating that "[I]t would lead too far to explain here in detail the laying out of an alignment chart; it suffices to state that the chart" takes the place of a couple of transmission line equations "and thus saves considerable time" in obtaining the values to be computed. Designed, however, to remain a pre-mechanical computing artifact, nomograms left something to be desired. C. Harold Berry concluded that the power nomogram for the chilling of condensate, the findings of which he presented in a 1921 issue of *Power*, "will prove useful for a moderate amount of use, but for an extended study a still better device is recommended. "This" he added, "is a special slide rule."[89]

In the hands of men like d'Ocagne, nomograms developed to the point where some of them could consist of an extended and complex combination of lines. The principle of all was that of the elementary nomogram that we find in the 1932 Audel popular technical handbook on calculating electrification, which consisted of three parallel lines. The one to the left, where the alignment started from, was called "present power factor." The one to the right, where the alignment ended, "desired power factor." After laying a straight edge across the present and the desired power factor value so as to connect the two, the reading of the value of the point of the

---

[88] See Ijzebrand Schuitema. 1999, Spring. Articles on Dutch contribution to slide rule history in the 20th century, Number 2: F.J. Vaes. *Journal of the Oughtred Society* 8(2): 39–42; G.S. Merrill. 1946, June. Slide-disk calculator. *General Electric Review* 49: 30–33; Antonin Svoboda. 1948. *Computing mechanisms and linkages*. New York: McGraw-Hill; Douglas P. Adams. 1964. *Nomography: Theory and application*. Hamden: Archon; Vladimir Kaparetoff. 1923, February. The 'Heavisidion': A computing kinematic device for long transmission lines. *AIEE Transactions* 42: 42–53; Ijzebrand Schuitema. 1993, October. The ALRO circular slide rule. *Journal of the Oughtred Society* 2(2): 24–37; and Steve M. Slaby's introduction in John H. Fasal. 1968. *Nomography*. New York: Frederick Ungar.

[89] See Kaparetoff, The 'Heavisidion': A computing kinematic device for long transmission lines: 53, and C. Harold Berry. 1921, August 2. The chilling of condensate. *Power* 54(5): 182.

intersection of the line produced by this alignment and a middle (third) chart line was pointing to how the engineer ought to react. Quite properly, this middle chart line was called "percent reactive kv-a" (reactive kv-a in percent of present kw load).[90] I would argue that standing for a generic instance of capitalist computing—by being as advanced as graphical calculation could be but, also, by being, still, a pre-mechanical mode of calculation—nomographical calculation affords us with a clear insight to the function of a calculating artifact as the imago (image) that links an engineer's start from the real (nature as it is) and his end in the ideal-symbolic (nature as it is supposed to be transformed through technology).

"Graphic Methods," wrote E. M. Horsburgh in his 1914 Edinburgh Exhibition handbook piece on nomograms and ruled papers (Section H), "are peculiarly the province of the engineer and the experimenter."[91] To explain why d'Ocagne started from the nomogram whereas Whittaker started in the same handbook from the calculating machine, I suggest that we look at the difference between the engineering and the scientific perspective on computation. As I understand it, against what the essentialist projection of the analog-digital demarcation would suggest, the perspectives of these two analysts were not antithetical but complementary. Engineering calculations were about the transformation of nature as it was (real) according to how it should be (ideal), scientific from the opposite end. As I read d'Ocagne, he was promoting the necessity of a dynamic mathematization-digitalization within graphical methods, which was complementary to the perspective of defending the same within mechanical methods. In other words, he was promoting a dynamic computing digitalization within what, by constitution, could only develop by the advance of the computing analogy between what existed and what was supposed to exist. Based on everything said so far, I agree that d'Ocagne's classification "may not come easily to the reader," but, "is based on sound logic."[92] Nomographic calculation aimed at additional mathematization (digitalization). In this sense, d'Ocagne was not a heretic of computing technology who went against digitalization. On the contrary, he was as orthodox as a promoter of computing technology could be, who properly respected the reality that engineering was starting from.

There is a general historiographical point to appreciate in reestablishing d'Ocagne as a contributor to (what we now call) digital computing technology. In his pioneering acknowledgment of the importance of nomograms in engineering, Eugene Ferguson assumes an essentialist contrast between computing with nomograms (and the rest of the tools of "visual analysis") and our (supposedly) digital electronic computing.[93] As I indicate later in this chapter (Sect. 5.8), the tradition of the visual

---

[90] See Graham, *Audels' new electric library, mathematics-calculations*, 93.

[91] Horsburgh, *Modern instruments and methods of calculation: A handbook of the Napier tercentenary exhibition*, 279.

[92] See the review of the recent English edition of d' Ocagne's book by H.A. Evesham in the *Annals of the History of Computing* 9 (no.3/4, 1988), 376.

[93] For Ferguson's introduction to nomography, see Eugene S. Ferguson. 1992. *Engineering and the mind's eye*, 151–152. Cambridge: MIT Press.

analysis afforded by nomography (and by the rest of the tools of visual analysis) was dynamically transformed into the visual analysis of electronic computing—it was not statically replaced by it. The nomogram was not simply a tool of engineering visualization (analog computing), but it was a tool of a visualization that served best the purpose of dynamic digitalization. I may refer here to to the relevant clarification of d'Ocagne, which he included in his communication to the 1914 Exhibition. D'Ocagne argued that a nomogram was superior to a numerical table to which it corresponded because it could provide with "a visual interpolation permitting the representation of all the values of the data within the limits of the figure" and because it could provide with more immediate familiarization with the relationship contained in the data of the numerical table—he referred to this as "the relief" of a topographical surface. But, he placed this argument within endorsing the assumption (he called it the "custom") that the phenomena to be engineered according to a nomogram ought to vary in digits (he called them "equal steps"), which were similar to the equal steps between the inscriptions on the lines of an alignment chart. It is not, as he moved on to explain, "simple empiricism" that he had in mind in proposing to compute with nomograms, but empiricism grounded in the "methods of analytical geometry."[94]

In the previous chapter, I argued that Vannevar Bush—the analyst that became the leader in the design of analyzers in general and analyzers for electric power analysis in particular—had actually started in 1920 with a "simple" analyzer for electric power analysis (Fig. 4.4). In doing so, he reconceptualized the electric power analysis machines of his ancestors as unnecessarily complex. In 1920, Bush had also published an article on an alignment chart for electric power analysis. In doing so, Bush reconfigured and renamed Kennelly's approach to charts of complex circular and hyperbolic functions, which was not based on nomograms but charts that privileged the visualization of the alleged beauty of electrical engineering: his (Bush's) was a simplifying chart of the same functions, which (like alignment charts in general) offered a minimum of visualization (Fig. 4.5). In the 1920s, Bush was then doing to the 1910s charts of his thesis advisor Kennelly the same thing that he did to his 1910s artificial lines (see Chap. 4): he pointed to the increased complexity of electrification in order to promote the design of his own calculating artifacts—alignment chart and network analyzer respectively—as more appropriate.[95]

---

[94] See Maurice d' Ocagne. 1915. Numerical tables and nomograms. In *Napier Tercentenary Memorial Volume*, ed. Gargil Gilston Knott, 279–280. London: Longmans, Green, and Company and Royal Society of Edinburgh.

[95] For Bush's 1920 analyzer and nomogram, see Vannevar Bush. 1920a, October. A simple harmonic analyzer. *AIEE Journal*: 903–905, and Vannevar Bush. 1920b, July. Alignment chart for circular and hyperbolic functions of a complex argument in rectangular coordinates. *AIEE Journal* 39: 658–659. For a comparison with Kennelly's charts, see Arthur Edwin Kennelly, *Chart Atlas of complex hyperbolic and circular functions.*

5.6 "Done Graphically Without the Computer Knowing Anything Whatever About the Mathematics"

In this section I start by comparing two graphs in order to indicate the dynamism of the increase in electric power transmission graph complexity. The first, by W. M. Schlesinger, was published in the March 5, 1892 issue of the *Electrical World*; the second, by Edith Clarke, in the May 1926 issue of the *General Electric Review*.[96] The two-page-long 1892 article included a diagram on the cost of power transmitted at various voltages and two diagrams with curves relating standard cost ($100 per HP) to variable voltage or variable cost to standard voltage (500 volts E.M.F. at the generator). By comparison, the variables treated in the six charts of the nine-page-long 1926 article were referring to only one component of electric power transmission calculations, namely, calculation of electric power transmission lines. Moreover, Clarke's article was explicitly restricted to a concern with technical variables, whereas Schlesinger's article was, also explicitly, concerned with technical variables, economic variables, and their interconnection. Had Clarke tried to be as holistic in her 1926 article as Schlesinger was in his 1892 one, she would have needed several books with graphs instead of one article. Noticeably, a decade before the publication of Clarke's article, Kennelly had to publish a full Atlas of charts to treat the issue from the technical end—moving on to explicitly add the economic end and the interconnection of the two would have required much more. The difference is not simply one of quantity. Implicitly, the economic side and its interconnection to the technical side were also included in Clarke's graphs. But calculation of electric power transmission as a whole had grown so much that the distance from explicitly economic to explicitly technical variables had become so great that the two appear to be separable. In 1892, the engineering and economics of power transmission could still be calculated by one person. By 1926, calculating electric power transmission was a subfield (electric power network analysis or simply power analysis) of a subspecialty (electric power engineering) of a subdiscipline of engineering (electrical engineering). Clarke had received graduate training in this subfield, which to her was autonomous enough to deserve its own history.[97]

The difference between the sets of graphs of the two authors can be also approached from the perspective of the degree of mathematization. Before he moved on to produce his graphs, Schlesinger introduced to both the technical and economic variables involved and moved on to extract the electrical engineering function that related them. He produced the graphs directly from this function. Clarke computed her graphs by electrical engineering functions indirectly, through the mediation of

---

[96] See William M. Schlesinger. 1982, March 5. Power transmission," *Electrical World* XIX(10): 154–155, and Edith Clarke. 1925, May. Simplified transmission line calculations. *General Electric Review* 29(5): 321–329.

[97] For Kennelly's charts, see Kennelly, *Chart Atlas of complex hyperbolic and circular functions*. For Clarke's history of power analysis, see Clarke, Trends in power analysis: 172–180.

some of the most complex mathematical functions, the hyperbolic ones. In addition to a reconfigured version of some of Schlesinger's technical variables, Clarke had to include new technical sub-variables. Frequency of transmission—introduced by the change from continuous current distribution to alternating current transmission—was a basic variable for Clarke, but unimportant for Schlesinger. Common to both articles was, however, the emphasis on the necessity and the sufficiency of graphs. Knowing that "hyperbolic functions, real or complex, are not popular with engineers," and that the engineering computations of transmission lines increasingly "laborious," Clarke decided to construct her graphs. The *General Electric Review* editor was more poetic:

> When we were young the multiplication table seemed most formidable, yet we eventually mastered it. But few of us have later been as completely successful in mastering some of the specialized branches of higher mathematics. Miss Clarke presents a simple medium for handling hyperbolic functions in a type of a problem frequently met.[98]

Schlesinger's graphs are a brief classic on the pursuit of individual profit that determined the development of electric power transmission:

> Looking at the problem from the standpoint of the owner of the power (either water or steam), it is not so much a question of making the cost per horse power delivered by the motor a minimum, as it is one of making the net profits derived from each horse power available at the generating plant a maximum. It is a well known fact that the condition of minimum cost of operating does not necessarily give a very efficient plant. If the power can be sold at a certain value, e, per horse power delivered by the motor, it can readily be conceived that, although the profits per horse power delivered will be a maximum, under the conditions of minimum operating expenses (that is, c = operating expenses per horse power delivered), yet by slightly increasing the cost of operating expenses the efficiency of the plant may be increased so that the product of available horse power delivered may become larger. When the product becomes a maximum we will have the plant giving the best returns for the money invested, or, in other words, we will have the conditions giving the most profitable plant.
>
> In the following I shall endeavor to give the laws covering the problem, and also to show how they can be applied for the purpose of answering the various questions of interest to owners of such properties. The owner of a power plant does not primarily care for the number of horse power actually delivered. His object is to desire most profit out of each horse power available at the source of power.[99]

My last point in interpreting the difference between the 1892 power transmission graphs by Schlesinger and the 1926 power line transmission graphs of Clarke is suggested by the word missing in 1892: lines. For Schlesinger, transmission could not be isolated from production (generation) of energy. Unlike Clarke, he would have found an isolated treatment of transmission lines meaningless.

The trade-off involved in computing electrical circuits by graphs was stated clearly in an editorial that introduced to an earlier *General Electric Review* article, that of H. C. Stanley of General Electric's San Francisco Office. Stanley was concerned with "graphical representations" of electrical circuits. "Frequently," argued

---

[98] See Clarke, Simplified transmission line calculations: 321.

[99] Schlesinger, Power transmission: 154.

the editor, "a number of resistances are connected in multiple and it is desired to know their total or combined value of resistance or reactance. The calculation necessary to obtain this combined value is usually simple in principle but at times laborious in practice. For approximate results and as a check on the more accurate calculations, a graphical solution is sometimes of value." Electrical engineers who approached electric transmission from the angle of (what we now call) electronics engineering had a similar interest in "graphic representations." Contemporaneous to Clarke's *General Electric Review* article on power transmission graphs was the article that Charles W. Carter, Jr., published in the *Bell System Technical Journal*, which was on "graphical representations" of aspects of electric transmission of communication. There also existed articles on graphs of electric power transmission for computing this transmission as a mechanical phenomenon, i.e., from the perspective the mechanical structure upon which the electric transmission of power rested. Until late, introducing to a graph for this type of computations was considered worth publishing an article. For example, Professor Fr. Jacobsen of Norway published an article on a diagram for calculating the sag and strain of conductors of overhead lines in the 1946 issue of the *International Conference for Large Electric Systems (CIGRE)*. This sample of articles on graphs added to the innumerable graphs in industrial or academic textbooks on power transmission that were written for a popular or an expert audience.[100]

I may add an example that introduces to the generation of a diagram registering the workings of an electric power network, which also involved computing artifacts that belong to three other classes, namely, a table, a planimeter, and a version of a slide rule—called "parallel slide ruler." It was "a station load diagram," to be produced by "operatives" and to be used by an "average manager." Its author, C. R. Van Trump of the Wilmington City Electric Company, was scheduled to present this diagram at the 24th National Electric Light Association Convention at Niagara Falls (1901). In his absence, the paper was read by somebody else. Trump wished to report the experience of 2 years of use of such diagram, which "has taught a valuable lesson of waste and how to prevent it, of leaks and how to choke them a bit":

> In the present day of great development in all lines of station apparatus, no detail has been so neglected by the average manager as the taking and development of station data; often despised by managers of plants of certain magnitude, some are apparently successful without it, but the station log cannot bear fruit in many ways.
> Important among these is the encouragement it gives to the operatives, firemen and engineers, and other stationmen, who, it must be remembered, are not like "dumb, driven cattle," but do their best work when they know the results of their efforts are recorded to their credit. It is a most healthful sign when the operatives evince great interest in the records.
> On the other hand, central station records are avoided because of cumbersome methods, of the expense of collecting a mass of data, and the work of putting it into intelligent shape:

[100] See H.C. Stanley. 1918, February. Graphical representation of resistances and reactances in multiple. *General Electric Review* 21(2): 133; Charles Carter, Jr. 1963. Graphic representation of the impedance of networks containing resistances and two reactances. *American Power Conference Proceedings* 25: 834–837, and Fr. Jacobsen. 1946. Diagram for calculating the sag and strain of conductors of overhead lines. *CIGRE* 2(214).

and further, unless the work is carried to the greatest detail, the story it unfolds is generally of very doubtful value....

The time required in recording is very slight, as the attendant has many other duties. It is also of great value, as it insures the station of the constant services of the attendant, who must keep wide awake for this service, which is difficult for him to reproduce unless taken regularly from the instruments. All of the work is done mechanically and requires no expert or supervision whatever after the clerk in the office has been drilled in the use of planimeter by which she does the averaging, and the benefit of the work has certainly many times exceeded the cost in arranging instruments and devising methods to take these data.[101]

Van Trump's passage captures the process of generation of a diagram by empirical data. In his book chapter on miscellaneous uses of charts, Allan C. Haskell mentioned the use of diagrams from the other end of the electric power industry, the one that had to do with the effort to sell the electricity produced. He found an "excellent example" of such use of charts in an article published in the June 16, 1917 issue of the *Electrical Review*. It was prepared by the National Lamp Works of General Electric Company of Cleveland. "One of the strong talking points of the electric lighting salesman, when he is required to show economy," explained Haskell, "is the steady reduction in both the cost of electrical energy and the cost of electric lamps." The mode of communicating this point actively shaped its perception. Publicity departments of various central stations have produced curves to argue the same point in the past, but, as Haskell claimed, no set of curves was "as complete and self-contained" as the aforementioned one.[102]

Haskell, who was Principal Assistant with the Construction Service Company, had published a lengthy handbook on how to make and use "graphic charts" in 1919, which was introduced by Richard T. Dana, a Consulting Engineer. "Graphic methods," he stated, "are rapidly superseding older methods" because "[t]hey can accomplish the same results more quickly and with less chance of error than was formerly possible, and they often produce results which are very valuable and which have not been achieved at all by other means." Haskell explained that he had been able to write his book after the publication of a "wealth of material" on graphs in engineering periodicals and technical proceedings "within the last few years." In his introduction, Dana added that, in the preceding years, the use of graphic methods "for accomplishing a great many functions of the engineer" was estimated to have developed "to a most astonishing degree." The publication of the works of d'Ocagne in France and Lipka in the United States were first in Dana's list.[103]

Some of the graphs, had stated Haskell in the preface, have "almost incredible labor-saving features." In elaborating on this statement, he left us with a 1919 presentation of graphs that is similar to Thorton Fry's 1941 presentation of analyzers as "examples of the use of mathematics so as to avoid the use of mathematics" (see Chap. 4): "[i]f mathematics were necessary to the use of charts most of the people now employ them would have been without their help. Charts, then, enable us to do

---

[101] C.R. Van Trump. 1901. A station load diagram. *National Electric Light Association (NELA) 24th Convention*: 363–364, and 368.

[102] Allan C. Haskell. 1919. *How to make and use graphic charts*, 527. New York: Codex.

[103] Ibid., iii–iv and 1.

a great deal of mathematical work without the mathematics." As I argued in inter-preting Fry (see Chap. 4), what we should look for after running into such a seem-ingly schizophrenic sentence by an analyst is the assumption of a second agent, a mathematically unskilled computor: "[n]ow," wrote Dana a few sentences below, "it is a fact that an enormous amount of computation is done graphically without the computer knowing anything whatever about the mathematics of the proceeding; all that is necessary to instruct the novice being to show him a similar chart and indi-cate the results to be achieved."[104]

Proper choice of a graph was important, and so was the sub-choice of the type of paper to use for a graph. Dana's list of the "principal functions," "principal kinds," and "general characteristics" of charts is the most exhaustive that I was able to locate. I thus choose it as an introductory contextualization of nomograms as a class of graphs. Dana's "classes" of the functions of charts and their subclasses included computation—mechanical (arithmetical and geometrical calculations, interpola-tion, calibration, integration), tabulation (statistical comparisons), plotting (sketches, maps, stadia surveys, organization plans and location of buildings and machinery), recording (filing, blue printing, photographic reproduction, statistical comparison), demonstration (for instruction, for advertising), statistical prediction (weather, pop-ulation, vital statistics, etc.), and notations (field notes). Dana's "classes" of kinds of charts included rectilinear coordinates, equally spaced, decimal divisions; rectilin-ear coordinates, equally spaced, other than decimal divisions; rectilinear coordi-nates, unequally spaced, various divisions; logarithmic; semilogarithmic; polar; isometric; trilinear; nomographic or alignment charts; and special forms, ruled and partly. It is indicative of how inclusive Dana was that the aforementioned Section H of the 1914 Exhibition was referring to only two of these kinds, namely, ruled paper and nomograms.[105]

As mentioned earlier in this chapter, following the publication of Lipka's book, d'Ocagne's nomograms were put to use by some US engineers. But many were not as enthusiastic as Lipka, who wrote for analysts. Dana, who was writing for more average engineers, was one of them:

> The alignment or nomographic chart on which the results are read by the application of the straight edge, or the straight line ruled on transparent celluloid, has become quite generally used and has a wide variety of applications. One disadvantage of it is that it has no pictorial value, but for obtaining its results it depends upon the mechanical operation rather than the visual operation performed by the person using it. Professor Lipka says that no charts are so rapidly constructed, nor so easily read, as those of this type, with which statement the writer hardly concur, although enthusiastically acknowledging the great value of these charts for many purposes.[106]

In comparison to the electronic computer of the recent decades, a nomogram of the first decades of the century appeared to be "visual." Hankins writes that "graphs

---

[104] Ibid. On Fry, see Thornton C. Fry. 1941, July. Industrial mathematics. *Bell System Technical Journal* 20(3): 280, and Haskell, *How to make and use graphic charts*, iii.

[105] Haskell, *How to make and use graphic charts*, 2 and 4.

[106] Ibid., 6.

do have limitations," but also "have one great advantage: They give a 'bird's eye view,' *a coup d'oeil*, that integrates an enormous amount of data into a single diagram." In 1919, Dana argued for the exact opposite. Initially, next to other charts, nomograms stood for a drive away from "visual operation."[107]

5.7   "Mention Should Be Made of a Circle Diagram that Picturizes in a Most Simple and Practical Manner"

A class of graphs that afforded visualization were the "circle diagrams," which were very popular in electrical engineering (Fig. 5.2). Steinmetz's "symbolic method" was based on the use of imaginary numbers for numerical calculation. Calculating with a circle diagram was introduced as preferable to the method of Steinmetz when a graphical orientation was necessary. In the early years, the Westinghouse electrical engineers were not eager to adopt the Steinmetz symbolic method of numerical calculation and insisted on graphical calculation. It has been suggested that this might have happened because Westinghouse's chief engineer Benjamin Lamme favored graphical calculation.[108] Oriented more toward economies of scope, in comparison to their colleagues at General Electric who were oriented toward economies of scale, the Westinghouse electrical engineers were less interested in pursuing an aggressive transformation of graphical to numerical calculation.[109] In Westinghouse's reference books on power transmission, until late (1940s), something as little dependent on the mechanization of computing, like circle diagrams, was treated as exhaustively as something that was symbolic of the state of the art in mechanized computing, like the network analyzer.[110]

Special power circle diagrams were constructed to provide with the graphical representation of the power transmission equations. In his academic handbook on electric power transmission, L. F. Woodruff, Professor of Electric Power Transmission at MIT, devoted a whole chapter to the persistently popular circle diagrams.[111] One circle was drawn to give the locus of power at the generation end and another at the distribution end, as the angle between sending and receiving voltage was varied. Aspects of the history of the introduction (1895) and the early use

---

[107] Hankins, Blood, dirt, nomograms: A particular history of graphs: 77.

[108] Ronald R. Kline. 1992. *Steinmetz: Engineer and socialist*, 91. Baltimore: The John Hopkins University Press.

[109] For a general introduction to the relative difference between the mode of production at General Electric and at Westinghouse, see Philip Scranton. 1997. *Endless novelty: Specialty production and American industrialization*. Princeton: Princeton University Press.

[110] Central Station Engineers of the Westinghouse Manufacturing Company, *Electrical Transmission and Distribution Reference Book*.

[111] Woodruff, *Principles of electric power transmission*.

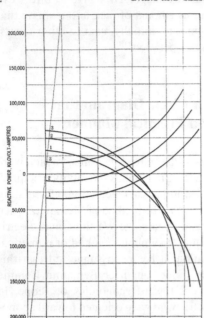

FIG. 6—CIRCLE DIAGRAM FOR 250-MILE TRANSMISSION LINE
This diagram is based on 750,000 cir. mil copper conductors, 21 ft. equivalent spacing, with 220-kv., 3-phase, 60-cycle supply. Circle 1 represents the condition for the receiver voltage equal to the supply voltage. Circles 2 and 3 represent the conditions with the receiver voltage equal to 90 and 80 per cent of the supply voltage respectively. The receiver power circles have their centers below the "X" axis, while the supply circles have their centers above the "X" axis.

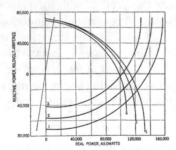

FIG. 7—CIRCLE DIAGRAM FOR 500-MILE TRANSMISSION LINE
This diagram is similar to Fig. 6, except for the increase in transmission distance. Curve 1 represents the receiver circle for a voltage equal to the supply voltage of 220 kv. Circles 2 and 3 represent the conditions with receiver voltages 90 and 80 per cent of the supply voltage respectively.

the circle diagram constants for these lines respectively. All of the previous figures except Figs. 4 and 5 have been plotted from the constants in Table II. The circle diagrams for each line have been plotted in Figs. 6, 7 and 8 for three-voltage conditions, so as to indicate the general shape of the diagram with respect to the voltage power surface. The supply power circle diagrams corresponding to the receiver power circle diagrams are also plotted in Figs. 6, 7 and 8.

Fig. 6 of the 250-mile line corresponds to the usual diagram for a short line indicating the amount of line charging kilovolt-ampere which must be taken care of. The diagram for the 500-mile line, Fig. 7, shows a large amount of charging kilovolt-ampere which completely

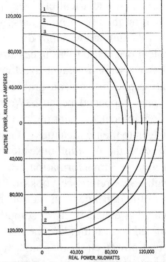

FIG. 8—CIRCLE DIAGRAMS FOR 750-MILE TRANSMISSION LINE
The transmission circuit is similar to that described in Figs. 6 and 7, except that the distance is increased to 750 miles. Circle 1 represents the condition with the receiver voltage equal to 100 per cent of the supply voltage of 220 kv. Circles 2 and 3 represent the diagrams with receiver voltages of 90 and 80 per cent of the supply voltage respectively.

overbalances the load, and requires the regulating equipment to handle very little reactive kilovolt-ampere leading. This illustrates the fact that as the length of line is increased, the voltage power surface is changed with respect to the operating range, so that in the case of the 500-mile line, improving the power factor to leading decreases the voltage at all loads and the operating range is at lagging power factor. This imposes a heavy requirement on the characteristics of the regulating equipment, since it must be designed for heavy lagging loads, and hence high reactance when,

Fig. 5.2 Page with circle diagrams of electric power transmission lines with lengths of 250, 500, and 750 miles in an article by engineers from an electrical manufacturer (R. D. Evans, Westinghouse) and an electric utility (H. K. Sels, Public Service Electric Co. of New Jersey) (1924)

of the circle diagram are described in an available biography of B. A. Behrend. Even though he was mathematically proficient, throughout his rich professional career, Behrend tended to stay more at graphical analysis in order to design electrical machinery, in contrast to Steinmetz who used graphical analysis only for tutorial purposes while coming to favor symbolic analysis for his own creative work.[112] An alternative to Steinmetz's symbolic method, Behrend's circle diagram was not only more suitable to those who were unable to use Steinmetz's complex quantities with. According to a master historian of electrical engineering, the circle diagram had "the additional advantage of providing a visual picture of a fairly complex system of interacting currents, voltages, and magnetic fluxes so that design decisions could sometimes be made without the necessity of the extended numerical calculations associated with the symbolic method."[113]

Over the course of the twentieth century, there was a considerable development of circle diagrams for many aspects of generation, transmission, and distribution of electric power. The advantage of calculating, with, for example, a stability circle diagram, had to do with the fact that, instead of a general calculation of stability, a load was assumed, and then the stability was calculated for this particular load. This had the advantage of providing with a less laborious calculation and the disadvantage of preventing from having a complete picture of the stability-load relationship. A method for obtaining the general circuit constants of transmission and the construction of the power circle diagram from these constants was described by R. D. Evans and H. K. Sels, who were with Westinghouse, at a 1924 AIEE paper (Fig. 5.2). Two years later, General Electric's Edith Clarke presented a paper on calculating the stability of transmission by circle diagrams or, alternatively, graphically or algebraically, by "equivalent circuits," that is, by replacing a complicated transmission structure by an equivalent simple one after applying connecting factors for correction. Just like the handbook by MIT's Woodruff, the aforementioned 1944 Westinghouse handbook on electric power transmission, which was full with references to the celebrated network analyzer, was stuffed with all kinds of the lowly circle diagram.[114]

At the 1948 International Conference of Large Electric Systems, *CIGRE*, P. J. Ryle, who was with the English firm of Merz and McLellan, presented a "circle diagram calculating board." Ryle's paper indicates the persistent popularity of transmission circle diagrams. It also indicates the limits of a definite classification of computing artifacts. Like so many other calculating artifacts, Ryle's circle dia-

---

[112] Brittain, *B. A. Behrend and the beginnings of electrical engineering, 1870–1920*, 142.

[113] Ibid., 139–140.

[114] See Robert D. Evans and H.K. Sels. 1924, February. Power limitations of transmission systems. *AIEE Transactions* 43: 26–38 and 71–103 (discussion); Edith Clarke. 1926, February. Steady-state stability in transmission systems: Calculation by means of equivalent circuits or circle diagrams. *AIEE Transactions* 45: 22–41 and 80–94 (discussion); Woodruff, *Principles of electric power transmission*, chapter VI, and Central Station Engineers of the Westinghouse Manufacturing Company, *Electrical Transmission and Distribution Reference Book*.

gram calculating board was a hybrid product of the combination of several traditions, including the circle diagram tradition and the tradition of calculating boards. The tradition of artifacts called "calculating boards" was much older and broader (see, also, Chap. 4). For example, a 1903 article in the *Electrical Review* was introducing to a "calculator board" as an "improved drawing board and apparatus for facilitating graphic methods of calculation and the like." It was promoted be E. Raymond-Barker as especially suitable to the "electrical localization of faults in submarine cables" and, also, as "adaptable for use in many and varied branches of quantitative research, whether electrical or mechanical, statistical or financial."[115]

In order to be used in fault localization and other electrical methods, the 1903 calculator board comprised "a permanent record of a great many useful curves, from which, by means of two intersecting sets of cursors acting at right angles to each other, calculations based on corresponding formulae may at once solved." This calculator board was advertised as affording "great facilities for graphic methods of calculation, and for the plotting of curves." For example, "[o]wing to the working surface of the board being a somewhat roughened, though transparent, sheet of celluloid, horn, or glass, al pencil lines, whether plotted curves or geometrical figures, remain visible thereon as long as they may be required." Tracing was made from the said pencil diagrams or plotted curves, after which the celluloid working surface could be cleaned "in readiness for fresh pencil work." In other words, just like the computer of the electronic era, the 1903 calculator board was constructed to provide with a stock of stored general-purpose (of what, in today's vocabulary, we could call) software along with the option of special-purpose software construction. Beyond this, the calculator board could be used as an ordinary drawing board, with extra facilities for perfect alignment and for drawings to scale." In fact the reverse side of it was an improved drawing board, promoted as having been "found very useful for drawing to scale, the ruling of equidistant parallel lines on blank paper, the drawing up of electrical summary forms during cable repairs, and many other purposes." A "strong" brass handle and a water-proof cover were adjuncts of the calculator board which rendered it "conveniently portable." "We have great pleasure," concluded the editor, "in being the means of placing before our readers this most ingenious and novel device, which is the fruit of arduous labours on the part of the inventor, and will be the means of saving, to enormous extent, the time and brains of its users."[116]

Yu Wang's computing artifact of the 1910s was quite similar. Patented on November 16, 1915, it was introduced through the pages of the *Engineering News* and the *Electrical Review and Western Electrician* in 1916 and in 1917. The 1916 article was signed by Yu Wang himself, who entitled his piece "The Slide Rule Replaced by A New Computer." The 1917 editorial was entitled "New Parallel-Line

---

[115] See P.J. Ryle. 1948. Practical long line A.C. Transmission line calculations and the design and use of a circle diagram calculating board. *The International Conference on Large Electric Systems*, *12th session* 8, no. 402: 1–12, and E. Raymond-Barker. 1903, August 28. The calculator board and graphic methods. *Electrical Review* 53: 329–331.

[116] Raymond-Barker, The Calculator Board and Graphic Methods: 329–331.

Computer to replace Slide Rule for Rapid Calculations." The instrument was being marketed by the Scientific Devices Company of New York City, of which Wang, a Chinese inventor of mathematical instruments, was the president. There were various versions of it, known as the "Z computer," the "Computing Board," and the "Wang Precision Computer." Based upon "the behavior of a pair of movable parallel lines," its "chief advantages" were supposed to be "its low cost," and the possibility, by "clever" combination of scales, to facilitate the calculation of complex problems by eliminating settings and by providing with that the slide rule was not supposed to provide with.[117]

Like the 1916 authors, Ryle claimed in 1948 that he had designed and constructed "a very convenient" artifact "by which all questions of finding suitable squared paper, choice of scales, and actual labor of drawing are eliminated." His device consisted of a fixed white background on which were engraved the axes of the elementary circle diagram of transmission, parallel vertical lines spaced at inches and tenths of an inch, and a convenient set of power factor lines. Over this background, Ryle laid a transparent celluloid sheet (the cursor), on which was engraved a convenient family of concentric circle arcs. Ryle gave operating and construction instructions, including details on how to overcome the difficulty of adjusting the celluloid sheet to a defined position over the background and to hold it firmly whilst a number of readings were taken. His solution was to build everything on a base that consisted of a small drawing, fitted for convenience and steadiness with back batters and rubber feet on the underside. Containing a number of inscriptions and allowing a number of motions, the artifact was all but simple. Parallel to the one edge of the board was cut a slot. A frame with short lugs (sliding on the upper and lower surfaces of the board for location normal to the surface) that carried hardwood blocks could be moved up and down the edge of the board, being locked thereto by a clamping screw. By means of a spring, the cursor could be set as needed and stay firmly set in position while the necessary readings were taken. The overall arrangement was designed to avoid backlash or shake of the cursor. For more accurate calculation, Ryle recommended an office model to about twice this scale.[118]

Ryle explained that he had preferred his much less costly mechanical circle diagram alternating current calculating board over a network analyzer because it was "generally acknowledged that the most convenient method of obtaining and recording performance figures for a given transmission line is that of the circle diagram," especially for an approximate calculation of a projected line within 1–2% calculating accuracy and for lengths up to 400 miles. For approximate calculation, he expected that by using his computing artifact, "the labour expended and time taken in calculating line performance can very much be reduced." For another line of

---

[117]Yu Wang. 1916, June 15. The slide rule replaced by a new computer. *Engineering News* 75(24): 1120, and Yu Wang. 1917. New parallel-line slide rule to replace slide-rule for rapid calculations. *Electrical Review and Western Electrician* 70(10): 22.

[118]Ryle, Practical long line A.C. Transmission line calculations and the design and use of a circle diagram calculating board: 6.

development of electric power transmission graphs that could be assembled so as to give elementary computing mechanization, I refer to the "graphic table" that Kennelly presented in 1895 and the "transmission line calculator" that Kennelly's student Clarke presented in 1923 (see Chap. 3, Figs. 3.1 and 3.2).[119]

Introducing to nomograms by comparing them to circle diagrams was not uncommon. Circle diagrams were provided along with nomograms in the set of contributions to calculating the regulation of transformers that I sample here. In the *Transactions of the First World Power Conference* (1923), the German professor O. S. Bragstad published an article on the determination of efficiency and phase displacement in transformers by measurement on open circuit and short circuit tests, which included a 15-page-long appendix on constructing and using a nomogram for alternating current calculations. "Technical calculations," explained Bragstad, "are often performed graphically by means of co-ordinate paper with special divisions of the co-ordinates, for instance, logarithmic paper, paper of sine and cosine division, etc." "Lately," he added, "also so-called nomograms have been used for this purpose." The nomographic method, wrote Bragstad, which "depends upon a transformation of the well-known vector diagram," is "supposed to be of some advantage for the numerical solution of different problems of alternating currents." For Bragstad's comparative angle, the nomogram was a more (we would now say) digital ("numerical") and, as such, a less visual (a more detached from a "physical conception") mode of computing than the circle diagram (here vector diagram):

> While the vector diagram is an excellent aid to the physical conception of alternating currents and to the laying down of the equations of an alternating current circuit, it is less adapted to numerical solutions, because the different vectors appear under different angles.
> The vectors, which in the vector diagram are drawn at different angles in relation to two generally right-angled axes, are in the new representation taken as parallel (vertical) lines issuing from a common (horizontal) base line. The direction of the vectors is determined by the position of the foot points of the vectors on the base line, which must accordingly be provided with a corresponding scale. In alternating currents, the vector angles are generally determined by the cosine, and therefore, a cosine scale is adopted to the base line.
> The right-angled axes of the usual vector diagram are in the transformed diagram or nomogram replaced by two parallel lines at right angles to the base line and with foot points on the base line.[120]

Similarly, in introducing to various charts for regulation of transformers in an article that was published in a 1925 issue of the *Journal of the Institution of Electrical Engineers*, Arthur Boelsterli started with a part on a complex alignment chart but added a second part because he thought that "mention should be made of a circle diagram that picturizes in a most simple and practical manner" the same relations.

---

[119] See Ryle, Practical long line A.C. Transmission line calculations and the design and use of a circle diagram calculating board: 1–2; Edith Clarke. 1923, June. A transmission line calculator. *General Electric Review* 26(6): 380–390; and Houston and Kennelly, Resonance in alternating current lines: 133–169.

[120] O.S. Bragstad. 1924a. Determination of efficiency and phase displacement in transformers by measurement on open circuit and short circuit tests. *Transactions of the First World Power Conference* 3: 1021.

A chart for the calculation of transformer efficiency that was copyrighted by J. F. Peters in 1911 and another, more complex one, for calculating the regulation of transformers were included in the chapter on power transformers and reactors of the Westinghouse influential handbook on electric power transmission. For a representative from the business side of computing a transformer's use in electric power transmission, I refer to the simple (three-line) alignment chart for calculating transformer demands for residential areas that was constructed at the Oklahoma Gas and Electric Company. It was presented by Perry Shelley at the 1946 (41st) meeting of the Edison Electric Institute Transmission and Distribution Committee.[121]

More general nomograms on calculating electric power transmission were presented by G. Combet in a 1929 article in the *Revue General de l'Electricite* and by Leonard H. Gussow in a 1946 issue of the *Electrical World*. Gussow, who was with the firm of Albert Kahn Associated Architects & Engineers of Detroit, was interested in calculating voltage drop in industrial alternating current circuits by correlating voltage drop, conductor size, circuit length, and current with line impedance and power factor. Instead of a drafting rule, the alignment in calculating with Gussow's nomogram required a drafting triangle. At the other end, there were also nomograms for as special as a calculating purpose could be. A nomogram for calculating various relay specifications that was offered by the Kurman Electric Company—entitled the "Kurman Calculator"—was covering a full page in the October 1941 issue of *Instruments*. In addition to the nomogram lines, a picture of the relays offered by Kurman and a table guiding to the Kurman relay specifications and their prices was included. It seems to me that this was a handy computing artifact that was intended to promote the Kurman relays through habituation to its use. In this sense, it was similar to the promotional slide rule hybrids discussed in earlier chapters (Chaps. 2 and 3).[122]

The contrast between the two *General Electric Review* articles that I consider below is indicative of the transition from general to special nomograms. The first, written in 1930 by Joergen Rybner who was formerly with the General Electric Research Laboratory, was a general summary of the theory of nomograms and a survey of their use for computing complex hyperbolic functions and for conversion between rectangular and polar coordinates. Sixteen pages long, it is the most inclusive article on nomography that I was able to locate in the electrical engineering press. By the time of the publication of the second article (1948), special uses of nomograms for computing exponential relationships were of more interest. Rybner was invited to translate his article from the official journal of the Danish Institute of

---

[121] See Arthur A. Boelsterli. 1925. Charts for regulation of transformers. *IEE Journal* 63: 692; Central Station Engineers of the Westinghouse Manufacturing Company, *Electrical transmission and distribution reference book*, 407 and 418; and Perry Shelley. 1947, January. The Oklahoma gas and electric company method for load determination on distribution transformers. *Edison Electric Institute Bulletin*: 17–19.

[122] G. Combet. 1929, April 6. Methode Graphique de Calcul des Reseaux de Distribution d' Energie Electrique. *Revue Generale de l' Electricite* 25(14): 535–542; Leonard H. Gussow. 1946, January 5. Calculating voltage drop in industrial A. C. circuits. *Electrical World*: 60–63; and Leonard H. Gussow. 1941, October. Kurman Calculator. *Instruments* 14(10).

Engineers, *Ingenioeren*. The editor of the *General Electric Review* justified this invitation by reference to the increase in computing complexity: "That problems in two variables are solved easily by the slide rule is familiar to all engineers. The facility with which the problems in three or more variables can be solved by suitable nomograms is not so well known." Like Bragstad, Rybner clarified that the one purpose of nomography is "to facilitate numerical computation." As far as presenting engineers with visual analysis—nomography's second purpose—he clarified that it was not an analysis of natural functions but "the properties of mathematical functions" that nomography should "illustrate." The author of the second article was A. H. Canada, who was with the General Electric General Engineering and Consulting Laboratory. Writing about two decades after Rybner, Canada thought of the nomography as special-purpose calculation: "[t]hese [his] and a number of other time-saving nomographs may be devised by engineers for routine calculations involved in various exponential or natural logarithmic relationships, and the possibilities are limited only by the engineer's ingenuity in adapting the nomograph to the specific applications at hand."[123]

5.8 "Time-Honored Graphical Procedures Within a Modern Technical Framework"

One can still find scattered presentations of nomograms in the technical press. Some thermography nomograms for use in connection to overhead power lines (and for many other uses) are mentioned by Richard E. Epperly, G. Erich Heberlein, and Lowry G. Eads in a 1999 issue of the *IEEE Industry Applications Magazine*. Nomographic charts remained popular until very late and book-length treatises on nomography were common. As late as in 1952, three Professors of General Engineering at the University of Illinois were predicting that "[g]raphical and mechanical aids in engineering computations are coming to occupy an ever-increasing field of usefulness. In particular the slide rule, of both standard and special types, and the nomogram have come into prominence." A 1932 nomography book by H. J. Allcock and J. Reginald Jones was edited for a fourth time in 1954, after being revised by J. G. L. Michel. It was eventually accompanied by a book that was focused on engineering, written by A. Giet (1954) and revised and translated by J. W. Head and H. D. Phippen. But, by then, the nomogram was classified differently. For Norman H. Crowhurst, an Engineering Consultant, nomograms were the one of the three basic calculator types, the other two being the slide rule and the graphical chart. The choice of calculator type to construct and use depended on "the adaptability to the formulae or data involved in the calculation or presentation," "the type of user and, possibly, his preferences in relation to calculator type," "the

---

[123] See Joergen Rybner. 1930, March. Nomograms. *General Electric Review* 33(9): 164, and A.H. Canada. 1948, March. Nomographs for computing exponential relationships. *General Electric Review* 51: 48.

precision and range of calculation required, and the nature of the calculation involved," and "the purpose and frequency of use and the location where the calculation or presentation will be used." For Crowhurst, "[G]raphical charts are informative to people who have the mathematical training to make them meaningful, but many lack this training. Nomograms, similarly, require mathematical 'reading' ability and unsettle the nonmathematical."[124]

As with the rest of the computing artifacts considered in this book, nomograms were developed along a transformation that subsumed them under electronic computing. In his 1968 foreword to John H. Fasal's treatise on nomography, Steve M. Slaby, Associate Professor of Graphics at the Department of Civil and Geological Engineering at Princeton's School of Applied Engineering and Applied Science, justified his insistence on nomography by its complementary role to electronic computing: "In many instances the use of the electronic computer in industry to perform certain types of repetitive computations cannot be economically justified. It is here that nomograms may justify this important need." Fasal sought to provide with an algorithm for the design of nomograms. Such algorithms were preparing for the subsuming of nomograms under electronic computing—along with the subsuming of other classes of computing artifacts—which defined electronic computing as such. With his 1964 treatise on nomography, Douglas P. Adams sought to incorporate in electronic computation the "magic and fun" of nomography, which "arrived full blown with d'Ocagne", and the "inner satisfaction that comes with each use of an alignment chart—as though somehow the operator were getting away with something that was quite smart and for which he could claim some portion of the credit."[125]

For his novel "nomographic-electronic computation" and his "NOEL-Nomographic-Electronic computer," Adams needed a new conception of graphs, which stated that wherever numerical value was correlated with space position, a graphical process has occurred. In bringing together "graphical work and modern electronic techniques so as to present time-honored graphical procedures within a modern technical framework," he claimed to have produced "a graphical computing technique which is fast, efficient and not subject to the conventional limitations on accuracy of the old-fashioned method" (Adams 1964, 173). Adams viewed the "nomographic technique as an organization of computation conducive" to be done "*very* quickly by IBM 7094 with oscilloscope output, and other methods." Like the rest of the computing artifacts considered in this book, nomograms were not

---

[124] See Richard A. Epperly, G. Erich Heberlein, and Lowry G. Eads. 1999. Thermography: A tool for reliability and safety. *IEEE Industry Applications Magazine* 5(1 and 3): 28–36 and 8, respectively; Randolph P. Hoelscher, Joseph Norman Arnold, and Stanley H. Pierce. 1952. *Graphic aids in engineering computation*. New York: McGraw-Hill, v; H.J. Allcock. 1950. *The Nomogram: The theory and practical construction of computation charts*. London: Pitman; A. Giet, J.W. Head, and H.D. Pippen. 1956. *Abacs or nomograms: An introduction to their theory and construction illustrated by examples from engineering and physics*. New York: Philosophical Library; and Norman H. Crowhurst. 1965. *Graphical calculators and their design*, 2–4. New York: Hayden.

[125] For Slaby, see Fasal, *Nomography*, v. For Adams, see Adams, *Nomography: Theory and application*, v.

replaced statically by electronic computers. They were dynamically transformed into something that could be integrated into electronic computing.[126]

5.9 Conclusion

Widely used tables and graphs have been an integral part of a broader chain of computing technology. In the context of the perpetual revolution in computing technology that sustained the course of the mechanical and the electrical eras, tables and graphs were not exempted from the complex and never-ending comparisons between and within the various classes of computing artifacts. These comparisons were inseparable from issues of relevance to the political economy of computing: the division of computing labor, the ownership of the means and therefore also of the products of computing, and the foundation of this political economy on the engendering of computing technology (issues that shaped the history of all the computing artifacts considered in the preceding chapters of this book). As for the ideology of presenting computing artifacts as intelligent (important variations between and within classes of graphs and tables aside), it is present in the history of tables and graphs but in a less aggressive version than the ones retrieved in the preceding chapters.

The chapter offers an elaboration on the way issues of relevance to the political economy of computing were manifested—for example, in disagreements concerning the accuracy of tables and graphs. It also elaborates on the issue concerning the normative role of computing artifacts as images that were indispensable in the context of the transformation of the real according to (what prevails socially as) the ideal (symbolic). Calculating with graphs could be central to presenting engineering as beautiful. The chapter offers several examples of debates on the visualization (we would now call it "virtualization") afforded by graphs versus other calculating artifacts or the lack of such virtualization in the case of classes of graphs (e.g., nomographs) that were used when the emphasis was placed on other computing values (e.g., speedy laboring with a nomograph even in the absence of developed skill, based on the highly skillful laboring appropriated and accumulated during the construction of this nomograph).

In comparison to a structure as imposing as that of a top-of-the-line analyzer (Chap. 4) or even a standard calculating machine (Chap. 6), a table and a graph appear to have been as humble as calculating artifacts could be. Yet, the history of comparisons between nomographs and other classes of graphs presents us with sur-

---

[126] See Adams, *Nomography: Theory and application*, 176. For references to the incorporation of graphic representation into electric power analysis by the use of electronic computers, see Don Bissell. 1998, April–June. Was the IDIIOM the first stand-alone CAD platform? *IEEE Annals of the History of Computing* 20(2): 17, and Kristine K. Fallon. 1998, April–June. Early computer graphics developments in the architecture, engineering, and construction industry. *IEEE Annals of the History of Computing* 20(2): 23.

prises. In comparison to other graphs—like circle diagrams, nomographs were usually regarded as sophisticated computing artifacts. Last but not least, from a broader perspective, the development of nomographs was not antithetical to the development of computers as we now define them. In fact the experience of computing with nomographs seems to be one of the many that was fed into that of electronic computing.

References

Allcock HJ (1950) The nomogram: the theory and practical construction of computation charts. Pitman, London

Bedell's F, Crehore AC (1893) Alternating currents: an analytical and graphical treatment for students and engineers. W. J. Johnston Company, New York

Bissell D (1998) Was the IDIIOM the first stand-alone CAD platform? IEEE Ann Hist Comput 20(2):17

Boelsterli AA (1925) Charts for regulation of transformers. IEE J 63:692

Brittain JE (1985) From computor to electrical engineer: the remarkable career of Edith Clarke. IEEE Trans Educ E-28(4):184–189

Brittain JE (2006) Arthur E. Kennelly. Proc IEEE 94(9):1773–1775

Brown JK (2000) Design plans, working drawings, national styles: engineering practice in Great Britain and the United States, 1775–1945. Technol Cult 41(2):195–238

Bush V (1920a) A simple harmonic analyzer. AIEE J 39(10):903–905

Bush V (1920b) Alignment chart for circular and hyperbolic functions of a complex argument in rectangular coordinates. AIEE J 39:658–659

Bush V (1943) Arthur Edwin Kennelly, 1861–1939. Natl Acad Sci Biogr Mem 22:89

Campbell-Kelly M, Aspray W (1996) Computer: a history of the information machine. Basic Books, New York. Chapter 1

Campbell-Kelly M, Croarken M, Flood R, Robson E (2003) The history of mathematical tables: from sumer to spreadsheets. Oxford University Press, Oxford/New York

Carson J (1919) Theory of the transient oscillations of the electrical networks and transmission systems. AIEE Trans 38(1):386

Carter C Jr (1963) Graphic representation of the impedance of networks containing resistances and two reactances. Am Power Conf Proc 25:834–837

Central Station Engineers of the Westinghouse Manufacturing Company (1944) Electrical Transmission and Distribution Reference Book. Westinghouse Electric and Manufacturing Company, East Pittsburgh, pp 612–618

Ceruzzi P (1991) When computers were human. Ann Hist Comput 13(1):237–244

Clark CA (2001) Evolution for John Doe: pictures, the public, and the scopes trial debate. J Am Hist 87(4):1278–1279

Clarke E (1923) A transmission line calculator. Gen Electr Rev 26(6):380–390

Clarke E (1925) Simplified transmission line calculations. Gen Electr Rev 29(5):321–329

Clarke E (1926) Steady-state stability in transmission systems: calculation by means of equivalent circuits or circle diagrams. AIEE Trans 45: 22–41 and 80–94 (discussion)

Clarke E (1943) Circuit analysis of A-C power systems: symmetrical and related components, vol I. Wiley, New York

Clarke E (1944) Trends in power system analysis. Midwest Power Conf Proc 7:177

Combet G (1929) Methode Graphique de Calcul des Reseaux de Distribution d' Energie Electrique. Revue Generale de l' Electricite 25(14):535–542

Croarken M, Campbell-Kelly M (2000) Beautiful numbers: the rise and decline of the British association mathematical tables committee, 1871–1965. IEEE Ann Hist Comput 22(4):44–46

d' Ocagne M (1915) Numerical tables and nomograms. In: Knott GG (ed) Napier tercentenary memorial volume. Longmans, Green, and Company and Royal Society of Edinburgh, London, pp 279–280

Daston L (1994) Enlightenment calculations. Crit Inq 21(1):182–202

Dellenbaugh FS Jr (1921) An electromechanical device for rapid schedule harmonic analysis of complex waves. AIEE J 40(2):142

Dellenbaugh FS Jr (1923) Artificial lines with distributed constants. AIEE Trans 42:803–819

Douglas P (1964) Adams, nomography: theory and application. Archon, Hamden

Dressel Dewit Ewing (1923) Tables of transmission line constants. Purdue University Press, Lafayette

Dwight HB (1925) Transmission line formulas: a collection of methods of calculation for the electrical design of transmission lines, 2nd rev and enlarged edn. Van Nostrand, New York. First edition, 1913

Epperly RA, Erich Heberlein G, Eads LG (1999) Thermography: a tool for reliability and safety. IEEE Ind Appl Mag 5(1 and 3):28–36 and 8

Eugene S (1992) Ferguson, engineering and the mind's eye. MIT Press, Cambridge, pp 151–152

Evans RD, Sels HK (1924) Power limitations of transmission systems. AIEE Trans 43:26–38 and 71–103 (discussion)

Evesham HA (1986) Origins and development of nomography. Ann Hist Comput 8(4):331

Fallon KK (1998) Early computer graphics developments in the architecture, engineering, and construction industry. IEEE Ann Hist Comput 20(2):23

Fasal JH (1968) Nomography. Frederick Ungar, New York

Ferguson E (1989) Technical journals and the history of technology. In: Cutliffe SH, Post RC (eds) In context: history and the history of technology (Essays in Honor of Melvin Kranzberg). Lehigh University Press, Bethlehem, pp 53–70

Franklin MW (1909) Transmission line calculations, part I. Gen Electr Rev 12(9):447–451

Fry TC (1941) Industrial mathematics. Bell Syst Tech J 20(3):280

General Electric Company (1909) Transmission line calculations. *Engineering Department Technical Letter* (no. 309, September 1909 and no. 309A, July 1911). Smithsonian Institution, National Museum of American History, Trade Catalogs Collections, Mezzanine Library, Washington, DC

General Electric Company (1911a) Hydro-electric calculations. *Engineering Department Technical Letter*, no. 316 and 316A (November, 1913). General Electric Archives, Schenectady/New York

General Electric Company (1911b) Tables for transmission line calculations. *Engineering Department Technical Letter*, no. 309-A. Smithsonian Institution, National Museum of American History, Trade Catalogs Collections, Mezzanine Library, Washington, DC

General Electric Company (1911c) Overhead line calculations. *Engineering Department Technical Letter*, no. 318. General Electric Archives, Schenectady

Giet A, Head JW, Pippen HD (1956) Abacs or nomograms: an introduction to their theory and construction illustrated by examples from engineering and physics. Philosophical Library, New York

Graham FD (1932) Audel's new electric library, mathematics-calculations, vol XI. Audel, New York

Gratan-Guinness I (1990) Work for the hairdressers: the production of de Prony's logarithmic and trigonometric tables. Ann Hist Comput 12(3):177–185

Grier DA (1997) Gertrude Blanch of the mathematical tables project. IEEE Ann Hist Comput 19(4):18–27

Grier DA (1998) The math tables project of the work project administration: the reluctant start of the computing era. IEEE Ann Hist Comput 20(3):33–49

Grier DA (2000) Ida Rhodes and the dreams of a human computer. IEEE Ann Hist Comput 22(1):82–85

Grier DA (2007) When computers were human. Princeton University Press, Princeton

Gussow LH (1946) Calculating voltage drop in industrial A. C. circuits. Electrical World 5:60–63

Hankins TL (1999) Blood, dirt, nomograms: a particular history of graphs. Isis 90:71

Hankins TL, Silverman RJ (1995) Instruments and imagination. Princeton University Press, Princeton

Harold Berry C (1921) The chilling of condensate. Power 54(5):182

Haskell AC (1919) How to make and use graphic charts. Codex, New York, p 527

Hawkins N (1895) Handbook of calculations for engineers and firemen. Audel, New York, pp 79–82. and 296

Hawkins N (1897) New catechism of electricity: a practical treatise. Audel, New York, p 331

Heard WL (1946) Coordinated graphic symbols for electric power and control drawings. Edison Electr Inst Bull 14(9):311

Hoelscher RP, Arnold JN, Pierce SH (1952) Graphic aids in engineering computation. McGraw-Hill, New York

Horsburgh EM (ed) (1914) Modern instruments and methods of calculation: a handbook of the Napier tercentenary exhibition. Bell and Sons, London

Houston EJ, Kennelly AE (1895) Resonance in alternating current lines. AIEE Trans 12:139

Imlay LE (1925) Mechanical characteristics of transmission lines II: span formulae and general methods of calculation. Electric J 22(2):part II, 53–57

Jacobsen Fr (1946) Diagram for calculating the sag and strain of conductors of overhead lines. CIGRE 2:214

Kaparetoff V (1923) The 'Heavisidion': a computing kinematic device for long transmission lines. AIEE Transactions 42:42–53

Kennelly AE (1913) A convenient form of continuous-current artificial line. Electrical World 61(24):1311

Kennelly AE (1914a) Tables of complex hyperbolic and circular functions. Harvard University Press, Cambridge, MA

Kennelly AE (1914b) Chart Atlas of complex hyperbolic and circular functions. Harvard University Press, Cambridge, MA

Kennelly AE (1925) The application of hyperbolic functions to electrical engineering problems. McGraw-Hill, New York. First edited in 1912 and reedited in1919

Kennelly AE (1928) Electric lines and nets: their theory and electrical behavior. McGraw-Hill, New York. First edited in 1917

Kirsten FK (1923–1929) Transmission line design, series of publications. University of Washington Press, Seattle

Kline RR (1987) Science and engineering theory in the invention and development of the induction motor 1880–1900. Technol Cult 28(2):283–313

Leonard JN (1932) Loki: the life of Charles Proteus Steinmetz. Doubleday, Doran, and Company, Garden City, pp 148–149

Light JS (1999) When computers were women. Technol Cult 40(3):455–483

Lipka J (1918) Graphical and Mechanical Computation. Wiley, New York

Lubar S (1995) Representation and power. Technol Cult 36(2 Suppl):54–82

Maggi L (1946) The calculation of block foundations for transmission line towers. Int Conf Large Electr Syst (CIGRE) 2(220):1

Rossiter MW (1980) 'Women's work' in science. ISIS 71(258):123–140

Merrill GS (1946) Slide-disk calculator. Gen Electr Rev 49:30–33

Nesbit W (1926) Electrical characteristics of transmission circuits, 3rd edn. Westinghouse Technical Night School Press, East Pittsburgh

Norman H (1965) Crowhurst, graphical calculators and their design. Hayden, New York, pp 2–4

Ocagne M d' (1928) Le Calcul Simplifie par les Procedes Mecaniques et Graphiques, troisieme edition. Gauthier-Villars, Paris

Pender H (1905) Formulae for the wire table. Electric Club J 11(5):327

Pernot DE (1916) Formulae and tables for the design of air-core inductance coils. University of California Press, Berkeley

Pernot FE (1918) Logarithms of hyperbolic functions to twelve significant figures. University of California Press, Berkeley

Pernot FE (1919) Formulae and tables for the design of air-core inductance coils and logarithms of hyperbolic functions to twelve significant figures and an extension of the step-by-step method of transmission line computation. University of California Press, Berkeley

Polachek H (1995) History of the journal 'Mathematical tables and other aids to computation' 1959–1965. IEEE Ann Hist Comput 17(3):67–74

Raymond-Barker E (1903) The calculator board and graphic methods. Electr Rev 53:329–331

Ronald R (1992) Kline, Steinmetz: engineer and socialist. The John Hopkins University Press, Baltimore, p 91

Rosebrugh TR (1919) The calculation of transmission line networks, Bulletin of the School of Engineering Research 1. University of Toronto Press, Toronto

Sakai Y (1905) How to use the slide-rule on the wire table. Electric Club J 11(10):632–633

Schlesinger WM (1892) Power transmission. Electrical World XIX(10):154–155

Schuitema I (1993) The ALRO circular slide rule. J Oughtred Soc 2(2):24–37

Schuitema I (1999) Articles on Dutch contribution to slide rule history in the twentieth century, number 2: F. J Vaes. J Oughtred Soc 8(2):39–42

Scott CF (1905) How to remember the wire table. Electr Club J 11(4):220–223

Scranton P, Novelty E (1997) Specialty production and American industrialization. Princeton University Press, Princeton

Serrell L (1889) Calculations for long-distance power transmission. Electrical World 25:292

Simons DM (1925) Calculation of the electrical problems of transmission by underground cables. Electr J 22(8):366–384

Smith SB (1983) The great mental calculators. Columbia University Press, New York, pp 343–344

Stanley HC (1918) Graphical representation of resistances and reactances in multiple. Gen Electr Rev 21(2):133

Steinmetz CP (1917) Engineering mathematics, 3rd edn Revised and Enlarged edn. McGraw-Hill, New York, p 283

Strange P (1979) Early periodical holdings in the IEE library. Proc IEE 126(9):941–994

Strange P (1985) Two electrical periodicals: the electrician and the electrical review 1880–1890 IEE Proc 132(part A 8):575–581

Svoboda A (1948) Computing mechanisms and linkages. McGraw-Hill, New York

(Tony) Furfari FA (1999) Benjamin Garver Lamme: electrical engineer. IEEE Ind Appl Mag 5(6):13

Walker M (1905) Calculating temperature rises with a slide rule. Electric Club J 11(11):694–696

Wang Y (1916) The slide rule replaced by a new computer. Eng News 75(24):1120

Wang Y (1917) New parallel-line slide rule to replace slide-rule for rapid calculations. Electr Rev West Electr 70(10):22

Warwick A (1994) The laboratory of theory or what's exact about the exact sciences? In: Norton Wise M (ed) The values of precision. Princeton University Press, Princeton, pp 311–351

Wiener AE (1894) Practical notes on dynamo calculation. The Electrical Engineer: 640–641 and 701–703

Wiener AE (1898) Practical notes of dynamo-electric machines: a manual for electrical engineers and a text-book for students of electro-technics. W. J. Johnston, New York

Woodruff LF (1938) Principles of electric power transmission. Wiley, New York, pp 115–116

Bragstad OS (1924a) Determination of efficiency and phase displacement in transformers by measurement on open circuit and short circuit tests. Transactions of the First World Power Conference 3:1021

Kennelly AE (1912) An investigation of transmission line phenomena by means of hyperbolic functions: the distribution of voltage and current over pi artificial lines in the steady state. Electrical World 60(6):306–311

Brittain JE (1989) The evolution of electrical and electronics engineering and the proceedings of the IRE: 1913–1937 and 1938–1962. Proc IEEE 77(6):837–856

General Electric Company (1919) Overhead line calculations, Engineering Department Technical Letter, no. 335D. General Electric Archives, Schenectady

Thielemans ML (1920) Calculs et Diagrammes Des Lignes De Transport De Force A Longue Distance. Comptes Rendus, 1170

Steinmetz CP (with the Assistance of Ernst J. Berg) (1897) Theory and calculation of alternating current phenomena. W. J. Johnston Company, New York

Tympas A, Tsaglioti F (2016) L'usage du calcul à la production: le cas des nomogrammes pour machines-outils au XXe siècle. In Le monde du génie industriel au XXe siècle: Autour de Pierre Bézier et de machines-outils, eds. Serge Benoit and Alain Michel. Collection Sciences Humaines et Technologie, Pôle editorial de l'UTBM, Paris, pp 63–73

Pebble JP (1908) The construction of graphical charts. American Machinist

Schlesinger WM (1982) Power transmission. Electrical World XIX(10):154–155

Van Trump CR (1901) A station load diagram. National Electric Light Association (NELA) 24th Convention: 363–364, and 368

Ryle PJ (1948) Practical long line A.C. transmission line calculations and the design and use of a circle diagram calculating board. The International Conference on Large Electric Systems, 12th session 8(402):1–12

Bragstad OS (1924b) Determination of efficiency and phase displacement in transformers by measurement on open circuit and short circuit tests. Transactions of the First World Power Conference 3: 1021

Shelley P (1947) The Oklahoma gas and electric company method for load determination on distribution transformers. Edison Electric Institute Bulletin: 17–19

Gussow LH (1941) Kurman calculator. Instruments 14(10)

Rybner J (1930) Nomograms. Gen Electr Rev 33(9):164

Canada AH (1948) Nomographs for computing exponential relationships. Gen Electr Rev 51:48

Eads LG (1999) Thermography: a tool for reliability and safety. IEEE Ind Appl Mag 5(1 and 3): 28–36 and 8

Chapter 6
"The Appearance of a Neatly Finished Box"

Contents

6.1   Introduction

The history of computing before the electronic era is frequently reduced to the history of calculating and tabulating machines, which are a posteriori designated as digital and therefore qualify to be considered direct ancestors of our electronic computer. As I perceive it, we face a two-dimensional historiographical challenge. We have to check if it is correct to privilege the history of computing with calculating and tabulating machines when it comes to the mechanical and the electrical eras. At the same time, we have to explain why computing with calculating and tabulating machines emerged as the privileged ancestor of electronic computing. The understudied history of the comparatively limited use of calculating and tabulating machines in engineering offers a contrast that is worth considering when it comes to address the aforementioned challenge. More specifically, in response to the first dimension of the aforementioned challenge, I will in this chapter present evidence that suggests that calculating and tabulating machines were not as important in engineering as we would expect based on the canonical emphasis on these machines as inherently technically superior. On the other hand, in response to the second dimension of this historiographical challenge, I will present evidence that shows that, in comparison to other computing artifacts of the 1914 Exhibition (e.g., in comparison to slide rules), calculating machines were more compatible with the pursuit of the further advancement of the capitalist division-of-computing labor.

The chapter starts with a section that offers an overview of the comparatively limited (e.g., next to a slide rule) use of calculating and tabulating machines in engineering (Sect. 6.2). This is followed by a detailed discussion of two revealing episodes from attempts at introducing the first commercially available calculating machine, the Arithmometer, to computations for electric lines of communication and, later, power (Sect. 6.3). The following section focuses on the political economy of computing with a calculating machine, especially in connection to labor and gender issues. It compares manifestations of these issues in the context of computing with calculating machines and computing with artifacts introduced in preceding chapters (Sect. 6.4). A special section is based on key World Fair and other comparisons between the calculating machine and the slide rule, as well as on comparisons within calculating machines. They were chosen so as to focus on the Arithmometer, which allows us to elaborate on the key difference between a calculating machine and a slide rule: the encasement (blackboxing) of the analog part of a calculating machine, which sharply demarcated between a private-concealed and analog part and a public-displayed and digital (numerical) one (Sect. 6.5). The chapter concludes with influential classifications of calculating artifacts that included calculating and tabulating machines, which were offered just before (just as they prepared for) the emergence of the electronic computer (Sect. 6.6).

6.2 "Cannot Be Altered Until the Operation Has Been Finished"

Over the course of this book, I have referred to the panorama of computing technology offered by the catalog of the 1914 Edinburgh Exhibition.[1] This catalog captures the junction formed by the end of the "long nineteenth century" (Industrial Revolution and French Revolution to World War I) and the beginning of the "brief twentieth century" (from World War I to the end of the Soviet Union).[2] In his infamous 1925 history of mathematics, David Eugene Smith made extensive use of this catalog.[3] Engineering was also influenced by what was exhibited at Edinburgh in 1914. In his influential 1918 MIT handbook of computing technology, MIT's Joseph Lipka referred explicitly to this catalog.[4] For an introductory classification to the class of computing artifacts under consideration in each of the preceding chapters, I have referred to the relevant section of the 1914 Exhibition catalog. The same catalog can also serve in this chapter as an introduction to the computing artifacts that

---

[1] Michael R. Williams. 1982. *Modern instruments and methods of calculation: A handbook of the Napier tercentenary exhibition*, Reprint Edition. Los Angeles: Tomash Publishers.

[2] For the expressions "long nineteenth century" and "brief twentieth century," see Eric Hobsbawm. 1987. *The age of revolution, 1789–1848*. New York: Pantheon; Eric Hobsbawm. 1996. *The age of capital, 1848–1875*. London: Weidenfeld & Nicolson; Eric Hobsbawm.1989. *The age of empire, 1875–1914*. New York: Vintage; Eric Hobsbawm. 1994. *Age of extremes: The short twentieth century, 1914–1991*. London: Michael Joseph.

[3] David Eugene Smith. 1925. *History of mathematics,* vol. II. Boston: Ginn.

[4] Joseph Lipka. 1918. *Graphical and mechanical computation*. New York: Wiley.

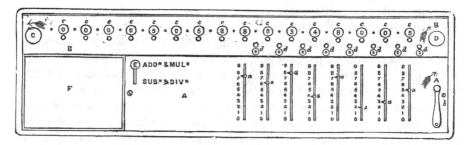

Fig. 6.1 Drawing of the Arithmometer in the Thomas T. P. Bruce Warren article that introduced it to electrical computations (1872)

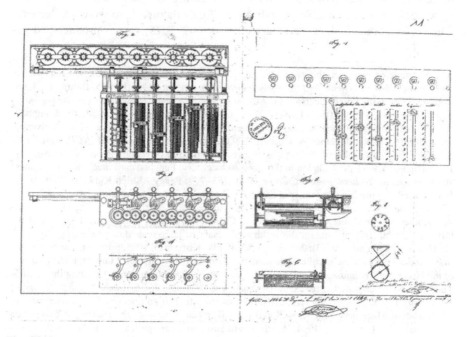

Fig. 6.2 Composite view of the Arithmometer from a French patent drawings (1849)

we now associate with the digital, namely, calculating machines ("mechanical calculators" or "desktop calculators") and tabulating machines (also called "punched card machinery" or "tabulators").

As shown in the preceding chapters of this book (especially Chaps. 2 and 3), at the time of the publication of this catalog, engineers were not excluding slide rules from their conception of calculating machines. This was not the case with the organizers of the 1914 Exhibition. Section D of the 1914 Exhibition described only calculating machines like the Arithmometer (see below, Sect. 6.3) (Figs. 6.1 and 6.2), machines in the tradition of Charles Babbage's calculating engines, and typewriters that could be used as calculating machines. With the addition of tabulating machines, we have everything that is now canonically presented as worthy of being considered as an ancestor to the electronic computer.

The available historiography on calculating machines and tabulating machinery is written mostly from the perspective of their invention and development. When the history of their use is mentioned, the emphasis is placed on stories from the successful introduction of such artifacts in business or state institutional environments, usually in reference to computational work processes that have already been subjected to a developed capitalist division of labor. The use of tabulating machinery by the census bureau of the state and by private financial enterprises (insurance and accounting companies or administration departments of companies like railroads) are some of the most recognizable cases. We also have a number of studies on the successful introduction of such artifacts for scientific computations.[5]

According to an available periodization of calculators, there were six "generations": "handcrafted adders and calculators" (1642–1875), "mass-produced adders

---

[5] For a sample of works on the history of calculating and tabulating machines, see Lars Heide. 2009. *Punched-card systems and the early information explosion, 1880–1945*. Baltimore: Johns Hopkins University Press; Goeffrey D. Austrian. 1982. *Herman Hollerith: Forgotten giant of information processing*, 105–111. New York: Columbia University Press; Martin Campbell-Kelly's contribution to *Computing Before Computers*, William Aspray ed. Ames: Iowa University Press, 1990), Chapter 4; James W. Cortada. 1993. *Before the computer: IBM, NCR, Burroughs, and the industry they created, 1865–1956*. Princeton: Princeton University Press; Arthur Norberg. 1990. High-technology calculation in the early 20th century: Punched card machinery in business and government. *Technology and Culture* 31(4): 753–779; Peggy Aldrich Kidwell. 2000, April–June. The adding machine Fraternity of St. Louis: Creating a center of invention, 1880–1920. *IEEE Annals of the History of Computing* 22(2): 4–21; Friedrich W. Kisterman. 1991. The invention and development of the Hollerith punched card: In Commemoration of the 130th anniversary of the birth of Herman Hollerith and for the 100th anniversary of large scale data processing. *Annals of the History of Computing* 13(3): 245–259; Friedrich W. Kisterman. 1995, Summer. The way to the first automatic sequence-controlled calculator: The 1953 DEHOMAG D 11 tabulator. *IEEE Annals of the History of Computing* 17(2) (): 33–49; Friedrich W. Kisterman. 1997. Locating the victims: The Nonrole of punched card technology and census work. *IEEE Annals of the History of Computing* 19(2): 31–45; Lars Heide. 1991. From invention to production: The development of punched-card Machinery by F.R. Bull and K.A. Knutsen. *Annals of the History of Computing* 13(3): 261–272; Lars Heide. 1994. Punched-card and computer applications in Denmark, 1911–1970. *History and Technology* 11: 77–79, and Lars Heide. 1997. Shaping a technology: American punched-card systems, 1880–1914. *IEEE Annals of the History of Computing* 19(4): 28–41; JoAnne Yates. 1993, Spring. Co-evolution of information-processing technology and use: Interaction between the life insurance and tabulating industries. *Business History Review* 67: 1–51 and Andrew Warwick. 1994. The laboratory of theory or what's exact about the exact sciences?. In *The values of precision*, ed. M. Norton Wise. Princeton: Princeton University Press. For an early account and its more recent reproduction, see George C. Chase. 1952, May. History of mechanical computing. *ACM Proceedings:* 1–28, and George C. Chase. 1980. History of mechanical computing machinery. *Annals of the History of Computing* 2(3): 198–226. For calculating and tabulating machines in scientific computing, see Peggy Aldrich Kidwell. 1990. American scientists and calculating machines: From novelty to commonplace. *Annals of the History of Computing* 12(1): 31–40; Mary Croarken. 1990. *Early scientific computing in Britain*. Oxford: Clarendon Press; Frederik Nebeker. 1995. *Calculating the weather: Meteorology in the 20th century*. San Diego: Academic Press, and Paul A. Medwick. 1988. Douglas Hartree and early computations in quantum mechanics. *Annals of the History of Computing* 10(2).

and calculators" (1875–1935), "low-cost mass-produced adders" (1920–1970), "electrical adders and calculators" (1920–1965), "electronic desktop calculators" (1960–1975), and "handheld LED calculators" (1971–1980).[6] Around the turn of the century, mass-produced calculating machines began to be used in the place of tables, especially for the elementary operations of arithmetic.[7] That the hopeful introduction of calculating machines to engineering was explicitly related to the pursuit of a more developed division-of-computing labor was clear to H. P. Skinner, who introduced himself as "chief computer" at the Surveyor's office in Washington, D. C. In an article entitled "Computing Machines in Engineering," published in the January 7, 1915 issue of the *Engineering News*, he introduced to his 10-year experience with testing various calculating machines for various purposes. In promoting the calculating machine, Skinner was recommending the extension to engineering computations of a mode of production that was explicitly connected to a new political economy of computing:

> The economy of the computing machine is due not only to its extreme rapidity but also to the fact that, by eliminating logarithms and otherwise simplifying calculating the work, it enables a less highly trained and therefore less highly paid man to perform the work. Thus it saves money in two ways: By reducing the time necessary for computation, and by reducing the money cost of the remaining time. The work must, of course, be supervised by a competent computer.

> To be of use to the engineer, a machine must be accurate, rapid, simple in operation, and durable, and its initial cost must not be too high.[8]

I choose to start with Skinner's article because it offers us a rare instance of the promotion of engineering uses of calculating machines and because it was contemporaneous to the 1914 Exhibition. More importantly, I start with Skinner because of his explicitness about the sources of computing value. Skinner analytically separated between two forms of computing value: value from making increased use of computing labor (from "reducing the time necessary for computation") and value from decreasing the value of this labor relatively to that of the computing machine (from "reducing the money cost of the remaining time"). They correspond to what is known as "absolute" and "relative" surplus value, respectively.[9]

The results of some of Skinner's tests, which were based on having tried "eleven different types of machines in various kinds of work, [and on] having performed computations for several branches of the government of the District of Columbia, for private individuals, and for research work," provide us with a good basis for comparisons. Skinner informed that the "initial cost" of machines "available for use of engineers ranged in price from $250 to $450." The "Brunsviga Midget," which he took as his example to "illustrate the application of machine work to engineering

---

[6] For Swartzlander's periodization, see Earl Swartzlander. 1995, Fall. Generations of calculators. *IEEE Annals of the History of Computing* 17(3): 76.

[7] Warwick, The laboratory of theory or what's exact about the exact sciences?, 336.

[8] P.H. Skinner. 1915, January 7. Computing machines in engineering. *Engineering News*: 25.

[9] Karl Marx. 1990. *Capital,* vol. 1. Penguin.

computation" because he had used one for several years, was selling for $275. In the conclusion to his article, Skinner also mentioned a Monroe calculating machine as offering a comparable option.[10]

This was a considerable machine-constant computing capital, beyond the reach of the average engineer. As for the cost of human-variable computing capital, it was presented as rather small.[11] For example, the initial cost of training to use a calculating machine was supposed to be very small. As Skinner claimed in the section on the "simplicity" in operation, "[a]ny clerical worker can learn to operate the machine for all ordinary work with a day's practice, and for all operations within a week."[12] Small was also supposed to be the cost of the maintenance labor. Skinner informed that a machine in constant use in his office for 4 years was "apparently in good condition, and no repairs have been made upon it."[13]

Skinner concluded his article by stating that he had found "Loomis' Logarithms of service in machine work, as this publication contains, in addition to the logarithms, the natural functions to 6 places of decimals, and 1-min. intervals, with means for interpolation, a feature lacking in most tables of natural function in use among engineers." The cost added by the purchasing of this handbook of logarithmic tables was only $1. The fact that a calculating machine was about 400 times more expensive than a book of cost above the average suggests that a calculating machine was quite costly: an investment equal to 400 handbooks was—and still is—considerable.[14]

Skinner claimed that "[i]t is impossible for the machine to give an incorrect result except by breaking down completely." He claimed so in the section on the "accuracy" of calculation, after emphasizing that "[a] number once set upon the machine cannot be altered until the operation has been finished, so that the operation indicated upon the machine is the operation that has been performed."[15] This was an important feature because, among other things, it sought to address the major concern of the mechanization of computing work throughout capitalist modernity, namely, the unintentional—or, worse, the intentional—alteration of the accuracy of the computation by a human computer.

By way of reminding about the centrality of this concern, I refer to Babbage's contemplation of a calculating machine that could "stop itself, and ring a bell" so as to draw the attention of its "attendant" in case of an unintentional error, whereas a "louder bell" would ring so as to draw the attention of its "guide" in case of an intentional mistake. "Knowing the kind of objections" that his countrymen could make to the invention of such machine, Babbage had proposed to himself the inquiry of the possibility of an analytical engine that could work unaffected by an attendant

---

[10] Skinner, Computing machines in engineering: 27.

[11] For the introduction of the differentiation between "constant" and "variable," capital, see Karl Marx, *Capital*, vol. 1.

[12] Skinner, Computing machines in engineering: 25.

[13] Ibid., 25.

[14] Ibid., 27.

[15] Ibid., 25.

who, "without breaking the machine," could "stop the machine in the middle of its work, whenever he chooses, and as often as he pleases" so as to "be at liberty" to occasionally "falsify as many numbers as he pleases." In this sense, Babbage contemplated a calculating machine that could literary run by itself, thereby turning the calculating worker into an "attendant." Similarly, "chief computer" Skinner's 1915 description of the accuracy of the calculating machine implied that the low-paid computors-clerks-attendants who were to be employed in engineering computations could not affect the accuracy of it without breaking it down completely.[16]

Being treated as the privileged ancestor of the electronic computer, the calculating machine is usually described as sharing with it the principle of being constructed as a general-purpose machine. Historians have just started to acknowledge that the electronic computer has not been a general-purpose machine to start with. For comparable initial investment, some electronic computers were actually more suitable to some purposes and other electronic computers to other purposes, depending on, for example, their differences in terms of internal organization of work ("computer architecture") or in terms of the external organization of their relationship to the human computing worker ("interface"). A history of the differences of the various calculating machines according to their intended use could provide help toward interpreting computating as a socially situated and therefore special purpose process.

In our example, Skinner admitted that there were actually computing purposes that were served better by "handwork" that by the calculating machine under consideration. In the section on rapidity, he mentioned tests that he made that had shown that "the machine is about six times as rapid in multiplication as hand work," and in division "seven times as rapid as hand work, requiring also much less time in checking." On the other hand, the machine was only "somewhat superior" in addition. Worse, in subtracting one number from another hand work was best. The machine was "more rapid" only in subtracting a number from a cluster of other numbers.[17]

Calculating machines were unfavorably compared to analyzers in regard to state-of-the-art calculations, like the ones concerning the stability of electric power

---

[16] See Charles Babbage. 1851. *The exposition of 1851: Views of the industry, the science, and the Government of England*. London: John Murray, 170. For an introduction to Babbage's machines, see Allan Bromley's contribution to *Computing before computers*, William Aspray ed., Chapter 2. For historical works that contain insightful links between the technical division-of-labor in Babbage's infamous writings on calculating engines and the social division of labor in Babbage's equally infamous writings on the society that he lived, see Gordon L. Miller. 1990. Charles Babbage and the design of intelligence: Computers and society in 19th-century England. *Bulletin of Science, Technology, and Society* 10: 68–76, and Simon Schaffer. 1994, Autumn. Babbage's intelligence: Calculating engines and the factory system. *Critical Inquiry* 21(1): 203–227. See also the entries by Simon Schaffer, Doron Swade, and Francis Spufford. 1996. *Cultural Babbage: Technology, time, and invention*, ed. Francis Spufford and Jenny Uglow. London: Faber and Faber.

[17] See Skinner, Computing machines in engineering: 25. For the dependence of electronic computing on use (purpose), see Richard E. Smith. 1989. A historical overview of computer architecture. *Annals of the History of Computing* 10(4): 277–303, and Eloina Pelaez. 1999, June. The stored program computer: Two conceptions. *Social Studies of Science* 29(3): 359–389.

transmission networks. In his 1921 survey, MIT's Frederick Dellenbaugh, Jr. compared a Marchant calculating machine favorably to a slide rule but found that the use of his analyzer was preferable to both.[18] After being trained to use only a slide rule in school, electrical engineer Edwin L. Harder worked with an electrically powered Marchant calculating machine for extensive but routine Westinghouse calculations on railroad electrification projects of the 1930s. Soon, however, in the process of becoming an analyst, he turned to network analyzers and the like described in a preceding chapter of this book (Chap. 4).[19] According to a 1944 comparison of network analyzers and calculating machines by the editor of the *Westinghouse Engineer*, network analyzers (also called "network calculators") had saved the day when the limits of calculating machines became apparent (Fig. 4.2):

> Engineers have a penchant for mathematics—so it is commonly believed. Yet the calculating board, often called the network calculator, was the result of a desire to solve problems with the least mathematics. When the plans for the electrification of the Virginian railroad were drawn, in the middle '20s, two crews of three men each worked several months with a battery of adding machines making the necessary calculations of short-circuit currents, voltage regulation, and telephone interference for the almost endless combinations of circuits and loads. Each team worked furiously for a couple of weeks and then spend the next week or so checking the results of the other team. With other railroad electrifications in the offing, with power systems growing so large and so complex in their interconnection, the solution of power-systems problems by mathematics was becoming a monumental task and in many cases utterly hopeless. Electrical systems threatened to become a Frankenstein out of control unless some simpler means of solving their involved problems was concocted. This led to the a-c calculator, first completed in 1929.[20]

I was unable to locate any argument to replace network analyzers by calculating or tabulating machines before the mid-1940s. L. A. Dunstan, an engineer in the Electrical Division of the Bureau of Power at the Federal Power Commission, was perhaps the most influential of those few who contemplated the "machine computation of power performance" or "machine computing of networks," by which he meant that artifacts like the network analyzer could be replaced by tabulating machinery. Dunstan's ideas attracted the attention of the community of the electronic computer. But by the time that we have the first (Dunstan's) attempts at replacing a network analyzer by a tabulating machine, both computing with tabulating machines and calculating with network analyzers were being absorbed by

---

[18] See Frederick, S. Dellenbaugh, Jr. 1921, February. An electromechanical device for rapid schedule harmonic analysis of complex waves. *AIEE Journal*: 135–144. For the Marchant calculating machine, see Peggy Aldrich Kidwell and Paul E. Ceruzzi. 1994. *Landmarks in digital computing: A Smithsonian pictorial history*, 36. Washington, DC: Smithsonian Institution Press, and several passages in Cortada, *Before the computer: IBM, NCR, Burroughs, and the industry they created, 1865–1956*.

[19] See, William Aspray. 1994. Calculating power: Edwin L. Harder and analog computing in the electric power industry. In *Sparks of Genius: Portraits of electrical engineering excellence*, ed. Frederik Nebeker, 163–164 and 194. New York: IEEE Press.

[20] "Network Calculator...Mathematician Par Excellence", *Westinghouse Engineer* 4 (July, 1944), editorial.

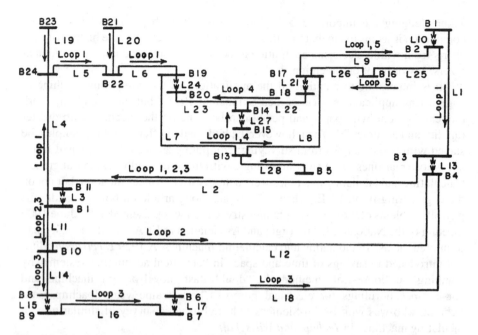

Fig. 6.3 Sample master diagram for machine computation of power network performance by L. A. Dunstan (1947a)

electronic computing. The substitution of tabulating machines for the network analyzers was by then therefore meaningless to start with.[21]

As it has been insightfully shown, there was important continuity between the architectural structure of the tabulating machines of the mid-1930s and the stored program electronic computer of the mid-1950s.[22] But that was not the only continuity. I find it very suggestive that when Dunstan sought to promote the use of tabulating machines for the computation of electric power analysis he relied on the tradition of the equivalent of "flow diagrams" or "flow charts" (the nucleus of electronic computing "programs") accumulated in calculating with the network analyzer (for a sample, see Fig. 6.3).[23] Put it in our vocabulary, we would say that the continuity in flow diagrams points to a continuity between the analog of the hardware of the network analyzer and the software of the digital calculating machine. As we start

[21] See L.A. Dunstan. 1947a. Machine computation of power network performance. *AIEE Transactions* 66: 610–620 and 621–624 (discussion), and L.A. Dunstan. 1947b, September. Machine computing of networks. *Electrical Engineering*: 901–906. For a similar case, see Philip D. Jennings, and George E. Quinan. 1946. The use of business machines in determining the distribution of load and reactive components in power line network. *AIEE Transactions* 65: 1045–1046.

[22] Paul Ceruzzi. 1997. Crossing the divide: Architectural issues and the emergence of the stored program computer, 1935–1955. *IEEE Annals of the History of Computing* 19(1): 5–12.

[23] Dunstan, Machine computation of power network performance: 611 and 613, and Machine computing of networks: 904.

acknowledging the importance of "flow charts" through perceptive histories of computing, it seems to me that that this continuity, which extends the history of flow charts from within electronic computing to between electronic computing and analyzers, is worthy of our attention.[24]

"It is impossible to mention all the applications of the computing machine to engineering applications," had argued Skinner in 1915, "but in general any work that can be done with paper and pencil can be done on the machine with greater rapidity and accuracy."[25] When, however, he had tried to offer specific examples, he stayed with two examples from surveying: computing adjacent lots of equal frontage whose rear lines make an oblique angle with the street and working out grades. Calculating and tabulating machines were actually used in electrification, but not on the engineering front. W. E. Freeman's 36 page long article on how to handle the payroll problems of the electric light industry, which was presented at the June 1909 meeting of the National Electric Light and Association (NELA) in Atlantic City, had promoted the use of tabulating and calculating machines. A 1929 *Electrician* editorial introduced to savings of time and space in "electrical accounting systems" by combing the "loose-leaf" method, the "double-fast" novel posting machine, and some "special rulings for electrical purposes." The same year, Joachim Hans Schultz, who was with Berlin-Siemensstadt, published a survey of similar uses of tabulating machines in *Technik und Wirtschaft*.[26]

I was able to locate only a few peripheral attempts at introducing calculating and tabulating machines to engineering and other technical computation. In 1943, Everett Kimball, Jr., at his capacity as Technical Advisor of the Machine Tabulating Division of the Bureau of the Census in Washington, D. C., wrote a pamphlet that was entitled "A Fundamental Punched Card Method for Technical Computations." This tabulating method became known as the "Kimball Method," particularly in the aircraft field where it was used. It was developed by Kimball at the Bureau of the Census at the request of E. F. Critshclow of the Vibration and Flutter Unit, CAA, in order to simplify their computational work. Kimball "intended to introduce the scientist to a fundamental method of punched card calculating; and also to provide tabulating technicians with an introduction to scientific computational methods, as well as a detailed means for performing specific fundamental operations." His was more of an effort to make the technology of punched card computation more scientific rather than a method for engineering and other technical computations. Kimball claimed that tabulating methods could "reduce the amount of skilled labor required," but he acknowledged that "such methods sometimes are not as economical financially as classical manual methods." For Kimball, it was only when the computation

---

[24] Nathan Ensmenger. 2016. The multiple meanings of a flowchart. *Information and Culture: A Journal of History* 51(3): 321–351.

[25] Skinner, Computing machines in engineering: 27.

[26] See W.E. Freeman. 1909. Pay-roll problems in the electric light industry. *NELA* 32nd Convention 3: 74–119; W.E. Freeman. 1929, November 15. Electrical accounting systems. *Electrician* 103: 598, and Joachim Hans Schultz. 1929, February. Lochkartenverfahren und Mitlaufende Kalkulation in der Elektrotechnischen Industrie. *Technik und Wirtschaft* 22: 41–45.

had to do with a long series of computations that machine tabulation was advantageous.[27]

Historians of calculating and tabulating machine manufacturers have argued that from the point of view of executives of IBM and Remington Rand, the scientific and engineering users were incidental to commercial ones.[28] This limited interest cannot be attributed only to the cost of these machines. After all, some engineers computed by analyzers that were even more expensive than calculating and tabulating machines. In my opinion, we cannot understand why most interwar engineers never developed a taste for calculating and tabulating machines without knowing what it was that they actually preferred to compute with. As we saw in the preceding chapters, the electrical engineering community had some unique requirements that could only be satisfied by developing expensive artifacts like the analyzers (Chap. 4). When engineers had to use a standard computing artifact, they preferred the inexpensive slide rules over the expensive calculating machine because it allowed them to maintain ownership of the computing artifact (Chap. 3).

There was actually some interest by manufacturers in promoting their calculating and tabulating machines to engineers. I will consider the example of the comptometer, which was one of the first practical calculating machines, and maybe the most popular desktop calculator between 1887 and 1902.[29] For the following two decades, the U.S. Navy standardized on the comptometer the mathematics required to design warships. At the time, its manufacturer, the Felt & Tarrant Manufacturing Company of Chicago, was competing with Burroughs for creating new markets. Copyrighted by Felt & Tarrant in 1914 and 1920, the 1920s first revised edition of *Applied Mechanical Arithmetic As Practiced on the Controlled Key Comptometer* was a volume of over 550 pages that reads both as an instruction manual and as a trade catalog. It contained distinct chapters on "electrical" and "engineering" applications of the comptometer. "The volume, variety, and peculiarity of the work in the engineering field," we read in the introductory page to the chapter on engineering, "called for a special machine,—one that would add and accumulate feet, inches and fractions of an inch in the one operation. Mr. Felt designed the 'Engineering Model,' shown in the opposite page, to meet these requirements. The model is especially adapted to the use of Architects, Building Contractors and Steel Fabricators, as well

---

[27] For Comrie, see L.J. Comrie. 1932. The applications of the Hollerith tabulating machine to Brown's tables of the moon. *Royal Astronomical Society Monthly Notices* 92(7): 694–707 and L.J. Comrie. 1944, August. Recent progress in scientific computing. *Journal of Scientific Instruments* 21: 129–135, and L.J. Comrie. 1946. The application of commercial calculating machines to scientific computation. *Mathematical Tables and Other Aids to Calculation* 2(16): 149–159. For Eckert, see W.J. Eckert. 1984. *Punched card methods in scientific computation*. Cambridge, MA: MIT Press. For Kimball, see Everett Kimball, Jr. *A fundamental punched card method for technical computations*, 1. Washington, DC: Bureau of the Census, Machine Tabulation Division, ca. mid-1940s.

[28] See Cortada, *Before the computer: IBM, NCR, Burroughs, and the industry they created, 1865–1956*, 136.

[29] Ibid., 39–41.

as to the Engineering Profession."[30] The "engineering comptometer" was ideologized as infallible:

> Soon after installing one of the Engineering Models, a prominent Chicago Architect had
> occasion to check a set of building plans containing a large number of detailed measure-
> ments. The work had been revised and two mental checkers and passed as correct. *But the
> Comptometer uncovered a dozen of more errors*; thus, as a *safeguard against mistakes*, the
> Comptometer was proven invaluable (emphasis in the original).[31]

A list of some hopeful uses of the "engineering or fractional model comptometer" by mechanical, civil, and architectural engineers was added, followed by several pages with examples and tables for use with the "engineering model
comptometer." The following example was offered as a typical example of savings
in computing labor: "[a] designer in the bridge department of a Western railroad
does three times as much work with the 12 column comptometer as by any other
method—and with accurate results." All of the examples described a sequence of
simple processes and settings for the calculation of simple formula. This was computing work for a computor-clerk, not for an analyst engineer. The exception of
examples from electrical engineering computations is noticeable. Electrical engineering computations were also excluded from the chapter on "electrical" uses,
which started with a detailed list of "where and how time is saved by the Comptometer
on electrical accounting work."[32]

The examples of the use of the comptometer mentioned referred mostly to computations based on the four basic operations by using tables from records like
monthly summaries of output, losses, consumption, and coal consumption. The
broad range of uses mentioned suggests that this calculating machine was promoted
as suitable for every computational work within electrification. To a non-engineer,
the link between a calculating machine and electrification seemed generally sponta-
neous. On the other hand, nothing in these two chapters could make an electrical
engineer to recommend the use of the comptometer in order to compute phenomena
as complex as the stability of electric power transmission. Noticeably, promoters of
calculating and tabulating machines tried hard to present them as electrical machines.
The comptometer catalog had to include a chapter on "electrical" uses even if the
uses mentioned were typical of the heydays of the mechanical era. In comparison to
an artificial line and a network analyzer (Chap. 4), calculating and tabulating
machines were not exemplars of an electrical computer. Their defining parts— those
that were constructed so as to materialize the computing analogy—consisted of
mechanical or, at best, electromechanical components.[33]

---

[30] For the comptometer catalog, see *Applied mechanical arithmetic as practiced on the controlled
key comptometer* (Smithsonian Institution, National Museum of American History, Mezzanine
Library, Trade Catalogs Collection), 239.

[31] Ibid.

[32] Ibid., 243 and 229.

[33] Ibid.

6.3 "The Miscalculation of Mains"

The rapid development of mass-produced calculating machines in the last parts of the nineteenth century was due, primarily, to wider commercial and bureaucratic purposes. We know that calculating machines were also tried in scientific computations.[34] The 1872 episode that we are about to consider adds the perspective of attempts at the introduction of these machines to the history of computing for engineering purposes.

It makes it all the more convenient that the 1872 telegraph engineers were discussing "electrical computations." The topic was stated in the title of the paper read by Thomas T.P. Bruce Warren, an electrician to Hooper's Telegraph Works, during the Fourth Ordinary General Meeting of the Society of Telegraph Engineers, on Wednesday, April 10, 1872: "On the Application of the Calculating Machine of M. Thomas de Colmar to Electrical Computations." The president of the society, C. W. Siemens, was chairing the meeting. Major General Hannyngton, who became known from his promotion of the Arithmometer against the celebrated table-maker Edward Sang, was present. In fact, Warren acknowledged that he was inspired to write his paper by Hannyngton. Mr. W. A. Gilbee, of South Street, Finsbury, the agent of the Arithmometer, had placed two such machines before the meeting. Warren's article started with an outline of the structure of the Arithmometer, repeated after a review of one of Hannyngton's articles which appeared in the *Engineer*, on May 20, 1870.[35]

The bulk of the article was about how to adjust the Arithmometer to "electrical computations" and "electrical computations" to the Arithmometer. Formulas and associated processes of electrical computation had to be modified so as to "admit machine assistance." In turn, the machine had to be operated in a modified manner. "In dealing so minutely with these numerical operations," Warren wrote, "my apology must be that the short cuts so familiar to us in calculating are extended to the machine, and that they are only developed by an acquaintance with its workings." The machine, he clarified, "requires peculiar methods, and in operating with it we have to present our formulae in a condition suited to its ready performance."[36]

Warren included several tables of computations produced by trying to follow this principle, along with some comparisons of how much labor was saved by the use of the Arithmometer. Computations considered "irksome and monotonous even to the most ardent admirer of figures" could now be performed not only with simple "rapidity," although additionally, in a manner which was "strictly and mechanically accurate." "Each of the tables accompanying this paper," boasted Warren, "represents

---

[34] See Warwick, The laboratory of theory or what's exact about the exact sciences?, 313.

[35] See Thomas T.P. Bruce Warren. 1872. On the application of the calculating machine of Thomas De Colmar to electrical computations. *Journal of the Society of Telegraph Engineers* 2: 141–169. For Hannyngton, see Warwick, The laboratory of theory or what's exact about the exact sciences?.

[36] Bruce Warren, On the application of the calculating machine of Thomas De Colmar to electrical computations: 145 and 164.

one hour's work on the Machine at full power, the results being recorded only with as many figures as in practice will be required." To draw such comparisons, Warren excluded from his account, among other things, both the capital required to modify the operation of the calculating machine and the formulas, and the capital required to purchase a calculating machine (as opposed to buy the paper and the pen needed for the same computations). "The object of my bringing this [his paper] before you," wrote Warren in his last paragraph, "rests on the assurance that the first step to be taken in bringing electrical testing within the limits of exact science must be to reduce the mental drudgery of calculating, for we must admit that the time occupied in testing bears a small proportion to the time spent on working out the results."[37]

Electric networking "had so much to do with calculations of an intricate kind" stated Siemens in opening the floor to discussion. "The more he had seen and heard about it the more he was satisfied the subject [using the Arithmometer] was one of great interest to Telegraph Engineers." Hannyngton was the first to speak. We get an idea of how much labor power was required to learn how to make proper use of the machine by considering that, as he admitted, after having used the machine for many years "he still regarded himself a learner." He also stated that "(I)t might require some ingenuity to adapt the machine to the various purposes to which it could be applied." To explain, however, why he "had no doubt of its value in electrical computations," he switched perspective. "They all knew," he claimed, "that even where calculations were not of an arduous nature, or such as to occasion any great strain upon the mind, after some hours' work the head would get weary, whereas this machine always remained perfectly cool." The majority of the discussants seized the opportunity to give impressive numbers of comparative savings, albeit, from different computing contexts. Peter Gray, to whom Hannyngton lent one of his Arithmometers for some weeks, thought that it required "some consideration as to the best way in which the formulae could be put." Perhaps, he added, "the most obvious way of proceeding was not always best for the machine." To find out the various applications, and apply them in the best manner, required "a scientific arithmetician." The discussion also revealed some doubts as to how "perfectly cool" the machine always actually was. There seemed to have been a problem with the machine getting out of order due to the springs.[38]

A comment made by another discussant connected the ideologizing of the Arithmometer as intelligent to the political economy of computing with it by referring to human computors:

Colonel WALKER, Superintendent of the Grand Trigonometric of India, (responding to the President's invitation) said hitherto he had not used this machine, because in India he had such a large number of computors, who could be obtained at comparatively small wages, he had had no necessity to do so; but since he had been in England he had not had equal facilities in the shape of computers. He had borrowed one of General Hannyngton's machines, which saved him a great deal of labour and gave accurate results. He was thinking of

---

[37] Ibid., 145–146 and 164.
[38] Ibid., 164–168.

employing it in India, where, notwithstanding they could get native computers who were very skillful, he thought it could be used with advantage.[39]

The motivation for introducing an Arithmometer, as Walker explained, was not simply one of pursuing a profit by replacing computing workers by a calculating machine, especially considering that this required a considerable capital—the majority of the discussants had, up to then, relied on Hannyngton to borrow an Arithmometer. Moreover, the profit was not to be produced by relying on the calculating machine in order to devaluate the computing labor power by deskilling it—Walker was explicit about using skilled "computors." Finally, one was not motivated by any necessity in order to accumulate the capital required in order to purchase and install a calculating machine—in India, as Walker explained, there was no such necessity because there was abundant inexpensive computing labor power. We will have to borrow the concept of "surplus value," which Karl Marx had introduced a little earlier, in order to grasp the prime mover of the attempt to introduce the Arithmometer to electrical computations. Walker was not talking about a liberal market exchange of equal values: "equal" to a calculating machine, "facilities in the shape of computers." As he clearly explained, he was interested in producing an "advantage," i.e., surplus computing value. Capitalist computing was not determined by exchange of equally valued commodities. It was determined by surplus value production that was based on the inequality between the value paid to the computor and the value in which his product is exchanged. This is exactly what Colonel Walker was interested in producing, by employing the abundant and skilled Indian computing labor.[40]

The episode adds the perspective of engineering in order to confirm what has already been insightfully observed regarding the labor involved in expanding the use of calculating machines from commerce to science, namely, that "increasing the scope and reliability of techniques of calculation requires labor," and, second, that "increased speed and accuracy will involve increased work."[41] It was only around the turn of the century that calculating machines began to be used in the place of tables, especially for the elementary operations of arithmetic.[42] It was not before the late 1890s that an Arithmometer could be used to undertake calculations themselves, not just to compute tables. To use relatively standard computing machinery required the relative standardization of electric power transmission, i.e., its relative mathematization. In the words of Warren, it required an engineering theory of electrification that was relatively more of an "exact science." The use of the Arithmometer to electric lighting and power network computations came along the professionalization of electrical engineering through its connection to science. This took place parallel to the emergence of electrical engineering, which incorporated in its subjects telegraphic communication, but also electric lighting (and, very soon, also, power).

[39] Ibid., 167.

[40] On the concept of surplus value, see Karl Marx, *Capital,* vol. 1.

[41] Warwick, The laboratory of theory or what's exact about the exact sciences?, 317.

[42] Ibid., 336.

In this context, the Arithmometer was one of the two calculating machines recommended by Joachim Teichmuller in 1893 as alternatives to the slide rule, for the purpose of solving the complex mathematical system (including as many as 30 equations) that one would arrive at by following his mode of computing an electric lighting and power transmission network.[43] As we shall immediately see, Teichmuller thought that a calculating machine ought to be used when the accuracy of the slide rule was not adequate. The resistance to Teichmuller's recommendation can help us elaborate on why the pioneers of the electric lighting network chose (what we now call) analog over digital computing—we know that for the calculation of his pioneering electric network (that at downtown New York), Thomas Edison brought in an expert in the slide rule and did not consider a calculating machine, but asked this expert to construct a miniature electric network, building on his previous exposure to artificial communication lines.[44]

Teichmuller's recommendation drew an ironic British editorial response, which was immediately answered by the German side. The detailed study of the German-English computing debate can also shed light on the years when the calculation of an electric network was becoming an activity that defined a chief electrical engineer as such. The German author protested against the empiricist irony launched against him by the English speaking world in the form of the charge that "nice calculation of mains is no doubt a pleasant pastime for mathematicians" by clarifying that "systematic calculation of mains is being carried out, not only by mathematicians, but more especially by electrical engineers engaged in practical work."[45]

Teichmuller referred explicitly to the Arithmometer in his 1893 article. The other calculating machine that he named was that of "Professor Selling." The Arithmometer was much more important at the time. In his 1925 survey of calculating machines, Ernst Martin devoted more space to the description of the Arithmometer than on any other calculating machine. By contrast, Selling's calculating machine was described very briefly. It dated back to 1886 and its distinct feature was the avoidance of "the tiresome turning of the crank, and the jerky tens-carry" by the incorporation of a mechanism known as the Nuremberg shears. Unlike the Arithmometer, neither the original calculating machine of Professor Dr. E. Selling of Wurzburg nor the larger calculating machine that he constructed later assumed much importance (the larger machine was electrically driven and with a mechanism for printing made by H. Welzer in Pfonten). Their manufacture was discontinued. Martin identified a sample of each in the Deutsches Museum in Munich.[46]

---

[43] See Johachim Teichmuller. 1893, September 15. Ueber die Stromvertheilung in Elektrischen Leitungsnetzen. *Elektrotechnische Zeitschrift* 37: 540.

[44] Aristotle Tympas. 2001. The computor and the analyst: Computing and power, 1870s–1960s. PhD diss., Georgia Institute of Technology, Atlanta, Chapter 2.

[45] See The miscalculation of mains. *The Electrician* (February 9, 1894): 384–385, and Johachim Teichmuller. 1894, March 16. The calculation of mains. *The Electrician*: 560–561. For the history of the journal *The Electrician*, see P. Strange. 1985. Two early periodicals: The electrician and the electrical review, 1880–1890. *IEE Proceedings* 132, part A(8): 575–581.

[46] See Ernst Martin. 1992. *The calculating machines: Their history and development*, 96–97. Cambridge, MA: MIT Press.

The bulk of Teichmuller's 1893 article was devoted to how one could analyze a network of electric lines so as to equate it to a linear system of first-degree mathematical equations. The mode of his analysis was based on adjusting the solution of an abstract system of mathematical equations to a system of mathematical equations best representing an electric distribution network. To do so, he started by selecting from the available work of professors of mathematics and he settled for some improvements that Professor Mehmke stated in his letters to Professor Nekrassof. Teichmuller was arguing for the coextensive constitution of electrical engineering and a mode of computing a distribution network which included the use of an Arithmometer. Warren recommended the Arithmometer for the computation of tables. Teichmuller recommended its use in order to undertake calculations themselves.[47]

This mode of computing was immediately attacked in an 1894 editorial of *The Electrician* entitled "The miscalculation of mains." By attacking directly the German mode of computing an electric transmission network as "superfluous," the British editorial indirectly attacked more local targets. "The diagrams and calculations which Prof. Forbes has more than one described," wrote the British editor, "serve to elucidate certain abstract principles rather than to guide engineers in the choice of section for any particular service main, or even in the selection of a feeding point." From so early on, the computing of the electric power network frequently attracted editorial attention. As with later editorials (like the one in the 1944 *Westinghouse Engineer*, see above), the 1894 edition was concerned with the proper choice of computing technology. More than once, the contrast between an old and new mode of computing took the form of a comparison between national computing styles. For the British editor of *The Electrician*, the Germans took pleasure in engaging themselves in an abstract mode of computing networks of electric conductors, suitable to mathematicians, but extremely inappropriate for the concrete computing problems of the fast-growing electric networks. "Nice calculation of mains is no doubt a pleasant pastime for mathematicians," charged the editorial, but "besides the considerations which depend on the mere geometry of conductors, such as the selection of the best site for a supply station by calculating the centre of gravity of all the proposed lamps, and the Kirchhoff relations of the currents in the supply network, there is no end to complications when losses and their cost come to be examined."[48]

Teichmuller strongly protested and drafted a letter in which he concluded that, in his country, "systematic calculation of mains is being carried out, not only by mathematicians, but more especially by electrical engineers engaged in practical work."[49] While they differed in regards to the way to calculate a solution, the two parties were in absolute agreement in respect to the cause and the magnitude of the computing problem. The British side offered the most vivid outline. The editor used the growth in London in order to capture the dynamic manner by which the electrification process "altogether upsets previous calculations":

---

[47] Teichmuller, Ueber die Stromvertheilung in Elektrischen Leitungsnetzen, 540.
[48] The miscalculation of mains. *The Electrician* (February 9, 1894), 384–385.
[49] Teichmuller, The calculation of mains. *The Electrician*, 561.

The steady growth of electric supply brings into prominence questions of adaptation of an existing system of conductors to a gradually changing load. ... If the load merely increased in streets already supplied, the loss on the feeders would rise until it became necessary to draw in more copper, and the loss on the network would rise until the Board of Trade limit was reached, unless the supply company for their own reputation increased the conductors. A simple case of that kind might be calculated in detail, but the addition of new streets, being those streets in which business is promised, or, on rare occasions, streets which lie in the route to new business, altogether upsets previous calculations; and though calculation might show whether a new feeder, a branch feeder, or the shifting of an old feeder would be the best course to adopt, business considerations would generally carry more weight with the engineer than mathematics, and as the chances of business are beyond the powers even of ellipsoidal harmonics, mathematics must give way to sound common sense.[50]

The British editor added that "in a socialist Utopia, where each man enjoyed a fixed 'living' income and lived rent free, a supply network might be pre-determined," which means "much more calculable," but even there "the necessity for guesses as to the probable demand renders any exact statement of the problem impossible; after supply has commenced, the demand is often found to grow in unexpected districts and to languish in street of which great things had been expected."[51] If even a planned socialist utopia would need complex computing, it was utopian to compute a capitalist city planning by a formal (mathematical) plan (which was a prerequisite to the use of a calculating machine):

Shrewd judgment and experimentation rather than algebra are required in determining the section of a feeder, for the mere C^2R losses present but a trifling difficulty compared with the forecasting of the probable future load, and the excess of copper which must be laid to-day in order to meet the conditions which may be expected a year or two hence. The study of existing gas supply cannot, of course, be ignored, but who can judge the character of a locality? Unless it can be expressed as a single coefficient it is of little use. Will future treatise on electric supply give us the proper constants for Piccadilly, London, and for Piccadilly, Manchester, and enable us to compare Belgrave-Square and the Broomielaw?[52]

In his response, Teichmuller claimed that he was speaking not only in his own name, "but in that of most German electricians engaged in projecting networks for electric supply." He was an electrical engineer from Mulheim am Rehein who had previously authored an 1893 article on "a new method of calculating systems of electrical supply," which appeared in a German journal. At that time, he was with the firm of Felten and Guilleaume. It is indicative of the importance of the issue of how to best calculate a conductor network that he mentioned a subspecialty of electrical engineering, that of the "conducting engineer." Teichmuller's argument was based on drawing a distinction between "projecting a plan" and "designing a network for immediate execution." While projecting a plan, the "greatest care must be bestowed on the mathematical determination of the site for the feeding points, and of the sections generally, much more care than there would be necessary in designing a network for immediate execution." This phase concluded with the decision of

---

[50] The miscalculation of mains, 385.
[51] Ibid., 385.
[52] Ibid., 385.

a "jury" as to the which was the best project submitted. It was during the next phase, that of the design of the actual network, that one "would be perfectly right to proceed in a more off-hand manner" because "the inexactitude of the elementary figures, the variability of those figures in the course of time, &c., would have to be taken into consideration."[53]

Up to here, his letter reads as simply adding a stage of calculation before that outlined in the British editorial. But things, as a more detailed examination of this second stage can show, were not that simple. Teichmuller's next paragraph connected the two stages in a manner that argued against the British approach. Teichmuller found the "off-hand manner" to require experience which could only be obtained by the careful study of existing networks. This was a problem, because "to draw more copper when the loss increases, will enable only a very limited number of people to obtain this experience, and even these after a very long time." In his opinion, a "much easier way" was "to design some network in the said off-hand manner and to *scrutinize the same afterwards by mathematical calculations* (emphasis in the original)" in order to determine the best course of action in the event of modification or expansion. "Such researches," he argued, were "particularly interesting; they will facilitate an insight into the properties which a network has, or should have, much better than the examination of the drop of existing networks, such an examination being moreover possible only on very rare occasions."[54] By contrast, the British editorial had argued that it would be inappropriate "to calculate the lost watts, and debit the cost of energy wasted per annum against the interest on the supply conductors." And moved on to suggest:

> (L)et the loss be reduced, if the company can afford it, either by shifting a feeding point or by drawing in more copper. This is where common sense comes in. When ardent mathematicians gets entangled in network-problems, he will not stop until he has debited a proportion of the interest and depreciation of the chimney stack to the watts wasted in the station ammeter.[55]

In connection to the introduction of the use of the calculating machine in scientific computations, it has been convincingly shown that the calculating machine "dictated both the form in which the mathematical results were expressed and the order of the work of the computer" as "the practice of calculating was reorganized, like so many aspects of Victorian culture, according to the rhythms of machines." And further, that the answer to a problem "is not given in advance. When I make a calculation I am doing an experiment to find out what answer I get."[56] This, in my view, is exactly what Teichmuller suggested in reference to engineering. As the passages by him quote above show, he was explicit about the experimental nature of every mode of computing. The German electrical engineer rejected the mathematization-experimentation dilemma—to draw in more copper or to draw in

---

[53] Teichmuller, The calculation of mains: 560–561.

[54] Ibid., 560.

[55] The miscalculation of mains: 385.

[56] See Warwick, The laboratory of theory or what's exact about the exact sciences?, 336, 343, and 315.

more mathematics—by arguing that mathematization ("to scrutinize") was a form of experimentation which allowed the calculation: "(t)o be executed in accordance with the easiest possible way, and—after the system has once been calculated—easily to modify the calculation according to the modifications of load and section; further to make calculations so lucid that the influence of the said modification will clearly appear in the course of the calculation."[57]

In his reminiscences of Edison's miniature network, Francis Jehl described how it was used in relation to the feeder patent. "The results," remembered Jehl, "were surprising" when the advantage of the "feeder-and-main" and "tree" conductor network arrangements were computed and quantitatively compared. Edison had applied for a patent of the feeder arrangement for electric networks on August 4, 1880, and he was granted a patent on September 19, 1882 (Number 264,642). The calculations by the miniature network showed that it required six less times of copper than the "tree" arrangement to maintain equal uniform pressure. Jehl inserted here the story of the answer that Lord Kelvin gave when he was asked why others have not thought of inventing the feeder arrangement: "(t)he only answer I [Kelvin] can think of is that no one else was Edison."[58]

Once Edison had settled for a certain calculating assumption, he actually needed no ingenuity in order to choose the "feeder-and-main" over the "tree" arrangement. In a "tree" circuit, like the one originally used to illuminate Menlo Park, the drop of pressure between the point of the production of electricity and the most remote point of its consumption was avoided by the use of thicker conductors of lower resistance near the generator and by the gradual use of thinner, higher resistance conductors toward the more distant points of the network. In the "feeder-and-main" arrangement, power was distributed to service mains through a number of smaller conductors called "feeders." Each feeder supplied a portion of the mains. This arrangement could save copper only by increasing the overall risk of pressure drop at the network level, i.e., the relative decrease of the amount of copper was haunted by an absolute increase of the risk of instability. The feeder arrangement was based on shifting the higher chance for a drop of the pressure at one particular point to the whole of the distribution network. In other words, in order to save copper, a big risk of a localized instability was transformed to a relatively small risk of network instability. The fact remained that, at the network level, all other things remaining equal, in relation to the "tree" arrangement, there was an absolute increase of the risk of instability. It was only after assuming this higher instability risk that the "feeder-and-main" circuit appeared to be technically superior—more profitable—than the "tree" circuit. How much more profit could be made? The higher the absolute increase in network instability, the higher the profits from savings in copper.

The rise of the instability risk due to Edison's feeder arrangement—conceptualized as a problem of regulation—remained a "cardinal" issue during the growth of electric networks. I here quote from an 1889 issue of the *Electrical World*:

---

[57] Teichmuller, The calculation of mains: 561.

[58] See Francis Jehl. 1939. *Menlo Park reminiscences*, 736–737. Dearborn: The Edison Institute.

Right here we encounter one of the cardinal difficulties of distribution for incandescent work—that of equalizing through the system the drop in potential occurring whenever its full capacity is approached. To secure practically perfect results, the resistance of all the feeders and the mains must be so proportioned and regulated that, however the resistance of any circuit or section of the lamp may vary, the current shall maintain a nearly uniform pressure in all the ramifications of mains and inside wiring of buildings, and each lamp give the same light as every other. An exact regulation is practically impossible, but we may far exceed the best results in water or gas pressure in our approach to the ideal condition. It is only necessary in addition to the proper calculation of the resistance of each of the several feeders, in their construction, to slightly vary their conductivity from time to time by means of resistance boxes known as "equalizers," introduced into their circuits at the station.[59]

Relatively better electric distribution economies corresponded to absolutely worse instability risks.[60] This trade-off was a fact that no calculation, including that by using the miniature network used by Edison to launch electrification or the Arithmometer recommended by Teichmuller to expand it, could transcend. As we have seen in the preceding chapters (especially Chaps. 3, 4 and 5), from the 1870s to the 1960s, the phantasm of instability permanently threatened the profits from electric circuits appeared to be technically superior (and therefore more profitable). Instability was the cardinal problem of profitability. Assuming that one type of electrification (the "feeder-and-main" arrangement) was technically superior over another (the "tree" arrangement) was downplaying the social trade-off involved: higher profit (from less copper) or higher instability. By focusing on the calculating machine, attention was drawn away from this social trade-off. This, to the British side, was a "miscalculation."[61] In our case, the British editor charged the German electrical engineer who wanted to invite attention to the Arithmometer with drawing the attention away from this trade-off.

---

[59] See *Electrical World XIV,* no. 3 (July 20): 42.

[60] For an account of the instability involved in early distribution networks and the stabilization techniques tried, see R.C.R. Brooke. 1985, December. Distribution diary. *IEE Proceedings* 132, (A8).

[61] For an introduction to the overall more cautious approach of the British, which resulted in more localized networks on the grounds of paying greater attention to the increase in instability, see Stathis Arapostathis. 2008. Morality, locality and 'Standardization' in the work of British consulting electrical engineers, 1880–1914. *History of Technology* 28: 53–74. As I read it, the attention by Arapostathis to morality and its manifestation in moving cautiously in the face of substantial instability and other risks in a local (in this case the British) context, moves us beyond the canonical attribution of the rapid increase of electric networks to a technical efficiency—see, for example, the celebrated account by Thomas P. Hughes. 1983. *Networks of power: Electrification in western society 1880–1930.* Baltimore: The John Hopkins University Press. For an introduction to the British context of the debate over the degree of the mathematization of electrical engineering, see Stathis Arapostathis, and Graeme Gooday. 2013, June. Electrical technoscience and physics in transition, 1880–1920. *Studies in the History and Philosophy of Science* 44, part A (2): 202–211.

6.4 "Can Be Put in the Hands of a Girl"

As with the artifacts considered in previous chapters, the political economy of calculating and tabulating machines was inseparable from presenting them as intelligent. We are introduced to this through the aforementioned connection between
human labor and the "perfectly cool" intelligence that we saw in the 1872 discussion of the Arithmometer. The 1893–1894 British-German debate about the
Arithmometer further introduced to the strategy of drawing attention to the calculating machine over the social trade-off that calculating with it was based on. This
strategy also fetishized the technical at the expense of the social. We know that
during this period the Arithmometer and the calculating machines were introduced
as "brains of steel."[62]

We lack a body of systematic studies of the long-run place of the ideology of
intelligent machines before the electronic era. I had attempted to start addressing
this lack through a study that started with the 1872 Arithmometer and concluded
with the 1844 network analyzer.[63] It now seems to me that the variant of the ideology of the intelligent machines displayed in the history of some top-of-the-line
analyzers is different from the ideology that has surrounded the introduction of
mass produced calculating and tabulating machines to fordist and taylorist work
contexts of mass production of calculations. In promoting the use of electrical analyzers that they have themselves designed as intelligent, just like in defending their
skillful use of slide rules, engineers were seeking to elevate themselves within the
world of analysts. The traditionally male analysts were defined by designing state-
of-the-art electrical analyzers or skillfully using slide rules in the context of producing a calculating analogy. In comparison, the ideology of intelligent machines as
displayed in connection with calculating machines pointed to the control of humans,
in these case usually females, by the machine. Using our vocabulary, we could say
that the ideology of intelligent machines as displaying in connection to slide rules
and electrical analyzers sought to advance the masculine control of the production
of the calculating analogy whereas in the case of calculating and tabulating machines
with the control of the feminine—the human computers—by the digital.

Central here is, I now think, the encasement of calculating and tabulating
machines that differentiated between a private-concealed and a public-revealed
view and the lack of a similar differentiation in the case of slide rules and electrical
analyzers. This encased part could be more appropriately presented as the mechanical equivalent to a human brain.[64] We will see the role of the encasement—an

---

[62] Warwick, The laboratory of theory or what's exact about the exact sciences?.

[63] Tympas, From digital to analog and back: The ideology of intelligent machines in the history of
the electrical analyzer 1870s–1960s.

[64] On the ideological connection of the masculine with the encased-private mind that controls the
analog parts of the electronic computer, and, the control of the revealed-public feminine body by
the digital parts of the electronic computer, see Aristotle Tympas, Hara Konsta, Theodore Lekkas,
and Serkan Karas. 2010. Constructing gender and computing in advertising images: Feminine and
masculine computer parts. In *Gender codes: Women and men in the computing professions*, ed.

exemplar version of what is nowadays now called "blackboxing"—in the following section, through retrieving and interpreting a representative line of classifications and comparisons between a slide rule and a calculating machine.

There was, to recapitulate, one variant of the ideology of intelligent machines that was connected to reaching to the top of the labor pyramid by an engineer-analyst and another for holding on its basis a clerk-computor. This difference may explains why, for example, in the three titles on tabulating machines from the *Scientific American* that I quote below the ideology of the intelligent machines is somewhat stronger than everything that I was able to find in the history of the artificial line of the same period—which was a history that did not usually made it outside the pages of the engineering press in the first place: "Keeping Books by Machine: The Punched Card as a Saver of Brain Energy"; "A Thinking Machine, Planning and Theories: Mechanical Reproduction of Mental Processes"; and "When Perforated Paper Goes to Work: How Strips of Paper Can Endow Inanimate Machines with Brains of Their Own."[65]

For the 1902 editor of *Engineering,* a tabulating machine was a "mechanical accountant." The "change from one gorgeous grouping to another" could "reveal" relations to the eye "as in a diagram." With this mechanical accountant a "mob of recorded facts," he wrote, "becomes a highly-drilled army, trooping off obediently at world of command, and capable of assuming a series of different formations in a short time." His aim was to transfer the mode of production of military formations to office computing work by substituting a manager for a general and a woman computor for a soldier. He suggested to do so by using a "system" that had an electric tabulating machine as its "superstructure" and the data "punched on cards," so that the job "can be put in the hands of the girl."[66]

In his 1905 *Engineering Magazine* article on tabulating machine cost-accounting for factories of diversified product, Morrell W. Gaines elaborated upon how such systems could differentiate men into classes because, like Taylor's unit-time measurements, "it puts men on their mettle," enabling the "proper choice to be made" of the class, the "best adapted to bring profits." "Cheap men," he continued, "can not be expected to be efficient. The pay should be proportioned to the importance of the job, and to the effectiveness of the incumbent":

Tom Misa, 187–209. IEEE Press.

[65] See H.S. McCormack. 1913, March 1. Keeping books by machine: The punched card as a saver of brain energy. *Scientific American*: 194–195; S. Bent Russell. 1915, September 18. A thinking machine, planning and theories: Mechanical reproduction of mental processes. *Scientific American* 113: 246–257, and Emanuel Scheyer. 1922, December. When perforated paper goes to work: How strips of paper can endow inanimate machines with brains of their own. *Scientific American*: 394–395 and 445. For Warwick, see, Warwick, The laboratory of theory or what's exact about the exact sciences?, 327–336. For the ideology of intelligent machines in connection to the network analyzer, see Tympas, From digital to analog and back: The ideology of intelligent machines in the history of the electrical analyzer, 1870s–1960s: 42–48.

[66] The Mechanical Accountant, *Engineering* (December 26, 1902): 840–841.

Cost accounting truly belongs, however, to the trained mind of larger grasp and firmer footing. It should be one of the paths by which the engineer pre-eminently, form the very nature of his training, aims to pass upward to a sphere of wider and more intimate contact with the external problems of the business. That way lies increase of influence, as well as increased usefulness.

The new system means facts for the "practical" man, insight for the analytical. For the trained engineer, as for the broad-minded executive, it offers knowledge that is power.[67]

Before the harsh unemployment of the 1930s was far from over in the hard-hit South, the 1938 editor of a journal like Georgia Power Company's *Snap Shots* could introduce to computing with tabulating as "Employees Operate 'Brainy' Accounting Machines" only because such machinery was for many years ideologized as being intelligent. In June 1922, in the *Snap Shots* of the Georgia Railway and Power Company, an earlier version of tabulating machines was presented as "Ingenious Machinery [that] Does Most of the Detail Work." The work was judged to be "Herculean": "When the task is considered in its entirety, Stone Mountain and the Egyptian pyramids become ant hills." Each month, the Georgia Railway and Power Company had to submit to the Railroad Commission of the State of Georgia a "distinctly and emphatically voluminous" book with every cent of money spent and received. The monthly entries were estimated to be about 120,000. The adding machine had lost its novelty "through long usage" but tabulating machines "that defy thought" were introduced. "The machines," we read, "do the work." But the pictures revealed that at least 20 humans worked with the machines.[68]

The use of tabulating machinery at the Georgia Power Company was typical of how such machinery was used in general by accounting in electrical utilities and electrical manufacturers. "The process of making up summary reports," we read in the 1938 *Snap Shots* piece:

> … is done almost entirely by machine. The machines are so versatile they apparently do everything but think; for instance, the dollar volume of a merchandise campaign can be computed without the use of an adding machine, or the total volume credited to an individual salesman, store, district or division can be obtained by merely running the cards through one of the machines.

The language of this passage implied a machine that, like the electronic computer (usually referred to as an electronic "brain"), was supposed to be general purpose and automatic. The fact was that the "brainy" accounting machine was used along a strict division-of-computing-labor. The ideology of intelligent machines was articulated to the political economy of a developed capitalist division-of-computing-labor. If the reader was left to form an opinion unassisted by this ideology, it is doubtful that she/he would ever conclude that the source of value was a "brainy" machine and not the labor power of workers to whom the labor was sharply divided. I quote the rest of the 1938 *Snap Shots* piece, which was accompanied by

---

[67] Morrell W. Gaines. 1905, December. Tabulating-machine cost accounting for factories of diversified product. *Engineering Magazine*: 372–373.

[68] Last word in equipment for accounting work. *Snap Shots* (June, 1922).

seven pictures (A-G), because I find it to be revealing of what was actually taking place at the Georgia Power Company:

> Under the direction of W. A. Brown, accounting supervisor, the following summaries are compiled on the machines: payroll departmental summaries, stores issues and receipts summary, sales bulletin figures, final figures for operating reports and other reports. Employees operating the tabulating card system machines above are: (A) "Key-punch" operators transferring original records to cards, left to right, Miss Ruth Campbell, Miss Janie Gardner, Mrs. Sara Boswell, Mrs. Frances Vaughn and Miss Mildred Bugg. (B) Mrs. Katherine O. Clonts and Mrs. Harriet Wright check and balance sales orders against originals on the tabulator. (C) Checking account numbers of material and stores requisitions against original records are Mrs. Katherine Freeman and Miss Dorothy Rountree. (D) Charles Kimsey feeds cards into the interpreter which prints information punched in the cards. (E) Charles Ratterree assorts account number cards in numerical order by use of the assorter. (F) Mr. Brown sets up the plug board which controls the operations of the tabulating machine on which summaries are tabulated. (G) A. H. Lewis and Frank Baumgartner at the alphabetical machine from which various accounting reports are tabulated.[69]

The fact that women "operators" were at the basis of the computing pyramid whereas a man "supervisor" was at the top is suggestive. I think that it can be seen as another instance of the analyst-computor distinction, which took advantage of the deep roots of engendered ideologies. The majority of women in computing with tabulating and calculating machines contrasted to the majority of men in computing with artificial lines and network analyzers. Generally, when we find articles on calculating and tabulating machines the division-of-labor implied was far more developed than when we find artifacts on analyzers or slide rules. In other words, what we now associate with digital computing corresponded to what was used along with a more developed division-of-labor. Computing with an artifact like an analyzer corresponded more to an analyst-computor division-of-computing-labor within engineering work. Computing with an artifact like a tabulating or a calculating machine corresponded more to an analyst-computor division-of-computing-labor between engineering and clerical work. In other words, computing with a calculating and tabulating machine corresponded to a deeper and wider reproduction of the analyst-computor division. Given the depth and the width of the analyst-computor division by the electronic era, this explains why tabulating and calculating machines are now canonically considered the privileged ancestor of the electronic computer.

6.5   "The True Automatic Machine Belongs to a Possible Rather Than an Actual Class"

J. A. Turck, in 1921, and Ernst Martin, in 1925, authored two books on the history of calculating machines. When Turck's and Martin's book were reedited in 1972 the and in 1992 respectively, the revolution that they thought that they were documenting in the 1920s went unnoticeable due to the assumption that the computing

---

[69] Employees operate 'Brainy' accounting machines. *Snap Shots* (September 1938): 8.

revolution had actually taken place in the 1940s. In other words, those who assumed that the electronic computer was revolutionary were spontaneously neglecting both the whole of the important history of artifacts like the slide rule and important parts of the history of calculating machines. Ironically then, the historiography that privileges the calculating machine as the main ancestor of the electronic computer is denying the calculating machine its own history as an artifact that was thought to have brought about its own computing revolution. To elaborate on the reason for this irony, in this section, I will focus on a few selected comparisons between, first, calculating machines and slide rules and, second, within calculating machines. I have so far purposely avoided providing with a "technical" description of a calculating machine. My hope is that we can best understand what a calculating machine was through the history of the social comparisons of technologies that to be presented in this section shortly.[70]

I begin with the comparison offered by Frederick A. P. Barnard, President of Columbia College and United States commissioner to the 1867 Paris Universal Exposition that was included in his 36 page long chapter on artifacts of "Metrology and Mechanical Calculation."[71] In his extensive history of mechanical calculation, Barnard briefly surveyed the history of the slide rule. "In theory," stated Barnard, "its powers are very great; in practice they are comparatively limited, from the facts that divisions must be either small, or the dimensions of the instrument itself be too great for convenience." "The circular form," he added, "possesses the advantage of admitting a greater length of scale conveniently within the reach of the operator; but still, without greatly exceeding the dimensions to which, for any practically useful purpose, such a machine must be limited, it is impossible to secure results which can be relied on beyond three places of figures." By contrast, Barnard devoted several pages of his report in order to explain the technical superiority of the Arithmometer.[72]

Barnard can be seen as a pioneer in decontextualized comparisons between the slide rule and the calculating machine. He was among the first given a formal forum to promote the use of the calculating machine. Barnard offers us an interesting case because he sought to explain the superiority of the calculating machine over the

---

[70] See J.A.V. Turck. 1972. *Origin of modern calculating machines.* Arno Press, and Martin, *The calculating machines: Their history and development.*

[71] I have first argued about the importance of studying the history of comparisons of computing technology at World Fairs in Tympas, The computor and the analyst: Computing and power, 1870s–1960s. A relevant extract from this dissertation was presented and discussed at a scholarly conference. See Aristotle Tympas, and Theodore Lekkas. 2006. Certainties and doubts in world fair comparisons of computing artifacts. *Proceedings of the XXV Scientific Instrument Symposium "East and West The Common European Heritage".* Krakow: Jagiellonian University Museum: 295–300. The importance of this study has been confirmed by: Kidwell, Peggy Aldrich, Ackerberg-Hastings, A. and Roberts, D.L. 2008. *Tools of American mathematics teaching, 1800–2000.* Johns Hopkins University Press. see pp. 105–122.

[72] See Frederick A.P. Barnard. 1869. *Paris universal exhibition, 1867: Report on machinery and processes of the industrial arts and apparatus of the exacts sciences,* 636 and 638–639. New York: Van Nostrand.

slide rule by drawing an essentialist technical demarcation yet without possessing the conceptual apparatus to support it. In describing the slide rule, Barnard placed the emphasis on sliding. He referred to it as "two rules sliding side by side" or "sliding rules" in the form of concentric circles. He described the slide rule once because there was no internal and external view of it. On the other hand, Barnard provided with a double description of the mechanical relationships materialized in the Arithmometer: one as they could be seen from outside and one as they could be seen from within, one external and one internal. The two were divided by the encasement of a certain part of the calculating machine. As far as the external view goes, Barnard reported that the Arithmometer "was constantly the center of the curious crowd" at the 1867 Fair. What the crowd could see was what we would now call a "black box": "The *arithmometer* of Mr. Thomas," wrote Barnard, "presents, externally, the appearance of a neatly finished box." Like the sliding rule, the Arithmometer was set up by sliding. Barnard stated that the "setting of the machine" was done by "sliding the indexes" (a rule or scale was called, among other things, an index). But the similarity in setting the slide rule and the calculating machine was not apparent to an external observer: in computing with the Arithmometer the effect of sliding could not be seen publicly.[73]

"So much for the machine as it appears to the spectator," continued Barnard by moving to an internal description, "now for the transmission of motion": "It will now be seen what is the effect of sliding the indexes as described above in the setting of the machine." In both cases, the human user set up the computing artifact in a certain position by the proper sliding indexes and then read the result. There was, however, one notable difference: unlike the calculating machine, the slide rule was not encased and the effect of sliding was publicly viewed. As a result, it was clear that it was the user (through sliding) that produced the result by setting up the artifact. When part of this production process became private by being encased into a box, the producer of the computation was still the human who was sliding the linked indexes. This, however, was no longer publicly visible in computing with a calculating machine. Following the general tendency of capitalist production, the production of computation by the human was here removed from public view to make it appear as if the source of computing value was the calculating machine, not the human that calculated with it.[74]

For a comparison that comes from the other end of the chronology covered in this book, I quote Norbert Wiener, one of the pioneer promoters of the electronic computer through the promotion of cybernetics:

> An example of an analogy machine is a slide rule, in contrast with a desk computing machine which operates digitally…Those who have used a slide rule know that the scale on which the marks have to be printed and the accuracy of our eyes give sharp limits to the precision with which the rule can be read. These limits are not as easily extended as one might think, by making the slide rule larger. A ten foot slide will give only one decimal point more accuracy than a one-foot slide rule, and in order to do this, not only must each

[73] Ibid., 631.
[74] Ibid., 640.

foot of the larger slide rule be constructed with the same precision as the smaller one, but the orientation of these successive feet must conform to the degree of accuracy to be expected for each one-foot slide rule. Furthermore, the problems of keeping the larger slide rule rigid are much more greater than those which we find in the case of the smaller rule, and serve to limit the increase in accuracy which we get by increasing the size. In other words, for practical purposes, machines that measure, as opposed to machines that count, are very greatly limited in their precision.[75]

Let us assume that the only way to increase the accuracy of the slide rule was by a corresponding increase in its size and, also, that other computing variables (portability, speed, cost, etc.) did not matter (this assumption is incorrect, see Chaps. 2, 3). What should still strike us here is that there was no mentioning of why the technical limits of the slide rule were not shared by the calculating machine. Wiener mentioned nothing about how to increase the accuracy of the calculating machine. Moreover, despite what he promised to do, he avoided offering a comparison in terms of "practical purposes."[76] In doing so, he assumed that which had to be proven, namely that a calculating machine was a counting machine that was different from (and superior to) a measuring machine like the slide rule. By the time of Wiener's comparison, the ideological weight accumulated by biased comparisons between the calculating machine and the slide rule had made the cover of the computing "black box" (the calculating machine) extremely heavy to lift. The (analog) measurement side of computing was well suppressed in the private space of the encasement so that computing could appear as consisted only of (digital) counting. As a result, Wiener could have the concepts that Barnard lacked: the calculating machine was now (and has been since) a "digital" computer and the slide rule an "analog" computer.

Wiener, who actually knew of the importance of computing with a slide rule during World War I—he had himself called World War I a "Slide Rule War," moved on to contradict himself when it came to actually discuss a concrete case.[77] He did so by referring to some "prejudices" about computing techniques: "[a]dd to this the prejudice of the physiologist in favor of all-or-none action, and we see why the greater part of the work which has been done in the mechanical simulacra of the brain has been on a machine that are more or less on a digital basis." As I hope to show, Barnard had his own doubts, which he expressed in discussing the trade-off between serial-sequential and parallel-simultaneous computing—these terms are usually employed in reference to digital and analog computing respectively. In computing with a slide rule, the user determines at which number the sliding must stop. In computing with a calculating machine, he could not do so because of the encasement. Put differently, the user could intervene in parallel to the open sliding of the slide rule but he could not intervene in parallel to the encased sliding of the calculating machine. As in

---

[75] Norbert Wiener. 1956. *The human use of human beings*, 64–65. Garden City/New York: Doubleday Anchor.

[76] Ibid., 65.

[77] For Wiener and World War I, see Thomas Wyman. 2001, Spring. Norbert Wiener and the slide rule or how American mathematicians came of age. *Journal of the Oughtred Society* 10(1): 46–47.

choosing between mass and flexible production in general, the trade-off between the efficiency of the sequential and the flexibility of parallel computation, i.e., the dilemma between automation and adaptability, was inescapable. The promoters of the electronic computer never solved the sequential-parallel computing dilemma that was inherited to them from the earlier history of computing. The dilemma marked the history of electronic computing since then, manifesting itself in several debates, from the analog-digital debate of the 1940s–1950s to the "connectionists"-"representationistists" debate of the 1980s–1990s.[78]

In the history of the calculating machines, the issue has been one of "carrying" the digits. The critical component of the calculating machine is the "carrying mechanism," usually known as the "accumulator." In the words of Barnard, "it is important that the resistances [to sliding] should not be allowed to accumulate. This is prevented by making the movements consecutive and simultaneous." After reviewing the development of calculating machines in general and the Arithmometer in particular, Barnard argued that in an "efficient calculating machine" additions are simultaneously made to all the dials." This, however, went against the consecutive motion because "if, in carrying, each [of the simultaneous additions to dials] acts directly on the next, its action will often arrive at a time when that one is in motion, so that the two actions will interfere, or the *carrying* action will fail to take effect." Earlier Barnard had dismissed Musina's machine in favor of the Arithmometer. The machine of Opradino Musina, of Mondovi, Italy, was the only other artifact exhibited under the class of calculating machines. Barnard had previously wondered if "[t]his little contrivance hardly deserves, perhaps, to be called a machine." After admitting the problem with sequential computing, he came back to it: "[t]he only remedy, while this direct action of one dial upon another is maintained as part of the system, is to cause the dials to move successively, as in the machine of Musina; an expedient which so far protracts the time of operation as to neutralize in great measure the advantage." Ironically then, moving from a comparison between a slide rule and a calculating machine to a comparison within calculating machines, Barnard encountered the same dilemma.[79]

In his introduction to calculating machines in the handbook of the 1914 Exhibition, F. J. W. Whipple did not include the slide rule but not because it was a calculating machine. He excluded it because he thought that it was not a "purely arithmetical" calculating machine. As I see it, the slide rule could not be a "purely arithmetical calculating machine" because there was no encasement to purify the product by concealing the process of its production. Whipple included in his article a description of a version of an Arithmometer, which was part of the exhibits from the University of Edinburg mathematical laboratory. Interestingly, P. E. Ludgate, another contributor to the section of the 1914 Exhibition handbook on calculating

---

[78] For the transmission of the serial-parallel dilemma from tabulating machines to electronic computers, see Paul E. Ceruzzi, "Crossing the Divide: Architectural Issues and the Emergence of the Stored Program Computer, 1935–1955."

[79] Barnard, *Paris universal exhibition, 1867: Report on machinery and processes of the industrial arts and apparatus of the exacts sciences*, 641, 638, and 645.

machines was not very satisfied with calculating machines like the Arithmometer. The title of his contribution was "automatic calculating machines." For Ludgate, the Arithmometer was not an "automatic calculating machine." It is doubtful that any of the existing calculating machines actually was:

> Automatic calculating machines on being actuated, if necessary, by uniform motive power, and supplied with numbers on which to operate, will compute correct results without requiring any further attention. Of course many adding machines and possibly a few multi-plying machines, belong to this category' but it is not to them, but to machines of far greater power, that this article refers. On the other hand, tide predicting machines and other instruments that work on geometrical principles will not be considered here, because they do not operate arithmetically. It must be admitted, however, that the true automatic calculating machine belongs to a possible rather than an actual class; for, though several were designed and a few constructed, the writer is not aware of any machines in use at the present time that can determine numerical values of complicated formulae without the assistance of an operator.[80]

Like Barnard, Ludgate would like both the adaptability of what we now call the analog and the automation of the digital. No wonder that both authors turned to Babbage for the conception of what they were looking for. "The first great auto-matic calculating machine," argued Ludgate, "was invented by Charles Babbage." Ludgate dreamt of what it could have been done "[i]f this engine was finished," but he acknowledged that it was never finished. He also clarified that Scheutz's differ-ence engine which was finished "was only suitable for calculating tables having small tabular intervals, its utility was limited." Babbage's second engine, the ana-lytical engine, which "was to be capable of evaluating any algebraic formula, of which a numerical solution is possible, for any given values of the variables," was also never finished. "I have myself," continued Ludgate, "designed an analytical machine, on different lines from Babbage's to work with 192 variables of 20 figures each." Even after the number of variables and figures was reduced from infinity to 192 and 20, respectively, Ludgate had to admit that he had not been able "to take any steps to have the machine constructed."[81]

Upon his return from the Exhibition that he was sent to, Barnard had a similar message to report to Americans:

> The alternative is to reject the direct action of dial upon dial, and to introduce a mechanism which may be *prepared for action* at the moment when the necessity of carrying occurs; but which shall not act until all the dials have completed the movements which the setting of the machine requires. This mechanism then taking separate and subsequent effect will com-plete the operation. That the special branch of the problem here considered is not simple, is illustrated by the fact that, since the time of Gerbert, it has occupied ineffectually the atten-

---

[80] For the passages by Whipple and Ludgate, see E.M. Horsburgh. 1914. *Modern instruments and methods of calculation: A handbook of the Napier tercentenary exhibition.* London: Bell and Sons, 69 and 124 respectively. For Ludgate, see Brian Randell. 1982. From analytical engine to elec-tronic digital computer: The contributions of Ludgate, Torres, and Bush. *Annals of the History of Computing* 4(4): 327–341.

[81] See Horsburgh, *Modern instruments and methods of calculation: A handbook of the Napier ter-centenary exhibition*, 127.

tion of so many ingenious men; and that Babbage himself confesses that it was the source of his greatest trouble in the construction of his great difference engine.[82]

To my knowledge, an ideal computer that could be used to take full advantage of both the serial computing of the Arithmometer and the parallel computing of Musina's calculating machine was never realized. The pursuit of this ideal was inherited to the history of the electronic computer by the history of the calculating and the tabulating machine.[83]

6.6 "No Short Summary Can Be at All Complete"

For Whipple, as we just saw, the slide rule was not a calculating machine. That the slide rule was a calculating machine was clear to the readers of Chas. A. Holden's article, which was published in the May 30, 1901 issue of *Engineering News*. Under the title "Use of Calculating Machines," Holden, an instructor at the Thayer School of Civil Engineering in Hanover, New Hampshire, was presenting the results of his survey on the important issue of "whether the Manheim pocket slide-rule and other calculating machines are appreciated and used to as great an extent as they should be" by engineering schools, engineers, and business firms. The most notable of the other calculating machines was also a slide rule.[84] But why engineers refused to award the status of the machine only to mechanical calculators?

As we show in preceding chapters (especially Chaps. 2 and 3), the cost of the slide rule was very low compared to that of a calculating machine, which could be afforded by an individual. Computing with calculating machines actually required proper institutional settings like the pioneering mathematical computing laboratory of E. T. Whittaker. For an introductory taxonomy of computing laboratories, I move on to distinguish conveniently between three variants. They all appear in the 1910s. In 1913, Whittaker set up his mathematical computing laboratory at the University of Edinburgh.[85] This was also the time of the appearance of the artificial line and other analyzer-related engineering computing laboratories that I have described elsewhere.[86] A third, hybrid variant was a mathematical computing laboratory that was set at an engineering environment. This was Joseph Lipka's MIT mathematical computing laboratory. A standard calculating machine was central to the mathemat-

---

[82] Barnard, *Paris universal exhibition, 1867: Report on machinery and processes of the industrial arts and apparatus of the exacts sciences*, 645.

[83] See Ceruzzi, Crossing the divide: Architectural issues and the emergence of the stored program computer, 1935–1955.

[84] Charles A. Holden. 1901, May 30. The use of calculating machines. *Engineering News* 45(22): 405.

[85] For Whittaker, see Warwick, The laboratory of theory or what's exact about the exact sciences?.

[86] Aristotle Tympas. 2012. A deep tradition of computing technology: calculating electrification in the American West. In *Where minds and matters meet: Technology in California and the West*, ed. Volker Janssen, 71–101. Oakland, CA: University of California Press.

ical computing laboratory, whereas an analyzer (e.g., an artificial line) was central to the engineering computing laboratory.[87]

Whittaker was actually the Convener of the 1914 Napier Tercentenary Exhibition, the contents of which were presented in a catalog that contained over 350 pages that was edited by Ellice Martin Horsburgh, Lecturer in Technical Mathematics at the University of Edinburg, under the title *Modern Instruments and Methods of Calculation*. Whittaker, who was the major promoter of the idea of a computing laboratory, was also pivotal in the classification of the 1914 exhibition. As we are informed by the Preface of the reprint edition, Whittaker has helped "with the general scheme and also in details."[88] A classification scheme was indispensable, especially considering the great number and variety of the computing artifacts exhibited. From the perspective of the classification of computers after the emergence of the electronic computer, the most striking feature of the volume of the 1914 Exhibition is the absence of an explicit demarcation of artifacts on the grounds of the concepts "analog" and "digital" computer. Quite simply, these concepts were not in use.[89]

Present-day classification of museum collections of computing artifacts according to the analog-digital demarcation run the risk of projecting our own reclassification of computing artifacts into the past. To borrow Eric Hobsbawm's appropriate expression, they run the risk of the "invention of the tradition" of the digital computer.[90] For instance, I think that we run the risk of projecting the present into the past when we edit a museum collection of computing artifacts by reclassifying them as if the digital was clearly separated from the analog before the postwar or by reediting an initial museum classification of computing artifacts by adding the analog-digital computing demarcation. In my opinion, projecting our own concepts into past computing classifications is like assuming that which has to be proven: that the 1914 classification contained the tendency that could conclude in the analog-digital computing demarcation is different from assuming that the analog-digital demarcation was already there. Stated differently, if we start by assuming that the analog and the digital was already there, we cannot understand that it was only after the successful historical development of Whittaker's classification that the analog-digital classification became possible. Accordingly, in this section, I will register a few observations that indicate that the tendency that concluded in the analog-digital demarcation existed as such without conflating this tendency with what was actually exhibited.[91]

---

[87] For Lipka, see Lipka, *Graphical and mechanical computation*.

[88] See Williams, in Horsburgh, *Modern instruments and methods of calculation: A handbook of the Napier tercentenary exhibition*, iii.

[89] For the general importance of classification, see Geoffrey C. Bowker, and Susan Leigh Star. 2000. *Sorting things out: Classification and its consequences*. Cambridge, MA: MIT Press. For Williams, see, Williams, "Introduction" in *The handbook of the Napier tercenary celebration or modern instruments and methods of calculation*, xx.

[90] Eric Hobsbawm, and Terence Ranger. 1983. *The invention of tradition*. New York: Cambridge University Press.

[91] See, Williams, "Introduction" in *The handbook of the Napier tercenary celebration or modern instruments and methods of calculation*, xviii.

The artifacts in the 1914 catalog varied from something as explicitly (now) analog and premodern as the sundial (included in the section "Loan Collection, Antiquarian") to something as explicitly (now) digital and modern (if not postmodern) as the parts of Babbage's unfinished difference engine (subsection in the section on calculating machines). Moreover, there was no concern to differentiate between something as complex of a machine as the "mechanical device for displaying printed tabulated matter" of the Robertson Rapid Calculating Machine Company that was set upon a desk table and something as simple of a tool as the "Espero" pocket calculator that was "really a form of abacus": in the handbook of the 1914 exhibition the two are placed in the same section (Section "Other Mathematical Laboratory Instruments," Subsection "Miscellaneous").[92]

To understand the implicit classification criterion of the 1914 Exhibition while we avoid presenting this criterion as something as explicit as our own analog-digital demarcation, I suggest that we start by paying attention to the subtle conceptual battle that underlined the momentum of (and the resistance to) the process of demarcating between the arithmetical from the non-arithmetical. "I propose," wrote F. J. W. Whipple in his introduction to calculating machines, "to confine my remarks to purely arithmetical machines, and say nothing of other apparatus, such as slide-rules or mechanical integrators." In contrast to present-day practice, Whipple implied that slide rules and mechanical integrators were actually also considered by some to be calculating machines. Without further explanation, he moved on to describe what he referred to as "arithmetical" calculating machines by excluding slide rules and mechanical integrators from consideration because they were not "purely" arithmetical calculating machines.[93]

As I mentioned in the previous section, Ludgate was not satisfied even with "purely" mathematical calculating machines because he was after "automatic" calculating machines. Similarly, in other sections of the same volume, the presence or absence of arithmetic alone did not actually suffice for classification purposes. The difference between arithmetical and non-arithmetical methods frequently intersected with the difference between graphical and mechanical methods to give various mixes. For example, in the subsection on "Harmonic Analysis" and in the subsection on "The Instrumental Solution of Numerical Equations" of the section on "Other Mathematical Laboratory Instruments" arithmetical computing is only one of three and five computing classes, respectively. In the first case, we find "arithmetical methods" placed next to "mechanical methods" and "graphical methods." In the second case, we find the "arithmetical or computing method" placed next to the "solution by means of radicals," the "solution by means of series," the "graphical method, " and the "instrumental method." In other words, even though it already offered a strong classification criterion, the demarcation between an arithmetical and a non-arithmetical computer could not provide with a classification

---

[92] Horsburgh, *Modern instruments and methods of calculation: A handbook of the Napier tercentenary exhibition*, 274–275.

[93] Ibid., 69.

criterion that was as encompassing as the present demarcation between an analog and a digital computer.[94]

To place the classification of the 1914 Exhibition within the overall context of self-conscious attempts at identifying and classifying the computing artifacts of modernity, we can start by comparing the 1914 Exhibition to the 1926 influential classification by William Henry Leffingwell. After arguing about the close relationship between the emergence of the Industrial Revolution and the appearance of office machines, Leffingwell claimed that bringing the "modern" to the office consisted in substituting mechanical for human effort. Leffingwell, who was a mechanical engineer, included what we now call "computers" in an impressive collection of office machines and other office artifacts that he described in a book that was entitled *The Office Appliance Manual*. The book was published by the National Association of Office Appliance Manufacturers, the sponsor, director, and supervisor of Leffingwell's exhaustive researches. The Taylorite Leffingwell referred to "function" as his explicit classification criterion—in Leffingwell's book we find an exhibition of computing artifacts according to their function as office machines. As a result, slide rules and calculating machines were placed together under the class of "accounting machines," which was different from, for example, the class of machines for "recording cash and credit transactions." More specifically, we find both the slide rule and the calculating machine under the sub-classes of machines for "bookkeeping" and "statistics." In Leffingwell's classification scheme, the demarcation between arithmetical and non-arithmetical machines was further weakened by placing "adding" and "calculating" machines—both exemplars of arithmetical computing—under distinct sub-classes of the sub-class of machines for "Statistics."[95]

We find the same approach in classifications of computers by electrical engineers. In 1921, when MIT's Frederick S. Dellenbaugh, Jr.—Director of Research at the MIT Electrical Engineering Laboratory—sought to promote his "electric analyzer" by presenting qualitative and quantitative results of his impressive survey of computing technologies, he offered a classification that is also different from ours. For Dellenbaugh, harmonic analysis could be done by three general methods, namely, "mathematical," "graphical," and "instrumental." For example, he mentioned the "Henrici-Coradi machine" and the "Westinghouse polar analyzer" as providing with the two best-known instrumental methods, a Marchant calculating machine, a slide rule, and his own electric analyzer without making any effort to differentiate between the analog and the digital. Noticeably, his electric analyzer (now an analog computer) was explicitly contrasted to all of them as belonging to a class of its own.[96]

---

[94] Ibid., 220 and 259.

[95] See William Henry Leffingwell. 1926. *The office appliance manual*. National Association of Office Appliance Manufacturers, chapters II–III.

[96] Dellenbaugh, An electromechanical device for rapid schedule harmonic analysis of complex waves.

On the other hand, Dellenbaugh's incidental comparison of the accuracy of the slide rule and the Marchant calculating machine suggests that what we now call "digital" was, for analysts, already implicitly considered to be technically superior to the what we call "analog." "The schedule analysis," wrote Dellenbaugh, "was performed upon a Marchant calculating machine. It can be done quicker with a slide rule, but the errors in the cosine components are then liable to be very great." This comparison anticipated the comparisons between the slide rule (as the representative of an analog computer) and a representative of the digital computer (a calculating machine or an electronic computer, see the example of Wiener's comparison in the preceding section of this chapter): of the many variables involved in evaluating a calculation—rapidity, accuracy, portability, cost, etc.—most were not taken into account by Dellenbaugh. By comparing a \$4 slide rule to a \$400 calculating machine, analysts like Dellenbaugh were contributing to the emergence of the essentialism of the encompassing technical demarcation between a superior digital and an inferior analog computer.[97]

Dellenbaugh's supervisor, Vannevar Bush, the chief perhaps analyst of his generation, has left us a more general comparison. "We are in an age of complex instruments," stated Bush in 1936 before moving on to predict that "[o]ut of it will come devices that will revolutionize the use of mathematics, and will profoundly influence some branches of mathematics itself. This process is now beginning, and it is probable that the next decade will see important advances."[98] Yet, calculating and tabulating machines were not the focus of Bush classification. This does not mean that Bush was in favor of what we now call the "digital." He sought to promote the digital through the evaluation of computers that was inherent in his classification of what we would now call "analog."[99]

Bush identified two classes of computing artifacts, which he called "operators" and "equations solvers," respectively. Slide rule, nomograms, harmonic analyzers and synthesizers, various integrators, and differentiators (including planimeters) were discussed as representative of "operators," in contrast to the three sub-classes of "equation solvers." All three sub-classes of "equation solvers" were designed along a computing analogy between a given system and a second, substitute system. When the entire equation was carried over from the system to its substitute, the analogy was simple. Bush sought to promote a different kind of computing analogy, one that relied on a minimum of analogy in the use of computers through a maximum of mathematization in the design of computers. As he explained, his network analyzer and his mechanical analyzer, which were typical of the second and the third class of "equation solvers," respectively, were defined by, first, "carrying over" only the constants (network analyzer) or, better, the terms of the equation (differential analyzer) individually and, then, by recombining them.

---

[97] Ibid., 142.

[98] Vannevar Bush. 1936. Instrumental analysis. *Transactions of the American Mathematical Society* 42(10): 666.

[99] For an elaboration on this, see Tympas, A deep tradition of computing technology: Calculating electrification in the American West".

An uncritical projection of our own classification into Bush's classification would be meaningless, because all three sub-classes of "equation solvers" as well as the class of "operators" would now be placed under the same class, that of analog computers. On the other hand, if we start by acknowledging that all computers are analog and that, by comparison, a digital computer is what historically appeared to be the most mathematical computer possible, then Bush's classification makes perfect sense. In this sense, in comparison to the 1914 classification, Bush's classification appears much closer to ours. Accordingly, Bush can be interpreted as someone whose classification contributed to the emergence of the analog-digital demarcation.[100]

Bush's classification can be also be read from the perspective of the history of the promotion of computing laboratories. For Bush, the prerequisite of a revolution in computing was progress to the point where "mass production of duplicate parts" could be possible. Implicitly, this is what he argued for by favoring a computing analogy that was based on "carrying over" mathematical parts that were removed from a specific computing analogy. Bush argued the same explicitly from a hardware perspective. In doing so, he introduced to the initial necessity of laboratory settings for computing experimentation:

> This development [mass production of duplicate parts] has had a large effect in the field of arithmetical computation. It will have a comparable effect, ultimately, in the field of other mathematical instruments. There is, nevertheless, a serious barrier to be overcome before this occurs. Reliability comes, in a complicated machine, only when a great deal of study and experiment is devoted to the design of individual parts, which are then fabricated by methods that produce large numbers of precise replicas at low unit cost. The spread between development and production cost may be enormous: thousands of dollars may be spent in perfecting a simple relay or lever which may later be produced for a few cents each, provided hundreds of thousands are made. This barrier militates heavily against the research tool, which is potentially useful in only a few laboratories. Otherwise there would be available a much greater variety of mathematical instruments than at present, and their performance would have be more satisfactory. Yet it appears, in spite of this inherent limitation that we are at the beginning of an important period of development of machines of higher analysis.[101]

Classifying just before the emergence of the electronic computer, Bush was as well positioned as a person could be in respect to having the opportunity to know of the whole of the available literature on computers that was accumulated during the mechanical and the electrical era:

"No short summary can be at all complete in regard to either the "operators" and the "equations solvers" [i.e., the classes of what we now call analog computers], for the literature of the subject is enormous, and each device requires much exposition if it is to be all understood. This is especially true since there is often such a wide

---

[100] Bush, Instrumental Analysis: 655. For Vannevar Bush's role at the time, see Larry Owens. 1986. Vannevar Bush and the differential analyzer: The text and context of an early computer. *Technology and Culture* 27(1): 63–95.

[101] Bush, Instrumental analysis: 651.

gap between the conception of such an instrument and its actual construction and use, so that details are often important. Hence, only a few will be selected for illustration in what follows, with full regret that every interesting development cannot be given its due recognition."[102]

We now focus on the literature on calculating and tabulating machines as representative of the whole of the history of computing before the electronic computer. What Bush had to say about the rest of the 1936 universe of computing artifacts is, I think, indicative of what we may be missing by such focus.

6.7 Conclusion

The argument that I advance in this chapter asserts that there was a considerable difference between what the calculating and the tabulating machines were supposed to be and what they actually were. More specifically, despite multiple attempts to introduce calculating and tabulating machines to the realm of engineering computations, it seems as if there were limits for the use of calculating machines by engineers (in general) and electrical engineers (in particular). The limited use of these machines in engineering becomes more apparent when we compare it to the more extensive use of the same machines in typical business purposes, e.g., accounting (including accounting in industries of relevance to electrification). Within this chapter, I sought to explain this contrast as the consequence of a difference regarding the division-of-computing labor. Simply, computing with calculating machines required a more developed capitalist division-of-computing labor. This explanation becomes more attractive after adding other contrasts, including that between the limits of the engineer's attachment to the calculating-tabulating machine and his strong ties to computing with a slide rule. Given that the calculating machine was much more expensive that the slide rule, it seems reasonable to hypothesize that the other side of the division-of-computing labor issue was the ownership of the means of computing production (this hypothesis is confirmed by the research presented in preceding chapters, especially Chaps. 2 and 3).

The chapter pays attention to the historical study regarding how the limits of the calculating machine were actually felt by the ideologues of the technical-essential superiority of the calculating machine, who constantly failed to construct the calculating machine of their dreams. I look at the same issue when I argue that the ideology surrounding the technical superiority of the calculating machine was founded on the division between the public and the private workings of the machine introduced by the encasement. Computing with a calculating machine appeared to be unlimited only because the material limitations were removed from public view.

---

[102] Ibid., 655.

References

Applied mechanical arithmetic as practiced on the controlled key comptometer. Smithsonian Institution, National Museum of American History, Mezzanine Library, Trade Catalogs Collection, 239

Arapostathis S (2008) Morality, locality and 'Standardization' in the work of British consulting electrical engineers, 1880–1914. Hist Technol 28:53–74

Arapostathis S, Gooday G (2013) Electrical technoscience and physics in transition, 1880–1920. Stud Hist Philos Sci 44(part A 2):202–211

Aspray W (1994) Calculating power: Edwin L. Harder and analog computing in the electric power industry. In: Nebeker F (ed) Sparks of genius: portraits of electrical engineering excellence. IEEE Press, New York, pp 163–164 and 194

Austrian GD (1982) Herman Hollerith: forgotten giant of information processing. Columbia University Press, New York, pp 105–111

Babbage C (1851) The exposition of 1851: views of the industry, the science, and the Government of England. John Murray, London, p 170

Barnard FAP (1869) Paris universal exhibition, 1867: report on machinery and processes of the industrial arts and apparatus of the exacts sciences. Van Nostrand, New York, pp 636 and 638–639

Bent Russell S (1915) A thinking machine, planning and theories: mechanical reproduction of mental processes. Sci Am 113:246–257

Bowker GC, Star SL (2000) Sorting things out: classification and its consequences. MIT Press, Cambridge, MA

Brooke RCR (1985) Distribution diary. IEE Proc 132(A8):533–542

Bush V (1936) Instrumental analysis. Trans Am Math Soc 42(10):666

Ceruzzi PE (1994) Landmarks in digital computing: a Smithsonian pictorial history, 36. Smithsonian Institution Press, Washington, DC

Ceruzzi P (1997) Crossing the divide: architectural issues and the emergence of the stored program computer, 1935–1955. IEEE Ann Hist Comput 19(1):5–12

Chase GC (1952) History of mechanical computing. ACM Proc: 1–28

Chase GC (1980) History of mechanical computing machinery. Ann Hist Comput 2(3):198–226

Comrie LJ (1932) The applications of the Hollerith tabulating machine to Brown's tables of the moon. R Astronomical Soc Monthly Notices 92(7):694–707

Comrie LJ (1944) Recent progress in scientific computing. J Sci Instrum 21:129–135

Comrie LJ (1946) The application of commercial calculating machines to scientific computation. Math Tables Other Aids Calculation 2(16):149–159

Cortada JW (1993) Before the computer: IBM, NCR, Burroughs, and the industry they created, 1865–1956. Princeton University Press, Princeton

Croarken M (1990) Early scientific computing in Britain. Clarendon Press, Oxford

Dunstan LA (1947a) Machine computation of power network performance. AIEE Trans 66:610–620. and 621–624 (discussion)

Dunstan LA (1947b) Machine computing of networks. Electr Eng 66:901–906

Eckert WJ (1984) Punched card methods in scientific computation. MIT Press, Cambridge, MA

Ensmenger N (2016) The multiple meanings of a flowchart. Inform Cult J Hist 51(3):321–351

Frederick SD Jr (1921) An electromechanical device for rapid schedule harmonic analysis of complex waves. AIEE J:135–144

Freeman WE (1909) Pay-roll problems in the electric light industry. NELA 32nd Convention 3:74–119

Freeman WE (1929) Electrical accounting systems. Electrician 103:598

Gaines MW (1905) Tabulating-machine cost accounting for factories of diversified product. Eng Mag: 372–373.

Heide L (1991) From invention to production: the development of punched-card Machinery by FR Bull and K A Knutsen. Ann Hist Comput 13(3):261–272

Heide L (1994) Punched-card and computer applications in Denmark, 1911–1970. Hist Technol 11:77–79

Heide L (1997) Shaping a technology: American punched-card systems, 1880–1914. IEEE Ann Hist Comput 19(4):28–41

Heide L (2009) Punched-card systems and the early information explosion, 1880–1945. Johns Hopkins University Press, Baltimore

Hobsbawm E (1987) The age of revolution, 1789–1848. Pantheon, New York

Hobsbawm E (1987) The age of empire, 1875–1914. Weidenfeld & Nicolson, New York

Hobsbawm E (1994) Age of extremes: the short twentieth century, 1914–1991. Michael Joseph, London

Hobsbawm E (1996) The age of capital, 1848–1875. Vintage, New York

Hobsbawm E, Ranger T (1983) The invention of tradition. Cambridge University Press, New York

Holden CA (1901) The use of calculating machines. Engineering News 45(22):405

Horsburgh EM (1914) Modern instruments and methods of calculation: a handbook of the Napier tercentenary exhibition. Bell and Sons, London

Hughes TP (1983) Networks of power: electrification in western society 1880–1930. The John Hopkins University Press, Baltimore

Jehl F (1939) Menlo park reminiscences, 736–737. The Edison Institute, Dearborn

Jennings PD, Quinan GE (1946) The use of business machines in determining the distribution of load and reactive components in power line network. AIEE Trans 66:1045–1046

Kidwell PA (1990) American scientists and calculating machines: from novelty to commonplace. Ann Hist Comput 12(1):31–40

Kidwell PA (2000) The adding machine Fraternity of St. Louis: creating a center of invention, 1880–1920. IEEE Ann Hist Comput 22(2):4–21

Kidwell PA, Ackerberg-Hastings A, Roberts DL (2008) Tools of American mathematics teaching, 1800–2000. Johns Hopkins University Press, Baltimore, pp 105–122

Kimball E Jr. A fundamental punched card method for technical computations, 1. Bureau of the Census, Machine Tabulation Division, ca. mid-1940s, Washington, DC

Kisterman FW (1991) The invention and development of the Hollerith punched card: In Commemoration of the 130th anniversary of the birth of Herman Hollerith and for the 100th anniversary of large scale data processing. Ann Hist Comput 13(3):245–259

Kisterman FW (1995) The way to the first automatic sequence-controlled calculator: the 1953 DEHOMAG D 11 tabulator. IEEE Ann Hist Comput 17(2):33–49

Kisterman FW (1997) Locating the victims: the nonrole of punched card technology and census work. IEEE Ann Hist Comput 19(2):31–45

Leffingwell WH (1926) The office appliance manual. National Association of Office Appliance Manufacturers, chapters II–III

Lipka J (1918) Graphical and mechanical computation. Wiley, New York

Martin E (1992) The calculating machines: their history and development, 96–97. MIT Press, Cambridge, MA

Marx K (1990) Capital, vol 1. Penguin, London

McCormack HS (1913) Keeping books by machine: the punched card as a saver of brain energy. Sci Am: 194–195

Medwick PA (1988) Douglas Hartree and early computations in quantum mechanics. Annals of the History of Computing 10(2):105–111

Miller GL (1990) Charles Babbage and the design of intelligence: computers and society in 19th-century England. Bull Sci Technol Soc 10:68–76

Nebeker F (1995) Calculating the weather: meteorology in the 20th century. Academic Press, San Diego

Norberg A (1990) High-technology calculation in the early 20th century: punched card machinery in business and government. Technol Cult 31(4):753–779

Owens L (1986) Vannevar Bush and the differential analyzer: the text and context of an early computer. Technol Cult 27(1):63–95

Pelaez E (1999) The stored program computer: two conceptions. Soc Stud Sci 29(3):359–389

Randell B (1982) From analytical engine to electronic digital computer: the contributions of Ludgate, Torres, and Bush. Ann Hist Comput 4(4):327–341

Schaffer S (1994) Babbage's intelligence: calculating engines and the factory system. Crit Inq 21(1):203–227

Schaffer S, Swade D, Spufford F (1996) In: Spufford F, Uglow J (eds) Cultural Babbage: technology, time, and invention. Faber and Faber, London

Scheyer E (1922) When perforated paper goes to work: how strips of paper can endow inanimate machines with brains of their own. Sci Am: 394–395 and 445.

Schultz JH (1929) Lochkartenverfahren und Mitlaufende Kalkulation in der Elektrotechnischen Industrie. Technik und Wirtschaft 22:41–45

Skinner PH (1915) Computing machines in engineering. Engineering News: 25

Smith DE (1925) History of mathematics, vol II. Ginn, Boston

Smith RE (1989) A historical overview of computer architecture. Ann Hist Comput 10(4):277–303

Strange P (1985) Two early periodicals: the electrician and the electrical review, 1880–1890. IEE Proc 132(part A 8):575–581

Swartzlander E (1995) Generations of calculators. IEEE Ann Hist Comput 17(3):76

Teichmuller J (1893) Ueber die Stromvertheilung in Elektrischen Leitungsnetzen. Elektrotechnische Zeitschrift 37:540

Teichmuller J (1894) The calculation of mains. The Electrician: 560–561

The miscalculation of mains. The Electrician (February 9, 1894), 384–385

Turck JAV (1972) Origin of modern calculating machines. Arno Press

Tympas A (2001) The computor and the analyst: computing and power, 1870s–1960s. PhD diss, Georgia Institute of Technology, Atlanta. Chapter 2

Tympas A (2012) A deep tradition of computing technology: calculating electrification in the American West. In: Janssen V (ed) Where minds and matters meet: technology in California and the West. University of California Press, Oakland, pp 71–101

Tympas A, Lekkas T (2006) Certainties and doubts in world fair comparisons of computing artifacts. Proceedings of the XXV Scientific Instrument Symposium "East and West the Common European Heritage". Jagiellonian University Museum, Krakow, pp 295–300

Tympas A, Konsta H, Lekkas T, Karas S (2010) Constructing gender and computing in advertising images: feminine and masculine computer parts. In: Misa T (ed) Gender codes: women and men in the computing professions. IEEE Press, Hoboken, pp 187–209

Warren TTPB (1872) On the application of the calculating machine of Thomas De Colmar to electrical computations. J Soc Telegraph Eng 2:141–169

Warwick A (1994) The laboratory of theory or what's exact about the exact sciences? In: Norton Wise M (ed) The values of precision. Princeton University Press, Princeton

Wiener N (1956) The human use of human beings. Doubleday Anchor, New York, pp 64–65

Williams MR (1982) Modern instruments and methods of calculation: a handbook of the Napier tercentenary exhibition, Reprint edn. Tomash Publishers, Los Angeles

Wyman T (2001) Norbert Wiener and the slide rule or how American mathematicians came of age. J Oughtred Soc 10(1):46–47

Yates JA (1993) Co-evolution of information-processing technology and use: interaction between the life insurance and tabulating industries. Bus Hist Rev 67:1–51

Chapter 7
Conclusion

The great number of classes (and subclasses) of computing artifacts introduced over the course of this book offers testimony of an extremely rich world of computing experiences throughout the mechanical and the electrical eras, which accumulated so as to prepare for the electronic one. Any attempt to place this world under one interpretative scheme seems destined to omit important details. On the other hand, without attempting to provide such a scheme, we run the risk of missing an important historical pattern. The scheme that I here advanced is organized around one thematic anchor: the relationship between human-variable and machine-constant computing capital. According to this scheme, in going from the highest to the lowest ratio of human-variable to machine-constant computing capital, the list of the artifacts encounter goes as following: graphs (Chap. 5), slide rules (Chaps. 2 and 3), calculating machines (Chap. 6), and analyzers (Chap. 4).

While developing this scheme, I was not only interested in considering how much we could gain by employing the variable-constant computing capital relationship to interpret the findings of my research. I also found it inviting how this relationship could gain specificity by employing it to make sense of my research findings. One appealing feature of the variable-constant computing capital concepts is that they accommodate the relative distinctions between different computing experiences without ontologically separating these experiences on the grounds of a technical criterion. In other words, they allow us to explain the emergence of the analog-digital demarcation while steering away from an essentialist perspective that would have to attribute it to the final discovery, in the 1940s, of this technical criterion of demarcation.

As I reflect over this book, it seems that it gives us a picture of a historically deep interest in the political economy of computing, manifested in an endless line of comparing and classifying computing technologies. That is comparing, for example, slide rules versus calculating machines, special versus universal slide rules, simple versus complex analyzers, nomographs versus the rest of the graphs, and, above all, real versus ideal analyzers or real versus ideal calculating machines. Taken together, these comparisons present us with the history of a systematic pursuit

© Springer-Verlag London Ltd. 2017
A. Tympas, *Calculation and Computation in the Pre-electronic Era*, History of
Computing, https://doi.org/10.1007/978-1-84882-742-4_7

of a technical-essentialist-ontological demarcation of computing perspectives—a pursuit that I read as a forerunner of the analog vs. digital computing debate that launched the electronic era of computing. But they also give us the history of how such demarcation turned out, repeatedly, to be illusory. Analogous to the variable-constant capital relationship—so typical of the capitalist mode of production as a whole—capitalism, which is programmatically defined by the systematic pursuit of development of machine capital supposedly to devaluate the human capital, is also historically defined by a constant paradoxical development of the need for human labor, and in fact skilled labor.

I have placed the social relationships that were shaped in the book's history through their interaction with technical relationships into a context determined by a prevalent perspective of the analyst as superior to the computor. My conclusion in regard to this is that in the period considered here, there was a battle but also a hegemony. The production and expansive reproduction of an analyst's work, as technically different from and superior to a computor's work, on the grounds of the specific development of computing artifacts, becomes the specific historical conclusion for this book.

The same conclusion reads: the production and expansive reproduction of an analyst's work as different from and superior to that of the work of a computor was as indispensable in departing from nature as it was to arrive at a historically specific form of nature, namely, that corresponding to modernity (historical capitalism). As I read through the chapters, I am struck by the force by which engineers thought of computing as bridging the two (nature as it was and nature as it was supposed to be) under a historically specific imaginary. From Steinmetz's "imaginary numbers" to Karapetoff's devising the idiosyncratic Heavisidion "as its own optical image," the conclusion of this book is that the computer has been capital's imago, not nature's reflection.

References

A Five-Place Calculating Device (1915) Electr World 66(11):604

Ackermann S, Kremer R, Miniati M (eds) (2014) Scientific instruments on display. Brill, Leiden/Boston

Adams RW (1915) A transmission line calculator. Gen Electr Rev 18(1):28–30

Adams DP (1964) Nomography: theory and application. Archon, Hamden

Agnew PG (1909) Experimental method for the analysis of E.M.F. Waves. Electr World 54(3):142–147

AIEE Journal XLI (1922):107

AIEE Transactions XXXVII, part I (1918):329

Alcott WJ Jr (1929) The decimal point with the slide rule. Eng News-Rec 102:686

Alger PL, Samson HW (1922) A new power-factor slide rule. Gen Electr Rev 25(7):455–457

Allcock HJ (1950) The nomogram: the theory and practical construction of computation charts. Pitman, London

Allen EC (1928) Slide rule calculation of vectors. Electr World 92(8):362

American Machinist 24 (1901):339

Amor CF (1986) The graphical methods of Sumpner, Drysdale, and Marchant: solving the Kelvin equation. IEE Proc 133(6):387–392

An Electrical Device for Solving Equations, Electrical World (1909) 54 (3): 144–146

Andrews H, Schure C (2001) A slide rule for wire drawing calculations. J Oughtred Soc 10(1):15–17

Applied Mechanical Arithmetic As Practiced on the Controlled Key Comptometer (Smithsonian Institution, National Museum of American History, Mezzanine Library, Trade Catalogs Collection), 239

Arapostathis S (2008) Morality, locality and 'standardization' in the work of British consulting electrical engineers, 1880–1914. Hist Technol 28:53–74

Arapostathis S, Gooday G (2013) Electrical technoscience and physics in transition, 1880–1920. Stud Hist Philos Sci 44, Part A(2):202–211

Aspray W (ed) (1990) Computing before computers. Iowa State University Press, Ames

Aspray W (1993) Edwin L. Harder and the Anacom: analog computing at Westinghouse. IEEE Ann Hist Comput 15(2):35–52

Austrian GD (1982) Herman Hollerith: forgotten giant of information processing. Columbia University Press, New York

Aylen J (2010) Open versus closed innovation: development of the wide strip mill for steel in the United States during the 1920s. R&D Manag 40(1):67–80

Aylen J (2012) Bloodhood on my trail: building the Ferranti Argus process control computer. Int J Hist Eng Technol 82(1):1–36

© Springer-Verlag London Ltd. 2017
A. Tympas, *Calculation and Computation in the Pre-electronic Era*, History of Computing, https://doi.org/10.1007/978-1-84882-742-4

Babbage C (1851) The exposition of 1851: views of the industry, the science, and the government of England. John Murray, London

Babcock BE (1993) An error on a slide rule for 50 years? J Oughtred Soc 2(2):15–17

Babcock BE (1994) A guided tour of an 18th century Carpenter's rule. J Oughtred Soc 3(1):26–34

Babcock BE (1995a) K&E Student's and Beginner's slide rules 1897 to 1954. J Oughtred Soc 4(2):41–49

Babcock BE (1995b) Two Noble attempts to improve the slide rule. J Oughtred Soc 4(1):41–45

Barnard FAP (1869) Paris Universal exhibition, 1867: report on machinery and processes of the industrial arts and apparatus of the exact sciences. Van Nostrand, New York

Barnes C (1997a) Dating Otis-king slide rules. J Oughtred Soc 6(2):35–36

Barnes C (1997b) Fuller's telegraph computer. J Oughtred Soc 6(2):37–38

Barth CG (1902a) Barth's gear slide-rule. Am Mach:1075

Barth CG (1902b) Barth's lathe speed slide rules. Am Mach:1684–1685

Barth CG (1919a) Supplement to Frederick Taylor's 'on the art of cutting metals' I and II. Ind Manag 58(3):169–175

Barth CG (1919b) Supplement to Frederick Taylor's 'on the art of cutting metals' I and II. Ind Manag 58(4):282–287

Barth CG (1919c) Supplement to Frederick Taylor's 'on the art of cutting metals' I and II. Ind Manag 58(5):369–374

Barth CG (1919d) Supplement to Frederick Taylor's 'on the art of cutting metals' I and II. Ind Manag 58(6):483–487

Bascome GH (1913) Calculating scales. Power 37(9):308–309

Bazerman C (1999) The languages of Edison light. The MIT Press, Cambridge

Beattie R (1912) The best form of the resonance method of harmonic analysis. Electrician 69:63–66

Bedell F (1942) History of A-C wave form, its determination and standardization. AIEE Trans 61:864–868

Bedell F, Crehore AC (1893) Alternating currents: an analytical and graphical treatment for students and engineers. W. J. Johnston Co, New York

Berkeley EC (1949) Giant brains, or, machines that think. Wiley, New York

Berry CH (1921) The chilling of condensate. Power 54(5):181–182

Bevan B (1822) A practical treatise on the sliding rule, London

Bissell D (1998) Was the IDIIOM the first stand-alone CAD platform? IEEE Ann Hist Comput 20(2):14–29

Bissell C (2007) The Moniac: a hydromechanical analog computer of the 1950s. IEEE Control Syst Mag 27(1):69–74

Blair M (1943) An improved current integrator. Rev Sci Instrum 14(3):64–67

Block W (1930) Measurements: industrial and scientific. Instruments:577–580

Blondel A (1925) Une Methode Potentiometrique d'Analyze Harmonique des Ondes des Comants Alternatifs des Alternateurs. Revue Generale de l'Electricite

Boelsterli AA (1925) Charts for regulation of transformers. IEE J 63:692–696

Bowker GC (2000) And Susan Leigh star. Sorting things out: classification and its consequences. The MIT Press, Cambridge

Bowles MD (1996) U.S. technological enthusiasm and British technological skepticism in the age of the analog brain. IEEE Ann Hist Comput 18(4):5–15

Bragstad OS (1924) Determination of efficiency and phase displacement in transformers by measurement on open circuit and short circuit tests. Trans First World Power Conf 3:1004–1039

Brain RM, Norton Wise M (1999) Muscles and engines: indicator diagrams and Helmholtz's graphical methods. In: Biagioli M (ed) The science studies reader. Routledge, New York, pp 50–66

Brittain JE (1970) B. A. Behrend and the beginnings of electrical engineering 1870–1920. Ph.D. dissertation, Case Western University

Brittain JE (1985) From computor to electrical engineer: the remarkable career of Edith Clarke. IEEE Trans Educ E-28(4):184–189

Brittain JE (1989) The evolution of electrical and electronics engineering and the proceedings of the IRE: 1913–1937. Proc IEEE 77(6):837–856

Brittain JE (1990) The evolution of electrical and electronics engineering and the proceedings of the IRE: 1938–1962. Proc IEEE 78(1):5–30

Brittain JE (2006) Arthur E. Kennelly. Proc IEEE 94(9):1773–1775

Brooke RCR (1985) Distribution diary. IEE Proc 132 A(8):533+

Brookes LE (1905) The calculation of horsepower made easy. Frederick Drake and Co, Chicago

Brown GS (1981) Eloge: Harold Locke Hazen 1901–1980. Ann Hist Comput 3(1):4–12

Brown JK (2000) Design plans working drawings national styles: engineering practice in great Britain and the United States 1775–1945. Technol Cult 41(2):195–238

Brown SL, Wheeler LL (1941) A mechanical method for graphical solution of polynomials. Franklin Inst J 231(3):223–243

Brown SL, Wheeler LL (1942) Use of mechanical multiarmonograph for graphing types of functions and for solution of pairs of non-linear simultaneous equations. Rev Sci Instrum 13:493–495

Bush V (1920a) Alignment chart for circular and hyperbolic functions of a complex argument in rectangular coordinates. AIEE J 39:658–659

Bush V (1920b) A simple harmonic analyzer. AIEE J:903–905

Bush V (1936) Instrumental analysis. Trans Am Math Soc 42(10):649–669

Bush V (1943) Arthur Edwin Kennelly, 1861–1939. Natl Acad Sci Biogr Memoirs 22:83–119

Bush V, Hazen HL (1927) Integraph solutions of differential equations. Franklin Inst J:575–615

Bush V, Gage FD, Stewart HR (1927) A continuous integraph. J Franklin Inst 203(1):63–84

Butcher WL A device for averaging certain kinds of continuous records by the planimeter. Eng News 53(26):685. λείπει η χρονιά

Cajori F (1909) A history of the logarithmic slide rule and allied instruments. The Engineering News Publishing Company, New York

Campbell GA (1924) Mathematics in industrial research. Bell Syst Tech J 3:550–557

Campbell GA (1928) The practical application of the Fourier integral. Bell Syst Tech J 7:639–707

Campbell GA, Foster RM (1931) Fourier integrals for practical applications, Bell telephone system monograph B-584. Bell Telephone System Laboratories, New York

Campbell-Kelly M (1995) Development and structure of the international software industry 1950–1990. Bus Econ Hist 24(2):74–110

Campbell-Kelly M, Aspray W (1996) Computer: a history of the information machine. Basic Books, New York

Campbell-Kelly M, Croarken M, Flood R, Robson E (2003) The history of mathematical tables: from Sumer to spreadsheets. Oxford University Press, Oxford/New York

Canada AH (1948) Nomographs for computing exponential relationships. Gen Electr Rev 51:44–48

Care C (2010) Technology for modelling: electrical analogies, engineering practice, and the development of analogue computing. Springer, London

Carlson WB (1988) Academic entrepreneurship and engineering education: Dugald C. Jackson and the MIT-GE cooperative engineering course 1907–1932. Technol Cult 29(3):536–567

Carpenter RC (1903) Experimental engineering (and manual for testing), Fifth revised and enlarged edn. Wiley, New York

Carson J (1919) Theory of the transient oscillations of the electrical networks and transmission systems. AIEE Trans 38(1):345–427. 458–488

Carter C, Jr. (1963) Graphic representation of the impedance of networks containing resistances and two reactances. Am Power Conf Proc 25:834–837

Catt C (1999) Slide rule accuracy. J Oughtred Soc 8(2):5

Central Station Engineers of the Westinghouse Manufacturing Company (1944) Electrical transmission and distribution reference book. Westinghouse Electric and Manufacturing Company, East Pittsburgh

Ceruzzi PE (1991) When computers were human. Ann Hist Comput 13(1):237–244

Ceruzzi PE (1997) Crossing the divide: architectural issues and the emergence of the stored program computer 1935–1955. IEEE Ann Hist Comput 19(1):5–12

Chamberlain EJ (1997) The Voith slide rule and mechanical pencil combination. J Oughtred Soc 6(1):27–28

Chamberlain EJ (1998) Slide rule decimal point location methods. J Oughtred Soc 7(1):38–52

Chase GC (1952) History of mechanical computing. Proc ACM:1–28

Chase GC (1980) History of mechanical computing machinery. Ann Hist Comput 2(3):198–226

Chubb LW (1914) The analysis of periodic waves. Electr J 11(2):91–96

Chubb LW (1915) Polar and circular oscillograms and their practical application. Electr J 11(5):262–267

Clark CA (2001) Evolution for John Doe: pictures the public and the scopes trial debate. J Am Hist 87(4):1275–1303

Clarke E (1923) A transmission line calculator. Gen Electr Rev 26(6):380–390

Clarke E (1926a) Simplified transmission line calculations. Gen Electr Rev 29(5):321–329

Clarke E (1926b) Steady-state stability in transmission systems: calculation by means of equivalent circuits or circle diagrams. AIEE Trans 45:22–41. 80–94

Clarke E (1943) Circuit analysis of A-C power systems: symmetrical and related components, vol I. Wiley, New York

Clarke E (1944) Trends in power system analysis. Midwest Power Conf Proc 7:172–180

Clason CB (1964) Delights of the slide rule. Thomas Y. Crowell Co., New York

Claudy CH (1914) A great brass brain. Sci Am:197–198

Clymer AB (1993) The mechanical analog computers of Hannibal ford and William Newell. IEEE Ann Hist Comput 15(2):19–34

Cockroft JD, Coe RT, Tyacke JA, Walker M (1925) An electric harmonic analyzer. IEE J 63(337):69–113

Combet G (1929) Methode Graphique de Calcul des Reseaux de Distribution d' Energie Electrique. Revue Generale de L' Electricite 25(14):535–542

Comrie LJ (1932) The applications of the Hollerith tabulating machine to Brown's tables of the moon. R Astron Soc Mon Not 92(7):694–707

Comrie LJ (1944) Recent progress in scientific computing. J Sci Instrum 21:129–135

Comrie LJ (1946) The application of commercial calculating machines to scientific computation. Math Table Other Aids Calc 2(16):149–159

Cortada JW (1993) Before the computer: IBM, NCR Burroughs, and the industry they created 1865–1956. Princeton University Press, Princeton

Cox WM (1891a) Equivalents of useful numbers for simplifying calculations and for slide rule practice. Eng News-Rec 25:5–6

Cox WM (1891b) The manheim slide rule. Keuffel and Esser, New York

Croarken M (1990) Early scientific computing in Britain. Clarendon Press, Oxford

Croarken M, Campbell-Kelly M (2000) Beautiful numbers: the rise and decline of the British Association Mathematical Tables Committee 1871–1965. IEEE Ann Hist Comput 22(4):44–61

Crowhurst NH (1965) Graphical calculators and their design. Hayden, New York

Cusumano MA (1991) Factory concepts and practices in software development. Ann Hist Comput 13(1):3–30

D' Ocagne M (1915) Numerical tables and nomograms. In: Knott GG (ed) Napier tercentenary memorial volume. Green and Company and the Royal Society of England, London, pp 279–280

D' Ocagne M (1928) Le Calcul Simplifie par les Procedes Mecaniques et Graphiques, Troisieme edn. Gauthier-Villars, Paris

De Beauclair W (1986) Alwin Walther, IPM, and the development of calculator/computer technology in Germany, 1930–1945. Ann Hist Comput 8(4):334–350

De Cesaris B (1998) The mechanical engineer. J Oughtred Soc 7(1):23–24

Dellenbaugh FS Jr (1921) An electromechanical device for rapid schedule harmonic analysis of complex waves. AIEE J:135–144

Dellenbaugh FS Jr (1923a) Another harmonic analyzer. AIEE J:58–61

Dellenbaugh FS Jr (1923b) Artificial lines with distributed constants. AIEE Trans 42:803–823

Der Praktische Maschinen-Constructeur 27 (Unland, 1894), 8

Dietzold RL (1937) The isograph: a mechanical root finder. Bell Lab Rec 36(4):130–140

Dovan JF (1950) The serial-memory digital differential analyzer. Math Table Other Aids Comput:102–112

Drew RL (1926) The slide rule and the power man. Power 63(25):967

Dunstan LA (1947a) Machine computation of power network performance. AIEE Trans 66:610–624

Dunstan LA (1947b) Machine computing of networks. Electr Eng:901–906

Durand WL (1922) Why not use a slide rule? Power 55(18):705

Dwight HB (1925) Transmission line formulas: a collection of methods of calculation for the electrical design of transmission lines (second edition revised and enlarged). Van Nostrand, New York

Eckert WJ (1984) Punched card methods in scientific computation. The MIT Press, Cambridge

Electric Journal 3 (1906):116–118

Electrical Accounting Systems (1929) Electrician 103:598

Electrical Review and Western Electrician (1909) 54(9):115, 399

Electrical World 50 (1907):402

Ellis JP (1961) The theory and operation of the slide rule. Dover, New York

Elzen B, Mackenzie D (1994) The social limits of speed: the development and use of supercomputers. IEEE Ann Hist Comput 16(1):46–61

Employees Operate 'Brainy' Accounting Machines (1938) Snap Shots:8

Ende JVD (1992) Tidal calculations in the Netherlands 1920–1960. IEEE Ann Hist Comput 14(3):23–33

Ensmenger N (2016) The multiple meanings of a flowchart. Inf Cult J Hist 51(3):321–351

Epperly RA, Erich Heberlein G, Eads LG (1999) Thermography: a tool for reliability and safety. IEEE Ind Appl Mag 5(1):28–36

Epperly RA, Erich Heberlein G, Eads LG Thermography: a tool for reliability and safety. IEEE Ind Appl Mag 5(3):8

Evans RD, Sels HK (1924) Power limitations of transmission systems. AIEE Trans 43:26–38. 71–103

Evesham HA (1986) Origins and development of nomography. Ann Hist Comput 8(4):323–333

Ewing DD (1923) Tables of transmission line constants. Purdue University Press, Lafayette

Extreme Accuracy With a Slide Rule (1923) Power 58(23):920

Fallon KK (1998) Early computer graphics developments in the architecture engineering and construction industry. IEEE Ann Hist Comput 20(2):20–29

Farey J (1927) A treatise on the steam engine. Longman, Rees, Orme, Brown, and Green, London

Fasal JH (1968) Nomography. Frederick Ungar, New York

Feazel B (1994a) Palmer's computing scale. J Oughtred Soc 3(1):9–17

Feazel B (1994b) Special Purpose Slide Rules. J Oughtred Soc 3(2):43–44

Feazel B (1995) Plamer's computing scale revisited. J Oughtred Soc 4(1):5–8

Feazel B (1997a) Electrical Wireman's combined gage and calculator. J Oughtred Soc 6(2):9–10

Feazel B (1997b) The Roylance electrical slide rule. J Oughtred Soc 6(2):39

Feely WE (1994) The engineer's rule. J Oughtred Soc 3(2):48–49

Feely WE (1996) Keuffel and Esser slide rules. Chron Early Am Ind Assoc Chron 49(2):50–52

Feely WE (1997a) The fuller spiral scale slide rule. Early Am Ind Assoc Chron 50(3):93–98

Feely WE (1997b) Thacher cylindrical slide rules. Early Am Ind Assoc Chron 50(4):123–127

Ferguson ES (1989) Technical journals and the history of technology. In: Cutliffe SH, Post RC (eds) Context: history and the history of technology. Lehigh University Press, Bethlehem, pp 53–70

Ferguson ES (1992) Engineering and the mind's eye. The MIT Press, Cambridge

Fifer S (1961) Analogue computation: theory, techniques, and applications, vols I–IV. McGraw-Hill, New York

Fisher HD (1916) Interpolating logarithms. Power 43(20):703–704

Flax S (1995) The tools to create. Trade Catalog, ca

Foster DE (1914) Engineers' improved slide rule. Power 39(15):537

Franklin MW (1909) Transmission line calculations, Part I. Gen Electr Rev 12(9):447–451

Franklin W (1967) Partners in creating: the first century of Keuffel and Esser. Keuffel and Esser, New York

Freeman WE (1909) Pay-roll problems of the electric light industry. NELA 32nd Conv 3:74–119

Fry TC (1941) Industrial mathematics. Bell Syst Tech J 20(3):255–292

Fry M (1945) Designing computing mechanisms. Mach Des:103–108

Furfari FA Benjamin Garver Lamme: electrical engineer. IEEE Ind Appl Mag 5(6):12–14

Gabbert M (1999) Slide rule competition in Texas High Schools. J Oughtred Soc 8(2):56–58

Gaines MW (1905) Tabulating-machine cost-accounting for factories of diversified product. Eng Mag:364–373

Garcelon DC (1996) Solving the Keuffel & Esser catalog problem. J Oughtred Soc 5(2):52–53

General Electric Company Transmission Line Calculations, Engineering Department Technical Letter (no. 309, 1909, September and no. 309A, July 1911) (Smithsonian Institution, National Museum of American History, Trade Catalogs Collections, Mezzanine Library, Washington, DC)

General Electric Company Tables for Transmission Line Calculations, Engineering Department Technical Letter (no. 309-A, July 1911a) (Smithsonian Institution, National Museum of American History, Trade Catalogs Collections, Mezzanine Library, Washington, DC)

General Electric Company Hydro Electric Calculations, Engineering Department Technical Letter (no. 316, 1911b, September, and 316A, November, 1913) (General Electric Archives, Schenectady, New York)

General Electric Company Overhead Line Calculations, Engineering Department Technical Letter (no. 318, November 1911c) (General Electric Archives, Schenectady, New York)

General Electric Company Overhead Line Calculations, Engineering Department Technical Letter (no. 335D, February 1919) (General Electric Archives, Schenectady, New York)

Get this Handy New Ohmite Ohm's Law Calculator Instruments (Index 1941):45

Giet A, Head JW, Phippen HD (1956) Abacs or nomograms: an introduction to their theory and construction illustrated by examples from engineering and physics. Philosophical Library, New York

Goldberg S (1992) Inventing a climate of opinion: Vannevar Bush and the decision to build the bomb. ISIS 83:429–452

Goodwin H (1923) Qualitative analysis of transmission lines. AIEE Trans 42:24–41

Graham FD (1932) Audel's new electric library: mathematics-calculations, vol XI. Audel, New York

Grattan-Guinness I (1990) Work for the hairdressers: the production of de Prony's logarithmic and trigonometric tables. Ann Hist Comput 12(3):177–185

Gray TS (1931) A photo-electric integraph. J Franklin Inst:77–102

Grier DA (1997) Gertrude blanch of the mathematical tables project. IEEE Ann Hist Comput 19(4):18–27

Grier DA (1998) The math tables project of the work project administration: the reluctant start of the computing era. IEEE Ann Hist Comput 20(3):33–49

Grier DA (2000) Ida Rhodes and the dreams of a human computer. IEEE Ann Hist Comput 22(1):82–85

Grier DA (2007) When computers were human. Princeton University Press, Princeton

Gross ETB (1959) Network analyzer installations in Canada and the United States. Am Power Conf Proc 21:665–669

Gussow LH (1946) Calculating voltage drop in industrial A. C. circuits. Electr World:60–63

Hankins TL (1999) Blood, dirt and nomograms: a particular history of graphs. ISIS 90:50–80

Hankins TL, Silverman RJ (1995) Instruments and the imagination. Princeton University Press, Princeton

Harmonic Analyzer for Power Circuits, NELA, Publication Number 278–22. Edison Electric Institute Library Archives, Washington, DC

Haskell AC (1919) How to make and use graphic charts. Codex, New York

Hawkins N (1895) Handbook of calculations for engineers and firemen. Audel, New York

Hawkins N (1897) New catechism of electricity, a practical treatise. Audel, New York

Heard WL Coordinated graphic symbols for electric power and control drawings. Edison Electr Inst Bull 14(9):311–312

Heide L (1991) From invention to production: the development of punched-card machinery by F. R. Bull and K. A. Knutsen. Ann Hist Comput 13(3):261–272

Heide L (1994) Punched-card and computer applications in Denmark 1911–1970. Hist Technol 11:77–79

Heide L (1997) Shaping a technology: American punched card systems 1880–1914. IEEE Ann Hist Comput 19(4):28–41

Heide L (2009) Punched-card systems and the early information explosion, 1880–1945. Johns Hopkins University Press, Baltimore

Helfand J (2006) Reinventing the wheel. Princeton Architectural Press, New York

Higgins WHC, Holbrook BD, Emling JW (1992) Defense research at Bell Laboratories. Ann Hist Comput 4(3):218–244

Hobsbawm E (1987) The age of revolution 1789–1848. Pantheon, New York

Hobsbawm E (1989) The age of empire 1875–1914. Vintage

Hobsbawm E (1994) Age of extremes: the short twentieth century 1914–1991. Michael Joseph, London

Hobsbawm E (1996) The age of capital: 1848–1875. Vintage

Hobsbawm E, Ranger T (1983) The invention of tradition. Cambridge University Press, New York

Hodgson JL (1928) Integration of diagrams. Instruments:479–482

Hodgson JL (1929a) Integration of 'orifice head' charts by means of special planimeters. Instruments:95–96

Hodgson JL (1929b) The radial planimeter. Instruments:227–231

Hoelscher RP, Arnold JN, Pierce SH (1952) Graphic aids in engineering computation. McGraw-Hill, New York

Holden CA (1901) The use of calculating machines. Eng News 45(22):405

Holst PA (1996) Svein Rosseland and the Oslo analyzer. IEEE Ann Hist Comput 18(4):16–26

Hopkinson J (1894a) The relation of mathematics to engineering. The Electrician:41–43

Hopkinson J (1894b) The relation of mathematics to engineering. The Electrician:78–80. 85

Hopp PM (1995) Otis-king update. J Oughtred Soc 4(2):33–40

Hopp PM (1996) Otis-king: conclusions? J Oughtred Soc 5(2):62–67

Hopp PM (1999) Slide rule: their history models and makers. Astragal Press, Mendham

Horsburgh EM (ed) (1914) Modern instruments and methods of calculation: a handbook of the Napier tercentenary exhibition. Bell and Sons, London. Reprinted with an 'Introduction' by Michael R. Williams. Tomash Publishers, Los Angeles, 1982:ix–xxi

Horton JW (1928) The empirical analysis of complex electric waves. Bell Telephone Laboratories Reprint B-320

Houghtaling W (1899) The steam engine indicator and its appliances. The American Industrial Publishing, Bridgeport

Hounshell DA (1984) From the American system to mass production 1800–1932: the development of manufacturing Technology in the United States. The John Hopkins University Press, Baltimore

Houston EJ, Kennelly AE (1895) Resonance in alternating current lines. AIEE Trans 12:133–169

How to Read a Slide Rule (1915) Power 42(6):192–194

Hughes TP (1983) Networks of power: electrification in western society 1880–1930. The John Hopkins University Press, Baltimore

Hunt BJ (1983) Practice vs. theory: the British electrical debate 1888–1891. Isis 74:341–355

Illuminating Laboratory Models Electrical Engineering (1948):636

Imburgia CA, Stagg GW, Kirchmayer L, Geiser KR (1955) Design and application of a penalty factor computer. Am Power Conf Proc 17:687–697

Imlay LE (1925) Mechanical characteristics of transmission lines II: span formulae and general methods of calculation. Electr J 22(2):53–57

Indicator Diagrams Electrician (1894):690–691

Jacobsen F (1946) Diagram for calculating the sag and strain of conductors of overhead lines. CIGRE 2(214)

Jehl F (1939) Menlo Park reminiscences. The Edison Institute, Dearborn

Jenkins AL (1917) Design of special slide rules, Parts I and II. Ind Manag:241–389

Jennings PD, Quinan GE (1946) The use of business Machines in determining the distribution of load and reactive components in power line network. AIEE Trans 65:1045–1046

Johansson M (1996) Early analog computers in Sweden—with examples from Chalmers University of Technology and the Swedish Aerospace Industry. IEEE Ann Hist Comput 18(4):27–33

Johnson JB (1932) The cathode ray oscillograph. Bell Syst Tech J 11:1–27

Jordan DW (1985) The cry for useless knowledge: education for a new Victorian technology. IEE Proc 132 A.8:587–601

Karapetoff V (1922) Generalized proportional dividers. Sibley J Eng:5–6

Karapetoff V (1923a) The 'Heavisidion': a computing kinematic device for long transmission lines. AIEE Trans 42:42–53

Karapetoff V (1923b) The 'Blondelion': a kinematic device which indicates the performance of a polyphase synchronous generator or motor. AIEE Trans 42:144–156

Karapetoff V (1925) Double integraph for electric line transients. Sibley J Eng 39:243–260

Kennelly AE (1912) An investigation of transmission line phenomena by means of hyperbolic functions: the distribution of voltage and current over Π artificial lines in the steady state. Electr World 60(6):306–311

Kennelly AE (1913) A convenient form of continuous-current artificial line. Electr World 61(24):1311–1312

Kennelly AE (1914a) Chart atlas of complex hyperbolic and circular functions. Harvard University Press, Cambridge, MA

Kennelly AE (1914b) Tables of complex hyberbolic and circular functions. Harvard University Press, Cambridge

Kennelly AE (1917) Artificial electric lines. McGraw-Hill, New York

Kennelly AE (1925) The application of Hyberbolic functions to electrical engineering problems, 3rd edn. McGraw-Hill, New York

Kennelly AE (1928) Electric lines and nets: their theory and electrical behavior. McGraw-Hill, New York

Keuffel & Esser Trade Catalog (1933) 18–19 (Smithsonian Institution, National Museum of American History, Trade Catalogs Collection, Mezzanine Library)

Kevles DJ (1977) The National Science Foundation and the debate over postwar research policy 1942-1945: a political interpretation of science—the endless frontier. ISIS 68(241):4–26

Kidwell PA (1990) American scientists and calculating machines—from novelty to commonplace. Ann Hist Comput 12(1):31–40

Kidwell PA (2000) The adding machine fraternity of St. Louis: creating a center of invention 1880–1920. IEEE Ann Hist Comput 22(2):4–21

Kidwell PA (2015) Useful instruction for practical people: early printed discussions of the slide rule in the US. IEEE Ann Hist Comput 37(01):36–43

Kidwell PA, Ceruzzi PE (1994) Landmarks in digital computing: a Smithsonian pictorial history. Smithsonian Institution Press, Washington, DC

Kidwell PA, Ackerberg-Hastings A, Roberts DL (2008) Tools of American mathematics teaching, 1800–2000. Johns Hopkins University Press, Baltimore, pp 105–122

Kimball E Jr (mid-1940s) A fundamental punched card method for technical computations. Bureau of the Census Machine Tabulation Division, Washington, CA

Kinter SM (1904) Alternating-current wave form analysis. Electr World Eng 63(22):1023+

Kirsten FK (1923–1929) Transmission line design. University of Washington Press, Seattle

Kistermann FW (1991) The invention and development of the Hollerith punched card: in commemoration of the 130th anniversary of the birth of Herman Hollerith and for the 100th anniversary of large scale data processing. Ann Hist Comput 13(3):245–259

Kistermann FW (1995) The way to the first automatic sequence-controlled calculator: the 1953 DEHOMAG D 11 tabulator. IEEE Ann Hist Comput 17(2):33–49

Kistermann FW (1997) Locating the victims: the nonrole of punched card technology and census work. IEEE Ann Hist Comput 19(2):31–45

Kleinman DL (1994) Layers of interests layers of influence: business and the genesis of the National Science Foundation. Sci Technol Hum Values 19(3):259–282

Kliever W (1941) Integrator for circular ordinates. Instruments 121:138

Kline RR (1987) Science and engineering theory in the invention and development of the induction motor 1880–1900. Technol Cult 28(2):283–313

Kline RR (1992) Steinmetz: Engineer and Socialist. The John Hopkins University Press, Baltimore

Kruger MK (1929) A slide rule for filter computations. Instruments:233–238

Kurman Calculator. Instruments (1941) 14(10)

Lacan J (1977) The four fundamental concepts of psycho-analysis, edited by Jacques-Alain miller and translated by Alain Sheridan. Hogarth Press, London

Larson M (1993a) The runner. J Oughtred Soc 2(1):40–43

Larson M (1993b) Runner indicator or cursor? J Oughtred Soc 2(1):47–48

Last Word in Equipment for Accounting Work Snap Shots (1922):8

Lecuyer C (1992) The making of a science based technological university: Karl Compton, James Killian, and the reform of MIT 1930–1957. Hist Stud Phys Sci 23(1):153–180

Lecuyer C (1995) MIT progressive reform and 'industrial service' 1890–1920. Hist Stud Phys Sci 26(1):35–88

Leffingwell WH (1926) The office appliance manual. National Association of Office Appliance Manufacturers, Chicago

Leonard JN (1932) Loki: the life of Charles Proteus Steinmetz. Doubleday, Doran and Co, New York

Light JS (1999) When computers were women. Technol Cult 40(3):455–483

Lighting Calculations Lightened Westinghouse Engineer 8 (1948):174

Lipka J (1918) Graphical and mechanical computation. Wiley, New York

Low FR (1910) The steam engine indicator, 3rd rev and enlarg edn. McGraw-Hill, New York

Low FR (1914) To find the number of integer places in a product or quotient. Power 39(12):400–401

Lubar S (1995) Representation and power. Technol Cult 36(Suppl 2):S54–S82

Lundberg KH (2005) The history of analog computing. IEEE Control Syst Mag:22–28

Lynch AC (1989) Sylvanus Thompson: teacher, researcher, historian. IEE Proc 136.A.6:306–312

Lyon R (1998) Dating of the Otis-king: an alternative theory developed through use of the internet. J Oughtred Soc 7(1):33–37

MacKenzie D (1990) The influence of the los Alamos and Livermore National Laboratories on the development of supercomputing. Ann Hist Comput 13(4):325–334

Maggi L (1946) The calculation of block foundations for transmission-line towers. Int Conf Large Electr Syst (CIGRE) 2(220)

Mahoney MS (1990) The roots of software engineering. CWI Q 3(4):325–334

Marble FG (1944) An automatic vibration analyzer. Bell Lab Rec 22(7):376–380

Marsden B (2004) Watt's perfect engine: steam and the age of invention. Columbia University Press, New York

Martin E (1992) The calculating machines: their history and development. The MIT Press, Cambridge

Mathematical Research Bell Laboratories Record (1925) 1(1):15–18

McCormack HS (1913) Keeping books by machine: the punched card as a saver of brain energy. Sci Am:194–195

McCurdy RG, Blye PW (1929) Electrical wave analyzers for power and telephone systems. Bell Telephone Lab Reprint B-439

McFarland SL (1995) America's pursuit of precision bombing 1910–1945. Smithsonian Institution Press, Washington, DC

Measuring Area of Indicator Diagram (1922) Power 55(18):693–696

Medwick PA (1988) Douglas Hartree and early computations in quantum mechanics. Ann Hist Comput 10(2):105–111

Mercner RO (1937) The mechanism of the isograph. Bell Lab Rec 26(4):135–140

Merrill GS (1946) Slide-disk calculator. Gen Electr Rev 49:30–33

Miller RN (1915) Slide rule quadratics. Power 42(12):422–423

Miller GL (1990) Charles Babbage and the design of intelligence: computers and society in 19th-century England. Bull Sci Technol Soc 10:68–76

Mindell D (2000) Opening Black's box: rethinking Feedback's myth of origin. Technol Cult 41(3):405–434

Mindell D (2004) Between human and machine. Johns Hopkins University Press, Baltimore

Montgomery HC (1938) An optical harmonic analyzer. Bell Syst Tech J 27:406–415

Moore AF (1913) Obtaining wire resistance on slide rules. Power 37(5):151

Moore CR, Curtis AS (1927) An analyzer for the voice frequency range. Bell Syst Tech J 6:217–247

Morrison JP (1915) Handy flywheel calculator. Power 42(20):683

Muller RO (1916) Pointing off decimals with the slide rule. Power 43(25):888

Murray FJ (1961) Mathematical machines: analog devices, vol II. Columbia University Press, New York

Nebeker F (ed) (1994) Sparks of genius: portraits of electrical engineering excellence. IEEE Press, New York

Nebeker F (ed) (1995) Calculating the weather: meteorology in the 20th century. Harcourt Brace, San Diego

NELA (1916) Bulletin 10, Part III, (New Series, no. 9), 782–783

Nesbit W (1919 and 1920) Electrical characteristics of transmission circuits. Electr J XVI–XVIII (Series of Articles)

Nesbit W (1926) Electrical characteristics of transmission circuits, 3rd edn. Westinghouse Technical Night School Press, East Pittsburgh

Network Calculator… Mathematician Par Excellence," Westinghouse Engineer 4 (1944): editorial (frontcover)

New Calculator Now Sold in United States Instruments (1928):294

Norberg AL (1990) High-technology calculation in the early 20th century: punched card machinery in business and government. Technol Cult 31(4):753–779

O'Neill EF (ed) (1985) A history of engineering and science in the bell system: transmission technology 1925–1975. AT&T Bell Laboratories, Indianapolis

Otnes R (1989) Keuffel and Esser Slide Rules. Historische Burowelt:15–20

Otnes R (1991) The Otis-king slide rule. J Oughtred Soc 0(0):7–8

Otnes R (1993) Thacher notes. J Oughtred Soc 2(1):21–25

Otnes R (1995) A page from the 1883 Keuffel & Esser catalog. J Oughtred Soc 4(2):14–15

Otnes R (1997) K&E instruction manuals. J Oughtred Soc 6(1):18–21

Otnes R (1998a) Notes on Frederick post slide rules. J Oughtred Soc 7(1):7–10

Otnes R (1998b) American slide rule instruction books before 1890. J Oughtred Soc 7(2):31–34

Otnes R (1999) Direct reading frequency response slide rule. J Oughtred Soc 8(1):49–50

Otnes R (2001) Keuffel & Esser—1880 to 1899. J Oughtred Soc 10(1):18–28

Otnes R. Keuffel and Esser and the American Engineering Slide Rule, Manuscript in the collection of the Division of Computers, National Museum of American History

Otnes R, Schure C (1996) The Blundell vector slide rule. J Oughtred Soc 5(1):18–19

Owen EL (1998) A history of harmonics in power systems. IEEE Ind Appl Mag 4(1):6–12

Owens L (1986) Vannevar bush and the differential analyzer: the text and context of an early computer. Technol Cult 27(1):63–95

Owens L (1990) MIT and the federal 'angel': Academic R&D and Federal-Private Cooperation before World War II. ISIS 81:188–213

Owens L (1994) The counterproductive Management of Science in the Second World War: Vannevar Bush and the Office of Scientific Research and Development. Bus Hist Rev 68:515–576

Owens L (1996) Where are we going Phil Morse? Challenging agendas and the rhetoric of obviousness in the transformation of computing at MIT 1939–1957. IEEE Ann Hist Comput 18(4):34–41

Payne H, O'Neill H (1922) A boiler-room slide rule. Power 55(14):543–544

Pebble JP (1908a) The construction of graphical charts. Am Mach

Pebble JP (1908b) The construction of graphical charts. Am Mach

Pebble JP (1908c) The construction of graphical charts. Am Mach

Pelaez E (1999) The stored-program computer: two conceptions. Soc Stud Sci 29(3):359–389

Pender H (1905) Formulae for the wire table. Electr Club J 11(5):327

Pernot FE (1916) Formulae and tables for the design of air-core inductance coils. University of California Press, Berkeley

Pernot FE (1918) Logarithms of hyperbolic functions to twelve significant figures. University of California Press, Berkeley

Pernot FE (1919) An extension of the step-by-step method of transmission line computation. University of California Press, Berkeley

Peters U (1903) The balance lever as a calculating machine. Iron Age 72:12–13

Peterson HA, Concordia C (1945) Analyzers...for use in engineering and scientific problems. Gen Electr Rev 48:29–37

Philips VJ (1985) Optical chemical and capillary oscillographs. IEE Proc 132.A.8:503–511

Pickworth CN (1903) Instructions for the use of a. W. Faber's improved calculating rule. A. W. Faber, London

Pinch T, Trocco F (2004) Analog days: the invention and impact of the moog synthesizer. Harvard University Press, Cambridge, MA

Polachek H (1995) History of the journal 'mathematical tables and other aids to computation' 1959–1965. IEEE Ann Hist Comput 17(3):67–74

Polakov WN (1913) Power plant log calculator. Power 37(17):596–597

Poulantzas N (1975) Classes in contemporary capitalism. New Left Books, London

Power (1915) 42(16):567

Power (1921) 53(8):329

Pray T (1899) Twenty years with the indicator, vol 1. Boston Journal of Commerce and Publishing, Boston

Preston F (2003) Vannevar Bush's network analyzer at the Massachusetts Institute of Technology. IEEE Ann Hist Comput:75–78

Puchta S (1996) On the role of mathematics and mathematical knowledge in the invention of Vannevar Bush's early analog computers. IEEE Ann Hist Comput 18(4):49–59

Puchta S (1997) Why and how American electrical engineers developed Heaviside's operational calculus. Arch Int Hist Sci 47:57–107

Ragland-Sullivan E (1986) Jacques Lacan and the philosophy of psychoanalysis. University of Illinois, Chicago

Randell B (1982) From analytical engine to electronic digital computer: the contributions of Ludgate Torres and bush. Ann Hist Comput 4(4):327–341

Raymond-Barker E (1903) The calculator board and graphic methods. Electr Rev 53:329–331

Richardson CG (1914) Fixing the decimal point in slide-rule calculations. Power 39(16):551–552

Roberts KD (1983) Carpenters and engineers slide rules (Part I, History). Chron Early Am Ind Assoc 36(1):1–5

Rosebrugh TR (1919) The calculation of transmission line networks. Bulletin: School of Enginering Research, University of Toronto 1

Rossiter MW (1980) 'Women's work' in science. Isis 71(258):123–140

Row JE (1928) Instruments for the solution of triangles and other polygons. Instruments:355–356

Russell SB (1915) A thinking machine planning and theories. Sci Am 113:246–257

Rybner J (1930) Nomograms. Gen Electr Rev 33(9):164–179

Ryle PJ (1948) Practical long line A.C. transmission calculations and the design and use of a circle diagram calculating board. Int Conf Large Electr Syst, 12th Session 8(402):1–12

Sakai Y (1905) How to use the slide rule on the wire table. Electr Club J 11(10):632–633

Schaffer S (1994) Babbage's intelligence: calculating engines and the factory system. Crit Inq 21(1):203–227

Schell HB (1916) Interpolating logarithms with the slide rule. Power 43(13):451–452

Scheyer E (1922) When perforated paper goes to work: how strips of paper can endow inanimate machines with brains of their own. Sci Am:394–395. 445

Schlesinger WM (1892) Power transmission. Electr World XIX(10):154–155

Schmitt OH, Tolles WE (1942) Electronic differentiation. Rev Sci Instrum 13:115–118

Schuitema Y (1993) The ALRO circular slide rule. J Oughtred Soc 2(2):24–37

Schuitema Y (1999) Articles on Dutch contributions to slide rule history in the 20th century. Number 2: F. J. Vaes. J Oughtred Soc 8(2):39–42

Schuitema IJ, van Herwijnen H (2003) Calculating on slide rule and disk. Astragal Press, Mendham

Schultz JH (1929) Lochkartenverfahren und Mitlaufende Kalkulation in der Elektrotechniscen. Industrie Technik und Wirtschaft 22:41–45

Schure C (1994a) The Scofield-Thacher slide rule. J Oughtred Soc 3(1):20–25

Schure C (1994b) The irony of it all. J Oughtred Soc 3(2):45

Schure C (1997) Slide rule watches. J Oughtred Soc 6(1):47–48

Scott CF (1905) How to remember the wire table. Electr Club J 11(4):220–223

Scott CF (1919) Finding the size of wire. Electr J 16(7)

Scranton P (1997) Endless novelty: specialty production and American industrialization. Princeton University Press, Princeton

Serrell LW (1889) Calculations for long-distance electric power transmission. Electr World:292

Shapiro S (1997) Splitting the difference: the historical necessity of synthesis in software engineering. IEEE Ann Hist Comput 19(1):20–54

Shapiro FR (2000) Origin of the term software: evidence from the JSTOR electronic journal archive. IEEE Ann Hist Comput 22(2):69–70

Shaw HS (1886) H. Mechanical integrators including the various forms of planimeters. Van Nostrand, New York

Shelley P (1947) The Oklahoma gas and electric company method for load determination on distribution transformers. Edison Electr Inst Bull:17–19

Sibley Journal of Engineering XXXII (1918):550

Simons DM (1925) Calculation of the electrical problems of transmission by underground cables. Electr J 22(8):366–384

Sinclair B (1986) 'inventing a genteel tradition': MIT crosses the river. In: Sinclair B (ed) New perspectives on technology and American culture. American Philosophical Society Library, Philadelphia, pp 1–18

Skinner PH (1915) Computing machines in engineering. Eng News, January 7, pp 25–27

Slichter CS (1909) Graphical computation of Fourier's constants for alternating-current waves. Electr World 54:146–147

Small JS (1993) General-purpose electronic analog computing: 1945–1965. IEEE Ann Hist Comput 15(2):8–18

Small JS (1994) Engineering technology and design: the post-second world war development of electronic analogue computers. Hist Technol 11:33–48

Smith DE (1925) History of mathematics, vol II. Ginn, Boston

Smith PH (1939) Transmission line calculator. Electronics 12:29–31

Smith SB (1983) The great mental calculators. Columbia University Press, New York

Smith RE (1989) A historical overview of computer architecture. Ann Hist Comput 10(4):277–303

Solomon AB (1919) An adding slide rule. Power 50(11):437

Special HP-35 Anniversary Edition International Association of Calculator Collector 17 (Summer 1997)

Spitzglass JM (1922, 1916) Slide rule and flow computer." Power 43(8):257

Spufford F, Uglow J (eds) (1996) Cultural Babbage: technology, time and invention. Faber and Faber, London

Stanley HC (1918) Graphical representation of resistances and Reactances in multiple. Gen Electr Rev 21(2):133+

Stanley VK (1922) Why not use a slide rule? Power 55(22):866

Stanley PE (1984) Carpenters' and engineers' slide rules (Part II, Routledges' rule). Chron Early Am Ind Assoc 37(2):25–27

Stanley PE (1987) Carpenters' and engineers' slide rules (Part III, Errors in the data tables). Chron Early Am Ind Assoc 40(1):7–8

Stanley PE (1994) Letters. J Oughtred Soc 3(1):35–37

Stanley PE (2004) Source book for rule collectors. Astragal Press, Mendham

Steinmetz CP (1897) Theory and calculation of alternating current phenomena (with the Assistance of Ernst J. Berg). W. J. Johnston Co., New York

Steinmetz CP (1917) Engineering mathematics (third edition revised and enlarged). McGraw-Hill, New York

Stocklmayer SM, Treagust DF (1985) Two electrical periodicals: the electrician and the electrical review 1880-1890. IEE Proc 132.A(8):575–581

Strange P (1979) Early periodical holdings in the IEE library. IEE Proc 126(9):941–942

Sumner J (2001) John Richardson, saccharometry and the pounds-per-barrel extract: the construction of a quantity. Br J Hist Sci 34(3):255–273

Svoboda A (1948) Computing mechanisms and linkages. McGraw-Hill, New York

Swartzlander E (1995) Generations of calculators. IEEE Ann Hist Comput 17(3):75–77

Task Force Plans System Expansion Electrical World (1959):88–89

Taylor FW (1907) On the art of cutting metals. ASME Trans 28:31–279

Teichmuller J (1893) Ueber die Stromverteilung in Elektrischen Leitungsnetzen. Elektrotechnische Zeitschrift 37(15):537–540

Teichmuller J (1894) The calculation of mains. The Electrician:560–561

Technology Review (1962):22

Teplow L (1928) Stability of synchronous motors under variable-torque loads as determined by the recording product integraph. Gen Electr Rev 31(7):356–365

The Analysis of Wave Forms Electric Journal 11(2) (1914)

The Hatchet Planimeter. The Electrician (1894):137–138

The Mechanical Accountant. Engineering (1902):840–841

The Miscalculation of Mains. The Electrician (1894):384–385

The Monogram Salutes... The GE Monogram 17(10) (1940):17

The Monogram Salutes... The GE Monogram 18(4) (1941):17

The Slide Rule I (1914) Power 39(6):210–211

The Slide Rule II (1914) Power 39(7):245–246

The Slide Rule III (1914) Power 39(8): 283–284

The Slide Rule I: Reading the Scales; Multiplication and Division. Power 57(20) (1922):774–775

The Slide Rule II: Proportion; Squares and Square Roots; Cubes and Cube Roots. (1922) Power 57(21):812–813

The Tag-Isom Blending Calculator Instruments (1928): 64–65

The Whythe Complex Slide Rule in Fuller Style (1999) J Oughtred Soc 8(1):15–17

Thielemans ML (1920a) Calculs et Diagrammes Des Lignes De Transport De Force A Longue Distance. Comptes Rendus:1170+

Thielemans P (1920b) Calculs Diagrammes et Regulation Des Lignes De Transport D' Energie A Longue Distance. Revue Generale De L'Electricite. 403, 435, 475, 515

Thielemans P (1921) Calculs Diagrammes et Regulation Des Lignes De Transport D' Energie A Longue Distance. Revue Generale De L'Electricite 451

Thompson SP (1905) Harmonic analysis reduced to simplicity. The Electrician:78–80

Thompson JE (1930) A manual of the slide rule. Van Nostrand, New York

Tomayko JE (1985) Helmut Hoelzer's fully electronic analog computer. Ann Hist Comput 7(3):227–241

Turck JAV (1972) Origin of modern calculating machines. Arno Press, New York

Turner AJ (1993) Of time and measurement: studies in the history of horology and fine technology. Varorium, Norfolk

Tympas A (1996) From digital to analog and back: the ideology of intelligent Machines in the History of the electrical analyzer 1870s-1960s. IEEE Ann Hist Comput 18(4):42–48

Tympas A (2001) The computor and the analyst: computing and power, 1870s–1960s. PhD dissertation, Georgia Institute of Technology, Atlanta, chap. 2

Tympas A (2003) Perpetually laborious: computing electric power transmission before the electronic computer. Int Rev Soc Hist 11(Supplement):73–95

Tympas A (2004) Calculation and computation. In: Horowitz MC (ed) New dictionary of the history of ideas, vol I. Charles Scribner's Sons, New York, pp 255–259

Tympas A (2005a) Computers: analog. In: Hempstead C (ed) Encyclopedia of 20th–century technology. Routledge, London/Great Britain, pp 195–199

Tympas A (2005b) Computers: hybrid. In: Hempstead C (ed) Encyclopedia of 20th–century technology. Routledge, London/Great Britain, pp 202–204

Tympas A (2007) From the historical continuity of the engineering imaginary to an anti-essentialist conception of the mechanical-electrical-electronic relationship. In: Heil R, Kamiski A, Stippak M, Unger A, Ziegler M (eds) Tensions and convergences: technical and aesthetic transformation of society. Verlag, Germany, pp 173–184

Tympas A (2012) A deep tradition of computing technology: calculating electrification in the American west. In: Janssen V (ed) Where minds and matters meet: Technology in California and the west. University of California Press, Oakland, pp 71–101

Tympas A, Dalouka D (2007) Metaphorical uses of an electric power network: early computations of atomic particles and nuclear reactors. Meta 12:65–84

Tympas A, Lekkas T (2006) Certainties and doubts in world fair comparisons of computing artifacts. In: Proceedings of the XXV scientific instrument symposium "east and west the common European heritage". Jagiellonian University Museum, Krakow, pp 295–300

Tympas A, Tsaglioti F (2016) L'usage du calcul à la production: le cas des nomogrammes pour machines-outils au XXe siècle" in Le monde du génie industriel au XXe siècle: Autour de Pierre Bézier et de machines-outils, Serge Benoit and Alain Michel eds., (Paris: Collection Sciences Humaines et Technologie, Pôle editorial de l'UTBM,), pp 63–73

Tympas A, Tsaglioti F, Lekkas T (2008) Universal machines vs. national languages: computerization as production of new localities. In: Anderl R, Arich-Gerz B, Schmiede R (eds) Proceedings of Technologies of Globalization. TU Darmstadt, Darmstadt

Tympas A, Konsta H, Lekkas T, Karas S (2010) Constructing gender and computing in advertising images: feminine and masculine computer parts. In: Misa T (ed) Gender codes: women and men in the computing professions. IEEE Press, pp 187–209

Van Trump CR (1901) A station load diagram. National Electric Light Association 24th Convention:363–370

Varney RN (1942) An all electric integrator for solving differential equations. Rev Sci Instrum 13:10

von Jezierski D (1995) Special slide rules of Faber-Castell. J Oughtred Soc 4(2):50–52

von Jezierski D (1996) Faber-Castell combination rule. J Oughtred Soc 5(1):24

von Jezierski D (2000) Slide rule: a journey through three centuries. Astragal Press, Mendham

von Jezierski D, Shepherd R (2000) Taylor, Taylorism, and machine time slide rules. J Oughtred Soc 9(2):32–36

Walker M (1905) Calculating temperature rises with a slide rule. Electr Club J 11(11):694–696

Wang Y (1916) The slide rule replaced by a new computer. Eng News 75(24):1120

Wang Y (1917) New parallel-line computer to replace slide-rule for rapid calculations. Electr Rev
Western Electrician 70(10):22

Warren TTPB (1872) On the application of the calculating machine of M. Thomas de Colmar to
electrical computations. J Soc Telegraph Eng 1(2):141–169

Warwick A (1994) The laboratory of theory or what's exact about the exact sciences? In: Norton
Wise M (ed) The values of precision. Princeton University Press, Princeton, pp 311–351

Wegel RL, Moore CR (1924) An electrical frequency analyzer. AIEEE Trans:457–466

Weinbach MP (1948) Electric power transmission. Macmillan, New York

Wess J (1997) The Soho rule. J Oughtred Soc 6(2):23–26

Westinghouse Electric Manufacturing Company Westinghouse Instruments and Relays (Catalogue
3-B). East Pittsburgh, 1916

Wheatley JY (1903) The polar planimeter and its use in engineering calculations together with
tables, diagrams and factors. Keuffel and Esser, New York

Wiener AE (1894a) Practical notes on dynamo calculation. The Electrical Engineer:640–641

Wiener AE (1894b) Practical notes on dynamo calculation. Electr Eng:701–703

Wiener AE (1898) Practical calculation of dynamo-electric machines: a manual for electrical engineers and a text-book for students of electro-Technics. W. J. Johnston, New York

Wiener N (1929) Harmonic analysis and the quantum theory. Franklin Inst J 207:525–534

Wiener N (1930) Generalized harmonic analysis. Acta Mathematica 55:118–258

Wiener N (1956) The human use of human beings. Doubleday Anchor, New York

Wildes KL, Lindgren NA (1985) A century of electrical engineering and computer science at MIT
1882–1982. The MIT Press, Cambridge

Williams MR (1982) Introduction. In: Williams MR (ed) The handbook of the Napier Tercenary
celebration or modern instruments and methods of calculation. Tomash Publishers, Los
Angeles, pp ix–xxi

Williams BO (1984) Computing with electricity 1935–1945. Diss. University of Kansas

Wines WE (1923) Why so many calculations in the boiler test code? Power 58(1):27–28

Wittgenstein L (1956) Remarks on the Foundations of Mathematics, edited by Wright GH, Rhees
R, and Anscombe GEM and translated by Anscombe GEM (Blackwell, Oxford)

Woodruff LF (1935) Complex Hyperbolic Function Charts. Electrical Engineering

Woodruff LF (1938) Principles of electric power transmission. Wiley, New York

Woolrich AP (2000) John Farey and his treatise on the steam engine of 1827. Hist Technol 22.
63–106, 531, 566–567, 567–568

Wyman T (1915) Using a slide rule. Power 42(24):825–826

Wyman T (1997) A five-piece combination gauging rod and slide rule. J Oughtred Soc 6(1):45–46

Wyman T (1998) The slide rule in college. J Oughtred Soc 7(2):57

Wyman T (2001) Norbert wiener and the slide rule or how American mathematicians came of age.
J Oughtred Soc 10(1):46–47

Yates JA (1993) Co-evolution of information-processing technology and use: interaction between
the life insurance and tabulating industries. Bus Hist Rev 67:1–51

Zachary G (1997) Pascal. Endless frontier: Vannevar bush engineer of the American century. Free
Press, New York

Index

© Springer-Verlag London Ltd. 2017
A. Tympas, *Calculation and Computation in the Pre-electronic Era*, History of
Computing, https://doi.org/10.1007/978-1-84882-742-4

Printed in the United States
By Bookmasters